POPULAR LOAN

This book is likely to be in heavy
demand. Please RETURN or RENEW it no
later than the last date stamped below

ENGLAND AND HER NEIGHBOURS,

1066-1453

ENGLAND
AND HER NEIGHBOURS,
1066-1453

ESSAYS IN HONOUR OF
PIERRE CHAPLAIS

EDITED BY

MICHAEL JONES
AND MALCOLM VALE

THE HAMBLEDON PRESS
LONDON   AND   RONCEVERTE

Published by The Hambledon Press, 1989

102 Gloucester Avenue, London NW1 8AX (UK)

309 Greenbrier Avenue, Ronceverte WV 24970 (USA)

ISBN 1 852850 14 0

British Library Cataloguing in Publication Data
England and her neighbours, 1066-1453: essays in honour
  of Pierre Chaplais.
  1. England. Foregin relations with Europe, 1066-1453
  I. Jones, Michael, *1940-*   II. Vale, M.G.A. (Malcolm
  Graham Allan), *1942-*   III. Chaplais, Pierre
  327. 4'204

Library of Congress Cataloging-in-Publication Data
England and her neighbours, 1066-1453: essays in honour
  of Pierre Chaplais / edited by Michael Jones and Malcolm
  Vale.
  p. 352. cm. 234 × 156.
  Includes bibliographical references.
  1. England – Foreign relations.
  2. England – Civilization – Medieval period, 1066-1453.
  3. Chaplais, Pierre.
  I. Chaplais, Pierre.   II. Jones, Michael (Michael C.E.)
  III. Vale, M.G.A. (Malcolm Graham Allan)
  DA45.E63 1989
  942 – dc20   89-15609 CIP

Typeset by Vitaset, Paddock Wood, Kent.
Printed and bound in Great Britain by
The Camelot Press, Southampton.

Contents

Preface

For over thirty years the classes held by Pierre Chaplais on diplomatic and palaeography served as the main introduction to research at Oxford for most post-graduates pursuing medieval history. The present collection is a small token of the affection and esteem in which he is held by all those who have passed through his hands; by colleagues who have occasionally consulted him for references or help with a recalcitrant hand or difficult manuscript and by the larger public reached through his meticulous scholarly work, especially as an editor of texts and documents. Whether in the formal surroundings of the History Faculty Library or in private conversation, he has shown remarkable patience and unflagging encouragement for the endeavours of countless beginners. His generosity with his time, not simply to those whom he was officially supervising, but for all those who brought their problems to him has been prodigious. His ability to decipher and interpret obscure texts (or, on occasion, to reconstruct what time and decay has destroyed) is legendary. He has sometimes observed that a trained mind reads what the eye does not see. During his time as an Editor at the Public Record Office, fragmentary and decayed documents classified as 'illegible' were apparently 'given to Chaplais' for successful elucidation. There can be few scholars who can range with such confidence and grasp over such long periods and in so many different areas of historical investigation, both in his own research and in the fruitful promotion of the work of others.

This volume has taken a theme and, whilst honouring Pierre in the traditional form of a Festschrift, seeks to reach a wider audience. This perhaps requires a word of explanation. Preliminary discussion revealed how easy it would have been to fill not one but several volumes with contributions from those whom he has influenced. In consultation with the publisher, it was decided that a particular need might be met by taking the theme of England and its neighbours from the Norman Conquest to the end of the Hundred Years War. While we were conscious that this would inevitably exclude some who might dearly wish to contribute, it was a theme which Pierre had particularly made his own. Moreover, not only had it been taken up by some former pupils, but by a wider circle of scholars (represented here by Drs. Carr, Frame and Zutshi). The volume

thus provides a review of many facets of England's external relations
during this long period, identifying both continuities and changes of
policy over the course of the middle ages. Most of the essays are intended
as surveys or reflections rather than detailed research papers, although
some take this form. However, it should be pointed out that references,
especially to source material, have often had to be ruthlessly abbreviated.
The volume will nevertheless serve as a guide to much recent literature.
We are conscious of certain gaps in the coverage; some were there from the
start, others appeared accidentally in the course of production. The
editors would particularly like to thank Alison McHardy and Patrick
Zutshi who very kindly stepped in at the eleventh hour to provide some
treatment of ecclesiastical affairs which would otherwise have been under
represented. They are very grateful, too, for the unstinted cooperation of
all other contributors. Finally, without the encouragement of our
publisher, Martin Sheppard, this particular tribute to Pierre Chaplais
from his pupils and friends would have been impossible.

Michael Jones   Malcolm Vale
Nottingham   Oxford

                                                      1 June 1989

List of Subscribers

Allmand, Dr Christopher, 111 Menlove Avenue, Liverpool L18 3HP
Altschul, Prof Michael, Dept of History, Case Western University, Cleveland, Ohio
    44106, USA.
Amt, Dr Emilie M, Dept of History, Washington College, Chestertown, MD 21620, USA
Arnold, Dr Benjamin, Dept of History, University of Reading
Ayton, Mr Andrew, Dept of History, University of Hull

Baker, Prof Derek, Dept of History, University of North Texas, Denton, Texas 76203,
    USA.
Ballard, Mr Mark, Hodges Wood, Groombridge, Tunbridge Wells, Kent TN3 9PN
Barron, Dr Caroline M., Dept of History, Royal Holloway and Bedford New College,
    University of London
Barrow, Prof G.W.S., 12 Lander Road, Edinburgh EH9 2EL
Bates, Dr David, School of History and Archaeology, University of Cardiff
Bennett, Mr Matthew, 48 Lye Copse Avenue, Farnborough, Hants GU14 8DX
Boulton, Dr D'A.J.D. & Dr M.B.M, University of Notre Dame, Indiana 46601, USA.
Brand, Dr Paul, 155 Kennington Road, London SE11 6SF
Brett, Dr Caroline J., Girton College, Cambridge
Brett, Dr M., Robinson College, Cambridge
Britnell, Dr R.H., Dept of History, University of Durham
Brooke, Prof Christopher and Dr Rosalind, Faculty of History, University of Cambridge
Brown, Prof A.L., Dept of Medieval History, University of Glasgow

Campbell, Mr James, Worcester College, Oxford
Carpenter, Dr David, Dept of History, King's College, University of London
Carr, Dr Anthony, Dept of History, University of Bangor
Church, Mr Stephen, 1 Orchard Hill, Faringdon, Oxon SN7 7EH
Clanchy, Dr M.T., Dept of History, Westfield College, University of London
Condon, Miss M.M., 28 Craigton Road, Eltham, London SE9 1QG
Cowdrey, the Revd H.E.J., St Edmund Hall, Oxford

Danbury, Miss Elizabeth A., Dept of History, University of Liverpool
Davies, Dr C.S.L., Wadham College, Oxford
Davies, Prof. R.R., Dept of History, University of Aberystwyth
Davis, Prof R.H.C., 349 Banbury Road, Oxford OX2 7PL
Ditchburn, Dr David, Dept of History, University of Aberdeen
Dobson, Prof R.B., Christ's College, Cambridge
Duncan, Prof A.A.M., Dept of History, University of Glasgow

Eales, Mr Richard, Eliot College, University of Kent
Elton, Sir Geoffrey, Clare College, Cambridge

Evans, Mrs Nesta, Crossings, The Green, Tostock, Bury St Edmunds, Suffolk IP30 9NY

Frame, Dr Robin, Dept of History, University of Durham
Fryde, Prof Edmund, Dept of History, University of Aberystwyth
Fukuda, Mr Makoto, Dept of History, Shujitsu Women's University, 1-6-1 Nishigawara, Okayama-Shi 703, Japan

Ganz, Dr David, Dept of Classics, University of North Carolina at Chapel Hill, NC 27599, USA
Genet, M Jean-Philippe, 147 avenue Parmentier, 75010 Paris, France
Gillingham, Mr John, 49 Old Shoreham Road, Brighton, Sussex BN1 5DQ
Giry-Deloison, Dr Charles, Institut Français du Royaume-Uni, 17 Queensberry Place, London SW7 2DT
Goldberg, Dr P.J.P., Dept of History, University of York
Goodman, Mr Anthony, Dept of History, Edinburgh University
Green, Dr Judith, Dept of History, The Queen's University, Belfast
Greenway, Dr D.E., Institute of Historical Research, Senate House, University of London
Griffiths, Prof R.A., Dept of History, University of Swansea

Haines, Prof Roy Martin, Dept of History, Dalhousie University, Halifax, Nova Scotia, Canada
Harding, Prof Alan, Dept of History, University of Liverpool
Hare, Miss Kathryn, 28 Chalcot Crescent, London NW1 8TD
Harper-Bill, Dr Christopher, 15 Cusack Close, Strawberry Hill, Twickenham TW1 4TB
Harvey, Miss Barbara, Somerville College, Oxford
Hayward, Mr J.M., 12 Preston Avenue, London E4 9NL
Highfield, Dr Roger, Merton College, Oxford
Holt, Prof J.C., Fitzwilliam College, Cambridge CB3 0DG
Housley, Dr Norman, Dept of History, University of Leicester
Hyams, Dr P.R., Dept of History, Cornell University, Ithaca, NY 14853, USA

Jones, Dr Michael C.E., Dept of History, University of Nottingham

Keen, Dr Maurice, Balliol College, Oxford
Kemp, Mr Anthony and Mrs Alison, 59 Princess Road, London NW1
Kennedy, Dr M.J., Dept of Mediaeval History, University of Glasgow
Kettle, Miss Ann J., Dept of Mediaeval History, University of St Andrews
Keynes, Dr S.D., Trinity College, Cambridge
King, Prof Edmund, Dept of History, University of Sheffield

Lewis, Mr P.S., All Souls College, Oxford
Leyser, Prof Karl Joseph, Manor House, Mill Street, Islip, Oxford OX5 2SZ
Lloyd, Dr Simon, Dept of History, University of Newcastle
Loud, Dr G.A., School of History, University of Leeds
Loyn, Prof H.R., 25 Cunningham Hill Road, St Albans, Herts AL1 5BX
Lydon, Prof James, Trinity College, Dublin

Maddicott, Dr J.R., Exeter College, Oxford
Mahony, Dr M.P., Mansfield College, Oxford
Martindale, Dr Jane, Dept of History, University of East Anglia
Mason, Dr Emma, Dept of History, Birkbeck College, University of London
McHardy, Dr A., Dept of History, University of Nottingham
Meek, Prof Christine, Trinity College, Dublin
Moore, Mr & Mrs A.R., St Hilda's College, Oxford

Moore, Mr D.J., 216 Badminton Road, Downend, Bristol BN15 6NP
Morgan, Dr Philip, Dept of Adult Education, University of Keele

Nicol, Mrs Alexandra, Public Record Office, Kew, Richmond, Surrey TW9 4DU

Ormrod, Dr W.M., St Catharine's College, Cambridge
Owen, Dr Dorothy, Old Manor House, Thimbleby, Horncastle, Lincs LN9 5RE

Patterson, Prof Robert B., Dept of History, University of South Carolina, Columbia,
    SC 29208, USA
Phillips, Dr J.R. Seymour, University College, Dublin
Powell, Mr Nicholas and Mrs Caroline, 115 Gloucester Avenue, London NW1
Prestwich, Prof Michael, Dept of History, University of Durham
Pryce, Dr Huw, Dept of History, University of Bangor

Richmond, Dr Colin, Dept of History, University of Keele
Robertson, Dr J.C., St Hugh's College, Oxford
Rogers, Dr Randall, Dept of History, Louisiana State University, Baton Rouge, LA 70803,
    USA
Rycraft, Mr Peter and Mrs Ann, 1 Mill Mount, York YO2 2BH

Saul, Dr N.E., Dept of History, Royal Holloway and Bedford New College, University of
    London
Sayers, Dr J.E., School of Library and Archive Studies, University College, London
Sellar, W.D.H., Dept of Scots Law, University of Edinburgh
Sheppard, Mrs G.T.F., Herne House, Weston Road, Bath, Somerset
Sheppard, Dr Evelyn I.M., Quantock House, Park Gardens, Bath, Somerset
Simpson, Dr Grant G., Dept of History, University of Aberdeen
Southern, Sir Richard, 40 St John St, Oxford OX1 2LH
Spufford, Dr Peter, Queens' College, Cambridge
Stadler, Dr Hubert M., Corpus Christi College, Oxford
Storey, Prof & Mrs R.L., Dept of History, University of Nottingham
Suppe, Prof Frederick, Dept of History, Ball State University, Muncie, IN 47306, USA
Swanson, Dr R.N., Dept of History, University of Birmingham

Thomson, Dr John A.F., Dept of Mediaeval History, University of Glasgow

Vale, Dr Malcolm, St John's College, Oxford

Watson, Prof A.G., School of Library and Archive Studies, University College, London
Wilks, Prof M.J., Dept of History, Birkbeck College, University of London
Wood, Dr I.N., School of History, University of Leeds
Wormald, Dr Jenny, St Hilda's College, Oxford
Wormald, Mr C.P., 60 Hill Top Road, Oxford

Yoshitake, Mr Kenji, Dept of History, Keio University, 2-15-45 Mita, Minato-ku,
    108 Tokyo, Japan

Zutshi, Dr Patrick, University Archives, University Library, West Road, Cambridge

Pierre Chaplais

Pierre Chaplais: a Personal Memoir

C.S.L. Davies

Pierre Théophile Victorien Marie Chaplais was born on 8 July 1920 at Châteaubriant, in the département of Loire-Atlantique in Brittany. His father was a postmaster, part of a family of civil servants, later moving to Redon, eventually, after the war, becoming postmaster of Deauville; he was to die in 1949. Pierre's mother died when he was a child. He has an elder sister who followed family tradition with a career in the telephone service at Nantes.[1]

Pierre was sent to school to the Collège St. Sauveur at Redon; a private religious foundation, with a seminary attached, built, appropriately, in the ruins of the ninth-century abbey. He did his *bac* largely in classics, philosophy, and mathematics (no history) and hoped to go in for the Navy, only to be turned down by the cadet school at Brest as colour-blind. Instead he went up to the university of Rennes to study classics and law. There he fell under the spell of one of his professors, Brejon de Lavergnée, a legal historian and historian of Brittany.[2]

His studies were, naturally, interrupted by the war. Pierre volunteered for military service in October 1939 and was sent to the artillery school at Fontainebleau as an officer cadet (*aspirant*), reaching the rank of *maréchal de logis* or sergeant. The school was mobilised to fight when the Germans attacked; during the *étrange défaite* they made their way south by horseback. After the armistice Pierre was demobilised, at Toulouse, in September 1940, returning then to Rennes to resume his studies.

Classics and law filled Pierre's time for most of the next three years; his aim was to be an academic lawyer. In France, as in England, it is useful for academic lawyers to at least qualify for practice; and to this end, at least ostensibly, Pierre was recommended by Brejon to his near namesake, an eminent Rennes lawyer, Maître Pierre Chaplet. Chaplet was involved in

---

[1] This memoir is based primarily on conversations with Pierre Chaplais over the years.
[2] 1911- Brejon's Poitiers thesis of 1937 was on *Un Jurisconsulte de la Renaissance: André Tiraqueau (1488-1588)*, a humanist, friend of Rabelais, as well as jurist. Brejon subsequently published *La Fraude à la Loi en Droit Romain* (1973), and *Rennes aux XVIᵉ et XVIIᵉ siècles* (1973) and was president of the federation of Sociétés Savantes de Bretagne from 1975-86.

the resistance movement Défense de la France.[3]

Défense de la France had been begun in 1940 by two Paris students, Robert Salmon and Philippe Viannay.[4] Strongly against the Armistice from the beginning, the movement began with some hope of Pétain as a symbol of national revolution. But this quickly evaporated, and in 1943 Défense de la France recognized de Gaulle. It produced in the cellars of the Sorbonne *La Défense de la France*, the most successful of the underground newspapers ('de tendance modérée et d'inspiration catholique').[5] It also produced false identity cards on a large scale. In 1943 it was building itself up as a military force; though something of the original 'boy-scout' (Pierre's words) inspiration remained, in the meetings in the Forêt de Paimpont, near Rennes, of small groups, eight or so, of would-be *francs tireurs*.[6] The movement did in fact succeed in constituting a military force which played a major part in the Liberation, both in Brittany and in Paris. Pierre and his group, however, were never armed. There was apparently a botched arms drop. Maître Chaplet was arrested at 7 a.m. on 21 December 1943; Pierre, turning up at Chaplet's home later in the same day, walked into the arms of the Gestapo.

After interrogation at Rennes, Maître Chaplet and Pierre were taken to Compiègne, then on a horrifying three day rail journey to Buchenwald, arriving there on 29 January 1944. There is no need to reproduce the familiar horror-story of the camp; the struggle to survive the cold, hunger, and fatigue, the struggle to retain human values in a régime systematically dedicated to degradation. Maître Chaplet's own account is one of the most vivid and moving. And he provides two brief glimpses of Pierre Chaplais. The first is at Compiègne: 'Mon jeune ami Ch..., qui marchait à côté de moi, avec ses lèvres grasses, ses yeux en amande et l'étrange

---

[3] Pierre Chaplet published an account of his prison experiences, under the title *Häftling 43485* (Editions Charlot, Paris 1947). (I must thank Dr. Michael Jones and Professor Brejon de Lavergnée for their help in procuring a copy.) Unfortunately Chaplet's book begins with his arrest and refers only briefly and in passing to his resistance activities. Maître Chaplet died on 11 Feb. 1974; I am grateful to his surviving son Monsieur Jean-Pierre Chaplet for his assistance.

[4] Marie Granet, *Défense de la France* (Paris, 1960); Marcel Baudot, *Libération de la Bretagne* (Paris, 1973).

[5] Baudot, p.60.

[6] Baudot, pp.79-80 also uses the scout analogy. Chaplet, p.52, mentions diffusion of underground newspapers, the production of false identity cards, and the formation of 'petits corps francs'. Pierre was with Chaplet at a clandestine meeting in the forest in August 1943 with Pierre Dunoyer de Segonzac. Segonzac had founded the École des Cardes at Uriage, near Grenoble, in 1940 dedicated to establishing a new concept of 'leadership' among French youth, despising both the intellectualist democratic tradition of the thirties and totalitarianism, and fostering a Catholic and soldierly ethos. By 1942 he had become disillusioned with the Pétain régime and raised a *maquis* in Tarn. See his memoir *Le Vieux Chef* (Paris, 1971), and W.D. Halls, *The Youth of Vichy France* (Oxford, 1981), esp. chapter xii.

turban dont il s'était coiffé, ressemblait à un fakir. On se le désignait du doigt. Il souriait imperturbablement comme un prince de carnaval.'

The second is of 'Ch.' discovering in a food parcel 'le portrait de sa fiancée qui fit le tour des tables. Le sourire d'Eliane eut un succès considérable. Ch... en rougissait de confusion, mais il était bien embarrassé pour dissimuler l'image qui était l'oeuvre d'un photographe d'art et prenait une grande place. Il la glissa, après avoir découpé l'entourage du carton, dans la doublure de sa veste rayée. Nous demandions à la voir de temps en temps'.[7]

At Buchenwald Pierre was employed making weapons, including a three-month period making cannon at the Gustoff-Werke in Weimar. In the camp he got to know some remarkable people; Julien Cain, head of the Bibliothèque Nationale and later Directeur des Bibliothèques de France;[8] Paul-Emile Janson, one time prime minister of Belgium;[9] Colonel Jean Ganeval, a professional soldier, resistance leader in Toulouse, later as military A.D.C. to President Coty, to play a key role in de Gaulle's coup of 13 May 1958.[10]

The camp itself was run in an extraordinary way. Early in the war the

[7] Chaplet, pp.108, 280-1. Chaplet was in Buchenwald until 1 October 1944, was then transferred to the subsidiary camp at Dora, returning to France at the end of the war via Bergen-Belsen. Eliane d'Eyron was awarded the *Croix de Guerre* for her work in the Resistance. She married Philippe Ragueneau, commander of a parachute unit dropped behind the lines in Brittany in 1944, subsequently a leading political journalist, press officer to de Gaulle, and director of a television chain.

[8] See *Humanisme Actif: Mélanges d'art et de littérature offerts à Julien Cain*, eds. Jean Porchier and André Masson, 2 vols (Paris, 1968).

[9] Born 1872. A Liberal. He served in numerous ministries between 1920 and 1940, and was prime minister 24 Nov. 1937 to 6 June 1938. As minister of justice he was responsible for the preventive arrest of political extremists of left and right when the Germans invaded. With the Belgian surrender he distanced himself from both King Leopold in Brussels and the government-in-exile in London, settling eventually in Nice. He was arrested for reasons which remain mysterious while attending a sanatorium in the French Alps, and arrived at Buchenwald in Feb. 1944. With no concessions made to his age or state of health, he died on 3 March 1944. See Paul van Molle, *Het Belgisch Parlement, 1894-1969* (Gent, 1969), pp.195-6; J. Gerard-Libois and J. Gotovitch *L'An 40* (Bruxelles, 1971); J. Stengers, *Leopold III et le Gouvernement* (Paris, 1980) and D. Rochette and J-M. Vanhamme, *Les Belges à Buchenwald* (Bruxelles, 1976), esp. annexe III. All this information was generously provided by my colleague, Dr. Martin Conway, of Christ Church, Oxford. Janson is one of the few individuals to earn more than passing mention by Pierre Chaplet. Chaplet mentions his love for France, and French culture, his faith in an ultimate allied victory, his 'personalité, demeurée si vivante et si jeune'. His death, according to Chaplet, was sudden. 'Il ne trahissait ni faiblesse, ni lassitude. Un jour, sans que l'on sût de quoi il souffrait, quelque chose se rompit. Il commença à descendre la pente. Rien ne pouvait le retenir. En quinze jours tout fut consommé . . .' Chaplet, pp.148, 211-2, 303, 434.

[10] Claude Bourdet, *L'Aventure Incertaine: de la Résistance à la Restauration* (Paris, 1975), p.130; Merry and Serge Bromberger, *Les Complots du 13 Mai* (Paris, 1959), p.13 suggest that he had acted for some time as liaison between the Elysée and de Gaulle. Ganeval joined the Senate as a U.N.R. member in 1959; *Who's Who in France, 1979-1980* (1979), p.658.

German political prisoners, mostly communists, had inserted themselves into positions of responsibility, displacing the 'criminals' who had, under the S.S., run the camp beforehand. In turn the German political prisoners encouraged the formation of national committees, again, naturally, dominated whenever possible by communists. The Comité des intérêts Français was formed in January 1944, about the time of Pierre's arrival. Its progenitor was the senior communist, Marcel Paul, though it was headed by the non-communist resistance leader, Colonel Manhès. Controversy has raged about the activities of these groups.[11] Pierre himself subscribes to the view that Marcel Michelin, head of the tyre firm (in the camp for the 'sabotage' of the German war effort by holding back supplies) was deliberately done to death as a class-enemy and suspected collaborationist, by being assigned the toughest working conditions.[12] Impossible choices had to be made, prisoners in effect condemned to death to save others; but some form of political organisation was necessary to maintain morale, to provide the will and the means for survival, and the communists were the best placed to provide this.[13] The logic of events, coupled with an admiration for the morale of the Russian officers, led Pierre to lean for a while to the left; he was approached to become a party member, though in the event he did not succumb.

The last few weeks of imprisonment in March and April 1945, as the Americans approached, were the most dangerous; the camp authorities might well destroy the prisoners to remove evidence of atrocities. Pierre's memory of this is hazy; he was in the infirmary, the result of the American bombing of Weimar, and played no part in the 'rising' which, according to the hagiography of the official prisoners' organizations, preceded the arrival of Paton's army at the camp.[14] He survived the hazards of the liberation; diarrhoea due to the sudden availability of food innocently pressed on the prisoners by the Americans. Via Eisenach where he scribbled some lines of Verlaine:

[11] For a positive view of these developments see, e.g. Walter Bartel and Klaus Trostorff, *Buchenwald, Mahnung und Verpflichtung, Dokumente und Berichte* (Berlin, 1983), and Pierre Durand, *Les Armes de l'Espoir; les Français à Buchenwald et à Dora* (Paris, 1977). A hostile account is provided by the English S.O.E. agent and prisoner, Christopher Burney, *The Dungeon Democracy* (1945) (several later editions up to 1984), esp. pp.61-3.

[12] Burney, *Dungeon Democracy*, p.24 alludes to this. For the Michelin Company's record of collaboration and/or sabotage, see John F. Sweet's study of Clermont-Ferrand, *Choices in Vichy France* (New York and Oxford, 1986), *passim*.

[13] Burney who himself attempted to negotiate with the S.S. camp authorities to prevent an evacuation (which would be tantamount to a death-sentence) or large-scale massacre, using well-placed non-communist prisoners as intermediaries, does not apologize for doing a deal which allowed the deportation of 8,000 *cretins*; 'few tears were shed and the camp relaxed a little' *Dungeon Democracy*, p.79. Cf. Durand, *Les Armes de l'Espoir*, pp.222-7.

[14] Bartel and Trostorff, and Durand, make this the heroic culmination of their accounts; Burney p.79, sourly comments, 'they were very childish, forming bands of different nationalities and marching about looking as if they had defeated the entire Wehrmacht'.

> Donc, ce sera par un clair jour d'été
> Le grand soleil, complice de notre joie . . .'[15]

he arrived in Paris on V.E. Day, 8th May, his group startling the more staid bourgeoisie as they sang the Internationale from the back of a lorry.

Pierre returned to Deauville, where his father was now postmaster; still keeping his options open as between Law and Classics. Indeed, he completed a thesis for the *Diplôme d'Etudes Supérieures* on the sea in the works of Seneca. In November 1945 he somewhat nominally qualified as an *avocat* (by dint of having war service credited) and was formally admitted to the Rennes Court. Academic law, however, was still his objective, and he set about preparing in Paris the substantial thesis demanded for the agrégation in law. He determined to work in legal history, and was introduced by Michel Debois, a communist and ex-déporté whom he had met at Deauville, to Edouard Perroy and to Robert Fawtier. Both had been heavily involved in the Resistance. Perroy wrote *La Guerre de Cent Ans* while on the run from the Gestapo in his native Forez. Fawtier had been arrested in 1942 and after a period in the notorious prison at Fresnes, was deported, ending the war in the camp at Mauthausen.[16] The spirit of comradeship amongst ex-resisters no doubt did something to open doors, but only Pierre's abilities would have earned him the good offices of such austere scholars. His thesis was on appeals from Gascony to England.

Pierre arrived in England on 2 September 1946, taking advantage of a three-week holiday paid for by the newspaper *France-Soir*, successor to *Défense de la France*. He carried letters of introduction from Fawtier and Perroy to Vivian Galbraith, then Director of the Institute of Historical Research; and stayed in England to pursue his researches for his thesis for the Law Faculty of Paris University. With his already greying hair (soon to turn almost pure white), Pierre elicited Galbraith's immediate sympathy and interest. He attended Galbraith's classes on palaeography and diplomatic and showed himself a scholar after Galbraith's own heart; very soon Pierre was induced to register for a London doctorate rather

---

[15] Pierre scribbled the three stanzas of Verlaine's best known poem, presumably from memory, with minor mistakes; of which the most revealing is 'notre joie' for 'ma joie' in the first line; cf. Paul Verlaine, *Choix de Poésies* (Paris, 1939), p.107. Pierre Chaplet, p.330, mentions among the activities organized by the 'comité des loisirs' of the French prisoners 'la causerie d'un universitaire sur Verlaine, avec lecture de poèmes par un élève du Conservatoire.'

[16] For Perroy see Etienne Fournial, *Cahiers de Civilisation Médiévale*, xvii (1974), 399-400. For Fawtier, see *Dictionnaire de Biographie Française*, vol.13 (publ. 1975), p.879. Pierre was also influenced by Robert Boutruche, who had been active in the Resistance, and was to dedicate his thèse to the memory of Marc Bloch; see Paul Lemerle's mémoire in P. Contamine, ed., *La Noblesse au Moyen Age: Essais à la mémoire de Robert Boutruche* (Paris, 1976), pp.7-13.

than continue climbing the French academic ladder. He supported himself meanwhile by teaching at the Linguists Club in Grosvenor Place, and by translating, notably for the B.B.C.; his work included talks by Bertrand Russell and introductions for light music concerts by Mantovani. In 1947 he got a British Council grant. In 1948 he married Doreen Middlemast, one time Wren serving in Ceylon, now working for the *Times of India* in Fleet Street, convenient for the P.R.O. In 1949 he was taken on as external editor of the Treaty Rolls at the P.R.O., at three guineas a day; Sir Hilary Jenkinson, apparently, at the interview commiserating with Pierre at his bad luck in being taught by Galbraith. This appointment, again, can only be explained by Pierre's natural gifts as a documentary scholar which had impressed those he had consulted, especially Harold Johnson, in the Round Room while working on his thesis.

Pierre was happy at the P.R.O.; had he been prepared to take British citizenship he might have joined the permanent staff.[17] But in 1955 he was appointed to succeed Kathleen Major as lecturer in Diplomatic at Oxford; Galbraith was by then Regius Professor and presumably influential in the appointment. The post was changed to a readership in 1957. In 1964 he became a Fellow of Wadham, to which he had been earlier introduced, as 'member of Common Room' by Lawrence Stone. (Stone was Fawtier's son-in-law, but the connection seems in fact to have been independent of this, and was at Galbraith's instigation.) Pierre has played a part in college affairs, characteristically and notably as Keeper of the Gardens. But as a Reader his main duties have been to the university, to the training of research-students. Not that his readiness to help has ever been limited. Anybody consulting him on, for instance, some small problem in medieval Latin finds himself spending the whole morning going over the document in all its ramifications and is subject thereafter to frequent enquiries about the progress of that piece of research.

Pierre's career in England has been that of the unflurried scholar. I am the last person to try to judge his technical work. What is striking to me, as a friend and colleague for over twenty years, comparing Pierre the scholar with the Pierre of the Resistance, is his lack of political *engagement*; not so much a lack of political opinions (he has plenty), but a reluctance to interpret history in the light of his wartime experiences. As a historian, he has been very much a professional's professional, not, apparently, interested in wider interpretation, perhaps too aware of the difficulty of deciding what really happened in Bordeaux, in that court case of 9 March 1348, to venture into the world of social change or intellectual development. As a scholar he has been superb; as an exemplar, too, to

[17] I am grateful to Sir Geoffrey Elton and Professor George Cuttino for their memories of this period.

generations of research students. He has devoted himself to his family; to Doreen, their sons Paul and Maurice, and now their grandchildren. He has cultivated his garden, and made a notable attempt at establishing a tolerable vineyard in Oxfordshire. He has put behind him the Catholicism of his Breton background along with the socialism of 1945. He has remained unmistakably French, not merely in his accent, but in his concern for food and wine and his meticulousness about the proprieties. He is the gentlest of men, always concerned that nobody should be hurt, by a harsh word or an impatient gesture. In a world increasingly threatened by financial imperatives, he has upheld the highest academic, aesthetic, and personal standards.

Abbreviations

BBCS	*Bulletin of the Board of Celtic Studies*
BEC	*Bibliothèque de l'école des chartes*
BEFAR	*Bibliothèque de l'Ecole française d'Athènes et de Rome*
BIHR	*Bulletin of the Institute of Historical Research*
BL	British Library
CCR	*Calendar of Close Rolls*
CChR	*Calendar of Charter Rolls*
CDI	*Calendar of Documents relating to Ireland*
CDS	*Calendar of Documents relating to Scotland*
Chaplais, *Essays*	P. Chaplais, *Essays in Medieval Diplomacy and Administration* (The Hambledon Press, London, 1981)
CLR	*Calendar of Liberate Rolls*
CM	Matthew Paris, *Chronica majora*, ed. H. R. Luard, 7 vols. (Rolls Series, 1872-83)
Complete Peerage	*The Complete Peerage*, revised edn. V. Gibbs *et al.*, 13 vols. (London 1910-59)
CPR	*Calendar of Patent Rolls*
CR	*Close Rolls*
Dip. Docs. I.	*Diplomatic Documents I, 1101-1271*, ed. P. Chaplais (H.M.S.O., 1964)
EHR	*English Historical Review*
Eng. Med. Dip.	P. Chaplais, *English Medieval Diplomatic Practice*, 2 vols. in 3 (H.M.S.O., 1975-82)
Foedera	Signifies the Record Commission edition of *Rymer's Foedera*, ed. A. Clarke *et al.*, 4 vols. (London, 1816-69) for the period to 1383 and the original edition, 20 vols., (LKondon, 1704-35) thereafter.
IHS	*Irish Historical Studies*
JMH	*Journal of Medieval History*
MGH	*Monumenta Germaniae Historica*
PRO	Public Record Office, London
RHF	*Recueil des historiens des Gaules et de la France*, ed. M. Boucquet *et al.*, 24 vols. (Paris, 1734-1904)
RS	Rolls Series
Rymer	See *Foedera*
SHR	*Scottish Historical Review*
Treaty Rolls	*Treaty Rolls, i. 1234-1325*, ed. P. Chaplais (H.M.S.O., 1955)
TRHS	*Transactions of the Royal Historical Society*
VCH	*Victoria County History*
WHR	*Welsh Historical Review*

Bibliography
of Pierre Chaplais (to 1989)

*Book reviews are not included: for items marked * see under 1981.*

1948

'English Arguments concerning the Feudal Status of Aquitaine in the Fourteenth Century', *BIHR*, xxi, 203-13.

1951

'Règlement des conflits internationaux franco-anglais au XIVe siècle (1293-1377)', *Le Moyen Age*, 1951, 269-302.*
'Chartes en déficit dans les cartons 'Angleterre' du Trésor des Chartes', *Bibliothèque de l'école des chartes*, cix, 96-103.*

1952

'The Making of the Treaty of Paris (1259) and the Royal Style', *EHR*, lxvii, 235-53.*
'Some Documents regarding the Fulfilment and Interpretation of the Treaty of Brétigny (1361-1369)', *Camden Miscellany*, xix, 1-84.

1953

'A propos de l'ordonnance de 1375 sur la bourgeoisie et la jurade de Bordeaux', *Annales du Midi*, 65, 113-8.*

1954

The War of Saint-Sardos (1323-1325). Gascon Correspondence and Diplomatic Documents (Camden Society, Third Series, lxxxvii).

1955

Treaty Rolls, i. 1234-1325 (H.M.S.O., London).
'Le Traité de Paris de 1259 et l'inféodation de la Gascogne allodiale', *Le Moyen Age*, 121-37.*
'Le sceau de la cour de Gascogne ou sceau de l'office de sénéchal de Guyenne', *Annales du Midi*, 67, 19-29.*

1956

'Documents concernant l'Angleterre et l'Ecosse anciennement conservés à la Chambre des Comptes de Lille (XIIe-XVe siècles)', *Revue du Nord*, 185-210.*

1957

(With T.A.M. Bishop) *Facsimiles of English Royal Writs to AD 1100 presented to Vivian Hunter Galbraith* (Oxford).
'Le duché-pairie de Guyenne: L'hommage et les services féodaux de 1259 à 1303', *Annales du Midi*, 69, 5-38.*
'The Chancery of Guyenne, 1289-1453', *Studies presented to Sir Hilary Jenkinson*, ed. J. Conway Davies (Oxford), pp.61-96.*

1958

'Le duché-pairie de Guyenne: L'hommage et les services féodaux de 1303 à 1337', *Annales du Midi*, 70, 135-60.*
'Privy Seal Drafts, Rolls and Registers (Edward I – Edward II)', *EHR*, lxxiii, 270-86.*

1959

'Une charte originale de Guillaume le Conquérant pour l'abbaye de Fécamp: la donation de Steyning et de Bury (1085)', *L'abbaye bénédictine de Fécamp (Ouvrage scientifique du XIIIe centenaire, 658-1958)* (Fécamp), i. 93-104, 355-7.*

1960

'The Seals and Original Charters of Henry I', *EHR*, lxxv, 260-75.*

1961

'Un message de Jean de Fiennes à Edouard II et le projet de démembrement du royaume de France (janvier 1317)', *Revue du Nord*, xliii, 145-8.*

1962

'The Original Charters of Herbert and Gervase, abbots of Westminster (1121-1157)', *A Medieval Miscellany for Doris Mary Stenton*, ed. Patricia M. Barnes & C.F. Slade, Pipe Roll Society, new series xxxvi, 89-110.*
'Some Private Letters of Edward I', *EHR*, lxxvii, 79-86.*

1963

'La souveraineté du roi de France et le pouvoir législatif en Guyenne au début du XIVème siècle', *Le Moyen Age, Livre Jubiliaire*, 449-69.*

1964

Diplomatic Documents, i. 1101-1272 (H.M.S.O., London).

1965

'The Origin and Authenticity of the Royal Anglo-Saxon Diploma', *Journal of the Society of Archivists*, iii, no.2, 48-61.

1966

'The Authenticity of the Royal Anglo-Saxon Diplomas of Exeter', *BIHR*, xxxix, 1-34.
'The Anglo-Saxon Chancery; From the Diploma to the Writ', *J. Soc. Archivists*, iii, no.4, 160-76.

1968

'Some Early Anglo-Saxon Diplomas on Single Sheets: Originals or Copies?', *J. Soc. Archivists*, iii, no.7, 315-36.

1969

'Who Introduced Charters into England? The Case for Augustine', *J. Soc. Archivists*, iii, no.10, 526-42.

1971

English Royal Documents. King John-Henry VI, 1199-1461 (Oxford).
'English Diplomatic Documents to the End of Edward III's Reign', *The Study of Medieval Records: Essays in Honour of Kathleen Major*, ed. D.A. Bullough & R.L. Storey (Oxford), pp.22-56.
'Master John de Branketre and the Office of Notary in Chancery, 1355-1375', *J. Soc. Archivists*, iv, no.3, 169-99.*
'English Diplomatic Documents, 1377-99', *The Reign of Richard II. Essays in Honour of May McKisack*, ed. F.R.H. Du Boulay & Caroline M. Barron (London), pp.21-45.

1973

'Les appels gascons au roi d'Angleterre sous le règne d'Edouard Ier (1272-1307)', *Économies et sociétés au Moyen Age. Mélanges offerts à Édouard Perroy* (Publications de la Sorbonne, Paris), pp.382-99.*
'Henry II's Reissue of the Canons of the Council of Lillebonne of Whitsun 1080 (?25 February 1162)', *J. Soc. Archivists*, iv, no.8, 627-32.*
Prisca Munimenta. Studies in Archival & Administrative History presented to Dr. A.E.J. Hollander, ed. Felicity Ranger (London), pp.28-107 (reprint of four articles originally appearing in *J. Soc. Archivists*, iii; see above).

1975

English Medieval Diplomatic Practice, Part II, Plates (H.M.S.O., London).

1978

'The Letter from Bishop Wealdhere of London to Archbishop Brihtwold of Canterbury: The Earliest Original "Letter Close" extant in the West',

Medieval Scribes, Manuscripts and Libraries. Essays presented to N.R. Ker, ed. M.B. Parkes & Andrew G. Watson (London), pp.3-23.*

1981

Essays in Medieval Diplomacy and Administration (The Hambledon Press, London) (reprint of twenty-two articles published between 1951 and 1978, marked * above).

1982

English Medieval Diplomatic Practice, Part I. Documents and Interpretation, 2 vols. (H.M.S.O., London).

1985

'The Royal Anglo-Saxon "Chancery" of the Tenth Century revisited', *Studies in Medieval History Presented to R.H.C. Davis*, ed. Henry Mayr-Harting & R.I. Moore (London), pp.41-51.

1987

'William of Saint-Calais and the Domesday Survey', *Domesday Studies*, ed. J.C. Holt (Woodbridge), pp.65-77.
'The Spelling of Christ's Name in Medieval Anglo-Latin: "Christus" or "Cristus"?', *J. Soc. Archivists*, vol.8, no.4, 1987, 261-80.

1989

'The Court of Sovereignty of Guyenne (Edward III–Henry VI) and its Antecedents', *Documenting the Past: Essays in Honour of George Peddy Cuttino*, ed. J.S. Hamilton and Patricia J. Bradley (Woodbridge), pp.137-53.

Chapter 1

Was it Infancy in England?
Some Questions of Comparison

James Campbell

Some of the most arresting work on the medieval development of western Europe has been that of Professor Robert Fossier, most recently in his *Enfance de l'Europe*, a tour de force of learning and imagination masquerading as an introductory manual.[1] In it his account of England is brief and somewhat casual.[2] The purpose of the present paper is to sketch possibilities and problems which arise when some of his arguments and suggestions are applied to this side of the Channel.

Among the most powerful of his theories is that on the extent to which 'encellulement dans le cadre de la seigneurie' became a dominant force in the life of *l'Europe chrétienne*. By *encellulement* he means 'la privatisation du pouvoir sur les hommes', the development of a system in which the effective units of power were localized *seigneuries*, and the most important political and economic relationships were within these, between lords and men.[3] The very comprehensiveness of his generalizations can lead to potentially contradictory emphases.[4] Nevertheless he is adamant on the general importance of *encellulement*; and on the extent to which it had beneficial economic effects; he is scornful of the notion of 'feudal anarchy', warning against 'l'historiographie jacobine, aveuglée par huit siècles des centralisations'.[5]

All the same, it is not altogether easy to disbelieve in 'feudal anarchy'; or in its harmful economic effects. For example Fossier himself has published a study which permits (most unusually) the quantification of the effects of an episode of feudal warfare.[6] A raid, of a few hours, made in 1298 on the village of Cagnoncles by a feudal lord did damage which was

---

[1] R. Fossier, *Enfance de l'Europe*, 2 vols. (Paris, 1982).

[2] Esp. i. 159, 386-7, 396-8, ii. 1032.

[3] *Enfance*, i. 288-601 (pp.288-90 for a forceful outline).

[4] P.8, n.50 below.

[5] *Enfance*, i. 294-5, cf. R. Fossier, *La terre et les hommes en Picardie jusqu'à la fin du XIIIᵉ siècle*, 2 vols. (Paris and Louvain, 1968), i. 260-1.

[6] R. Fossier, 'Fortunes et infortunes paysannes au Cambrèsis à la fin du XIIIᵉ siècle', *Economies et Sociétés au Moyen Age. Mélanges offerts à Edouard Perroy* (Paris, 1973), pp.171-82. (I owe this reference to Professor R.W. Kaeuper.)

the equivalent in value of 40,000 hours' work by a mason or a reaper. For an earlier period, such a work as the *De Administratione* of Suger would seem to go far to show how 'feudal anarchy' could be economically harmful. Suger brings out how great a hindrance to the prosperity of an estate was the proximity of an unfriendly aristocrat: harrying the countryside, oppressing the peasantry, taking all the good timber for his castle.[7]

The questions of how far there was *encellulement* in England and of whether, and where, there was such a thing as 'feudal anarchy' there are major ones. Fossier contends that the later Anglo-Saxon period saw a great extension of private jurisdiction: 'Au Xe siècle, depuis 956 plus exactement, la faiblesse des cours comtales avait abouti à autoriser les maîtres du sol, les lords, à juger des causes foncières, domaniales, puis des causes banales, au moins pour une categorie d'hommes, les "hommes de justice", les sokemen . . .'[8] This is a view related to Maitland's on the extent of franchisal jurisdiction in late Anglo-Saxon England; it neglects the refutation of Maitland's case by N.D. Hurnard, who demonstrated the strong probability that the evidence which he used for the existence before 1066 of numerous high franchises, shows, in fact, the reverse.[9]

Fossier is on much stronger ground when he points to 'fort contrôle public' in England.[10] The absence, not the presence, of *encellulement* is crucial, in both the political and the economic development of England. In various basic ways the power of the English kings and the prosperity of the English economy were closely associated. The relationship cannot always have been a positive one. If the *Chronicle* is to be believed then English and Anglo-Danish kings raised at least £272,147 in gelds between 991 and 1018.[11] Perhaps such taxation was an economic stimulus, in that it led to dethesaurization;[12] but it cannot have been more than a very mixed economic blessing, not least since much of the bullion went to Scandinavia.

Hardly questionable are the advantages of an abundant silver coinage, of good quality, and uniform. That such a currency circulated within the dominions of the English kings is plain; and its nature, after the introduction or reintroduction of *renovatio monetae* late in Edgar's reign, makes it possible to estimate with some reliability the number of coins

---

[7] *Sugerii . . . Opuscula et Epistolae*, ed. J.-P. Migne, *Patrologia Latina*, vol.186 (Paris, 1854), cols.1214-9.

[8] *Enfance*, i. 396-7.

[9] N.D. Hurnard, 'The Anglo-Norman Franchises', *EHR*, lxiv (1949), 289-321, 433-59.

[10] *Enfance*, i. 159.

[11] M.K. Lawson, 'The Collection of Danegeld and Heregeld in the Reigns of Aethelred II and Cnut', *EHR*, xcix (1984), 721-38. Dr. Lawson has shown me a forthcoming, and convincing, paper of his, re-arguing the acceptability of these figures as indications at least of orders of magnitude.

[12] Fossier, *La terre et les hommes*, i. 382-5; Lawson, *op.cit.*, p.727.

struck in successive issues; even to make some kind of guess at the number in circulation. Dr. D.M. Metcalf's calculations suggest that the amount struck in different issues *c*.973-*c*.1059 varied between 47 million pennies and 2.5 million; the amount in circulation from 12 million to 1.3 million.[13] The uniformity of the English currency over a wide area contrasts sharply with, for example, the circumstances in Picardy, where *c*.1050-70 twenty different coinages were in circulation.[14] This uniformity favoured the economic interconnection of the different areas of England. Such interdependence is demonstrated by the extent to which coins are found at a distance from their places of minting. Of coins of the period 1018-87 found singly more than a third were at places more than a hundred kilometres from their mints.[15] The mechanisms for such dispersal could have been in part fiscal; but such a hoard as that from Chester, deposited *c*.980 (i.e. before the period of heavy gelds), strongly suggests the importance of commercial factors. Of its 120 coins, which cannot have been in circulation for more than about six years, only eight were from the Chester mint, and twenty one other mints were represented.[16]

Aspects of the impact of the state on the English economy which deserve special emphasis have to do with public works and public order. A great deal of civil engineering underlay the prosperity of eleventh-century England. The capacity of the Dark Ages in such matters was great. In the Carolingian world one has only to consider the bridge which Charles the Bold threw across the Seine at Pont de l'Arche, or in Scandinavia the oak-piled causeway, a kilometre long, at Ravning Enge (*c*.979).[17] The English were capable of comparable works. Consider Offa's Dyke; or the complete rebuilding of Winchester at about the end of the ninth century;[18] or the extensive reconstruction of the wharves and docks of London at about the same time.[19] Such works were probably undertaken under the direct control of the king.

Even more important were the systems and laws which sought to ensure the maintenance of the communications system as a whole.

---

[13] 'Continuity and Change in English Monetary History, *c*.973-1086, Part 1,' *British Numismatic Journal*, l (1980), 20-49, Part 2, *ibid.*, li (1982), 52-90.

[14] *Enfance*, ii. 1046-7.

[15] D.M. Metcalf, 'Continuity and Change . . .', Part 1, esp. 24-31.

[16] D.M. Metcalf, 'The Ranking of Boroughs: the Numismatic Evidence from the Reign of Aethelred II', *Ethelred the Unready: Papers from the Millenary Conference* (Oxford, 1978), p.168.

[17] D.M. Wilson, *Civil and Military Engineering in Viking Age Scandinavia* (Greenwich, 1978), p.7.

[18] M. Biddle and D.J. Keene, 'The Late Saxon *Burh*', *Winchester in the Early Middle Ages*, ed. M. Biddle (Oxford, 1976), p.450.

[19] B. Hobey, *Roman and Saxon London, a Reappraisal* (London, 1985), pp.18-20, 22; T. Dyson and B. Schofield, 'Saxon London', *Anglo-Saxon Towns in Southern England*, ed. J. Haslam (Chichester, 1984), pp.207-30.

Bridges were especially important in this period. This is brought home by, for example, the *Gesta* of the bishops of Cambrai which relate how the *rustici* rejoiced when the bishop repaired the bridges.[20] In England the obligation to maintain bridges was one which was stressed in a large proportion of charters from the eighth century on. It appears as a widely enforced public duty. A case in point is that of the bridge at Cambridge.[21] This was built at some time in the Anglo-Saxon period and probably before 875. In the middle ages, and later, the responsibility for its maintenance lay on the holders of some thirty estates, scattered in Cambridgeshire west of the Cam. From the earliest relevant document to survive, which is of 1236, to the latest, which is of 1752, these obligations are invariably expressed in hides, the normal unit of assessment up to the twelfth century, but one which thereafter fell into desuetude. This suggests the probability of a pre-thirteenth-century origin for the maintenance system, and, quite likely, of a pre-Conquest one. The case for the latter is strengthened by the evidence for the maintenance of the great bridge over the Medway at Rochester by a similar system; for there the earliest list of the estates responsible is in Old English. It is not clear whether this list is pre-Conquest or immediately post-Conquest.[22] That a later document (1340) assesses the obligations for maintaining the bridge in terms of the archaic Kentish unit, the sulung, suggests that they went a long way back.[23] What we have, almost certainly at Rochester, probably at Cambridge, very likely at other places for which we lack documents, are systems for the maintenance of bridges, which were publicly enforceable and which antedate the Conquest, it may be considerably. Our evidence is always local; but generally suggests the context of a wider system; the direct ancestor of, often the same as, that which prevailed until quite modern times.

It is an important question what the pre-Conquest system was for the maintenance of roads. Here we are largely dependent on the compilations of the earlier twelfth century which claim, in general plausibly, to tell us about Anglo-Saxon law. These indicate that some (possibly all) main roads and waterways were royal; with two consequences: one, that damaging or encroaching upon them was punished by an extremely heavy fine of £5 or £8; two (less, but almost, certain) that offences against people

---

[20] *La terre et les hommes*, i. 257.

[21] H.M. Cam, 'Bridges', *Victoria County History of Cambridgeshire*, iii, ed. J.P.C. Roach (Oxford, 1959), p.114.

[22] *Anglo-Saxon Charters*, ed. A.J. Robertson (Cambridge, 1939), pp.106-9, 351-2.

[23] *Public Works in Medieval Law*, ed. C. Flower, Selden Society, xxxii and xl (1915, 1922), i. 203-9. The assessment of the liabilities for the maintenance of a particular pier corresponds closely to the relevant part of that printed by Robertson, except that it is expressed in 'sullyng', which Flower translates as 'shillings', *recte* 'sulungs'.

travelling on them were similarly punished.[24] Lesser roads and waterways seem to have been protected by a second tier system run at the shire level.[25]

The maintenance of communications was not undertaken by public authority alone; for example, considerable works on the Thames were undertaken by the abbey of Abingdon at about the time of the Conquest.[26] But the maintenance of public systems of control in relation to roads and bridges must have mattered. It is worth noticing that what little evidence we have suggests that speed of movement in the late Anglo-Saxon period was hardly different from what it was to be much later.[27]

The greatest economic advantage which the wide and effective exercise of royal power brought was peace. Fossier provides an illuminating description of the 'peace movement' in western Europe: developing under ecclesiastical influence in the later tenth century, and afterwards to become integrated into the operation of secular power.[28] The relationship between this movement and English circumstances has not been much regarded. On much of the Continent, public peace needed to be restored after Carolingian order crumbled; but in England there was no need for a peace movement because the concept of public peace was never broken as it was on the Continent, and the control and extension of peace remained the responsibility of kings. A demonstration of this is the way in which the oath taken by all freemen to keep the peace (corresponding to the Carolingian peace oath) can be traced as a continuous English institution from at least the tenth century up to the eighteenth.[29] A striking feature of the *Anglo-Saxon Chronicle* from Alfred's reign onwards is to what an extent it is a record of peace, if the wars against Scandinavians are set aside. Indeed, there was some dynastic violence, in particular in 900 and 978.[30] Certainly, the internal politics of Ethelred II's reign were neither calm nor clean. It is true that the annalists of the *Chronicle* could be misleadingly

[24] *Leges Henrici Primi*, ed. L.J. Downer (Oxford, 1972), cc.10.1, 10.2, 12.2, 35.2, 80.3a, 80.5; *Leges Edwardi Confessoris*, in *Die Gesetze der Angelsachsen*, ed. F. Liebermann, 3 vols. (Halle, 1898-1916), i. 627-72, cc.12, 12.1, 12.7; *Domesday Book*, ed. A. Farley, 2 vols. (1784), i. la, 280a, 298c; *Public Works*, ed. Flower, ii; 51. W.S. Holdsworth, *A History of English Law*, x (1938), pp.299-311, 322-8.

[25] *Leges Edwardi Confessoris*, ed. Liebermann, cc.12.9, 12.10, 12.11.

[26] R.H.C. Davis, 'The Ford, the River and the City', *Oxoniensia*, xxxviii (1973), 263-4.

[27] D. Hill, *An Atlas of Anglo-Saxon England* (Oxford, 1981), p.115; P.H. Sawyer, 'The Royal *Tun* in Pre-Conquest England', *Ideal and Reality in Frankish and Anglo-Saxon Society*, ed. P. Wormald, D. Bullough and R. Collins (Oxford, 1983), pp.286-7.

[28] *Enfance*, i. 313-8, 596-7. B.S. Bachrach, 'The Northern Origins of the Peace Movement at Le Puy in 975', *Historical Reflections/Réflexions historiques*, xiv (1987), 405-21 puts more stress on the importance of secular authority in the early days of the movement.

[29] W. Kienast, *Untertanheid und Treuvorbehalt in England und Frankreich* (Weimar, 1952).

[30] *Two of the Saxon Chronicles Parallel*, ed. C. Plummer and J. Earle, 2 vols. (Oxford, 1892-9), i. 92, 123.

discreet, not least about dissidence.[31] But, when all that is said, it is still significant that so little civil strife is recorded. In nearly two centuries the nearest England seems to have come to civil war was in the crisis of 1051-2; and in that crisis war was avoided. It is worth noticing the nature of some of the violence which *is* chronicled. '952 . . . And in this year also the king ordered a great slaughter to be made in the borough of Thetford in vengeance for Abbot Eadhelm, whom they had slain'.[32] Compare Wendover's account of Edgar's punishing the men of Thanet for robbing merchants from York.[33] He 'despoiled all of them of their possessions and even deprived some of life'. Royal violence maintained peace.

The economic advantages of peace are easily exemplified by the way in which the Conqueror's path to London can be traced by the reduced value of estates years after 1066.[34] In this context we should consider the special vulnerability of oxen. No army can destroy more·than one year's crops: but if it kills oxen it kills capital. A repeated feature in the peace legislation of southern France and Spain is the desire to protect plough-beasts. The peace of Cerdanya (1118) was thus described: '. . . mittimus pacem in predicto comitatu de bubibus atque ceteris animalibus et omnibus hominibus tangentibus illos vel arantibus . . . '.[35] The plough-beasts come first. Their crucial importance is brought home by an account of bishop Conrad of Liège's charity during the famine of 1042. He gave twopence a week to each of his tenants so that they should not be driven to sell their *boves*, and thus have to leave the land uncultivated, and either to live in miserable beggary or to die, with all their families, by a death sharper than the sword.[36] Such an account helps to explain the wording of the *Chronicle*'s obituary notice for Henry I: 'He had peace for man *and beast*' (my emphasis).[37] One can, indeed, see that there was good peace for beasts in England. Domesday's recording of approximately 650,000 oxen,

[31] E.g. *ibid.*, ii. 137-8.

[32] *Ibid.*, i. 192.

[33] D. Whitelock, *English Historical Documents c.500-1042*, 2nd edn. (1979), p.284 and n.

[34] H.C. Darby, *Domesday England* (Cambridge, 1977), pp.242-7 and Chapter VIII in general.

[35] T.N. Bisson, *Conservation of Coinage. Monetary Exploitation and its Restraint in France, Catalonia and Aragon, c.1000-c.1225 AD* (Oxford, 1979), pp.60-1.

[36] *Anselmi Gesta Episcoporum Leodiensinum*, ed. R. Koepke, *MGH, Scriptores*, vii (Hanover, 1846), p.221. (I am indebted to Professor K.J. Leyser for this reference.)

[37] *The Peterborough Chronicle, 1070-1154*, ed. C. Clarke, 2nd edn. (Oxford, 1970), p.54, cf. his being described as 'keeper of the beasts and guardian of the flocks', F. Liebermann, 'A Contemporary Manuscript of *Leges Anglorum Londoniis Collecta*', *EHR*, xviii (1913), 739. The Dialogue of the Exchequer says that insolvent debtors should, if possible, be left with their plough oxen 'lest the debtor being unable to farm is reduced to penury', ed. C. Johnson, with corrections by F.E.L. Carter and D.E. Greenway (Oxford, 1983), p.111. (I owe the last reference to Dr John Hudson.)

many the property of peasants, is a sufficient demonstration.[38] The presence of such a stock of motive power had more than agricultural significance. For example, an entry in Worcestershire Domesday says: 'Ibi sunt boves ad i carucam sed petram trahunt ad ecclesiam'; the capacity to build largely depended upon the availability of traction.[39]

The relationships between peace and prosperity were in some ways intricate, in others simple. One of the simplest lay in the protection of frontiers. Take Helmold's account of this in his *Chronicle of the Slavs*. He says that in the days, when through the mercy of God and the valour of Otto I, lasting peace had been established in Wagria and Schleswig the countryside began to be thickly inhabited. In his own day (he is writing in 1172) that peace had long gone: but in the vast and almost impenetrable forest were still to be seen the traces of lost settlements: ridge and furrow, the remains of walls indicating the plans of settlements, mill-dams in the streams.[40] Helmold's observations give him some claim to be considered the father of medieval archaeology: they add a dimension to, for example, the numerous Domesday references to waste in shires on the Welsh border.[41] It is true that 'waste' can be a term of fiscal art rather than of literal description.[42] Nevertheless Helmold's description is a reminder of what the hard reality of an inadequately defended frontier could be; and the history of the Welsh frontier from the time of Offa to that of Edward I demonstrates that recurrently its defence required forces much more powerful than local resources provided. *Encellulement* would not keep out the Welsh.

There was a juncture at which England looked as if it might be in the process of *encellulement*, namely the reign of Stephen. That something which could be so described was in train is made plain by the totally unprecedented appearance of baronial coinages.[43] The locus classicus for the economic impact of such *encellulement* is the much quoted *Peterborough Chronicle*. Let me quote it again: '. . . they (sc. the rebellious barons) filled the country full of castles. . . . they took those people whom they thought

[38] Darby, *Domesday England*, p.336 (81,184 teams of 8); E. Miller and J. Hatcher, *Medieval England and Economic Change, 1086-1348* (Cambridge, 1978), pp.23-4. Contrast the exceedingly small numbers of oxen recorded in ninth century polyptychs, Fossier, *La terre et les hommes*, i. 234, though it may well be that this is in part an indication of the use of tenants' oxen. (For the reasons for accepting that the ploughteam as recorded in Domesday was normally of eight oxen, Darby, *op.cit.*, pp.121-6.)

[39] *Domesday Book*, i. 175^b; cf. Fossier, *La terre et les hommes*, ii. 447.

[40] *Helmoldi Chronica Slavorum*, ed. H. Stoob (Darmstadt, 1963), pp.69, 71.

[41] H.C. Darby and I.B. Terrett, *The Domesday Geography of Midland England* (Cambridge, 1974), pp.95-8, 142-6; C.P. Lewis, 'English and Norman Government and Lordship in the Welsh Borders, 1039-87', Oxford D.Phil. thesis, 1985, Chapter 5.

[42] Lewis, *loc.cit.*

[43] E.g. M. Archibald, 'Coins', *English Romanesque, 1066-1200* (Exhibition catalogue, Hayward Gallery, 1984), p.320 and nos.440, 441, 442, 443, 452.

had any goods . . . and tortured them with indescribable torture to extort gold and silver . . . Many thousands they killed by starvation . . . They levied taxes on the villages . . . When the wretched people had no more to give they robbed and burned the villages, so that you could easily go a whole day's journey and never find anyone occupying a village, nor land tilled. Then corn was dear and meat and butter and cheese, because there was none in the country. Wretched people died of starvation: some lived by begging for alms, who had once been rich men: some fled the country'.[44] Efforts are made to minimise this account, e.g. by indicating that conditions were not the same everywhere; that this description is one which reflects quasi-conventional moralizing rhetoric; and that the *Chronicle* also emphasizes how relatively well the abbey of Peterborough did in Stephen's reign.[45] These contentions are questionable. There are other comparable descriptions derived from other areas.[46] The allowances for 'waste' in the Pipe Roll of 2 Henry II suggest extensive devastation, even though the element of fiscal deceit is unquantifiable.[47] It is not the case that this description 'conformed to a standard pattern used for centuries';[48] I can find no such descriptions earlier or later in England. That Peterborough itself was not badly hit shows that the chronicler was not generalizing from merely local or interested experience. Rather does he seem to be describing a widespread economic catastrophe. There is some evidence which would fit with this. Henry II's early revenues, as recorded in the Pipe Rolls, were low by comparison with those of 1129-30.[49] The chronicler's attitude accords with that of those whom Professor Fossier regards as blinded by centuries of Jacobin centralization.[50] One might do better to see this monk as enlightened by centuries of West Saxon centralization: his norm was a world in which kings had long maintained *pax*, the *gode frith* for which another chronicler praised William I, otherwise detestable to him.[51]

A provocative feature of Professor Fossier's theses is the restricted role he attributes to towns; he regards them as external to the main concerns of society until *c*.1200 more than once describing them as 'cysts'.[52] His view is shared by some English historians: Professor Miller and Dr. Hatcher,

---

[44] *Peterborough Chronicle*, ed. Clark, pp.55-6.
[45] H.A. Cronne, *The Anarchy of Stephen's Reign* (London, 1970), pp.2-23, esp. pp.3, 10-14.
[46] E.g. *ibid.*, p.183.
[47] *Ibid.*, pp.224-5. Doubts about the literal reality of 'waste' were forcefully expressed by A.L. Poole, *From Domesday Book to Magna Carta* (Oxford, 1955), pp.151-3; but he to a large extent begs a crucial question, that of how far the 'waste' of the Pipe Rolls may reflect otherwise unrecorded devastation due to war.
[48] Cronne, *The Anarchy*, p.14.
[49] J.C. Holt, *Magna Carta and Medieval Government* (London, 1985), pp.34-5.
[50] P.1. above.
[51] *Peterborough Chronicle*, ed. Clark, p.12.
[52] *Enfance*, ii. 980.

for example, regard the eleventh-century English economy as characterized by 'the absence of manufacture as a significant specialised activity'.[53] These contentions raise major difficulties.

Professor Sawyer, in a crucial paper, contends that 'England was as heavily urbanized in the eleventh century as in the fourteenth';[54] the figures he uses do not quite demonstrate this; but other calculations indicate that the proportion of the population living in settlements with a population of more than 450 in 1086 probably approached, and may indeed have reached, what it was in 1377.[55] It is well within the bounds of possibility that the major provincial towns were of the same order of magnitude in the late eleventh as in the late fourteenth century.[56]

That many people lived in towns itself suggests that the economic integration of town and countryside was already established. The author of the *Leges Edwardi Confessoris* seems to share this view when he sees waterways as essentially the means of conveying supplies from countryside to town: 'aque quarum navigio de diversis partibus deteruntur victualia civitatibus et burgis'; 'aquis minoribus, naves ferentibus, cum eis que necessaria sunt civitatibus et burgis, ligna scilicet et cetera'.[57] Note the *ligna*; fuel was the most bulky item of urban

---

[53] Miller and Hatcher, *Medieval England*, p.1, cf. *ibid.*, p.12, but note the modifying observations, p.10.

[54] P.H. Sawyer, 'The Wealth of England in the Eleventh Century', *TRHS*, 5th ser., xv (1965), 164.

[55] I hope to go into this matter more fully elsewhere; but, briefly, Professor Sawyer used J.C. Russell's figures for the proportion of the population living in burghal settlements in 1086: 10.2%; and for the proportion living in settlements with a population of more than 450 in 1377: 11.6%. It is better to compare the 1377 figure with Russell's figures indicating the proportion of the population living in settlements with on his estimation a population of over 450 in 1086: 8.6%. There are various reasons (e.g. his omission of Bury St. Edmunds) for regarding the second figure as an underestimate. (J.C. Russell, *British Medieval Population* (Albuquerque, 1948), pp.45-54, 140-6.) On the estimates of H.C. Darby and his colleagues, reduced to exclude places likely to have had a population of less than 450, the 'burgess etc' proportion of the whole population, as they estimate it, is between 6.6% and 8.9%: *Domesday England*, pp.89, 302-9, 364-8. The authors of the *Domesday Geographies* commonly indicate that their estimates for urban populations are minima. I am aware of the questionability of taking population as a criterion of urban status. However, it is that which makes it easiest to compare centuries; and an inspection of the Russell and Darby lists for 1086 used in the way I have indicated above will show that one obvious objection, viz. that they could include places whose apparently high population is due to a number of settlements being comprised under the name of one, does not apply.

[56] Thus in 1066 York was the second most populous town after London, Oxford the fifth (assuming Winchester to be higher than fifth); a multiplier of 5 suggests populations of 9,000 for the one, and 5,000 for the other. In 1377 York was the second most populous town, Lincoln the fifth: the poll tax records suggest populations of 10,872 and 5,353: C. Stephenson, *Borough and Town, a Study of Urban Origins in England* (Cambridge, Mass., 1933), p.221; W.G. Hoskins, *Local History in England* (London, 1959), p.176.

[57] Ed. Liebermann, *op.cit.*, 12, 12.11 (pp.638, 639-40).

consumption. In the early fourteenth century Norwich Cathedral Priory could burn 400,000 peats a year.[58] This use of the peat-mines which became the Broads probably reflects the exhaustion of timber. Behind *defrîchement* lay not only the demand for land, but also that for fuel for domestic and perhaps above all for industrial use.

In England, such a demand could have been quite sharp, quite early. For there were towns with important industries in England before the Conquest. From the later ninth century pottery-manufacture became important in a number of towns, chiefly in the east.[59] Stamford is the best-known instance: its abundant products were distributed over a radius of a hundred and twenty miles.[60] Though pottery shouts loudly in the archaeological record other manufactures were probably more important. At York there is evidence for wood and leather working and other manufactures on a considerable scale.[61] A likely tannery was housed in a building 27.5 metres by 6: not so much a workshop, more a factory.[62] The early (not later than the early tenth century) herring-processing establishment there deserves special notice.[63] The herring was the potato of the middle ages: its preservation and distribution, and the urban role in either, are both important. Although only in the case of pottery is it possible to demonstrate that some of what was produced in the towns was consumed in the countryside, nevertheless the same was very probably true of other manufactures also, not least metal goods, tools.[64] In emphasizing the importance of these Professor Fossier associates it with the proliferation of rural smiths.[65] The capacity of such smiths would, however, be limited. We meet one who would not even make hunting-arrows.[66] If one may draw on a continental source to indicate English possibilities, the earliest Arras toll-list is relevant. It shows both that tools could be bought in the town, and that so also could iron and steel. Rural smiths were not the only sources of tools; and for their raw materials they could look to a town.[67] Another continental source indicates a further important possibility in the town/country relationship. Guibert of Nogent describes country people coming to town (*c*.1110) to provision themselves

---

[58] J.M. Lambert and others, *The Making of the Broads* (London, 1960), pp.84-5.

[59] J.G. Hurst, 'The Pottery', *The Archaeology of Anglo-Saxon England*, ed. D.M. Wilson (London, 1976), pp.314-39; J. Haslam, *Medieval Pottery* (London, 1978), pp.10 et seq.

[60] K. Kilmurry, *The Pottery Industry of Stamford, Lincs., AD 850-1250* (Oxford, 1980).

[61] A. MacGregor, 'Industry and Commerce in Anglo-Scandinavian York', *Viking Age York and the North*, ed. R.A. Hall (London, 1978), pp.45-51.

[62] *Ibid.*, pp.51-6.

[63] R. Cramp, *Anglian and Viking York* (York, 1967), pp.18-19.

[64] G.M. Knocker and R.G. Hughes, 'Anglo-Saxon Thetford', *Archaeological News Letter*, ii (1950), 118; MacGregor, 'Industry and Commerce', pp.42-5.

[65] *Enfance*, ii. 631-2; *La terre et les hommes*, i. 370-2.

[66] *The Chronicle of Battle Abbey*, ed. E. Searle (Oxford, 1980), pp.36-7.

[67] *Cartulaire de l'Abbaye de Saint Vaast d'Arras*, ed. E. van Drival (Arras, 1875), p.168.

with vegetables, corn and other produce.[68] This would be consonant with specialized production: peasants selling some agricultural products and buying others.

Important in the relationships with which I am concerned may have been those between townsmen and landowners. The early eleventh-century tract saying that a trader who had prospered to the extent of crossing the sea three times at his own expense was worthy of the rights of a thegn is relevant here.[69] The evidence from Domesday and later sources for such a town as Cambridge shows a close relationship between burgess and thegnly status.[70] Similarly indicative is the position in the eleventh and twelfth centuries of such a family as that of Deorman: moneyers, goldsmiths, landowners, and more.[71] Even such a quasi-apocryphal story as that in the *Gesta* of Hereward the Wake that he had a godfather called Gilbert of Ghent, who lived at York and sounds like a merchant, is suggestive of the kind of link of which we could know much more if our knowledge of late Anglo-Saxon prosopography were better than it is.[72] After the Conquest there is no doubt that some aristocrats were important urban property-owners; and one may wonder how far they had other commercial concerns.[73]

The general involvement of the eleventh-century English polity with towns may be seen in more ways than one. English kings had control over towns to an extent unparalleled elsewhere: e.g. there were no towns over which bishops exerted firm control in England. The Conqueror's determination to maintain that control partly explains why the great majority of his castles were urban.[74] A singular aspect of the association of towns with the state appears in the ceremonies associated with the coronation. Special functions at the feast were attributed to the representatives of London, Oxford, Winchester and the Cinque Ports.[75] The London and Winchester services are first mentioned in connection with the coronation of Richard I. Most of our earliest information about what happened outside the *ordo* comes from this date. The services in question could be much older. This possibility is strengthened by evidence that those of Oxford go back at least to Henry II's time and by

---

[68] *Guibert de Nogent: Histoire de sa vie*, ed. G. Bourgin (Paris, 1907), iii, 7, pp.155-6.

[69] *Gesetze*, ed. Liebermann, i. 458.

[70] H.M. Cam in *VCH, Cambridgeshire*, iii. 3-4.

[71] P. Nightingale, 'Some London Moneyers and Reflections on the History of English Mints in the Eleventh Century', *Numismatic Chronicle*, cxlii (1982), 33-50.

[72] E.A. Freeman, *The History of the Norman Conquest of England*, 2nd edn. (Oxford, 1876), iv. 828.

[73] E.g. *Domesday Book*, i. f.298 for Norman aristocratic landowners at York.

[74] Well illustrated by R. Allen Brown's map in R. Allen Brown, H.M. Colvin and A.J. Taylor, *The History of the King's Works*, i (1963), fig.5.

[75] J.H. Round, *The King's Sergeants and Officers of State with their Coronation Services* (London, 1911), pp.166-72.

the description of the same three towns, London, Winchester and Oxford, as having special rights of pre-emption in a twelfth-century document generally agreed to reflect Anglo-Saxon circumstances.[76] I can find no continental parallel to such urban involvement in coronation ceremonial; its appearance in England represents an integration between towns and monarchy not in accord with Fossier's view of the gap between towns and the rest of society before *c*.1200.

That he should hold such a view is the more surprising in the light of the extremely illuminating arguments he puts forward on the development of the countryside: in particular on its penetration, as he puts it, by iron and by silver. He sees this process as taking place in different areas at somewhat varying times; in Picardy between *c*.1050 and 1125.[77] It involved more participation in markets and the diffusion of better techniques and more tools. One of the determinative contrasts between the Carolingian and the medieval countryside is, he maintains, that in the former smiths and materials were rarely met with, in the latter, often. He relates these developments to social changes: in particular to the appearance of a substantial knightly class.[78] Put too simply the argument is this. Horses and armour were not cheap. (In eleventh-century Normandy a horse could cost between £2 and £30, a hauberk £7.[79]) A countryside whose economy was developing (growth in mechanical milling and in the supply of metal goods playing important parts in such development) could support more gentlemen of the horse and hauberk owning kind than heretofor.[80]

Apply such thoughts to England. Consider, for example, armour. In 1008 Ethelred II ordered the provision of 'a helmet and a hauberk from every eight hides'.[81] Perhaps he did not get them; but this is something more than *a priori* evidence to suggest that his demand was not

[76] J. Cooper, 'Medieval Oxford', *VCH, Oxford*, iii, ed. A. Crossley (1979), p.50; M.W. Bateson, 'A London Municipal Collection of the Reign of John', *EHR*, xvii (1902), 499-500.

[77] *La terre et les hommes*, i. 252-5.

[78] *Enfance*, ii. 615, 625-6; *La terre et les hommes*, i. 236-40, 370-4, 382, 387.

[79] L. Musset, 'La vie économique de l'abbaye de Fécamp sous l'abbatiat de Jean de Rouenne 1028-78', *L'abbaye bénédictine de Fécamp, ouvrage scientifique du XIIIᵉ centenaire*, 4 vols. (Fecamp, 1959-63), i. 71 suggests that the mid-eleventh-century price-range was (in Norman pounds) from £2-3 for a mediocre horse to £10 for a good one. However, a charter of 1041 x 1048 mentions 'equum xxx librorum' and another of 1063 'xii librorum equo': M. Fauroux, *Recueil des actes des ducs de Normandie de 911 à 1066* (Caen, 1961), nos.113, 156. The former charter also refers to 'unum halberc vii librorum'; N.P. Brooks, 'Arms, Status and Warfare in Late Saxon England', *Ethelred the Unready*, ed. D. Hall, p.81 cites a Norman reference of 1133 indicating that a *lorica* and a stirrup were worth £15. Fossier, *Enfance*, i. 428 puts the cost of a *lorica c*.1080 at about £5, and that of an equipped warhorse at £5-£12.

[80] R. Fossier, 'Land, Castle, Money and Family in the Formation of Seigneuries', *Medieval Settlement*, ed. P. Sawyer (London, 1974), pp.159-68, esp. 164-8.

[81] *Two Saxon Chronicles*, i. 138.

unrealistic.[82] That armour and helmets first appear in English wills in the early eleventh century suggests that their availability on a large scale was new.[83] The knights of Norman England 'served by their hauberks':[84] thousands of hauberks before and after the Conquest are implied. How were they provided? No doubt, often by lords. Tostig had a store of weapons at York in 1065.[85] In 1130 we find a Cheshire knight on his death-bed returning armour and horse to his lord.[86] But many men, Saxon and Norman, presumably provided their own equipment. Using very rough rules of thumb (e.g. that a hide of land was worth about a pound a year) and prices of the order of magnitude quoted above, it would seem that something like the annual income from quite a big village would have been required to provide a hauberk; and the capital represented, in principle, by the horses and armour required for the Anglo-Norman *servitia debita* must have been vast.

Such considerations almost demonstrate the marked economic development of England. But thanks to Domesday, we have more direct evidence. Of particular interest in the light of Fossier's observations are the six thousand odd mills recorded.[87] The abundance of these, the most elaborate machines of the day, suggests an economy as much developed as developing. Fossier reminds us also of the importance of smiths. Domesday provides no more than casual references to these: their appearance at centres of authority is noteworthy; the eight smiths at Glastonbury are a striking instance.[88] The significance of smiths is more directly brought home by Aelfric's *Colloquy*: his smith says that the ploughman depends on him for his plough, the fisherman for his hook, the shoemaker for his awl.[89] The sense of the smith as the specialist upon whom other specialists depended is deepened by the early eleventh-century tract on estate management, *Gerefa*; it provides a long list of required instruments, tools, many of metal.[90] One may suppose that

[82] J. Campbell, *Essays in Anglo-Saxon History* (London, 1987), p.200; *Thietmari Merseburgensis Episcopi Chronicon*, ed. J.M. Lappenbergh and F. Kurze (Hanover, 1889), viii. 40 (p.217).

[83] N.P. Brooks, 'Arms, Status and Warfare . . .', pp.81-103.

[84] F.M. Stenton, *The First Century of English Feudalism*, 2nd edn. (Oxford, 1961), pp.14-18.

[85] *Two Saxon Chronicles*, i. 191(d).

[86] G. Barraclough, *Facsimiles of Early Cheshire Charters* (London, 1957), p.20.

[87] R. Lennard, *Rural England, 1086-1135* (Oxford, 1959), pp.278-87 provides the best account.

[88] H.C. Darby and R. Welldon Finn, *The Domesday Geography of South West England* (Cambridge, 1967), pp.162, 166.

[89] *Aelfric's Colloquy*, ed. G.N. Garmonsway (London, 1939), pp.39-40.

[90] *Gesetze*, ed. Liebermann, pp.453-5; translated W. Cunningham, *The Growth of English Industry and Commerce in the Early and Middle Ages*, 5th edn. (Cambridge, 1910), pp.573-5: over a hundred different kinds of tool, implement and vessel are listed, over twenty of them metal.

improved techniques and more abundant tools went hand in hand with increased investment, so that a more heavily capitalized countryside – more oxen, more mills, more iron tools – created more demand, for manufactures and for luxury goods, in towns, which in turn were creating an increased demand for agricultural produce and fuel.

Fossier's work is in the tradition of Marc Bloch, bringing home above all the inseparability of the history of the economy and the history of power. Three things stand out if one asks, for England, some of the questions he raises. First, the importance of the power of the state; second, the need to recognize that some determinative factors are barely discernible so that, alas, it may follow that others are not discernible at all; third, the crucial importance of comparison.

Leading examples of the economic significance of the power of the state are sketched above: in regard to currency, communications and towns. It is not hard to think of others. For example, the absence of Jews from late Anglo-Saxon England is strongly suggested by the evidence of the Hebrew *responsa*. The same evidence shows the Rhineland Jews in the tenth and eleventh centuries active in trade from Bohemia to Spain.[91] Granted the closeness of the connections between England and the Rhineland, it is not easy to explain the absence of Jewish involvement in England by anything other than royal decree. The consideration of systems, or possible systems, of economic organization raises many possibilities. For example, Dr. Britnell's excellent article on the relationship between hundreds and markets, in arguing against there having been a system of one market to each hundred in fact establishes at least the possibility that there was such a system.[92] Or again, Henry I's charter of 1131 granting a monopoly of waterborne commerce in Cambridgeshire to Cambridge may be in effect a confirmation and relate to a long-standing system which prevailed in other shires.[93] Very important is the almost complete absence of castles from England.[94] Here we seem to have an example of the maintenance of a royal prerogative, of control over fortification, which had existed on the Continent, but which had been extensively lost. The more one looks at England, the less helpful does the doctrine of *encellulement* seem. One might add, the more one reads the work of Fossier, the less is one assured that he is so convinced of the near-universal validity of that doctrine as the vigour

[91] I.A. Agus, *Urban Civilisation in Pre-Crusade Europe*, 2 vols. (Leiden, 1965), *passim*: the one possible reference to trade with England (early eleventh century) probably relates to North Africa (i. 61). See also H.G. Richardson, *The English Jewry under the Angevin Kings* (London, 1960), p.1, n.4.

[92] R.H. Britnell, 'English Markets and Local Administration before 1200', *Economic History Review*, 2nd ser., xxxi (1978), 183-96.

[93] H.M. Cam in *VCH, Cambridgeshire*, iii. 6. My observations are in the light of, regrettably, unpublished work by Mr Neil Middleton.

[94] R. Allen Brown, *English Castles*, 3rd edn. (London, 1976), pp.40-51.

of some of his statements suggests. Rather might one consider what he has to say, for example, about the *modèle de Flandre* or about the extent to which something like public power survived in Picardy.[95]

To seek to understand the tenth and eleventh centuries is to face a jigsaw with many missing pieces. The temptation to jam what we have together without leaving gaps is one to resist. Consider, for example, Professor Sawyer's brilliant hypothesis that the abundance of silver in late Anglo-Saxon England is best explained by the assumption that the export of wool was already of major importance.[96] His evidence was entirely inferential. It can be strengthened. First, Dr. Metcalf has now demonstrated in great detail that it is indeed likely that there was a very large inflow of silver in the early eleventh century.[97] Second, Sawyer, uncharacteristically, missed a passage in Henry of Huntingdon (writing in the 1140s) stating that, although little silver is mined in England, much is brought 'a proxima parte Germaniae per Rhenum' on account of England's wonderful fertility in fish and meat, in most precious wool, in cattle without number. Thus, says Huntingdon, a larger supply of silver is to be found there than in Germany itself.[98] Dr. Nightingale's hypothesis that the adoption of new weight-standards in the Rhineland, Flanders and Scandinavia in the early eleventh century was under the influence of England partly depends on, but partly reinforces Professor Sawyer's hypothesis.[99] None of this had been thought of twenty-five years ago. One wonders how much we still do not know; above all about the determinative influence of major international trade.[100]

Problems of comparison press very hard. Crucial here is the superiority of the English evidence, above all, Domesday Book. Thus Domesday proves that the clearing of woodland had progressed a very long way by 1086. It permits calculations on more than one basis which establish the strong possibility that there was as much land under the plough in 1086 as in *c*.1900.[101] The principal reasons for doubting this evidence seem to be

[95] *Enfance*, i. 379-401; *La terre et les hommes*, i. 268-9.

[96] 'The Wealth of England in the Eleventh Century', pp.161-3.

[97] D.M. Metcalf, 'Continuity and Change in English Monetary History . . .'.

[98] *Historia Anglorum*, ed. T. Arnold (London, 1879), pp.5-6. This reference cannot be probative for the eleventh century; but not until the early twelfth century do English sources provide such information.

[99] P. Nightingale, 'The Evolution of Weight Standards and the Creation of New Monetary and Commercial Links in Northern Europe from the Tenth Century to the Twelfth Century', *Economic History Review*, 2nd ser., xxxviii (1985), 192-209.

[100] *La terre et les hommes*, i. 248 for a bold suggestion along these lines.

[101] F.W. Maitland, *Domesday Book and Beyond* (Cambridge, 1879), pp.435-7; R. Lennard, *Rural England 1086-1135*, pp.4-7; H.C. Darby, *Domesday England*, pp.129-33. Local studies, e.g. C. Taylor, *The Cambridgeshire Landscape* (London, 1973), pp.70-80 and C. Dyer, *Lords and Peasants in a Changing Society* (Cambridge, 1980), pp.21-5 support the impression of very extensive pre-Conquest clearing.

little more than a priori. (A good deal that seems fairly clear about late Anglo-Saxon England is doubted a priori.) Furthermore, a very high proportion of the settlements of medieval and later England are mentioned in Domesday. Of course many changed their nature, and/or, within limits, their sites, after 1086. It is still an astonishing fact that if you wish to write the history of an English village within the area covered by Domesday Book, some four times out of five you will find an account of it there. Were we reduced to collecting the first references to particular settlements in chronicles and charters, to plotting references to clearing as they appear in such sources, our picture would be one of the major growth of settlement and of clearing having taken place in the twelfth and thirteenth centuries. We might well, of course, suspect that the distribution of the evidence had skewed that picture; but we would have no means of verifying the suspicion (other than by far more pollen-analysis than has so far been possible). In short we should be in the position of those who study settlement in France or Germany.[102] It by no means follows, of course, that because settlement and clearing were far advanced in England by 1086 that the same applied anywhere, let alone everywhere, across the Channel. But the English evidence does raise questions: not least, about the true implications of the polyptych evidence for exceedingly high populations in the ninth century. The normal endeavours to minimize the significance of this can seem a little forced.[103] And one notices with interest such an observation as that of Fossier on the extent of woodland in Picardy, which in the twelfth century seems to have been about what it was in the eighteenth.[104]

It could be that there was something really extraordinary about England. Certainly contemporaries lauded the English wealth. William of Poitiers does so, for example. The land, he says, is itself fertile, but its wealth has been increased by foreign trade. There are many treasures there − put to pious uses by good King William.[105] But the wealth of England may have been something of a topos, a necessary preliminary to a ritual observation on *luxus Anglicanus*.[106] The topos and the ritual may indeed tell us something; it is interesting that William of Malmesbury should characterize the Confessor's reign as one of peace: 'pro pacis

---

[102] Fossier himself in his brief consideration of clearing in England adopts the technique of looking for direct evidence rather than considering the unmistakable general implication of Domesday: thus he substantially post-dates the bulk of clearing in England, *Enfance*, i. 100, 172-3, 186.

[103] E.g. R. Doehaerd, *Le haut Moyen Age Occidental: Economies et Sociétés* (Paris, 1971), pp.110-3.

[104] *La terre et les hommes*, i. 306.

[105] *Guillaume de Poitiers: Histoire de Guillaume le Conquérant*, ed. R. Foreville (Paris, 1952), pp.222-6.

[106] *William of Malmesbury: De Gestis Pontificum*, ed. N.E.S.A. Hamilton (London, 1870), p.179.

affluentia fervebat luxus'.[107] We are very short of figures which would permit serious comparison. Professor Sawyer's observation that the cash income of Christ Church, Canterbury in the late eleventh century seems to have been more than twice that of Cluny is an exception.[108] There is a wide field for enquiry here.

It is also worth making comparisons with later centuries and other lands. 'Mixed farming techniques have also been introduced . . . aimed . . . at the introduction of oxdrawn ploughs in order to eliminate the tillage bottleneck and make possible larger farms.' This observation (1977) relates to Syria.[109] The eighty odd thousand plough teams of Domesday England look the more impressive in its light. They look yet more so if one considers C. Uzereau's account of 'Animal Draught in West Africa' (1974).[110] For example, in Dahomey animal draught was almost unknown until *c.*1964 and ten years later there were only some 3,600 plough oxen there.

The changes which took place in late Dark Age and early medieval Europe were of determinative importance and not for the history of Europe alone. We are looking at the accumulation of the resources and techniques which were the necessary preliminary to the European conquest of most of the world. No one has brought out the nature and intricacy of these processes more effectively than has Professor Fossier. There are two major respects in which the case of England does not fit with, and to an extent raises questions about, his brilliant interpretative scheme. First, it suggests the importance not of *encellulement* but, rather, of royal and public power. Second, it suggests that some of the development to which he refers, not least that of towns as an integral part of society and the economy, not as mere alien growths, had taken place much earlier in England than he argues to have been the case abroad. That the English evidence is unusually good raises a question as to whether he has post-dated such transformations elsewhere.

Such matters abound in cause for doubt. *Dubito ergo sum* must be the motto of the dark age historian. On one point there can be no doubt: the heavy debt which English historians owe to French. The present paper is doubly illustrative of this. Provoked by the boldly deployed learning of Professor Fossier, it is offered as part of a tribute to Pierre Chaplais, the Madox of our day.

---

[107] *The Vita Wulfstani of William of Malmesbury*, ed. R.R. Darlington, Camden Society, 3rd ser. xl (1928), p.23.

[108] 'The Wealth of England . . .', p.156. (£650 compared to £300: I cannot compare the pounds but assume the English were worth more.)

[109] W.B. Morgan, *Agriculture in the Third World* (London, 1977), p.195.

[110] *World Crops*, xxvi (1974), 112-4

Chapter 2

Succession and Politics in the Romance-speaking World, c. 1000-1140*

Jane Martindale

'This evil conflict brought low a rich and prosperous land. In that calamity the fertility of the soil was destroyed through ravaging, wealth by plunder and – or so it is said – a third of the population of the kingdom and its surrounding parts was wiped out through its inhabitants' great wickedness, and as a result of the envy and divisions among barons, earls and powerful men of the kingdom.'[1]

Suger, abbot of St. Denis

This description of the Anglo-Norman kingdom after the death of Henry I (1135) resembles so many of the set-pieces cataloguing the disorders of the anarchy that, despite its relative unfamiliarity to English historians, it may seem scarcely worth a second thought. It is part of an extended account of the most serious political crises with which European rulers were confronted in the early twelfth century; moreover it was written by a man who provided surprisingly modern explanations of why 'disorders, scandals and rebellions are liable to occur . . . at the deaths of kings'.[2]

Suger, abbot of St. Denis from 1122-51, inserted it as a preface to his unfinished *Life* of Louis VII (1137-80); and even if he did not have first hand experience of conditions in England and Normandy, Suger was an exceptionally well-informed observer of political affairs. As counsellor to two Capetian rulers his comments deserve close attention, whilst his administration of the kingdom during Louis VII's absence on crusade lends even greater weight to his views. Additionally he was acquainted with many prominent individuals involved in the struggle between Matilda and Stephen for Normandy and England; while his contribution in securing the peaceful succession of the young Louis VII also suggests

---

* Limitations of space prevent full discussion of the technical aspects of much of the original material used here, nor can the very full secondary literature be extensively cited in this paper which represents only some of the detailed topics (e.g. on family structure) of studies now in hand. I should like to thank Michael Jones for encouragement in preparing this contribution.

[1] *Vie de Louis le Gros par Suger suivie de l'histoire du roi Louis VII*, ed. A. Molinier (Paris, 1887), cited as *Hist. Louis VII*, p.149.

[2] *Ibid.*, p.147; for authorship, see p.xxxiv and G. Spiegel, *The Chronicle Tradition of St. Denis* (Leyden, 1978), pp.49-51.

that his views on succession to high office need to be taken seriously.[3]

The problems of political succession and of inheritance were closely related in his opinion. Suger expressed this conviction with especial emphasis in an assertion that even the lands of the mighty and very famous King Henry were exposed to the dangers of war and faction because he was deprived of his heir at sea. For lack of an heir – and it seems that Suger thought in terms of a male descendant when he wrote 'heir' – the way was opened up for the events with which all English historians are familiar: 'The king's nephew, Count Stephen of Boulogne (younger brother of the palatine Count Theobald), assumed the crown after he entered the kingdom. He did not pay any attention to the fact that the count of Anjou had taken as his wife King Henry's daughter (who had been empress of the Romans) . . . and that the count had sons by her'.[4] Although unfortunately no judgement is passed on whether a sister's son had better rights of inheritance than a daughter, the dynastic problems of the Norman royal house are comprehensively summed up in that tortuous sentence; and Suger makes similar remarks on the nearly contemporary disorders in the 'empire of the Romans'. For lack of an heir their territory ruled by Matilda's first husband, Emperor Henry V, was also brought 'almost to ruin', destroyed by the conflicts among competing dynastic rivals. By contrast the French (*Franci*) could rejoice because they were ruled by Louis VI's *nobilissima proles*, already consecrated and crowned before his father's death. The stability of the kingdom had been assured – at least in Suger's view – by the son's inheritance of his father's lands.[5]

Suger must have had an ulterior motive in drawing attention to the disasters which had befallen the Capetians' most powerful neighbours: the state of the French kingdom would inevitably appear all the brighter for the sombre contrast. In spite of this fairly obvious bias, the direct connection made between aristocratic inheritance methods and the maintenance of political and social order is of great interest in considering politics and property in the eleventh and twelfth centuries. Suger appears to have drawn attention to problems which arose when inheritance practices were unclear, or hereditary claims advanced by different contenders were weighed against other considerations. The system of heredity with which he was familiar – and which he thought equally applicable to the great kingdoms of England, Germany, France and to their greatest principalities – was not so tidily arranged that the problems

---

[3] *Ibid.*, pp.v-vii; Suger, *Vie de Louis VI le Gros*, ed. H. Waquet (Paris, 1929), pp.v-xvii; A.W. Lewis, *Royal Succession in Capetian France. Studies on Familial Order and the State* (Harvard, 1981), pp.56-7; E. Bournazel, 'Suger and the Capetians', *Abbot Suger and Saint-Denis*, ed. P.L. Gerson (New York, 1986), esp. pp.55-60, 66; M. Bur, 'Suger's Understanding of Political Power', *ibid.*, pp. 73-5.

[4] *Hist. Louis VII*, p.149. The interest of Suger's terminology cannot be discussed here.

[5] A.W. Lewis, 'Suger's Views on Kingship', *Abbot Suger and Saint-Denis*, esp. p.51.

of political succession could be solved by reference to some body of rules, universally acknowledged. He does not say that Stephen had no right to his maternal uncle's inheritance, but he does note that Stephen was a younger son. For many contemporaries the elbowing out of his elder brother might have been more important than Stephen's disinheritance of Matilda. Suger also hints that, even though Matilda might be repugnant to her father's barons, she did have sons by her second husband who might be regarded as suitable successors to their grandfather.[6] A churchman might have particular distaste for the idea of a woman's succeeding to the throne but, on the other hand, this churchman could not deny the legitimacy of female inheritance without undermining the means by which Louis VII had benefited from his marriage to Eleanor of Aquitaine *cum tota terra sua*. Suger had helped to engineer that marriage and to ensure the establishment of Louis in Eleanor's duchy.

Suger's interpretation of these crises has found various modern echoes, especially in discussions of the difficulties which beset the Norman dynasty and the princes who contributed towards the making of the Angevin empire. There would probably now be general agreement that it was the remoter contingencies of the prevailing system of heredity which provoked the bitterness of the disputes for the Anglo-Norman inheritance, and frequently forced descendants of William the Conqueror to fight for the succession between 1087 and 1154. It is more readily accepted, too, that the dynastic interests of the royal family were widely supported by those of the aristocracy; but this reinterpretation – grossly oversimplified here – inevitably makes it necessary to re-examine also the relationship between property and politics.[7]

The boundaries between the normal and remoter contingencies have been brilliantly explored in recent years. Yet certain puzzles remain. In the nature of things it is difficult to give an authoritative answer to the questions raised by Professor J.C. Holt: 'What underlay a family alliance? What provoked a family conflict?' These questions were still unanswered

[6] A reference in Suger's treatise *De rebus in administratione sua gestis* to his purchase of jewels for St. Denis which came from Count Theobald of Champagne *via* Cîteaux and Fontevrault raises the question of whether Stephen may not in some way have compensated his elder brother for the loss of the Anglo-Norman inheritance. These jewels were of great value and had been obtained from the 'treasures' of King Henry, *Abbot Suger on the Abbey Church of St. Denis*, ed. E. Panofsky, 2nd edn. (Princeton, 1979), pp.59, 107, references kindly provided by my husband.

[7] J. Le Patourel, *The Norman Empire* (Oxford, 1976), pp.190-2, cf. pp.104-9, 270-1, 288-9, 327; R.H.C. Davis, *King Stephen* (London, 1976), pp.13-15, 121-8 (and in 1980 edn., pp.154-5); J.C. Holt, 'Feudal Society and the Family in Early Medieval England', *TRHS*, 5th ser. 32-35 (1982-5), esp. 32 (1982), 194; *idem*, 'Politics and Property in Early Medieval England', *Past & Present*, no.57 (1972), 3-52; J.Gillingham, *The Making of the Angevin Empire* (London, 1984), pp.4-16.

in the Norman Empire of the 1120s.[8] The question of what was considered a normal hereditary succession, and how remoter contingencies should be settled were affected by disputes which took place on an even wider front. Here some of the more striking cases, where succession and politics appear to have been closely interconnected within the Capetian kingdom and the Romance-speaking world during the eleventh and twelfth centuries, will be examined in order to elucidate problems which have occasionally received rather different treatment from French and English scholars. It is offered as a tribute to a scholar whose own work has so illuminatingly crossed the boundaries of the Anglo-French medieval world.

Even without reminders from Suger, it is clear that the Anglo-Norman crises of Henry I's reign and earlier need to be discussed within their European setting. The view that Matilda could be presented as a 'marriageable widow' who might 'entangle England with a foreign power' seems inappropriate today, when far more emphasis is placed on the shared background of the contestants for Henry I's throne.[9] The paternal origins of both Stephen of Blois and Henry of Anjou lay deep in the Loire valley where their distant ancestors had fought to establish political control over the city of Tours. By the twelfth century also both dynasties had a strong interest in the new Christian kingdom of Jerusalem; but, whereas Stephen's father died in the futile but heroic defence of Ramleh in 1102, Henry's grandfather left for Jerusalem after his son Geoffrey was chosen as second husband for the Empress Matilda;[10] in his later years Geoffrey took the high sounding title *Goffridus Fulchonis regis Jerusalem filius et Dei gratia Andecavorum comes*. Involvement in crusading went even further than this, since Stephen's paternal uncle renounced his own county to serve with the newly founded knighthood of the Temple; while Henry of Anjou's marriage to Eleanor later added the princes of Antioch to the aristocratic connections of this group with the Holy Land.[11] Even without going so far afield, it is striking that Henry I's own outlook was European rather than insular. Walter Map was undoubtedly exaggerating when he wrote that Henry sent for every *iuvenis* of promise 'this side of the Alps' to join his court, but Henry presumably gathered together many who were French or Romance-speaking. Significantly, too, the ceremonies which

---

[8] Holt, *TRHS*, 32 (1982), 193-6.

[9] A.L. Poole, *From Domesday Book to Magna Carta* (Oxford, 1951), pp.128, 131-2; cf. M. Chibnall, *Anglo-Norman England* (Oxford, 1986), p.5.

[10] Davis, *King Stephen*, pp.1-5; S. Runciman, *A History of the Crusades*, 3 vols. (Cambridge, 1953-8), ii. 78; J. Chartrou, *L'Anjou de 1109 à 1151* (Paris, 1928), pp.23-5.

[11] Chartrou, *L'Anjou*, pp.225-39; *Regesta Regum Anglo-Normannorum (1066-1154)*, ed. H.A. Cronne & R.H.C. Davis (Oxford, 1968), iii, nos.19, 1002; A.J. Forey, 'The Emergence of the Military Orders in the Twelfth Century', *Journal of Ecclesiastical History*, 36 (1985), 180; below n.46 for Raymond of Antioch, Eleanor's paternal uncle.

prepared the way for the acceptance of Matilda by the Anglo-Norman baronage took place at Rouen (where Henry knighted Geoffrey of Anjou) and Le Mans (where he married Matilda).[12]

The problems of politics and succession at this level transcended the frontiers of a single county or principality and throw into relief any uncertainties over the 'familial' order. Whether or not there was a throne involved, it seems likely that the succession to William I would have caused (as Suger put it) *scandala et motiones*. Given Matilda's various handicaps, the revolts which followed her father's death do not seem especially surprising. At a time when the acquisition of power and the exercise of authority were so closely dependent on the system of heredity changes in the organization of the family, or in the rules governing descent and inheritance (e.g. relating to the succession of women), would have a great impact on the transmission of honours and the transfer of land. It has indeed been claimed that the late twelfth century represents the point at which a profound, although long drawn out, revolution in the organization of the family was brought to a close. Instead of the earlier loosely organized medieval groupings, aristocratic families were transformed into lineages which traced descent and affiliation in the masculine line alone. At the material level, it is argued, this general change from clan into lineage was accompanied by the consolidation of dynastic resources and a gradual reluctance to endow all children born in a single generation with family property. These changes produced the triumph of primogeniture as a system of inheritance, but also had important repercussions for aristocratic perceptions of family and kindred. This model (based essentially on northern French genealogical literature) has received much attention, although its applicability to the development of political structures surely needs further evaluation.[13]

The great aristocratic families which had built up principalities and established themselves in counties before the end of the tenth century seem already at the material level to have based their inheritance practices on a principle of patrilineal transmission. The counts of Flanders, for instance, transmitted their lands directly from father to son

---

[12] Walter Map, *De Nugis curialium*, ed. M.R. James, C.N.L. Brooke and R.A.G. Mynors (Oxford, 1983), pp.470-1; J.O. Prestwich, 'The Military Household of the Norman Kings', *EHR*, 96 (1981), 26, 30-5; cf. G. Duby, 'Les "jeunes" dans la société aristocratique dans la France du nord-ouest au xiie siècle', in his *Hommes et structures du moyen âge* (Paris, 1973), pp.213-25. For Geoffrey of Anjou's knighting and marriage, *Historia Gaufredi Ducis* in *Chroniques des comtes d'Anjou*, ed. L. Halphen and R. Poupardin (Paris, 1913), pp.178-81.

[13] G. Duby, 'Remarques sur la littérature généalogique en France au XIe et XIIe siècles', *Hommes et structures*, pp.287-97; K. Schmid, 'The Structure of the Nobility in the Earlier Middle Ages', *The Medieval Nobility*, ed. T. Reuter (Amsterdam, 1978), pp.47-8 (and cf. pp.6-7); Holt, *TRHS*, 32 (1982), 199; K.-F. Werner, 'Kingdom and Principality in Twelfth-Century France', *The Medieval Nobility*, ed. Reuter, pp.277-8; J. Dunbabin, *France in the Making, 843-1180* (Oxford, 1985), pp.45-100, 162-222, 295-321.

for nine generations; and, although this record does not seem to have been matched by any other princes who had acquired such great structures of command in general, the pattern is repeated again and again.[14] The counts of Poitiers succeeded each other from father to son for five generations following the seizure of Poitiers by night in 902 by Ebles.[15] Their competitors for the title *dux Aquitanorum*, the counts of Toulouse, also transmitted their county patrilineally for six generations until a succession dispute erupted in the 1090s.[16] The counts or dukes of the Normans (originally intruders into the late Carolingian world) also passed Normandy from father to son for five generations in spite of a potentially dangerous minority following the assassination of William Longsword in 942.[17]

The case of Burgundy cannot, however, be presented in such clearcut fashion, since the Capetians intervened in the succession to this duchy on a number of occasions; but their most significant intervention was made because the claimant, Otto-William, was not descended by blood from the preceding duke.[18] The most important counts of the Loire valley also transmitted their honours from father to son, although with the counts of Anjou the historian's problems are complicated by genealogical literature composed at a later date.[19] The descent of their rivals, the counts of Tours (later of Blois), is even more difficult to disentangle because of claims to inherit the counties of Troyes and Meaux in the early eleventh century; lands which later coalesced into the county of Champagne.[20]

The establishment of the Capetian dynasty as the royal house after 987

[14] J. Dhondt, *Études sur la formation des principautés territoriales en France* (Bruges, 1948) for the basis of later discussion; cf. E. Hallam, 'The King and Princes in Eleventh-Century France', *BIHR*, 53 (1980), 143-56; Pirenne, *Histoire de Belgique*, 3rd edn. (Brussels, 1909), ii. 53-5, 98-105, 438-9; F.-L. Ganshof, *La Flandre sous les premiers comtes* (Brussels, 1949), pp.1-47, 125-7; *idem*, 'La Flandre', *Histoire des institutions françaises au moyen âge*, ed. F. Lot and R. Fawtier, 3 vols. (Paris, 1957-9), i, *Institutions seigneuriales*, p.356; Dunbabin, pp.73-4.

[15] *Chronique de St. Maixent*, ed. J. Verdon (Paris, 1979), p.78; A. Richard, *Histoire des comtes de Poitou, 778-1204*, 2 vols. (Paris, 1903), i. 44-234; Dhondt, *Principautés*, pp.217-26.

[16] L. Auzias, *L'Aquitaine carolingienne* (Toulouse, 1937), pp.337, 352, 372, 427-8; Dhondt, pp.228-9; Dunbabin, pp.84-6.

[17] D. Douglas, *William the Conqueror* (London, 1964), p.24; D. Bates, *Normandy before 1066* (London, 1982), pp.9-13, 99-100; R.H.C. Davis, *The Normans and Their Myth* (London, 1976), pp.26-8.

[18] J. Richard, *Les ducs de Bourgogne et la formation du duché du XIe au XIVe siècles* (Dijon, 1954), pp.2-16. Otto-William was not allowed to succeed to his step-father's honours; instead Robert the Pious eventually appointed his own son Henry *c.* 1002-16.

[19] *Chroniques des comtes d'Anjou*, ed. Halphen and Poupardin, pp. xxvi-xxxvi; L. Halphen, *Le comté d'Anjou au XIe siècle* (Paris, 1906), pp.1-12; O. Guillot, *Le comte d'Anjou et son entourage au XIe siècle*, 2 vols. (Paris, 1972), i. 1-101.

[20] M. Bur, *La formation du comté de Champagne, v. 950-1150* (Nancy, 1977), pp.257-8; E. Hallam, *Capetian France, 987-1328* (London, 1980), pp.43-8; J. Longnon, 'La Champagne', *Institutions seigneuriales*, ed. Lot and Fawtier, pp.124-7; Werner, *The Medieval Nobility*, ed. Reuter, p.250 n.24.

conforms to a similar pattern. If interpreted in the light of rivalry for the throne which had long marred the stability of the kingdom, then this may cause surprise; but, as Fawtier remarked, 'there does not seem to have been any very determined opposition' to the Capetians' establishment of a hereditary royal dynasty. There are few signs that this patrilineal transmission was regarded as contravening custom, or that kingship in this respect obeyed different rules from those of lesser honours.[21] In practice the Capetian house was exceptionally fortunate because no king ever failed to obtain a son, so that the *regnum Francorum* was transmitted in a unbroken male line for seven generations between the consecration of Hugh in 987 and the accession of Philip Augustus in 1180. On the other hand, there was one protracted period when the inheritance probably seemed in doubt, since Louis VII's son Philip was only born after twenty-eight years of marriage – and to his third wife. Moreover it was twice necessary to transfer the succession between brothers during their father's lifetime, thus illustrating some of the familial problems associated with patrilineal transmission of property.[22]

All these instances of direct succession from father to son are well-known and frequently cited in studies of the Capetian kings and of the great secular aristocracy of the *regnum Francorum*. Written custom, generally of a rather late date, preserves evidence for the survival of some more complicated regional tenurial arrangements. These customs often seem to have been designed to preserve family lands intact by means other than unremitting patrilineal descent and primogeniture. They generally relate to the transmission of *châtellenies* or viscounties and are rarely applicable to counties or large agglomerations of honours.[23] Nevertheless, there is a distinct possibility that some disputed successions – notably the protracted conflict between the sons of William the Conqueror – represent the survival of more archaic systems of heredity and resistance to newer methods of disposing of the family patrimony.

The chief obstacle for historians interested in the years before the late twelfth century is the difficulty of making a connection between legal texts of late date and the information available for earlier years of actual successions. Except for the southern part of Languedoc, few documents

[21] R. Fawtier, *The Capetian Kings of France* (London, 1958), p.49; Le Patourel, *The Norman Empire*, p.190; Duby, 'Remarques', p.297.

[22] Fawtier, pp.49-53; Lewis, *Royal Succession*, p.64; J.-F. Lemarignier, *Le gouvernement royal aux premiers temps Capétiens, 987-1108* (Paris, 1965), pp.37-65; *idem*, 'Autour de la royauté française du IXᵉ au XIIIᵉ siècle', *BEC*, 113 (1956), 13-25; *Hist. Louis VII*, pp.165-6, 176-7.

[23] P. Ourliac and J. Gazzaniga, *Histoire du droit privé français de l'an mil au Code Civil* (Paris, 1985), pp.241-9; cf. Ourliac, *Etudes d'histoire du droit médiéval* (Paris, 1979), pp.211, 217-8; Bates, *Normandy before 1066*, pp.127, 258 (parage); Guillot, *Anjou*, i. 102-3; P. Hyams, 'The Common Law and the French Connection', *Proceedings of the Battle Conference*, 4 (1981), 77-81, 87-90. Considerations of space prevent a more varied regional bibliography.

record transactions between laymen over the transmission of honours (lands, castles and even ecclesiastical property).[24] Thus generalizations are based, as Georges Duby emphasized, on 'indications of affiliation and alliance' scattered throughout 'cartularies, collections of charters and necrologies', as well as in chronicles or genealogical literature whose significance Duby has also expounded. The documentary evidence for inheritance practices is often allusive and indirect; and, even for the royal dynasty, opposition to a particular succession cannot always be traced, let alone the grounds for more obvious disputes.[25] Some weight needs to be attached to the traces of mental perceptions provided by linguistic usage, and to texts which had wide currency and authority. The importance of the firstborn, for instance, may have been impressed on men's minds by many passages of the Old Testament, and even through Christ's primogeniture, mentioned both literally and figuratively.[26] Perhaps, too, the Carolingian royal tradition of deference for the *primogenitus* had been perpetuated. It is never easy to assess the degree of influence exercised by such ideas in a different context.[27]

There is a further sign that notions of heredity were in practice associated in men's minds with patrilineal descent to the exclusion of all other forms of affiliation and, moreover, that a son was regarded as a man's only natural successor. The use of the term *heres* in narrative and literary texts suggests that this word (which originally had a very much wider meaning) came to be regarded almost as the equivalent of 'son'. This is the implication of an anecdote retailed by the chronicler Adémar of Chabannes, that St. Gerald of Aurillac allegedly refused the offer of an advantageous marriage alliance with the retort that it was better to die son-less than to leave bad heirs ('Utile est', inquit, 'mori sine filiis quam relinquere malos heredes').[28] In the account with which this chapter began, too, it is noteworthy that, although Suger applied the term *heres* to William Aethling, whose death deprived King Henry of a direct masculine successor, he never described Matilda as *heres*, although she was eventually the king's designated successor, and his daughter. Confirmation of this narrowed range of meaning comes also from

---

[24] C. Brunel, *Les plus anciennes chartes en langue provençale* (Paris, 1926), no.1; cf. R.W. Southern, *The Making of the Middle Ages* (London, 1953), pp.189-9 (Carcassonne and Narbonne).

[25] 'Remarques', pp.287-8; J. Dhondt, 'Élection et hérédité sous les Carolingiens et premiers Capétiens', *Revue belge de philologie et d'histoire*, 18 (1939), 939-47.

[26] *Genesis*, 27; *Exodus*, 12; *Luke*, 2 vii; *Colossians*, 1 xv.

[27] *Capitularia Regum Francorum*, ed. A. Boretius and V. Krause, *MGH*, 2 vols. (Berlin, 1883-97), i. 270-3 for a single crucial text.

[28] Adémar de Chabannes, *Chronique*, ed. J. Chavanon (Paris, 1897), pp.141 and 199; cf. *Chron. St. Maixent*, p.78.

Ordericus Vitalis's use of the term *legitimus heres* when he wished to stress that a succession was to be transmitted from father to son.[29] The most curious proof of the strength of this usage comes from a mid-twelfth century source which, although it does not directly concern the French kingdom, relates to a case widely known in aristocratic circles of this world. When Pope Hadrian IV referred to the extremely troublesome problems surrounding the succession to Alfonso I of Aragon, he wrote that the ruler died 'without an heir'. This wording is strange because Alfonso had designated the recently founded military orders as the successors to his kingdom. He had a brother who was regarded by many Aragonese nobles to be his rightful heir.[30] The Pope can only have meant that he did not have a son.

Marc Bloch wrote that in the earlier middle ages 'men believed in the hereditary vocation, not of an individual but of a dynasty'.[31] There can be few doubts that both men and women preserved a perception of a kindred wider than that of the nuclear family, and that at aristocratic levels this was symbolised by the continued employment of small groups of personal names whose resonance it is now not always easy to hear. Names like Fulk and Geoffrey would be chosen within each generation of the Angevin counts, William by Poitevins and others, while Raymond is scarcely found before the early twelfth century outside the family of the counts of Toulouse and the neighbouring aristocracy who were linked to them by blood. In practice a sense of dynastic identity was apparently compatible with the transfer of family honours and property from father to son, since there are few indications that a wider range of kin was normally regarded as being eligible to inherit. Daughters, too, were excluded although notable changes took place before the end of the eleventh century. Maternal kin always had an important role in other spheres, but women were only gradually admitted to the ranks of those who could inherit or transmit important honours. At the highest levels within the Romance-speaking world, it seems possible that this exclusion of women from inheritance was linked to the recognition that transmission of property could also involve succession to high office, for which women were disqualified. There are few contemporary pronouncements on these important topics, so that changed attitudes and practices are peculiarly

---

[29] Ordericus Vitalis, *The Ecclesiastical History*, ed. M. Chibnall, 6 vols. (Oxford, 1969-80), vi. 52, 300, 328; cf. ii. 214, 262, 352, 356; iii. 192, 210; v.196 for sons as heirs.

[30] *Liber Feudorum Maior*, ed. F.M. Rosell, 2 vols. (Barcelona, 1947), i. no.13; see Szabolcs de Vajay, 'Ramire II le Moine, roi d'Aragon et Agnès de Poitou', *Mélanges René Crozet*, 2 vols. (Poitiers, 1966), ii. 741.

[31] M. Bloch, *Feudal Society* (London, 1964), p.384, cf. Werner in *The Medieval Nobility*, ed. Reuter, pp.37-59, 149-53, 157-60, 166-8; Lewis, *Royal Succession*, pp.8-10, 57-8.

difficult to trace or explain.[32] Before any of these problems can be considered, however, it is necesary to return to some ramifications of descent and succession in the masculine line.

There was often a gulf between the ideal of a son's succession and the reality, which was not always a question of remoter contingencies but of the dynastic or family strategies essential to secure patrilinear descent. As long as it was possible for members of the greater aristocracy to employ serial monogamy and an illegitimate son was accepted as a man's successor, then even where marriage had produced none it might still be possible to ensure direct lineal succession. The history of the Poitevin counts and the dukes of Normandy would have been very different if Ebles Manzer and William the Bastard had been excluded from their father's honours.[33] Even when an aristocratic marriage resulted in the birth of a son and heir, more than one son was frequently needed to secure the succession. The Capetian line, for instance, would have been endangered if there had not been another son to step into the place of King Robert's son Hugh, whose death (1025) had occurred after his official designation as his father's successor in 1017. This episode has been widely discussed because it both illustrates the practice of anticipatory association of the heir and raises doubts about whether the succession to the throne may not still have been regarded as elective. The hereditary principle was endorsed by the consecration of Henry, the son next in line after Hugh,[34] and indeed has appeared to be so firmly established that a similar crisis during the reign of Louis VI has sometimes been overlooked. Louis VII only came to the throne after the death of his elder brother Philip (consecrated 1129, died 1131), who was killed in Paris after a 'devilish pig' ran into his horse's path. By 1131 it was taken for granted that Louis as next son would automatically move into the position of heir. The presence of Innocent II in the kingdom provided the opportunity for an especially ceremonious consecration.[35]

These Capetian examples of fraternal succession support Bloch's

[32] K.J. Leyser, 'Maternal Kin in Early Medieval Germany, a Reply', *Past & Present*, no.49 (1970), 126-34 (problems of terminology); cf. J. Heers, *Le clan familial au moyen âge* (Paris, 1974), pp. 23-7 (broad survey). Reasons for a woman's disqualification from inheritance can be glimpsed from the arguments of a famous letter to King Robert edited by Halphen, *A travers l'histoire du moyen âge* (Paris, 1950), p.242.

[33] Douglas, *William the Conqueror*, pp.15, 31-2; Richard I (942-66) was also allegedly the son of William Longsword *de concubina Brittana* (Flodoard, *Annales*, ed. Ph. Lauer (Paris, 1905), p.86). For aristocratic ideas on marriage see G. Duby, *Medieval Marriage: Two Models from Twelfth-Century France* (Johns Hopkins, 1978), pp.1-81 but cf. C. Bouchard, 'Consanguinity and Noble Marriages in the Tenth and Eleventh century', *Speculum*, 56 (1981), 267-87.

[34] Lewis, *Royal Succession*, pp.24-7; cf. Dhondt, n.25 above.

[35] Suger, *Vie de Louis VI*, p.266; *La Chronique de Morigny*, ed. L.Mirot (Paris, 1912), p.57. Lewis, *Royal Succession*, pp. 55-6 and *idem*, 'Anticipatory Association of the Heir in Early Capetian France', *American Historical Review*, 83 (1978), 909.

dictum that the dynasty was more important than the individual, although they may seem to be of relatively restricted political significance because they occurred during the father's lifetime. They still demonstrate the general point that, whatever other problems might be raised by this lineal mode of succession, the direct transmission of an inheritance from father to son would sometimes depend upon the survival of two or more brothers. Sometimes, however, there was no way of avoiding fraternal succession. This was a dilemma which faced a number of princely houses, since 'the most ruthless unigenture must allow for occasional reversion to a collateral line . . . the provision of a plurality of heirs [is] a measure of common prudence'.[36] The most remarkable series of fraternal successions between members of a single generation occurred in the Poitevin dynasty following the death of William the Great (when four brothers in turn succeeded to the paternal honours). These successions were complicated by the coincidence that, although two of them were married, neither had a son; it was not until 1058 that the youngest brother (who was known at different stages of his career as Guy, Geoffrey and William) found himself in a position to consolidate the dynasty's possessions and the important acqusitions of the previous decades. As a local chronicler put it, he then 'successit in regno': his third wife produced the much longed-for son which established his lineage.[37] Few examples illustrate the need for a plurality of sons quite so spectacularly, but we may argue that fraternal succession was widely accepted at this time as normal if it would ensure a smooth transmission of power; and this could happen even *inter vivos*, as when Hugh of Burgundy decided to enter the monastery of Cluny and his place was immediately taken by his brother Odo.[38]

Whereas the practice of fraternal succession could preserve the identity of a dynasty and allow its subsequent reorganisation along patrilineal lines, the need for several sons was also potentially dangerous. The threat posed by frustrated ambition or disappointed fraternal expectations can be recognized from rumours which sometimes circulated when one brother succeeded another, for instance when Robert of Normandy was suspected of poisoning his brother Richard.[39] All too often fraternal rivalry prevented the peaceful transmission of authority and raised the spectre of deeper conflicts. Measures might be taken to forestall the dangers posed by the spectacle of brothers at each other's throats; but before the end of the twelfth century not even the greatest princes evolved

[36] J. Goody, in *Succession to High Office* (Cambridge Papers in Social Anthropology), 1966, p.27.
[37] Richard, *Comtes de Poitou*, i. 220-65; *Chron. St. Maixent*, p.130; W. Kienast, *Der Herzogstitel im Frankreich und Deutschland (9 bis 12 Jahrhundert)* (Munich, 1968), pp.178, 196; Werner, 'Kingdom and Principality', pp.248-9.
[38] J. Richard, *Les ducs de Bourgogne*, p.14 (Hugh ruled 1075-8; his brother d.1102).
[39] Douglas, *William the Conqueror*, pp.408-15; Bates, pp.99-100.

any rites which were comparable to royal consecration, or which would be successful in designating a prince before he acceded to power.[40] Even where some arrangement had been made,[41] conflict might simply be postponed, as happened after Count Geoffrey Martel had settled Anjou on Geoffrey le Barbu (before November 1060). The long struggle over the Anglo-Norman inheritance sprang originally from fraternal rivalry lasting from 1087 until Henry I established his authority in Normandy.[42]

Division of lands and honours provided one means of averting dynastic conflict; but there are often difficulties in determining whether a partition followed established custom or was the outcome of a specific political crisis. For instance, did the partition of England and Normandy after 1087 prove that the Conqueror was making a division between William and Robert which followed a separation of patrimony and acquisition? Or did the designation of a younger son as king represent William I's reaction to Robert's disloyalty and rebellion and thus prove that a political solution had been found to the king's dilemmas?[43] Similar problems of interpretation are raised in other contemporary cases – even if less was politically at stake than in the conflicts between the three sons of William I.

One of the most puzzling episodes is the struggle for Anjou after Geoffrey Martel's death in 1060. The conflict only became serious after Fulk Réchin lost Saintes and its county (*c.* 1062) with which he had been invested before his elder brother's succession to Anjou; because Saintes was an acquisition of the Angevin house, it might have been regarded as the younger brother's portion with the patrimony reserved for the elder. On the other hand, that particular division may have been a once and for all political settlement designed to avert fraternal conflict (in this it was unsuccessful). Detailed examination of the inheritance practices of the counts of Blois during the earlier eleventh century, and of the Poitevin dukes of Aquitaine (who twice used Gascony as a younger brother's portion), reveal similar ambiguities.[44] The Capetians, too, had endowed younger sons with the duchy of Burgundy in the first half of the eleventh century.[45]

[40] H. Hoffman, 'Französische Fürstenweihen des Hochmittelalters', *Deutsches Archiv*, 18 (1962), 115-6 but cf. Lewis, *Amer. Hist. Rev.* 83 (1978), 915-21.

[41] Designation occurred, but any apparent examples of anticipatory assocation in the ranks of comital or princely families need to be treated with some care, given the poor survival rate of original documents, and the alterations made to these in transcripts subsequently.

[42] F. Barlow, *William Rufus* (London, 1983), pp.40-2 provides a select survey of the large bibliography on this point.

[43] *Ibid.*, and Le Patourel, *Norman Empire*, pp.341-51.

[44] Below nn.54, 55, for these cases.

[45] Fawtier, *Capetian Kings*, p.163; Lewis, *Royal Succession*, pp.2, 58-63, which differs from C.T. Wood, *The French Apanages and the Capetian Monarchy* (Cambridge, Mass., 1966), pp.3-10.

Partitions might solve the problem of endowing several sons from the resources of a single county or some other large unit, duchy or principality; but there were other possible solutions such as an emigration or the pursuit of an expansionist policy. By the early twelfth century the crusading states were especially favoured by French dynasties, although oddly enough not always for the establishment of younger sons. The departure of Raymond (son of William IX of Aquitaine) for Antioch in the 1130s undoubtedly involved the establishment of a younger son by marriage to an heiress; the involvement of the counts of St. Gilles in Tripoli, was far more complicated.[46] And when Count Fulk of Anjou left the Loire valley with the prospect of becoming king of Jerusalem, he left his patrimony to his son Geoffrey, who from then on exercised power in Anjou. In general there was difficulty in dividing an honour repeatedly; divisions could sometimes scarcely be maintained during a single generation. The actions of William Rufus and Henry I also suggest that partition could not solve the twin problems of personal rivalry and political instability. The Poitevin dynasty displayed similar reactions to partitions at a slightly earlier date, when Duke William the Great's second son made a determined (but unsuccessful) bid to unite Gascony with the patrimonial lands north of the Garonne, an aim which was only eventually achieved by his youngest half-brother.[47]

The movement towards consolidation of family property seems to have become so strong that by the early twelfth century few princely or comital houses any longer made substantial partitions. The process of unification was often achieved by violence and then rarely reversed. The fates of Geoffrey le Barbu and Robert of Normandy show what could happen to losers in a fraternal struggle even if they were *primogeniti*.[48] Other notable instances of this tendency involved bids made by a father's brother to secure the family patrimony at the expense of a brother's children. Theobald of Blois-Champagne (d. 1090) deprived his nephew Odo II of Champagne of his portion of the family's principality; Odo had to be

---

[46] Raymond had appeared in Antioch before Feb. 1136, *Cartulaire général de l'Ordre des Hospitaliers de St. Jean de Jérusalem*, ed. J. Delaville Le Roulx, 4 vols. (Paris, 1894-1906), i, nos.129, 170, 183. J. Richard, 'Les St. Gilles et le comté de Tripoli', *Islam et chrétiens du Midi (XII-XVᵉ s.)*, *Cahiers de Fanjeaux*, 18 (1983), 65-75.

[47] The date at which Odo succeeded is difficult to determine because so many early Gascon documents are suspect also along with much regional genealogical information, see e.g. F. Lot, 'L'évêché de Bayonne', *Mélanges d'histoire du moyen âge dédiés à la mémoire de Louis Halphen* (Paris, 1951), esp. pp.436-42 and cf. E. Nortier in *Saint-Sever, millénaire de l'abbaye* (Mont-de-Marsan, 1985), pp.99-126. However, Odo's return to Poitou on the death of his elder brother, and then Guy-Geoffrey's despatch to Gascony are known from the *Chron. St. Maixent*, pp.118, 132-4, 192 events taking place *c.* 1038 onwards. The year of Guy-Geoffrey's despatch to Gascony is not given.

[48] R.W. Southern, 'The Place of Henry I in English History', *Proceedings of the British Academy*, 48 (1962), 153; Halphen, *Le comté d'Anjou*, pp.148-50; Guillot, i. 109 n.483.

content with emigration to England and acquisition of the honour of Holderness.[49] Two other causes célèbres also involved the intervention of wicked uncles. Robert le Frison actually won the county of Flanders through the defeat of his nephew, Arnulf, at the battle of Cassel (1071), thus disinheriting the lineage of his brother Baldwin VI and replacing it by his own.[50] Raymond of St. Gilles, however, did not have to go to those lengths in the 1090s to obtain his brother's county of Toulouse, probably because his brother's only surviving child was a girl, married to a traditional enemy of the dynasty.

In the Anglo-Norman realm 'a woman inherited . . . because, in the absence of male heirs in the same generation, she was the only means of continuing the lineage'.[51] That was certainly the principle on which Henry I of England was acting when he designated his daughter to succeed him and arrange her marriage, to Geoffrey of Anjou. Ironically before Henry's death Matilda's chief competitor Stephen had already greatly increased his power through marriage to the woman who was the only survivor of her generation among the family of the counts of Boulogne.[52] There can be little doubt that by the first decade of the twelfth century female succession came to be widely regarded as a feasible method of transferring a county or principality – perhaps even a kingdom – to another generation. Although a number of ramifications of this principle were explored empirically and applied to what was still often an abnormal tenurial situation, a comparative historical approach to this aspect of inheritance reveals that a woman's succession (and consequently her husband's) was often a source of political dispute.[53]

Before the end of the eleventh century a great honour seems never to have been transmitted *to* a woman in the Capetian kingdom. Succession and inheritance might be claimed *through* descent from a female, but where such proceedings are at all clear, the woman did not enjoy this inheritance in person. Even in the eleventh century claims might be advanced which depended on this type of descent; they were certainly not always

[49] A. Fliche, *Le règne de Philippe Ier* (Paris, 1912), pp.246-7; Hallam, *Capetian France*, p.48; M. Bur, 'Les comtes de Champagne et la Normannitas: sémiologie d'un tombeau', *Proceedings of the Battle Conference*, 3 (1980), 29-30; Chibnall, *Anglo-Norman World*, pp.23, 52.

[50] Pirenne, *Hist. Belgique*, i. 80, 105-7; Fliche, pp.173-88, 252-66; Ganshof, *La Flandre*, pp.47-50; *idem, Feudalism*, 3rd edn. (London, 1964), pp.94-5; below nn.64-70 for Toulouse.

[51] Holt, *TRHS*, 35 (1985), 3 (and 5 for the twenty Norman baronies which had descended in the female line before 1130); E. Searle, 'Women and the Legitimation of Succession at the Norman Conquest', *Proceedings of the Battle Conference*, 3 (1980), 159-70.

[52] Le Patourel, pp.76-7, 214-5. Matilda of Boulogne's brother died young and her father retired from the world, Davis, *King Stephen*, pp.7-10.

[53] Cf. Sir Frank Stenton, *The First Century of English Feudalism*, 2nd edn. (Oxford, 1961), pp.49-50; S.F.C. Milsom, 'Inheritance by Women in the Twelfth and Early Thirteenth Centuries', *On the Laws and Customs of England* (Univ. of North Carolina Press, 1981), pp.60-6; *idem, The Legal Framework of English Feudalism* (Cambridge, 1976), pp.154-5.

successful. Odo II of Tours and Chartres, for instance, acquired Champagne via a grandmother who was also a distant relative of the count of Troyes (Stephen d. 1022); on the other hand, his claim to the kingdom of Burgundy was rebuffed. Instead Odo's maternal uncle transferred the royal insignia to the German king and a hereditary claim through his mother was disregarded.[54] The Poitevin acquisition of Gascony was also justified by transmission of his mother's rights to another Odo, who was son of William the Great and the Gascon Brisca or Prisca; although that claim was not disputed, by the time Odo got possession of Bordeaux, his mother was long since dead. Eventually the Poitevins' transmission of Bordeaux and Gascony by hereditary right owed as much to force of arms and money, as it did to actual lineal succession.[55]

The county of Anjou in the mid-eleventh century provides the clearest indications of the way in which a woman could be bypassed, even where she was the vehicle through which hereditary succession was claimed. Geoffrey Martel was childless after four marriages: he had no surviving brothers, and some years before he died in 1060 two sisters' sons had appeared in Anjou. Only one of these nephews was intended to succeed to the dynastic lands and comital title, and the count made his arrangements well before his death. The younger son was knighted and Angevin acquisitions outside the county were transferred to him (Fulk Réchin in his autobiography describes that his uncle 'me fecit militem', 'me ornavit in militem'); while the patrimony was granted to the elder, Geoffrey le Barbu.[56] Two important features for the history of female inheritance have often been overlooked in discussion of this important case. First, as Guillot remarked, comital designation was all-important because Geoffrey Martel had passed over the rights of another nephew, Fulk of Vendôme, whose mother was probably an older sister than Geoffrey and Fulk Réchin's.[57] Perhaps Geoffrey Martel was able to make this choice

---

[54] Bur, *La formation de Champagne*, pp.507-13 (table p.96); Hallam, pp.45-6; Dunbabin, pp.191-2. Odo's paternal uncle was Rudolf III who had no sons (R. Poupardin, *Le royaume de Bourgogne (808-1038)* (Paris, 1907), pp.148, 159-73).

[55] Brisca was the duke's second wife, generally assumed to have died *c.* 1018-9, although it seems that she was probably already dead by 1016, BN, MS. latin 12765 pp.208-12, cf. Richard, *Comtes de Poitou*, i. 177 n.2. On the succession to Gascony see *Bordeaux pendant le haut moyen âge*, ed. C. Higounet (Bordeaux, 1961), pp.53-7 and p.305 (though corrections are necessary), and cf. Ch. Samaran, *Institutions seigneuriales*, ed. Lot and Fawtier, p.186; but for the Poitevin point of view see *Chron. St. Maxient*, pp.130-2; and for the purchase of rights from the count of Armagnac *Cartulaire du prieuré de St. Mont*, ed. J. de Jaurgain, *Archives historiques du Gascogne*, 2ème sér.7 (1904), no.7; BN, MS. latin 11826 pièce no.11.

[56] *Chrons. des comtes d'Anjou*, pp.232, 236-7. The date established by Guillot, i. 102-5 and ii. Catalogue nos.212, 278 disproves the assertion that this was a deathbed bequest, G. Duby, *The Knight, the Lady and the Priest*, pp.91-2.

[57] Guillot, i. 104 n.465; Halphen, *Le comté d'Anjou*, pp.65-6; and below n.77.

because he had no *naturalis heres*. Even more significantly, he did not regard either of his own sisters as being qualified to possess Anjou in person as her *hereditas*, although at a slightly later date that would not have been unusual for a daughter, as is reflected in the title born by Melisende of Jerusalem before the death of her father, Baldwin II, in 1131.

The county of Maine provides a further example of an important honour in which female succession aggravated the political problems which resulted from the conflicting external pressures exercised by the neighbouring Normans and Angevins. Maine also supplies evidence of a change in attitudes to female inheritance between the mid and late eleventh century. Although some care needs to be taken in assessing this evidence, the outlines are clear. The struggle to control this strategically placed county was justified by appeals to the hereditary right of a number of women. After the death of Robert of Normandy's fiancée, claims had to be traced back to the daughters of Count Herbert Eveille-chien (d. between 1032-5). After Azzo of Este and his son were unable to establish themselves in Maine, the young Hugh V sold out to the lord of La Flèche whose mother, like Hugh's, was Count Herbert's daughter. Presumably it was easier for a regional lord who had close links with other local castellans to establish himself. Uncertainty and conflict lasted for nearly thirty years (*c.* 1065-92). In the end Count Hélie of La Flèche (d. 1110) also left a daughter to succeed.[58] The marriage of this girl, Aremburgis, to Count Fulk of Anjou brought Maine as her *hereditas* to her husband. As a woman she had a more assured position than in an earlier generation, but in practice the Angevins absorbed Maine into their patrimony, and this was transmitted without partition to the eldest son of Fulk and Aremburgis.[59]

Female succession as a practical proposition became a political issue towards the end of the eleventh century. Because there was still great variation in the way such successions were treated, attention needs to be paid to some of the more important. One of the earliest – and least well-known to English historians – concerns Bigorre. In this Pyrenean county Beatrice had succeeded her father, Count Bernard, some time before the late 1070s. She became the second wife of Centulle, viscount of Béarn, who took the comital title after their marriage,[60] although his wife disposed of

[58] R. Latouche, *Le comté du Maine au XIᵉ siècle* (Paris, 1910), pp.37-53, 113-26; Chartrou, *L'Anjou*, p.29; Holt, *TRHS*, 35 (1985), 5 n.13.

[59] Latouche, *loc. cit.*; Chartrou, *L'Anjou*, p. j. nos.18, 27 (a distinction is made between *hereditas* and *dos*). Contrast the view that partition was customary in Angevin lands, T. Keefe, 'Geoffrey Plantagenet's Will and the Angevin Succession', *Albion*, 6 (1974), 268-74.

[60] P. Tucoo-Chala, *La vicomté de Béarn et le problème de sa souveraineté* (Bordeaux, 1961), pp.33-5 (needs some correction), 146 docs. no.4 (in my view this should be dated *after* Sept. 1086). Centulle's second marriage is likely to have taken place after Feb. 1079, see *Registrum Gregorii VII*, ed. E. Caspar, 2 vols. (Berlin, 1955), ii. 431-2 (letter assuming that he had not yet separated from his first wife).

land and churches in the county *hereditario iure*.[61] In many respects this inheritance and the subsequent transmission of their honours could serve as a textbook model for female succession; it also appears to have been achieved without conflict. One of its more unusual features, at least by northern standards, was that, after Centulle's death, Béarn and Bigorre descended separately, possibly because Béarn was already provided with an heir by Centulle's first wife. More remarkably, no fraternal ambitions marred these arrangements: the sons of the two marriages were both deeply involved in the Spanish campaigns of the early twelfth century and acquired honours in Aragon.[62]

All other instances of female succession which occurred throughout the huge region between the Loire, the Mediterranean and the Pyrenees suggest that Countess Beatrice's succession was untypically peaceful. In most known cases a woman's inheritance was disputed and, whether or not a claim was vindicated, it generally involved the use of force. The Poitevin chronicle of St. Maixent, for instance, suggests that the county of La Marche was transmitted immediately to a woman after the deaths of Count Audebert and his son Boso (1088 and 1091): 'Aumodis his sister succeeded him. She had two sons by Count Roger.'[63] The affair does not seem to have been so simple, however, since before his death Boso had apparently designated his paternal uncle, Odo, to succeed in 'all his county'. If the details of subsequent events in La Marche were better known it might be possible to decide whether resistance to Aumodis was expressed because there was hostility in principle to the succession of a woman, or perhaps because of political and personal suspicion of her husband Roger, one of the many sons of the powerful Roger of Montgomery. Eventually, Aumodis was treated as her ancestors' legal successor and took the title *comitissa de Marchia*, but her uncle remained active until *c.* 1098. It certainly cannot be maintained that she was regarded from the first as her brother's legitimate heiress, or that she succeeded him unopposed.[64]

The details of how (or even when) Count Roger and Aumodis established their position in La Marche cannot be determined. Equally there are many gaps in the evidence relating to the disputed succession to

[61] *Cartulaire de St. Victor de Marseille*, ed. V. Guérard (Paris, 1857), nos.818 (a.1080), 483-4, (a.1091, confirmation by *Beatrix comitissa Bigorritana*).

[62] M. Defourneaux, *Les français en Espagne* (Paris, 1949), pp.125-82, 214-30; cf. C. Higounet, *Le comté de Comminges de ses origines à son annexation à la couronne* (Toulouse, 1949, new edn. St. Gaudens, 1984), i. 36-40, 236.

[63] *Chron. St. Maixent*, pp.148, 150.

[64] G. Thomas, *Les comtes de la Marche de la Maison de Charroux* (Paris, 1928), catalogue nos. ix, lxviii, lxxv; *Chartes et documents de l'abbaye de Charroux*, ed. P. de Monsabert, *Archives historiques de Poitou*, 39 (1910), no.33; Richard, *Comtes de Poitou*, i. 306; J.F.A. Mason, 'Roger of Montgomery and his Sons, 1067-1102', *TRHS*, 5th ser.13 (1963), 14-17, 23, 27; Le Patourel, *Norman Empire*, pp. 191-2, 292-3, 308.

the county of Toulouse. Raymond of St. Gilles certainly acquired his brother's county and disregarded any claims his niece may have put forward to inherit, but some of the most basic information for an understanding of this complicated dispute is lacking, for instance the year of Raymond's succession, and even the date of his brother's death. The political position Raymond had built up for himself in the region around Toulouse and in the Rhône valley may have been as important as hereditary right in determining his acceptance as count in Toulouse for, although he was accepted by Pope Urban II, it was still possible to find support for his niece, Philippa.[65] She had married the young duke of Aquitaine, William IX, in 1094;[66] from then until *c.* 1123 the lineage of St. Gilles had to be prepared actively to defend possession of Toulouse against the claims of the Poitevin dynasty.

It is unfortunate that most discussions of this important affair have been based on later Anglo-Norman chroniclers who were chiefly interested in explaining the Angevin Henry II's attack on Toulouse in 1159. These accounts are not only inaccurate, but also viewed the issue of female succession from an anachronistic standpoint.[67] It is, for instance, incorrect to suppose that the Poitevin duke soon gave up his wife's pretensions to the county (whether from lack of ambition or means), since Toulouse was twice occupied by a Poitevin party (in 1098 and again *c.* 1112 onwards). It was only lost after war between Duke William and Raymond's youngest son, Alfonso (1123).[68] An original charter from St. Sernin de Toulouse (surviving together with Urban II's magnificent bull naming Raymond as count) describes William of Aquitaine both as count of Poitiers and *Pictavensis et Tolose*; while his wife's hereditary claims would be understood by reference to her as *nomine Philippa . . . filia W. comitis.*[69] Both from these references of 1098 and from later ones it emerges that Duke William, far from wishing to assert suzerainty over Toulouse, intended to rule the county directly as his wife's inheritance. Philippa's

---

[65] L. and J. Hill, *Raymond IV de Saint-Gilles, comte de Toulouse* (Toulouse, 1959), pp.4-5, 19-20 are almost alone in assuming that Raymond's succession to his brother was based on customary practices; cf. now R. Benjamin, 'A Forty Years War: Toulouse and the Plantagenets, 1156-96', *Historical Research* (formerly *BIHR*), 61 (1988), 270-5, 278.

[66] *Chron. St. Maixent*, p.150; Richard, *Comtes*, i. 405-6 (but the legal position was far less clear-cut than is assumed in this work).

[67] Cf. William of Malmesbury, *De gestis regum Anglorum*, ed. W. Stubbs, ii. 455-6 and Orderic Vitalis, *Ecc. Hist.*, ed. Chibnall, v.276 with the Angevin chroniclers, Robert of Torigny and William of Newburgh, who misleadingly asserted that the duke of Aquitaine had sold or mortgaged his wife's county before *c.*1100, *Chronique*, ed. L. Delisle, i. 319-20; *Chronicles of the Reigns of Stephen, Henry II, Richard I*, ed. R. Howlett, 4 vols., iv. 201-2.

[68] *Chron. St. Maixent*, pp.192-4; *Cartulaire de l'abbaye de Lézat*, ed. P. Ourliac and A.-M. Magnou (Paris, 1984), i. pp.xli-xlii.

[69] Arch. dép. de la Haute-Garonne, 101 H 586 no.1; and for a slightly different reading *Cartulaire de St. Sernin de Toulouse*, ed. C. Douais (Toulouse, 1887), nos.291-2.

disinheritance by her paternal uncle therefore takes on an altogether greater importance than has often been assumed.[70]

No contemporary document sets out any legal arguments in favour of female inheritance in the three cases just considered, but in Mediterranean Languedoc a number of transactions among the laity were recorded in writing.[71] Among these are two charters enabling us to obtain much needed information on the succession of Provence c. 1112, concerning the marriage of Dulcia, daughter of Countess Gerberga, to Count Raymond-Berengar III of Barcelona. The terms of settlement may have been the result of disorder in the region since Gerberga made over to her future son-in-law 'all the *honor* which I have, or ought to have, in any way whatsoever'. Dulcia also made a grant ceding her life interest in Provence to Raymond-Berengar, though the eventual succession of their children was guaranteed.[72] In legal terms therefore the count was assured of Provence, but in practice his position was by no means so certain; and, even though Dulcia's hereditary right to succeed was acknowledged, only a very determined series of military campaigns actually secured Provence for the counts of Barcelona.

As Suger suggests, the problems of political succession were acute during the decade which saw the deaths of Henry I of England, his son-in-law Emperor Henry V, and the Capetian Louis VI, even though only one of these kingdoms was also affected by the special difficulties associated with its transmission to a woman. All these rulers would have been aware of the difficulties recently produced by claims traced through women, since all the claimants for the fiercely disputed county of Flanders based their hereditary right on descent stemming originally from the female line. Between the death of Baldwin VII, the assassination of Count Charles and the death of William Clito (the years 1119-28), all pretenders to Flanders were descended either from a daughter of Robert le Frison (d. 1093) or Baldwin V (d. 1067).[73]

The actual inheritance by a woman of a great honour was virtually unknown within the Capetian kingdom until the very late eleventh

---

[70] J. Boussard, *Le gouvernement d'Henri II Plantagenêt* (Paris, 1956), p.417; W.L. Warren, *Henry II* (London, 1973), pp.83-5.

[71] *Liber Feudorum Maior*, ed. Rosell, ii, nos.875-7.

[72] J.-P. Poly, *La Provence et la société féodale, 879-1166* (Paris, 1976), pp.318-30, 347-8; C. Higounet, 'Un grand chapitre de l'histoire du XIIe siècle: la rivalité des maisons de Toulouse et de Barcelone pour la prépondérance méridionale', *Mélanges Louis Halphen* (Paris, 1951), pp.312-8. This marriage provided the political foundations for a century of Catalan domination of the region.

[73] F.-L. Ganshof, 'Le roi de France en Flandre en 1127 et 1128', *Revue historique du droit français et étranger* (1949), 204-28. Count Charles the Good (murdered 1127) and the eventually successful candidate Thierry of Alsace were both descended from the usurper Robert le Frison; while William Clito (killed 1128) was a claimant via Baldwin V; Suger considered that his was the rightful claim, *Vie de Louis VI*, p.246.

century. The demands of heredity were so pressing that in difficult cases choice would be made among those who could establish blood-ties with the ruling dynasty. Where necessary candidates included males who traced their connections in the female line; that did not mean that a woman succeeded in person. Considerable changes had surely taken place when Beatrice succeeded her father in Bigorre in the 1070s, and Aumodis followed her brother as *comitissa de Marchia*. Such developments have been interpreted as proof of the transformation of noble kin-groups into the more narrowly defined lineages of the twelfth century, but most of the known instances of female succession show that there was still great resistance to a daughter following her father. A daughter would never be regarded as the *naturalis heres* as a son would be. Against this background, opposition to Henry I's daughter Matilda may be regarded as inevitable and comparable to the resistance met by Philippa of Toulouse or Aumodis of La Marche. The disputes over those southern counties suggest that close relatives generally presented the greatest threat to a woman's chances of succession. An adult male established in the region was in a position to build up his own resources and a body of supporters in a fashion that would not have been possible for a girl. Whether a sister's son (like Stephen of Blois in relationship to Henry I of England) or a father's brother (like Raymond of St. Gilles or Odo of La Marche) he was well-placed to lay hands on a disputed *honor*, whatever the rights of the woman with whom he was competing.[74]

It seems possible that practices and attitudes in the Romance-speaking world may have been influenced by the Spanish kingdoms and the crusading states. When Henry I decided to designate Matilda as his probable successor, her prospective father-in-law was about to retire from his county of Anjou. He began a new career as the bridegroom of Melisende, daughter of Baldwin II of Jersusalem, and became king on Baldwin's death.[75] Even though no one in the Anglo-Norman kingdom may have known that Melisende was styled *heres* before her father's death, this precedent must have been widely known, and would have influenced the attitudes of both Geoffrey of Anjou and his son Henry towards Matilda's claims to succeed her father.[76] Slightly earlier the kingdom of Leon-Castille had been not only inherited but also ruled by a woman. Queen Urraca's reign (1109-26) was turbulent and she did not lack opposition. Her first husband was from the family of the counts of Burgundy and closely related to Pope Calixtus II and it seems probable

[74] Cf. Milsom, *The Legal Framework of English Feudalism*, pp.147-8.

[75] Fulk was about forty years old: Aremburgis of Maine died *c*.1126, as a widower Fulk took the cross in 1128, and was in Jerusalem by the early summer of 1129, Chartrou, *L'Anjou*, pp.23-4, 225-39.

[76] B. Hamilton, 'Women in the Crusader States: the Queens of Jerusalem', *Medieval Women*, ed. D. Baker (Oxford, 1978), pp.149-52.

that her case was widely known.[77] This example of a woman's inheritance of a kingdom may have provided a precedent for a practice which would have been unthinkable only a few decades earlier. The 'scandals and revolts' which followed Matilda's attempts to establish her own position in the Anglo-Norman kingdom show how many difficulties still stood in the way of a woman's succession to high office.[78] Even Eleanor of Aquitaine's succession was less troublefree than is sometimes imagined.

Eleanor's marriage to Louis VII (aged about fifteen or sixteen in 1137) was carefully prepared by his father. A privilege of unprecedented lavishness was first bestowed on the bishops of Aquitaine,[79] but secular needs were not neglected. A large body of men was collected to accompany the young king on his progress through the lands ruled by Eleanor's ancestors which 'none of his [i.e. the king's] forefathers had ever possessed'. This company of over five hundred of 'the best knights of the kingdom' sounds more like an army prepared to deal with trouble and put down resistance than a peaceful wedding-escort.[80] It was headed by some of the most powerful men north of the Loire and shows that far more was involved than an ordinary inheritance making sure of 'the hand and dowry of a minor'.[81] When the death of Eleanor's father at Compostela became known, important political decisions must have been taken before the marriage was solemnized; the most significant of these would have been to exclude Eleanor's younger sister from the succession. Perhaps that could be taken for granted as Aquitaine had been transferred undivided for three generations. Another problem was avoided more by good luck than good management. Eleanor's only paternal uncle, Raymond, had been recently established as prince in the conveniently distant principality of Antioch. If he had still been in Aquitaine, the Capetian party would surely have had to move more rapidly than it did between April and July 1137.[82]

The Poitevin dukes had traditionally displayed considerable loyalty to the Capetians. The 'troubadour' duke, Eleanor's grandfather, even sang

---

[77] B.F. Reilly, *The Kingdom of Leon-Castilla under Queen Urraca, 1109-26* (Princeton, 1982); R. Fletcher, *Saint James's Catapult: The Life and Times of Diego Gelmire of Santiago de Compostela* (Oxford, 1984), pp.129-62 (esp. 130, 148-51).

[78] Reilly, p.352 compares Urraca's political difficulties with those facing Matilda in England, as does Gillingham, *Angevin Empire*, p.8.

[79] A. Luchaire, *Louis VI le Gros* (Paris, 1890), no.581; J. Gaudemet, *Institutions ecclésiastiques*, ed. Lot and Fawtier, pp.169-73; Richard, *Comtes*, ii. 18-45.

[80] *Vie de Louis VI*, pp.280-2 and *Chron. de Morigny*, pp.67-70 ('royalist' accounts); cf. Orderic, ed. Chibnall, vi. 490.

[81] Luchaire, *Louis VI*, p.264. Eleanor's contemporaries would surely have described Aquitaine as her *hereditas*, not her *dos*.

[82] Eleanor's paternal uncle is sometimes overlooked, Werner, 'Kingdom and Principality', p.264; cf. above n.46.

of the king 'from whom I hold my *honor*' in one of his most famous poems.[83] All the same Louis VI was undoubtedly pressing home a political advantage when he intervened in Aquitaine in 1137 for, as a local chronicler observed, by accepting the elder daughter of the dead duke as his wife, his son 'was able to obtain the whole principality of that land'.[84] No king since the ninth century had been successfully involved in the transmission of power in this region. It seems that Louis VI and his counsellors were creating norms, rather than acting in accordance with ones already clearly established, when the king took charge of Eleanor's inheritance. The significance of this intervention has been obscured by interpreting it in too legalistic a fashion.

Inheritance and doubts over succession in a county, principality or, still more, a kingdom, could have repercussions which would destroy political equilibrium and endanger the conduct of government. Abbot Suger saw clearly that the time of succession was often the moment when the flames of revolt were lit and a fire kindled which could consume a ruler's subjects, and into which his kin and greatest magnates would inevitably be drawn. Historians have often paid more attention to institutional forms of government and the increasing elaboration of administration than they have to the problems considered here. Changes in a system of heredity should not be discussed in isolation from the other problems which beset medieval rulers, or detached from broader questions of economic and social change. The recent concentration on the connection between politics and property has surely been of particular value because it draws attention to the fragility of institutional achievements if these were not linked to changes which would also procure political stability. During Suger's lifetime most aristocratic dynasties in the Capetian kingdom and Romance-speaking world were still attempting to evolve methods of inheritance that would also allow peaceful succession, the unquestioned transmission of property from one generation to the next, and undisturbed transfer of political authority. Possibly conflict precipitated social and even political change, and contributed towards the definition of law and custom on matters of inheritance; but these are aspects of early medieval kingship which lead to other topics and issues which need separate treatment.[85]

All the issues considered here revolve around notions of family and descent, affiliation through blood and marriage, and a psychology of the family which cannot easily be understood if historians proceed from the preconceptions of a more modern world. Discussion is complicated by the fact that so often the 'pattern of ways, habits . . . and norms' was largely

---

[83] *Les chansons de Guillaume IX*, ed. A. Jeanroy, 2nd edn. (Paris, 1927), no.xi.

[84] *Chron. St. Maixent*, pp.194-6.

[85] Cf. M. Gluckman, 'The State and Civil Strife', *Politics, Law and Ritual in Tribal Society* (Oxford, 1965), pp.163-6.

unspoken, or at least unwritten.[86] There was some survival of the view that office and honour were matters of suitability for the job and performance, but in practice the exercise of secular authority was almost invariably linked to notions of heredity, and to increasingly precise rules of succession. There can surely be little disagreement with the view that the dynastic and familial concerns of royal kin-groups were supported and reinforced by those of the great aristocracy established throughout the former West Frankish kingdom. All alike were apparently concerned to adapt their family strategies to solve the problems of how to secure a son's inheritance despite increasing external pressures imposed by changed attitudes towards marriage and legitimacy, the tensions created by rivalry among brothers, and competition for patrimonial lands among members of different generations. Historians have to make allowances for calculations which mostly went unspoken, for although examples of fraternal rivalry were there for all to see, so were cases of the death of sons through hunting or war.[87] A generation might be thinned or destroyed through these occupational hazards of the secular aristocracy, so that the need to establish means by which women could inherit may in part be regarded as the outcome of demographic pressures. There are few signs that ideals were transformed to keep pace with the problems confronting these dynasties. No amount of clerical commiseration would wipe out the misery of the childlessness of Henry I's second wife, Adela of Louvain. Louis VII hastened to remarry, fearful that he would only be survived by daughters.[88] As Innocent II reminded a sorrowing father in 1131, if a man had may sons, at least one of these should survive to rule after his death.[89]

---

[86] Hyams, 'The Common Law and the French Connection', p.79; cf. P. Ourliac, '*La convenientia*', *Études d'histoire du droit privé offertes à Pierre Petot* (Paris, 1959), pp.413-22.

[87] Two counts of Flanders at least were killed in military operations; so were Count Odo II of Blois-Chartres, the eldest son of Robert I of Burgundy, two Poitevin counts and the elder son of Fulk Réchin. Others may have died of wounds; while numbers would be instantly increased if deaths in Jerusalem and Spain were added.

[88] See the letter of Hildebert of Le Mans in Migne, *Patrologia Latina*, vol.171, cols.179-81; Werner, 'Kingdom and Principality', p.268.

[89] *Chron. de Morigny*, p.59.

Chapter 3

England and Germany, 1050-1350

Benjamin Arnold

The Norman Conquest of England confirmed the severance of the kingdom from the Scandinavian political sphere, whose expansive ambition was laid to rest at Stamford Bridge in 1066. The German annalist Lampert of Hersfeld noted the event, telling us that Harold *rex Anglisaxonum* destroyed three kings there,[1] meaning Harald of Norway, Eystein Orri, his designated son-in-law, and an unnamed Irish king who had joined the Norwegian expedition.[2] It must be admitted that the Anglo-Saxon realm did not figure prominently upon the mental horizon of the Germans, in spite of Otto the Great's marriage to Edith of Wessex, and the subsequent descent of the Salian ducal and imperial house from their daughter Liudgard. It is true that the eleventh century saw the assimilation, after the disruptions of the Viking age, of the Rhineland, the Low countries, and south-east England into a single trading region based upon the profitable route between London, Bruges, and Cologne. Ethelred II had already recognized the significance of German trade, in confirming valuable commercial rights in London to *homines imperatoris*, amongst other continental merchants.[3] Commerce, however, did not strike aristocratic German churchmen at all favourably, and Lampert specifically warned his readers against the outrageous political pretension of the Cologne merchants.[4] He also appears to have been suspicious of the upstart Anglo-Norman régime, and included an unfounded report that William the Conqueror intended to raid the Empire and to occupy the imperial palace and town of Aachen. Germans had some reason to suspect the intentions of French princes towards imperial Lotharingia, and Lampert's story is probably based upon memories of the West Franks' great raid into Aachen in 978, of which he had read in the earlier Hersfeld

---

[1] A. Schmidt and W.D. Fritz, *Lampert von Hersfeld: Annalen*, Ausgewählte Quellen zur deutschen Geschichte des Mittelalters, xiii (Darmstadt, 1957) p.110.

[2] E.A. Freeman, *The History of the Norman Conquest of England*, 2nd edn. (Oxford, 1875), iii. 364-77.

[3] H.E.S. Fisher and A.R.J. Jurica, *Documents in English Economic History. England from 1000 to 1760* (London, 1977), p.274.

[4] Lampert, *Annalen*, pp.236-48 (1074).

annals.[5]

Since the seafaring proclivities of the Frisians were greatly curtailed by the Vikings, it was not until the mercantile triumph of the North German Hansa in the thirteenth century that subjects of the German Empire again took to the sea on a great scale. Before this, the North Sea rendered the Anglo-Norman realm somewhat remote from German awareness. This was underlined in the regional law of Lotharingia and Saxony regarding the security of the sea-coast, custom distinctly hostile to navigators. Ancient right of wreck delivered distressed ships, persons, and goods into the power of the imperial crown. The Stade Annals record an occasion when, in the eleventh century, Anglo-Saxon women were shipwrecked in the estuary of the Elbe, lost their liberty, and were assigned to the household of the margraves of Stade.[6]

Although the sea was a physical barrier, the growing significance of the Anglo-Norman kingdom motivated a diplomatic reappraisal in German circles, leading to Emperor Henry V's marriage to Henry I's daughter Matilda of Normandy at Mainz in 1114, and her subsequent imperial coronation in 1117 at Rome.[7] Although the marriage proved childless, it paved the way for a regular Anglo-German alignment sustained by marriages, or at least their negotiation, for a century and a half. If concord was punctuated by disasters such as Henry VI's incarceration of Richard I and King John's support of Otto IV, it culminated in Earl Richard of Cornwall's promotion to the German throne in 1257, and the possible establishment of the Angevin dynasty as the German imperial house.

In the time of Henry I the new alliance of England and Germany had immediate consequences in European diplomacy. It was a threat to the Capetian dynasty, nearly always on bad terms with the dukes of Normandy, and eventually resulted in the abortive invasion of northern France by the Henries in 1124. From 1120 the empress was herself the heiress of England and Normandy, and had her marriage to Henry V proved fruitful, then the imperial dynasty would have acquired a new kingdom, just as the emperor's collateral descendant Henry VI was to acquire the Sicilian kingdom through his marriage in 1186 to the Hauteville royal heiress, Constance. In 1125, however, Henry V died at an early age, probably of cancer; Matilda returned to her father, with the Hand of St. James in her luggage;[8] and the Germans elected Duke Lothar of Saxony as their monarch.

[5] *Ibid.*, pp.252 (1074) and 34 (978).

[6] H. Conrad, *Deutsche Rechtsgeschichte. Frühzeit und Mittelalter*, 2nd edn. (Karlsruhe, 1962), p.277 and J.M. Lappenberg, *Annales Stadenses*, MGH, Scriptores xvi (Hanover, 1859), 320.

[7] K.J. Leyser, 'England and the Empire in the Early Twelfth Century' in *Medieval Germany and its Neighbours, 900-1250* (London, 1982), pp.191-214.

[8] Leyser, 'Frederick Barbarossa, Henry II, and the Hand of St. James', *ibid.*, p.225.

If Matilda's first marriage inaugurated closer Anglo-German ties, the results were on the whole disappointing to the Anglo-Norman and Angevin houses, simply because the Empire could not share the tradition of suspicion, hostility, even contempt, with which the Normans and Angevins regarded the monarchy of France down to the treaty of Paris in 1259. The imperial court certainly had its disagreements with the French crown, especially in backing rival popes in the intermittent schisms of the eleventh and twelfth centuries. But there was no fundamental conflict of interests, over spheres and frontiers, between France and Germany until the fourteenth century. The alliance of King John's England and Germany, or at least that part of it loyal to Otto IV, against Philip II of France, prompted more by family feeling than political sense, was an interlude. Until the time of Charles of Anjou, the Capetians tended to regard papal diplomacy or intrigue directed against the Hohenstaufen imperial house with chilly respect and practical misgiving.

In the 1160s Empress Matilda's son by her second marriage, Henry II of England, reverted to his grandfather's scheme of an Anglo-Imperial alliance to be confirmed by marriages. This was most opportune for Emperor Frederick I Barbarossa, who needed support in his diplomatic and military endeavours against Pope Alexander III and his supporters. With the promulgation of the Constitutions of Clarendon in 1164, Henry II also found himself in conflict with the pope. In 1165 the emperor's principal adviser, Archbishop Rainald of Cologne, promptly arrived in Rouen for negotiations with the Angevin monarch. The king's eldest daughter Matilda was betrothed to Henry the Lion, duke of Saxony and Bavaria, first cousin and close friend of the emperor. Her younger sister Eleanor was betrothed to the emperor's only son Frederick, both being infants. Henry II promised to recognize Paschal III, the imperial candidate for the papacy. The marriage of Matilda and Henry the Lion duly took place at Minden in Saxony in 1168, but the other, more significant betrothal never came to a marriage.[9] Frederick did not survive childhood, and Eleanor was betrothed to Alfonso VIII of Castile instead. If Henry II had hoped that a daughter would, like his own mother, one day be an empress, it was the subordinate betrothal of 1165 which was to have consequences, and these quite unexpected. They followed from Henry the Lion's deposition as duke of Saxony and Bavaria in 1180.

The fall of Henry the Lion, and his subsequent terms of exile at the Angevin court, did not directly affect the fundamentally pro-imperial attitude of the Angevin monarchy. The reason for this is that Duke Henry had fallen victim, not to the machinations of Frederick Barbarossa, but to the opposition of the Saxon aristocracy, which had cited him before the imperial court as a malevolent lord in 1179. It was not Barbarossa's

[9] K. Jordan, *Henry the Lion: A Biography*, transl. P. Falla (Oxford, 1986), pp.144, 147.

hostility but Henry's own arrogance in refusing to answer the charges which compelled the emperor, with obvious regret, to fulfil a sequence of legal procedures resulting in the expulsion of a friend and cousin who had, for nearly twenty-five years, served the imperial cause with distinction. Henry II's impartial attitude is therefore easy to explain. On the one hand he was free to pursue a new marriage-alliance with the Empire, by negotiating another possible betrothal, of Richard Lionheart to Frederick Barbarossa's daughter Agnes.[10] Nothing came of this. On the other hand, Henry II was also free to do generous things for his daughter, son-in-law, and grandchildren. Possibly he wished, as years advanced, to compensate for earlier shortcomings in Angevin domestic felicity. A further motive touched the mutual prestige of their houses. We learn that when the magnificent new church of St. Blaise in Brunswick was dedicated by Duke Henry and Duchess Matilda in 1188, the citation mentioned their mutual descent from imperial forbears, his from Emperor Lothar III, hers from Empress Matilda.[11] Not only had the Welf and Angevin dynasties, by means of outstanding marriages, risen from comital rank to ducal or royal titles, but both felt they shared the lustre of imperial descent.

The Angevins therefore did something for Henry the Lion's children. Richenza, renamed Matilda, was married off to Count Geoffrey II of Perche in 1189; William, born at Winchester in 1184, did not return to Germany with his parents, but was brought up at his grandfather's expense;[12] and Otto, subsequently emperor, was given one of his grandmother Eleanor's possessions, the county of Poitou, in 1196.

The fall of Henry the Lion did not at first disturb the pro-Hohenstaufen diplomatic outlook of the English crown. But once Henry II and Frederick Barbarossa were dead, the formula of amity inherited from their Anglo-Norman and Salian predecessors was permitted to lapse when the next generation allowed personal interest to override their better judgement. It is well known how Barbarossa's son Henry VI extorted a huge ransom from the imprisoned Richard I, and compelled him to submit as an imperial vassal. Richard had not the time, means, or inclination to seek revenge, but his brother John did decide to turn England against the Hohenstaufen alignment. In supporting his Welf nephew Otto IV (1198-1214) against the Hohenstaufen monarchs Philip of Swabia (1198-1208) and Frederick II (1212-50), John was expecting German assistance in recovering his Norman and Angevin possessions confiscated by Philip II of France in 1204. At first Otto IV kept clear of this entanglement, intending that his marriage to Beatrice of Swabia in 1209 would reconcile the Hohenstaufen party in Germany to his own imperial candidature. This policy came to grief through Otto's arrogant handling of Italian

[10] *Ibid.*, p.184.
[11] *Ibid*, p.202; Henry the Lion's gospel-book makes the same point, *ibid.*, p.158.
[12] A.L. Poole, 'Die Welfen in der Verbannung', *Deutsches Archiv*, ii (1938), 133.

affairs. He insisted upon German imperial authority over the whole peninsula, causing Pope Innocent III to withdraw his support. Since the pope was also on bad terms with King John, a consequence of the latter's high-handedness against the English Church, he reverted, with some reservations, to the previous papal constellation established between 1177 and 1197, a cautious alliance between the Hohenstaufen, the French monarchy, and Rome. For the purpose, the young Hohenstaufen king of Sicily, Frederick II, was sent to Germany in 1212.

In order to protect themselves from this new coalition, King John and Otto IV decided upon the strategy of dealing with the most formidable partner, Philip of France, in spite of the fact that Frederick II was already at large in southern Germany. Their plans made some sense, for success in the Bouvines campaign ought to have restored Anjou and Normandy to King John in the French king's rear, and the lower Rhineland to Otto IV, where it was essential to prevent the advance of Frederick II. King Philip's victory was, of course, a disaster for the Welf-Angevin alliance, which fell apart for good as the parties tried to save themselves from the wreckage. Otto IV resigned the Empire, his brother Henry was deprived of the Rhine-Palatinate, and the ex-emperor retired to his estates in Saxony where he died childless in 1218. King John was constrained to submit to all the demands of Innocent III, the English Church, and the disaffected barons. Frederick II was properly crowned king of the Romans at Aachen, and opened negotiations with the pope for his imperial coronation, while securing the whole of Germany to his allegiance. Innocent III celebrated the triumph of his schemes by summoning the Fourth Lateran Council, and Philip II by founding the church of Notre-Dame de la Victoire at Senlis as his votive-offering.[13]

The new king of the Romans was a man of many talents, and bore no lasting grudge against the Welfs and the Angevins for the damage done to the Hohenstaufen interest under Otto IV and King John. Frederick II sought to restore the confidence of all his neighbours in the wisdom of imperial diplomacy, which secured his coronation as emperor in 1220. The mutual regard of the Capetian and Hohenstaufen houses was not seriously disturbed until Charles of Anjou, with the reluctant consent of his brother Louis IX, wrested the crown of Sicily from Frederick II's successors in the 1260s. Once the generation of Henry the Lion's children had passed away, Frederick II reconciled himself to the Welfs. In 1235 Otto IV's nephew Otto the Child, son of that William born in Winchester, was created duke of Brunswick and Lüneburg.[14] From him descended all

[13] J.W. Baldwin, *The Government of Philip Augustus* (Berkeley, Los Angeles, and London, 1986), p.389.
[14] L. Weiland, *Constitutiones et Acta Publica*, MGH, Leges sectio iv. 2 (Hanover, 1896), 197, pp.263-5.

future Welfs, including the electoral house of Hanover which reigned over Great Britain from 1714 to 1901.

As King John's children grew up, Frederick II also reverted to the traditional policy of close ties with the Angevin dynasty. Having buried three wives, Constance of Aragon, Isabella of Brienne and Jerusalem, and Bianca Lancia, whom he married *in articulo mortis*, he married Henry III of England's sister Isabella in 1235. They are thought to have produced four children, Isabella dying in childbed in 1241.[15] Charles-Otto, later renamed Henry, was born in 1238, and according to Frederick II's will in 1250, was declared heir of his elder half-brother Conrad IV.[16] But his claim to the Hohenstaufen crowns was overtaken by the birth of Conradin in 1252, and within two years Henry was himself dead. Isabella's other surviving child Margaret had greater political significance. Through her marriage in 1255 to Margrave Albert of Meissen, she transmitted the cause of Hohenstaufen legitimacy in Germany to the Saxon house of Wettin, just as her niece Constance transmitted the claim to the Sicilian crown to the house of Aragon. For a long time there was a party in Germany and Italy which advocated the election of Margaret's son Frederick of Meissen (1257-1323) as German monarch, but nothing came of it. Henry III of England showed no interest in his niece or in the future of her family, simply because he was enticed by the papacy into promoting, at huge expense, his son Edmund of Lancaster and his brother Richard of Cornwall as candidates to the thrones of Sicily in 1254 and Germany in 1257 respectively.[17] It appears that as an obedient son of the church, Henry was impressed by Gregory IX's excommunication of Frederick II in 1239, and turned against the Hohenstaufen even before his sister's early death in 1241.

The new policy proved a disaster to Henry III in that the enormous cost of the preparatory diplomacy again raised the spectre of serious baronial opposition to the English crown. It marked a decisive break with the norms of Anglo-Angevin diplomacy, which went back to the initial negotiations of Henry I of England and Henry V of Germany in 1109. It also indicates how the initiative which Frederick II had grasped with international success after the battle of Bouvines had crumbled away under pressure from the papal curia, settled since 1239 in the final phase of its antipathy to the Hohenstaufen. First Henry III and then Louis IX of France, Frederick's erstwhile allies, were persuaded to permit their

[15] H. Decker-Hauff, 'Das staufische Haus' in *Die Zeit der Staufer: Katalog der Ausstellung im württembergischen Landesmuseum*, (Stuttgart, 1977), iii. 358-9, 366.

[16] T.C. van Cleve, *The Emperor Frederick II of Hohenstaufen* (Oxford, 1972), pp.374f, 380f.

[17] W.E. Rhodes, 'Edmund, Earl of Lancaster', *EHR*, x (1895), 19-40, 209-37; C.C. Bayley, 'The Diplomatic Preliminaries of the Double Election of 1257 in Germany', *ibid.*, lxii (1947), 457-83, and A. Wachtel, 'Die sizilische Thronkandidatur des Prinzen Edmund von England', *Deutsches Archiv*, iv (1941), 98-178.

kinsmen to try to seize the Sicilian kingdom from Frederick II's descendants, whose expulsion was secured by Charles of Anjou's military victories in the mid 1260s.

Less decisive was the intervention of Earl Richard of Cornwall in Germany. In 1256, when William of Holland, anti-king of the Romans since 1247, was killed in battle with the Frisians, Richard presented himself as the candidate of the archdiocese of Cologne, that region of the Empire which, by reason of its prosperous trade, had always favoured the English connection. With the support of Archbishop Conrad, Richard at first made a reasonable showing, but his rival for the German throne, Alfonso X of Castile, also recruited considerable backing amongst the German princes. Both men were elected in 1257.[18] Alfonso had already laid claim to the duchy of Swabia, the original patrimony of the Hohenstaufen dynasty, when Conrad IV died in 1254, since the Castilian ruler's mother Beatrice was a daughter of Philip of Swabia. In retaliation Richard confirmed the duchy to the better claimant, the infant Conradin, in 1257.[19] Neither of the foreign kings was a success. Alfonso never visited Germany, and Richard, who 'poured out money like water at the feet of the princes',[20] achieved nothing by his several armed parades up and down the Rhineland.

The advent of Anglo-Angevins as empress in 1235 and king of the Romans in 1257 proved quite peripheral to German politics and to international diplomacy, yet the tradition of an Anglo-German royal marriage-alliance persisted into the next generation. Richard of Cornwall's successor as German king, Rudolf of Habsburg (1273-91), was a political pupil of Frederick II, the affairs of Italy excepted, so that it is not surprising still to find him negotiating with Edward I of England for such a connection. In 1277 Edward's infant daughter Joan of Acre was affianced to King Rudolf's second son Hartmann, the marriage postponed *sine die*.[21] In the event, the groom was accidentally drowned in the Rhine in 1281, and in adulthood Joan married Gilbert de Clare, earl of Hertford and Gloucester.

This was not the end of Edward I's interest in Anglo-Imperial ties. He married off three other daughters, to Duke John of Brabant, Count John of Holland, and Count Henry of Bar, a vassal of the French crown, but most of whose lands were situated in the Empire. The reign of Adolf of Nassau

---

[18] Weiland, *Constitutiones*, ii. 376-87, pp.479-86; C.C. Bayley, *The Formation of the German College of Electors in the Mid-Thirteenth Century* (Toronto, 1949), pp.63-77, 152-63; N. Denholm-Young, *Richard of Cornwall* (Oxford, 1947), pp.86-117, 139-55; R. Reisinger, *Die römisch-deutschen Könige und ihr Wähler 1189-1273* (Aalen, 1977), pp.71-88.

[19] Weiland, *Constitutiones* ii. 386, 485.

[20] J.M. Lappenberg, *Annales Hamburgenses*, MGH, Scriptores xvi (Hanover, 1859), 384.

[21] F. Trautz, *Die Könige von England und das Reich, 1272-1377* (Heidelberg, 1961), pp.117-27.

(1292-98) coincided with Edward's confrontation with Philip IV of France over the duchy of Aquitaine and other issues. Casting about for allies, Edward entered into an anti-French agreement with King Adolf in 1294, but the German monarch, with worsening domestic political threats to face, backed out in 1297, possibly induced by a French bribe.[22] In spite of this contretemps Edward III reverted to his grandfather's policy in 1337, perhaps with greater hopes of constructive action against France, since Emperor Louis the Bavarian and Margrave William of Jülich were his brothers-in-law, and Edward's sister Eleanor was married to Duke Rainald of Guelders. England provided cash-subsidies and Germany was to find troops. The emperor also appointed Edward as vicar of the Empire in the field.[23] This alliance had divided aims; Edward was planning to invade northern France; Louis was hoping for a campaign against the papacy in Avignon; and the princes of the Low countries desired more English money. By 1341 the coalition had fallen apart. In hopes of a reconciliation with the papacy, the emperor abandoned Edward III for an alignment with the French crown, although the latter proved unable to bring about Louis' ultimate aim.

Three times the Anglo-Angevin monarchy, under Henry III, Edward I, and Edward III, had attempted, by use of its superior income, to draw Germany into an effective alliance, and in the time of Richard of Cornwall, to purchase its crown. But the political needs and interests of the two countries were not at all compatible. It can be seen that the intermittent careers of Norman and Angevin princesses and princes, from Empress Matilda to Richard of Cornwall, at the courts of the Empire made little lasting impact upon the course of English or German affairs. The essential task which more truly related the two countries was not diplomacy but commerce, and here the Germans were the dominant partner. By the thirteenth century the north German Hansa was coming into control of the trade of the Baltic and North Seas, the privileged Stalhof in London being one of the four principal terminal points of the huge Hanseatic system reaching out to Scandinavia, the Baltic states, and Russia, as well as England, Flanders, and all of northern Germany.[24] The growth of this trade into the fourteenth century is well documented, and in spite of a quite marked deterioration in Anglo-Hanseatic relations in later

---

[22] G. Barraclough, 'Edward I and Adolf of Nassau. A Chapter of Mediaeval Diplomatic History', *Cambridge Historical Journal*, vi (1940), 225-62 and F. Bock, 'Englands Beziehungen zum Reich unter Adolf von Nassau', *Mitteilungen des österreichischen Instituts für Geschichte*, Ergänzungsband xii (1933), 198-257.

[23] H.S. Lucas, *The Low Countries and the Hundred Years War, 1326-1347* (Ann Arbor, 1929) and H.S. Offler, 'England and Germany at the Beginning of the Hundred Years War', *EHR*, liv (1939), 608-31. See also below p.241.

[24] P. Dollinger, *La Hanse, XIIe-XVIIe siècles* (Paris, 1964), pp.56-8, 77-80, 96-9, 129-30, 301-5, 371-81 on the Hansa and England.

times, English demand for Rhenish wine, Baltic timber, Prussian grain, and Russian furs constituted a great tradition in commerce which never died out.

If the seas, rivers, and estuaries of northern Europe eventually facilitated the commercial ties of Germany and England, the sea also represented, as we have seen, a formidable barrier in medieval times. Gottfried von Strassburg may have derived his *Tristan* (about 1210) from Thomas of Britain, but his geographical knowledge of England is shaky because, as Professor Hatto reminds us,[25] it was hundreds of miles from the upper Rhineland. The era of the crusades, and of common expeditions as far afield as Portugal, Prussia, and Byzantium, did notoriously little to erode the provincial xenophobia of western Europe. The Swabian chonicler Otto of St. Blaise, writing early in the thirteenth century, records 'English perfidy' on the Third Crusade, by which he means the behaviour of an Angevin, Richard I.[26] John of Salisbury composed similar platitudes about the Germans, stigmatising them as reckless, barbarous, and treacherous.[27]

Despite such strictures, the remote but cordial connection of Germany and England supported by imperial and royal diplomacy was also reflected in the sphere of cultural influences. In the tenth century the people of Cologne developed the strange legend of St. Ursula, supposedly the daughter of a British king, and said to have been martyred with her 11,000 virgin companions on the banks of the Rhine in the fifth century. Her cult resulted in one of the fine new churches of twelfth-century Cologne. To the Germans, England was a realm just distant enough for fantasy, rather in the style of attributing Iceland in the *Nibelungenlied* to Brunhild as her kingdom. The *Carmina Burana* texts preserve the ambiguous snatch where, according to the sex of the singer,

> Were the world all mine
> from the sea to the Rhine,
> I would give it all up
> for the king (or queen) of England
> lying in my arms![28]

---

[25] A.T. Hatto, *Gottfried von Strassburg, Tristan* (Harmondsworth, 1960), appendix 5.

[26] A. Hofmeister, *Ottonis de Sancto Blasio Chronica*, MGH, Scriptores in usum scholarum (Hanover and Leipzig, 1912), p.55.

[27] M. Chibnall, *John of Salisbury's Memoirs of the Papal Court* (London, 1956), pp.12, 66, 76, and T. Reuter, 'John of Salisbury and the Germans' in M. Wilks (ed.), *The World of John of Salisbury*, Studies in Church History, Subsidia iii (Oxford, 1984), 415-25.

[27] A. Hilka and O. Schumann, *Carmina Burana* i, part 2; *Die Liebeslieder* (Heidelberg, 1941), 145 A, p.247.

Chapter 4

Anglo-Scottish Relations, 1066-1174

Judith Green

The issue at the forefront of Anglo-Scottish relations between 1066 and 1174 was that of control of the northern counties of England or, to put it another way, whether the border between the two realms was to be fixed along the Solway-Tweed line or further south.[1] The issue was not new in 1066, for its roots lay in the growing power of the Scottish monarchy and its potential for southward expansion; nor was it resolved in 1174, for the recovery of northern England was to remain an objective of the Scottish crown until 1237.[2] More was at stake than territory, for kings of Scotland on occasion were prepared to recognize the overlordship of kings of England. How far did such acts of submission compromise the independence of Scotland? This question is significant not only in the context of the eleventh and twelfth centuries, but also in the light of Edward I's claim to overlordship of Scotland in the later thirteenth century. Although relations between the two monarchies were not always peaceful, from the late eleventh century the states were in closer contact than before, and the coming of the Normans provided a channel through which outside influences could flow into Scotland. The nature of those influences, which Professor G.W.S. Barrow has done so much to unravel,[3] is one that belongs more appropriately to a history of Scotland than of Anglo-Scottish relations, but the ebb and flow of relations between the

---

[1] G.W.S. Barrow, 'The Anglo-Scottish Border', *The Kingdom of the Scots* (London, 1973), pp.139-61.

[2] For the background see D.P. Kirby, 'Strathclyde and Cumbria: a Survey of Historical Development to 1092', *Cumberland and Westmorland Antiquarian and Archaeological Society*, new series, lxii (1962), 77-94; M.O. Anderson, 'Lothian and the Early Scottish Kings', *S[cottish] H[istorical] R[eview]*, xxxix (1960), 98-112; B. Meehan, 'The Siege of Durham, the Battle of Carham and the Cession of Lothian', *SHR*, lv (1976), 1-19; and a recent appraisal by A.P. Smyth, *Warlords and Holy Men, Scotland, A.D. 80-1000, New History of Scotland*, i (London, 1984), especially chapter 7; there is a brief account of Anglo-Scottish relations between 1174 and 1237 in A.L. Poole, *From Domesday Book to Magna Carta*, 2nd edn. (Oxford, 1955), pp.278-82.

[3] See especially *Kingdom of the Scots*; *[The] Anglo-Norman Era [in Scottish History]* (Oxford, 1980); *Kingship and Unity; Scotland 1000-1306, New History of Scotland*, ii (London, 1981). The earlier work by R.L.G. Ritchie, *The Normans in Scotland* (Edinburgh, 1954) is still useful.

two monarchies has to be set in the context of growing cross-border contacts, especially in the ecclesiastical sphere and in the families of the lay aristocracy.

The period falls naturally into four phases. The first lasted until the death of King Malcolm III (Canmore) of Scots in 1093. Malcolm had already demonstrated hostile intentions by launching an invasion of Northumberland in 1061, and in the summer of 1066 had sheltered Harold Godwinson's enemies: his brother Tostig and Harald Hardrada of Norway.[4] Malcolm invaded the north on four other occasions after 1066, the last in 1093, but after his death Anglo-Scottish relations entered a more peaceful phase. His sons initially used the support of Rufus and Henry I to establish themselves on the throne against rival contenders, and Henry in particular built up a close relationship with David I (1124-1153). A reappraisal of that relationship is offered below, and it is suggested that the resulting period of peace was of special importance for the advance of Norman settlement in northern England. After Henry's death David used the disputed succession in England to advance his power south of the border; for some years the Scots controlled Northumberland, Cumbria (Cumberland and Westmorland), and at least part of Lancashire; in 1157, however, Henry II resumed the northern counties. The fourth and final phase lasted from 1157 until 1174 when William the Lion's attempt to recover the lost counties which he regarded as his patrimony ended so disastrously for Scotland.

When he became king of England, William the Conqueror was thus faced with a hostile northern neighbour. In 1066 England north of the Humber and the Dee fell into several regions:[5] royal authority seems to have been strongest in Yorkshire; to the north lay the bishopric of Durham and then Northumberland where local aristocratic families, especially that based at Bamburgh, were still powerful; in the north-west, Cumbria lay outside the power of the English crown, though further south King Edward and Earl Tostig had held land in Lancashire. Tostig had been appointed in 1055, and his had been the unenviable task of representing royal authority in the north; his efforts had ended in failure in 1065 when expelled by the Northumbrians and the men of York.[6] William's approach to governing the north was to continue the practice of appointing earls – in 1066 there was no practicable alternative – but none of his candidates lasted long. Copsi, his first choice, had been Tostig's deputy in Yorkshire, but Copsi was soon murdered by a member of the powerful Bamburgh

---

[4] Symeon of Durham, *H[istoria] R[egum]*, in *Opera omnia*, 2 vols, ed. T. Arnold, *RS*, 1882-5, ii. 174-5; *The Anglo-Saxon Chronicle, a revised translation*, ed. D. Whitelock, D.C. Douglas and S.I. Tucker (London, 1961) (hereafter cited *ASC*), *s. a.* 1066.

[5] W.E. Kapelle, *The Norman Conquest of the North* (London, 1979), Chapter 1.

[6] *Ibid.*, Chapter 4.

family.[7] The second earl, Cospatric, was descended on his mother's side from an earlier earl, Uhtred, and on his father's side was related to King Malcolm. Cospatric seems to have taken part in the resistance to the Normans recorded in 1068, for in that year he made his way into exile at the Scottish court.[8] William tried next Robert de Commines, but he was murdered at Durham early in 1069.[9] These ill-fated appointments were only one dimension of William's problems in the north where the Norman advance met with stubborn resistance. The revolt of 1068 was renewed in 1069; the local rebels were then joined by Englishmen who had taken refuge in Scotland, including Cospatric and Edgar Aetheling, together with a fleet from Denmark. On two occasions in 1069 the situation was so serious as to demand the presence of the Conqueror himself. On his second expedition William decided to prevent a recurrence of rebellion by harrying the north in the winter of 1069-70.[10]

Until 1070 Malcolm did not intervene directly. English exiles did find a refuge at his court, and *c*.1070 Malcolm married Margaret, sister of Edgar Aetheling. The bridegroom was said to have been more eager for the marriage than the bride, and its political significance in terms of a bond between the royal houses of Scotland and Wessex cannot be ignored.[11] In 1070, however, Malcolm launched his first invasion since the accession of William, attacking Northumberland from the north-west.[12] William did not respond immediately, but two years later collected forces for an invasion of Scotland by sea and by land. He advanced as far north as Abernethy, where Malcolm submitted to him and became his man (*homo suus devenit*) according to the chronicle of Florence of Worcester.[13] The phrase used here is redolent of continental vassalage, but it is unlikely that Malcolm regarded his submission as significantly different from those which kings of Scotland had made before the Norman Conquest, nor that the independence of Scotland was being breached.[14]

Malcolm's third invasion took place in 1079, and the situation in the north remained dangerous in the following year when Bishop Walcher of

---

[7] Symeon of Durham, *HR*, ii. 198.

[8] Kapelle, p.108; Symeon of Durham, *HR*, ii. 199.

[9] Symeon of Durham, *HR*, ii. 186-7.

[10] For a detailed account of events in the north see Kapelle, pp.112-19.

[11] *ASC* 'D' *s. a.* 1067. The four eldest sons of this marriage were named after Anglo-Saxon kings. For a valuable study of Queen Margaret see D. Baker, 'A Nursery of Saints: St. Margaret of Scotland Reconsidered' in *Medieval Women*, ed. D. Baker, Studies in Church History, Subsidia 1 (Oxford, 1978), 119-41.

[12] Symeon of Durham, *HR*, ii. 190.

[13] F[lorence of] W[orcester], *Chronicon ex Chronicis*, ed. B. Thorpe, 2 vols. (London, 1848-9), ii. 9.

[14] A.O. Anderson, 'Anglo-Scottish Relations from Constantine II to William', *SHR*, xlii (1963), 1-20 discusses the early submissions pp.2-10; cf. Smyth, *Warlords and Holy Men*, pp.199-214.

Durham was murdered at Gateshead. Walcher was a Lotharingian appointed in 1071, and after the downfall of Waltheof, earl of Northumbria between 1072 and 1075, Walcher had enjoyed the powers of earl.[15] Two expeditions were sent north in 1080. The first was led by Odo of Bayeux, the second by William's son Robert. Robert advanced as far as Falkirk but retreated without achieving anything, though he did lay the foundations of a castle at Newcastle on the River Tyne, protecting the north-south route.[16] William continued in his search for an effective earl. He next tried Aubrey (probably Aubrey de Couci) who evidently soon surrendered his lands and office and left England and then, probably at the very end of the reign, Robert de Mowbray, nephew of the king's leading minister, Geoffrey, bishop of Coutances.[17] William's appointments thus failed to be effective, and military expeditions evidently did not deter the Scots from invading. The limited progress of Norman settlement in the north by the end of the reign was reflected in Domesday Book. Northumberland, Durham, Cumberland and Westmorland were not surveyed at all; and in Lancashire and Yorkshire the tenurial map was still incomplete, especially in the upland areas. Great compact lordships had been created guarding the routes across the Pennines at Richmond, Pontefract and, to the south, at Tickhill; north of the Tyne castles had been built at Durham and Newcastle, but the north was still vulnerable to attack.[18]

Initially it appeared that Rufus would be no more successful than his father in establishing a secure northern frontier. In 1088 he was faced with a major revolt in which Robert de Mowbray and the bishop of Durham took part.[19] Having surmounted this challenge, he then had to deal with an invasion by Malcolm (his fourth) in 1091. Rufus marched north, as his father had done in 1072, and extracted from Malcolm a renewal of the submission he had made in 1072.[20] Rufus, however, was evidently not prepared to let matters rest there, for in the following year, as reported in a terse entry in the Anglo-Saxon Chronicle, he advanced into Cumbria, drove out Dolfin the native ruler, and built a castle at Carlisle supported by a colony of peasant farmers dispatched thither.[21] Exactly what was the significance of these actions? It is thought that before 1092 Cumbria had been in the orbit of the Scottish king, though not all historians accept this

---

[15] Symeon of Durham, *HR*, ii. 199; 208-11.

[16] *Ibid.*, ii. 211.

[17] *Ibid.*; for comment see F. Barlow, *William Rufus* (London, 1983), p.161 n.

[18] For a brief review of the castleries, Kapelle, pp.144-5; the foundation of Durham castle is mentioned by Symeon of Durham, *HR*, ii. 199-200.

[19] Barlow, *William Rufus*, Chapter 2.

[20] Symeon of Durham, *HR*, ii. 218; FW, ii. 28.

[21] *ASC s. a.* 1092.

view.[22] Moreover it is not certain whether the new military lordship of Carlisle was committed by Rufus to Ranulf Meschin, nephew of the earl of Chester, or whether the grant to Ranulf was made by Henry I.[23] Rufus did begin to distribute land to his followers both in Cumbria and in Northumberland. Ivo Taillebois, his steward, received the lordship of Kendal in the south Lakes,[24] and in the north-east he seems to have established Guy de Balliol at Bywell on the Tyne west of Newcastle, and Robert d'Umfraville at Prudhoe and Redesdale.[25] Neither Guy nor Robert had held lands in Domesday Book, and it looks as though they were men who owed their advancement to Rufus rather than his father. In this respect they are comparable with Robert de Rumilly and Robert de Stuteville, who were both given lands in Yorkshire by Rufus.[26] Northern England was one area where Rufus had land at his disposal with which to reward his followers.

The determination displayed by Rufus in 1092 may well have been one of the reasons why Malcolm went south to meet Rufus at Gloucester in 1093, though also at issue was the marriage of Malcolm's daughter Edith, educated in England under the aegis of her aunt Christina.[27] Malcolm seems to have wanted her to marry Alan, count of Brittany and lord of Richmond, one of the Yorkshire castleries, a marriage which Rufus may well have regarded as a threat to his own security. The meeting between the two kings did not in any case go well. According to the chronicle of

---

[22] Smyth, *Warlords and Holy Men*, pp.229-31 follows the line taken by the majority of commentators; Kapelle, however, is more sceptical, *Norman Conquest of the North*, pp.151-2.

[23] The only information about the date of Ranulf's appointment seems to derive from his foundation charter of Wetheral priory near Carlisle, which referred to Abbot Stephen of St. Mary's, York who died in 1112, *The Register of Wetheral*, ed. J.E. Prescott, Cumberland and Westmorland Antiquarian and Archaeological Society (1897), no. 1. Ranulf may be presumed to have been in Rufus's favour from his marriage to Roger FitzGerold's widow, Lucy, an heiress in her own right: I.J. Sanders, *English Baronies* (Oxford, 1960), p.18.

[24] Ivo gave churches in the lordship of Kendal to St. Mary's, J.F. Curwen (ed.), *Records Relating to the Barony of Kendale by W. Farrer*, i (Kendal, 1923), appendix no. 1, p.377. Ivo died *c*.1094: *Complete Peerage*, vii, appendix J, 743.

[25] For the former: *Book of Fees: Liber Feodorum, The Book of Fees Commonly Called Testa de Nevill, Reformed from the Earliest MSS, by the Deputy Keeper of the Records* (London, 1920-31), i. 397. This, though a late source, probably records an authentic tradition. Guy was evidently established in the north by the start of Henry I's reign, but the following references probably relate to his land in co. Durham: *R[egesta] R[egum] A[nglo-] N[ormannorum]*, 4 vols., ed. H.W.C. Davis and others, (Oxford, 1913-69), ii. nos.575, 709. See also G.A. Moriarty, 'The Balliols in Picardy, England and Scotland', *New England Historical and Genealogical Register*, cvi (1952), 273-90. For Robert d'Umfraville see L. Keen, 'The Umfravilles, the Castle, and the Barony of Prudhoe, Northumberland', *Proceedings of the Battle Conference on Anglo-Norman Studies*, v (1982), at 170-1.

[26] For the former see *Early Yorkshire Charters*, ed. C.T. Clay, vii. 31-5, and for the latter *ibid*., ed. C.T. Clay, ix. 1-2.

[27] Barlow, *William Rufus*, pp.309-17.

Florence of Worcester, Rufus was only prepared to deal with Malcolm as a lord with his vassal, terms which Malcolm indignantly rejected.[28] It may be that the chronicler was adding his own gloss to events, but if correct it suggests that Rufus may have been seeking to enforce a stricter interpretation of his overlordship than Malcolm was prepared to allow. At any rate, Malcolm retreated in anger to Scotland where he hastily prepared to launch his fifth and final invasion, during which he met his death at the hands of Robert de Mowbray's men.[29]

Malcolm had invaded northern England five times in all. For the impact of his expeditions on northern England there is only the testimony of the chroniclers, especially Symeon of Durham. Symeon referred to destruction, to the burning of churches, and to the enslavement of the young.[30] Malcolm does not seem to have tried to fortify strongholds, or to have established a permanent presence. He was therefore presumably aiming for booty, and a recognition of Scottish overlordship rather than a thoroughgoing conquest of the kind carried through in England by the Conqueror.

His death marked the end of an era in Anglo-Scottish relations, for his sons were less hostile than he had been to the Norman kings. In the first instance this was because Duncan and then Edgar turned to Rufus for assistance in establishing their claims to the throne. In 1093 Malcolm's brother Donald took the throne. Malcolm's son Duncan did displace Donald for a short time with Rufus's help, but was killed.[31] Rufus thereupon backed the claim of Duncan's half-brother Edgar, who evidently acknowledged Rufus's overlordship before his accession in 1097, for there survives at Durham a remarkable charter of 1095, in which Edgar refers to himself as king of Scots and Lothian by the gift of his lord King William. If the charter is, as it seems,[32] authentic, it provides a remarkable insight into Rufus's perspective of his overlordship. Rufus's reign had witnessed a more vigorous, aggressive, policy towards the north which was beginning to pay dividends, and during the reign of his successor, Henry I, these foundations were built on.

Henry was unmarried when his brother's death in the New Forest and his elder brother Robert's absence on crusade gave him the chance of seizing the English throne. Henry needed to marry to get an heir, and he also needed security from Scottish attack in the event of his brother's return. His speedy marriage to Edith, now renamed in Norman fashion

[28]   FW, ii. 31.
[29]   Symeon of Durham, *HR*, ii. 221.
[30]   *HR*, ii. 190-1; on Malcolm's motives see Ritchie, *Normans in Scotland*, p.26.
[31]   *ASC s. a.* 1093; FW, ii. 32 suggests that Duncan was possibly a member of Rufus's military household; *Early Sources of Scottish History A.D. 500-1286*, collected and translated A.O. Anderson, 2 vols. (Edinburgh, 1922), ii. 88.
[32]   A.A.M. Duncan, 'The Earliest Scottish Charters', *SHR*, xxxvii (1958), 103-35.
[33]   *RRAN*, ii. nos.601, 648, 689, 701, 703, 706, 818a, 828, 832-3.

Matilda, achieved both of these aims, for Matilda was sister to the king of Scotland and, through her mother, descended from the old royal line of Wessex. King Edgar was at the English court in 1101 and soon another of Matilda's brothers, David, also appeared there.[33] Edgar was succeeded on the Scottish throne in 1107 by Alexander 'with the consent of King Henry' according to Henry of Huntingdon.[34] Alexander married an illegitimate daughter of Henry, and he also seems to have been prepared to recognize the overlordship of the English crown, for in 1114 he accompanied Henry I's expedition into Wales.[35]

Not long before this expedition, either late in 1113 or early in 1114, Henry had bestowed on his brother-in-law David one of the richest matrimonial prizes of the Anglo-Norman world, Matilda, daughter of Earl Waltheof and Countess Judith, the Conqueror's niece.[36] Queen Matilda had urged the marriage,[37] and the king may not have needed much persuading, for he was generous to members of his family. It may indeed have been at about this time that one of his nephews, Stephen of Blois, received the honour of Eye, the first tranche of what was to be a vast accumulation of estates.[38] Henry also seems to have had a good opinion of David personally, for the latter acted as a royal justice in England on more than one occasion.[39] Yet Henry's decision cannot have been made lightly. David was by 1114 heir-presumptive to the Scottish throne, and already heir by Edgar's will to land in southern Scotland.[40] Lothian had for a time come under the sway of the kingdom of Bernicia and thus of Northumbria, and David's interest in acquiring land south of the Tweed may have been strengthened by his marriage to the daughter of Earl Waltheof and the grand-daughter of Earl Siward of Northumbria.

Of more immediate importance was the material wealth the marriage brought to David. It is possibly significant that the earliest indications of his activity in southern Scotland come after rather than before his marriage, for Alexander is said to have been reluctant to accept the terms of his brother's will.[41] If this was the case, then David may be envisaged as

[34] Henry of Huntingdon, *Historia Anglorum*, ed. T. Arnold (RS, 1879), 236.

[35] William of Malmesbury, *De Gestis Regum Anglorum libri quinque, historiae novellae libri tres*, ed. W. Stubbs, 2 vols., (RS, 1887-9), ii. 476; *Brut y Tywysogyon or the Chronicle of the Princes, Red Book of Hergest Version*, ed. T. Jones, Board of Celtic Studies, University of Wales History and Law Series, no.16 (Cardiff, 1955), pp.78-9.

[36] *ASC* 'H' *s. a.* 1114 (*recte* 1113).

[37] 'Life of Waltheof' in *Early Sources of Scottish History*, ii. 147.

[38] *RRAN*, ii. no.932 n.

[39] *R[egesta] R[egum] S[cottorum]*, ed. G.W.S. Barrow (Edinburgh, 1960), i, no.5; *RRAN*, ii, no.1505; *The Ecclesiastical History of Orderic Vitalis*, ed. M. Chibnall, 6 vols. (Oxford, 1969-80), iv. 277.

[40] Ailred of Rievalux, 'Relatio de Standardo', in *Chronicles of the Reigns of Stephen, Henry II and Richard I*, ed. R. Howlett, 4 vols. (RS, 1884-90), iii. 193.

[41] As preceding note.

using his new wealth to help him in securing his inheritance. Kapelle has suggested that David may have worked in conjunction with his great friend and ally, Robert de Brus, and with Ranulf Meschin, to bring a degree of order to the border region.[42] Robert was one of those men from western Normandy whose early support for Henry I had been rewarded by grants of land in England; and his friendship with David was similarly rewarded by the grant of a vast tract of land in south-west Scotland.[43] David could count other Normans amongst his friends before his accession in 1124,[44] but Robert stands out because he alone seems to have had large estates on both sides of the border.

The more peaceful course of relations between England and Scotland suffered a setback soon after 1120.[45] In 1121 the bishop of Durham built a castle at Norham on the River Tweed,[46] and Walter Espec was probably established at nearby Wark at about the same date.[47] Walter, with Eustace FitzJohn, was to be a key figure in Henry's government of the north after 1120. Eustace and he were both present at a great meeting of northern magnates at Durham in 1121, so it is likely that Eustace also had already been established in his Northumberland lordship of Alnwick.[48] The reason for this assembly is not mentioned, but it was probably connected with the security of the northern border.[49] In 1122 King Henry paid his only recorded visit to Carlisle, where he ordered the fortifications to be strengthened.[50] It seems that Henry was afraid David might take advantage of the removal of Ranulf Meschin from Carlisle to invade. David evidently did not regard Cumbria south of the Solway as permanently lost to the Scottish crown at this date, and he may have felt

---

[42] Kapelle, pp.206-7.

[43] L.C. Loyd, *The Origins of Some Anglo-Norman Families*, Harleian Society, ciii (Leeds, 1951), 42-3; *Early Yorkshire Charters* ed. W. Farrer, ii. 10-19; *Early Scottish Charters Prior to A.D. 1153*, ed. A.C. Lawrie (Glasgow, 1905), no.54.

[44] David's charter for Selkirk (founded 1113) was witnessed amongst others by Robert de Brus, Robert d'Umfraville, Walter de Bolebec, Hugh de Morville, and Odard sheriff of Bamburgh: *Early Scottish Charters*, no.35 (there dated *c*.1120).

[45] H.S. Offler, 'Ranulf Flambard as Bishop of Durham 1099-1128)', *Durham University Journal*, xxxiii (1971-2), at 20-1.

[46] Symeon of Durham, *Historia Dunelmensis Ecclesiae* in *Opera omnia*, i. 140; *HR*, ii. 260.

[47] Walter gave land and the church of Wark to the priory he founded at Kirkham *c*.1122: W. Dugdale, *Monasticon Anglicanum*, new edn. 6 vols. in 8 (London, 1817-30), vi. 208. Henry I's queen Matilda had earlier given the church of Wark to Durham: *RRAN*, ii, no.1143.

[48] Symeon of Durham, *HR*, ii. 261-2; Eustace was pardoned geld in Northumberland in 1130 and this remission probably represents Alnwick: *Pipe Roll 31 Henry I*, ed. J. Hunter for Record Commission (London, 1833), p.35.

[49] In this context see the fifteenth-century account of Adelulf's entry into Nostell priory in 1122 cited by D. Nicholl, *Thurstan Archbishop of York (1114-1140)* (York, 1964), p.134. This refers to Henry I advancing towards Scotland at that time with an army for the suppression of rebellion.

[50] Symeon of Durham, *HR*, ii. 267.

aggrieved that Carlisle was not granted to him in 1121.[51] David may also have had designs on Northumberland, but if so held back from attack, remaining on such good terms with Henry that, when he became king of Scotland in 1124, Henry allowed him to keep the earldom of Huntingdon.

It was as one of Henry's leading vassals that David attended the court which Henry held at Christmas 1126, and was the first of the laymen to swear an oath of allegiance to the Empress Matilda as Henry's successor.[52] The occasion was of critical importance to Henry I, and the motives underlying David's public gesture of support deserve closer examination than previously accorded. By 1126 Henry had evidently decided that his second marriage was unlikely to produce a male heir, whilst the death of Matilda's husband had opened up the possibility of her succession. It was not a welcome prospect for the magnates, as it would presumably be Matilda's husband who would rule England, and there are signs of opposition to Henry's plans at this time.[53] David may well have chosen to support his niece in default of any other candidate, and perhaps at this stage nurtured hopes that her hand would be bestowed on his own son.[54] There were other considerations. There is no indication that during David's stay at the English court Henry exacted from him a public renewal either of homage for Huntingdon, or an act of submission such as earlier Scottish kings had performed. The silence of the sources is not conclusive on this point, but it is suggestive that Henry was prepared to be conciliatory.[55] He could offer another inducement to David: his influence

---

[51] An awareness that historically Cumbria had been a larger area than that under Scottish control by the 1120s is shown in the inquest into the lands held by the bishopric of Glasgow about this time which listed lands north of the Solway 'in those provinces of Cumbria which were under [David's] lordship and power (for he did not rule the whole region of Cumbria)': *Early Scottish Charters*, no.50.

[52] William of Malmesbury, *Historia Novella*, ed. K.R. Potter (Edinburgh, 1955), pp.1-4.

[53] C. Warren Hollister, 'The Anglo-Norman Succession Debate of 1126: Prelude to Stephen's Anarchy', *Journal of Medieval History*, i (1975), 19-41.

[54] It is not apparent that Henry had informed the magnates, or had even decided himself, that Matilda should marry Geoffrey of Anjou at the time the oath was taken. William of Malmesbury attributed to Roger of Salisbury the comment that Roger did not feel obliged to keep his oath because the king had promised not to marry his daughter outside the kingdom without taking the advice of his magnates but had not kept his word: *Historia Novella*, p.5. It was not until Louis VI recognized William Clito's claim to the county of Flanders that an Angevin alliance became an urgent priority to protect the security of Normandy, J. Gillingham, *The Angevin Empire* (London, 1984), pp.8-10 explains the context.

[55] Alexander is nowhere stated to have made a formal act of submission to Henry I, though his acceptance of the latter's overlordship is suggested by his participation in the campaign of 1114. J. Le Patourel pointed out there is no direct evidence of David having performed homage in 1126-7, but believed it likely to have happened: *The Norman Empire* (Oxford, 1976), pp.209-10, n.5. David, however, might well have been reluctant to make any personal submission to Henry I after 1124, and in this context Henry's own refusal to do homage to Louis VI of France for Normandy is highly relevant: William of Malmesbury, *De Gestis Regum Anglorum*, ed. W. Stubbs, 2 vols. (RS, 1887-9), ii. 496.

in persuading Archbishop Thurstan of York to drop his insistence on receiving a profession of obedience before consecrating a new bishop for St. Andrews.

The background to this dispute was the attempts of Scottish kings from the late eleventh century to establish an episcopate independent of the primatial claims of York. When David's chaplain was consecrated bishop of Glasgow (*c.*1117), he had not made a profession to Thurstan, and the latter's subsequent struggles to avoid professing obedience to Canterbury himself had prevented him from taking effective action against John of Glasgow. By 1125 Thurstan was not only pressing for John's profession but was also insisting on a profession from the bishop-elect of St. Andrews.[56] He might well have secured the latter, for Robert, prior of Scone, was a canon of York,[57] but his success would not have pleased David, who may already have envisaged the setting up of an archbishopric at St. Andrews.[58] The case was heard at Rome in 1126; the pope postponed his decision for a year; and it was during this period that the Christmas court of 1126 was held. The account of Hugh the Chantor describes how both kings persuaded Thurstan to seek a further postponement from Rome and permission to reach an out-of-court settlement.[59] Accordingly early in 1127 Thurstan consecrated the new bishop without a profession.[60] The case is very revealing of the aims of both kings. David's role in promoting reform and renewal in the Scottish church can hardly be exaggerated, but he did not wish to see that church as a subordinate province of York, or even of Canterbury. Henry could have chosen to back his archbishop, whose claims at Rome that Scotland was subordinate to England fitted in with a claim to temporal overlordship, but instead he persuaded Thurstan to back down.[61] He may have extracted from David two concessions on behalf of Thurstan, though this is by no means certain. The first was permission for Thurstan to consecrate a bishop for Whithorn in Galloway; the date of Gillaldan's consecration, however, is unclear.[62] More important was Thurstan's

---

[56] Nicholl, *Thurstan of York*, pp.78-110.

[57] FW, ii. 89.

[58] When the case was heard at Rome in 1126 the York party found that the Scots had been trying to secure an archbishopric for St. Andrews, Hugh the Chantor, *The History of the Church of York, 1066-1127*, ed. C. Johnson (Edinburgh, 1961), p.126.

[59] *History of the Church of York*, p.129.

[60] *Early Scottish Charters*, nos.75, 76.

[61] C.W. Hollister and T.K. Keefe, 'The Making of the Angevin Empire', *Journal of British Studies*, xii (1973), 3-4 argue that Henry's general outlook was not imperialistic, and his relations with David lend support to their case.

[62] *Fasti Ecclesiae Scoticanae Medii Aevi ad annum 1638*, 2nd draft by D.E.R. Watt, Scottish Record Society, New Series, i (1969), 128 dates the consecration as falling between 1128 and 1140.

consecration of a bishop of Carlisle in 1133. It has been suggested that the new see, comprising the southern part of the old bishopric of Glasgow, may have been mooted several years beforehand, and therefore that David's tacit acquiescence may have been secured.[63] Yet it is possible that David refused to countenance Thurstan's action. The new bishop, Adelulf, does not seem to have entered his see before 1139, though whether he was prevented from doing so is not clear.[64]

Peace between England and Scotland in the early twelfth century created an environment more favourable to Norman settlers in the far north than before. The boundaries of the new lordships reflected earlier units, larger in the north-west than the north-east.[65] Several Cumbrian lordships were founded in the time of Ranulf Meschin: his brother William was established at Egremont, his brother-in-law Robert de Trivers at Burgh by Sands, and Richer de Boivill at Kirklinton.[66] Two others went to non-Normans: Waldeve son of Cospatric held Papcastle (Allerdale below Derwent), and Forne son of Sigulf, a Yorkshire thegn favoured by Henry I, the lordship of Greystoke.[67] In Northumberland also two holders of the new baronies were of native extraction.[68] Little can be discovered of the origins of others, whose names suggest that they were Norman-French. The earliest references to these families is usually a statement in the inquest of 1166 that the lordship had been established

[63] Nicholl, *Thurstan*, pp.146-7; M. Brett, *The English Church under Henry I* (Oxford, 1975), pp.26-8.

[64] Adelulf was consecrated by Thurstan in August 1133: Nicholl, *Thurstan*, p.149. He then seems to have followed Henry I to Normandy where he appears as a witness to royal charters: *RRAN*, ii, nos.1900-2, 1908, 1910, 1911, 1913, 1915. In 1136 he attested charters for Stephen, and in the following year was with the king in Normandy: *RRAN*, iii, nos.99, 271, 335, 717, 718, 818, 919, 942, 975.

[65] G.W.S. Barrow, 'The Pattern of Lordship and Feudal Settlement in Cumbria', *Journal of Medieval History*, i (1975), 117-38; 'Northern English Society in the Twelfth and Thirteenth Centuries', *Northern History*, iv (1969), 1-28; for the jurisdictional powers of the new lordships, R.R. Reid, 'Barony and Thanage', *EHR*, xxxv (1920), 161-99; see also T.A. Gwynne, 'Society in the Anglo-Scottish Border Region in the Twelfth and Thirteenth Centuries', unpublished M. Litt. thesis, University of Newcastle, 1974.

[66] Sanders, *English Baronies*, pp.115, 23, 58; Barrow, *Anglo-Norman Era*, p.176.

[67] Sanders, pp.134, 50. Liddel was granted to Turgis Brundos, also styled Turgis of Rosedale (North Yorkshire). See T.H.B. Graham, 'Turgis Brundos', *Cumberland and Westmorland Antiquarian and Archaeological Society*, new series, xxix (1929), 49-56. Barrow suggested he may have been a Fleming, *Kingdom of the Scots*, p.146. Kendal passed after the death of Ivo Taillebois, possibly first to Robert de Stuteville and then after 1106 to Nigel d'Aubigny: *Charters of the Honour of Mowbray, 1107-1191*, ed. D.E. Greenway, British Academy Records of Social and Economic History new series, i (London, 1972), xxii.

[68] W. Percy Hedley, *Northumberland Families*, 2 vols. (Newcastle upon Tyne, 1968-70), i. 54, 235-6, and see the comments on p.16.

before 1135.[69] There are exceptions: Walter de Bolebec,[70] Walter Espec, and Eustace FitzJohn came from families holding land as tenants-in-chief of the crown.[71] It has been suggested above that Walter Espec and Eustace FitzJohn received their Northumberland estates when Henry was anxious about the security of the border, but the fact most of the other men established in the north were not leading magnates or royal officials is interesting. It may be surmised that such estates were not a particularly attractive proposition for wealthy men, but, had this been a highly vulnerable area, the king may have been compelled to draft in powerful magnates with the resources of men and money to hold the frontier, as the Conqueror had done on the Welsh Marches, and as Henry I did in his redistribution of lordships in south Wales.[72] The impression that the new lordships were being established in an environment less hostile perhaps than in other regions is also suggested by consideration of castle-building. By comparison with the frontier with Wales, or that between Normandy and France in the Vexin, the Anglo-Scottish border does not seem to have been heavily fortified in the twelfth century.[73]

[69] E.g. Walter son of William (Whalton), Gilbert of Newcastle (Bolam), William Bertram (Mitford and see also Bothal), Richard Bertram (Bothal), Nicholas de Grenville (Ellingham), Hubert de Laval (Callerton), William de Merlay (Morpeth): *Red Book of the Exchequer*, ed. H. Hall, 3 vols. (RS, 1896), i. 436-7, 444; Percy Hedley, i. 22, 26, 191, 34, 145, 196; Sanders, pp.150, 17, 131, 107, 41, 109, 65. Hugh, son of Eudo of Chevington, should also be included in this category. It was suggested Hugh was a son of Eudo *dapifer*, but there is no evidence for the claim. Hugh's son Ernulf attested a charter of William de Vesci as *dapifer*, but he could have been William's steward: A.M. Oliver, 'Early History of the Family of Morwick', *Archaeologia Aeliana*, 4th series, xii (1935), 263-76; Hedley, *Northumberland Families*, i. 29.

[70] Sanders, pp.84-5. Sanders does not tie the Northumberland family in with that of Whitchurch, Bucks. (p.98), but the connection is made by Loyd, *Anglo-Norman Families*, p.17. Walter I gave Walton to Ramsey abbey with the services pertaining to two knights' fees, except castleguard at Newcastle: *Cartularium monasterii de Ramesia*, ed. W.H. Hart and P.A. Lyons, 3 vols. (RS, 1884-93), i. 154. J.H. Round demonstrated that Hugh, son of the benefactor of Ramsey, was the holder of Whitchurch and under-tenant of the Giffard honour at his death in 1164 or 1165: *Rotuli de Dominabus et Pueris et Puellis de Donatione Regis in XII Comitatibus, 31 Henry II, 1185*, Pipe Roll Society (1913), xxxix-xl.

[71] J.A. Green, *The Government of England under Henry I* (Cambridge, 1986), pp.245-6, 250-2.

[72] *Ibid.*, pp.14-15.

[73] For surveys of castles in the north see J.F. Curwen, *The Castles and Fortified Towers of Cumberland, Westmorland and Lancashire North-of-the-Sands, together with a brief Historical Account of Border Warfare* (Kendal, 1913); C.H. Hunter Blair, 'Castles', *Archaeologia Aeliana*, 4th series, xxii (1944), 116-68. The relative paucity of eleventh and twelfth-century castles in the border region is an impression gained from the relevant sections of D.J. Cathcart King, *Castellarium Anglicanum* (London, 1983). It may well be therefore that future archaeological work will revise the dating of some castles whose first appearance in the sparse documentary sources is relatively late. Notwithstanding, the contrast with the numerous castles of the Welsh border is striking. For brief comment on the castles of the Vexin see J.A. Green, 'Lords of the Norman Vexin', in *War and Government in the Middle Ages*, ed. J. Gillingham and J.C. Holt (Woodbridge, 1984), p.49.

Another significant feature of the northern border is that although holders of the new lordships had cross-border links, only Robert de Brus in the early twelfth century was able or allowed to establish a major cross-border lordship of the kind which had come into being, for instance, in the Norman Vexin in the eleventh century.[74] The development of cross-border interests by families living near the Anglo-Scottish border during the twelfth century is a topic which would repay further investigation. Dr. Stringer has recently pointed to the neglected subject of Anglo-Scottish proprietorship by historians of the English and Scottish aristocracies,[75] and it has immediate significance for our understanding of border society.

Peace barely survived the death of Henry I, for as soon as the news reached David of Stephen of Blois' coup, he crossed the border and seized the castles of Carlisle, Wark, Alnwick, Norham, and Newcastle for the Empress, and was preparing to attack Durham when Stephen marched north to negotiate.[76] It was agreed that David could keep Carlisle, that he should receive Doncaster in addition, and that his claim to Northumbria would be considered; in return he handed back the other four castles he had taken. These generous terms were not enough to satisfy David, for in the following year he invaded again while Stephen was in Normandy. Thurstan negotiated a truce until the king's return, but Stephen still refused to cede Northumbria.[77] In 1138 the Scots invaded once more, and after a futile attempt to capture Wark, they ravaged the countryside, destroying homes and churches, and killing the inhabitants as far south as the Tyne.[78] Stephen marched north, crossed into Scotland and was preparing to attack Roxburgh when, fearing betrayal by Eustace FitzJohn, he retreated. Another invasion by the Scots followed and on this occasion they penetrated Yorkshire. The district of Craven was put to the sword and the women taken off into captivity at Carlisle, after which it was the turn of county Durham to suffer.[79] Once again it was left to Thurstan to organize resistance. An army of local levies led by northern magnates faced the Scots near Northallerton. This was a critical moment: the northern magnates included Robert de Brus and Walter Espec, whose ties of friendship with David stretched back many years. The conflict of loyalties for these men was acute. Robert de Brus and Bernard de Balliol negotiated with David and were said to have offered him the earldom of

---

[74] J.A. Green, 'Lords of the Norman Vexin', pp.50-2.

[75] K.J. Stringer, *Earl David of Huntingdon* (Edinburgh, 1985), Chapter 9.

[76] The principal accounts of the Scottish invasions are to be found in Richard of Hexham, *De Gestis Regis Stephani et de Bello Standardi* in *Chronicles of the Reigns of Stephen, Henry II and Richard I*, ed. R. Howlett, iii, 139-78; Ailred of Rievaulx, 'Relatio de Standardo', *ibid.*, 181-99; and in John of Hexham's continuation of Symeon of Durham, *HR*, pp.284-332.

[77] Richard of Hexham, p.162; John of Hexham in Symeon of Durham, *HR*, ii. 288.

[78] Richard of Hexham, pp.151-4; John of Hexham in Symeon of Durham, *HR*, ii. 289-90.

[79] Richard of Hexham, pp.155-9; John of Hexham, pp.291-2.

Northumbria, but the offer was firmly rejected. In the battle that followed Robert, Bernard and Walter, all fought against David, whose only important adherents among the northern magnates were Eustace FitzJohn, angered by the confiscation of his castles, the son of Robert de Brus, Alan de Percy, and Edgar son of Cospatric.

Although the battle of the Standard was a crushing defeat for the Scots, David undoubtedly did best out of the negotiations for peace.[80] These were set in hand by the papal legate Alberic, who travelled to Carlisle where he reconciled David to Bishop Adelulf and negotiated the return of women captured by the Scots. Queen Matilda also had an important part to play, for she, like the Empress, was David's niece and said to be much attached to her mother's kindred. It was accordingly agreed that Northumbria should be held by David's son Henry as earl with the same customs as in the reign of Henry but excluding the castles of Newcastle and Bamburgh. Henry did homage to Stephen for the earldom, an act which Stephen was particularly anxious to secure and which presumably explains his willingness to make concessions. Henry married Ada de Warenne, sister of William III of Warenne, half-sister of the Beaumont twins and, perhaps equally importantly, descended from King Henry I of France.[81] From 1136 David controlled Cumbria and from 1139 his son held Northumberland. What consequences did this transfer have for the local aristocracy?

There can be little doubt of the reality of David's lordship of Cumbria, first of all. He visited Carlisle on more than one occasion and is thought to have built the castle keep there.[82] Some of his silver coins were issued from Carlisle in the name of Erebald, a moneyer who was probably a member of the family which held the silver mines at Alston from Henry II.[83] The honours of Egremont and Skipton passed by marriage to David's nephew William FitzDuncan,[84] and David established one of his most faithful supporters, Hugh de Morville, in Westmorland.[85] Papcastle was at that time in the hands of Alan son of Waldeve. In 1150 the abbey of Holm

[80] The sources for this paragraph are again Richard of Hexham, pp.167-76 and John of Hexham, pp.297-300.

[81] V. Chandler, 'Ada de Warenne, Queen Mother of Scotland', *SHR*, lx (1981), 119-39.

[82] For David's itinerary, *RRS*, i. 114; for the attribution of the keep to David: Curwen, *The Castles and Fortified Towers of Cumberland*, p.54, citing *Scotichronicon*, v. xxxii.

[83] I.H. Stewart, *The Scottish Coinage* (London, 1955), p.5. Erebald minted coins for Stephen: G.C. Brooke, *A Catalogue of English Coins in the British Museum, The Norman Kings*, 2 vols. (London, 1916), ii. 337; R.P. Mack, 'Stephen and the Anarchy, 1135-1154', *British Numismatic Journal*, xxxv (1966), 41. For the Carlisle mint under Henry II, D.J. Allen, *A Catalogue of English Coins in the British Museum Cross and Crosslets (Tealby) Type of Henry II* (London, 1951), p.xcviii.

[84] This marriage must have taken place after 1135. Ranulf Meschin, who held the honour before it passed to his sister Cecily, was still living in 1135 but dead by 1140: *Early Yorkshire Charters*, vii (ed. C.T. Clay), 11.

[85] Barrow, *Anglo-Norman Era*, p.73.

Cultram was founded with the grant of those parts of the vill held by Prince Henry and that which he had granted to Alan.[86] Subsequently Papcastle also passed to William Fitz Duncan. Finally, the lordship of Burgh by Sands passed to an heiress married to a man named Ranulf Engaine.[87] Ranulf's parentage has not been identified, but his son was a benefactor of Dunfermline abbey and it seems likely that Ranulf belonged to one of the Engaine families which had entered the service of King David.[88] David's power in the north-west did not however end at the River Duddon, for at some date, probably in 1141, he took over the honour of Lancaster, which had been granted to Stephen by Henry I.[89] David transferred the honour to Ranulf earl of Chester in 1149, Ranulf having earlier received a grant of it from Stephen.[90]

In the north-east Scottish overlordship after 1139 was also not merely nominal. David was able to capitalize on his friendships with Walter Espec, Eustace FitzJohn, and Bernard de Balliol.[91] Close links were built up with the Umfravilles of Prudhoe and Redesdale, Gilbert d'Umfraville becoming Prince Henry's constable.[92] Other Northumberland lords occur as witnesses to Henry's charters as earl, notably Ralph de Merlay, whose wife was a daughter of Cospatric II, earl of Dunbar.[93]

David's ambitions did not stop at the Tyne in the north-east, however, for on the death of Geoffrey Rufus, bishop of Durham in 1141 he sought to secure the appointment of his own chancellor, William Cumin. His candidate had the backing of the Empress, but Cumin's heavy-handed tactics aroused opposition within the diocese; a protracted contest ensued, and Cumin eventually had to admit defeat.[94] Still more glittering prospects were opened up by the vacancy at York after Thurstan's death in 1140, when the candidature of Waldef, prior of Kirkham and David's stepson, was mooted. Stephen unsurprisingly vetoed the proposal on the grounds of Waldef's kinship with David, but the candidature of his own nephew was to be disputed in another lengthy contest.[95] Had Waldef been consecrated, however, David's influence in the north, already considerable in ecclesiastical circles, would have been greatly increased.

---

[86] *Early Scottish Charters*, no.244.

[87] Sanders, p.23.

[88] Barrow, *Anglo-Norman Era*, p.100 n.

[89] G.W.S. Barrow, 'King David I and the Honour of Lancaster', *EHR*, lxx (1955), 85-9.

[90] John of Hexham, p.323; *RRAN*, iii, no.178.

[91] At the battle of the Standard Bernard was chosen with Robert de Brus to negotiate with the Scots, and it was said that Bernard had taken an oath of fealty to David: Richard of Hexham, p.162.

[92] Keen, 'The Umfravilles, the Castle and Barony of Prudhoe', p.171.

[93] *Early Scottish Charters*, no.247; *RRS*, i, nos.11, 32, 33.

[94] A. Young, *William Cumin: Border Politics and the Bishopric of Durham 1141-1144*, University of York, Borthwick Paper no.54.

[95] Jocelin of Furness, 'Life of Waldef', *Acta Sanctorum*, 3 August, p.257a.

David had achieved remarkable success in extending the overlordship of the Scottish crown south of the border. He was in effect using those methods which Professor Le Patourel described as Norman imperialism against the Normans themselves.[96] Yet he had undoubtedly benefited from the disputed succession in England, and the acid test of his success was to be the accession of a strong king to the English throne. David evidently did what he could to secure the future, for according to William of Newburgh when he knighted his great-nephew Henry of Anjou in 1149, he exacted a promise that Henry would not take back Cumbria and Northumbria.[97]

It was David's grandson Malcolm (Prince Henry having predeceased his father) who arrived at the court of King Henry II in 1157 to do homage for Cumbria and Northumbria. Henry 'not wishing to see his kingdom diminished', took back Cumbria and Northumbria, but restored Huntingdon, lost to the Scots in the 1140s. His decision was in accordance with his policy of returning to the situation of 1135, but it left Malcolm's brother William, already invested as earl of Northumbria, with only the lordship of north Tynedale, and a burning sense of grievance at the loss of his patrimony.[98]

Malcolm had little choice but to accept the situation in the face of *force majeure*, but Henry's actions then, and subsequently, injected a degree of tension into Anglo-Scottish relations. In 1158 Henry was at Carlisle; he refused to confer knighthood on Malcolm and his brother, and the honour was deferred until their return from the Toulouse campaign.[99] Malcolm's participation in this venture, though similar to that of Alexander in the Welsh campaign of 1114, aroused criticism in Scotland, and on his return he faced a major revolt.[100] Nor did his military service allay Henry's suspicions, for in 1163 Malcolm was summoned to attend a great council at Woodstock. Henry had returned to England in January, evidently concerned about the situation in the west and in the north. He led an expedition into Wales and then proceeded to Carlisle where he met Malcolm. In July the Welsh princes and Malcolm were summoned to Woodstock where they did homage both to Henry and to his heir; Malcolm handed over hostages including his brother David.[101] It has

---

[96] Le Patourel, *Norman Empire*; for recent assessments of David's achievements: G.W.S. Barrow, *David I of Scotland (1124-1153). The Balance of New and Old*, University of Reading Stenton Lecture 1984 (University of Reading, 1985); Stringer, *Earl David of Huntingdon*, pp.1-5.

[97] William of Newburgh, *Historia Rerum Anglicarum*, in *Chronicles and Memorials . . . Stephen, Henry II, and Richard I*, i. 105.

[98] *Ibid.*

[99] Chronicle of Melrose, *Early Sources of Scottish History*, ii. 235; 240-3.

[100] *Ibid.*, 244.

[101] Ralph of Diceto, *Opera Historica*, ed. W. Stubbs, 2 vols. (RS, 1876), i. 311.

been pointed out that Scotland seems narrowly to have escaped a military expedition in 1163.[102] Specific reasons for Henry's disquiet are hard to pinpoint, though his treatment of the Scots had been cavalier. It was not surprising that in arranging royal marriages in 1160 and 1162 the Scots had looked outside the Angevin sphere of influence. These marriages may have made Henry uneasy.[103]

Henry may also have been alarmed at the increasingly likely prospect that Malcolm would be succeeded by his brother William,[104] an eventuality that materialized in 1165. Relations between Henry and William were far from cordial: it was on hearing someone speak well of the Scottish king that Henry fell to the ground biting the straw in his anger,[105] and a chance allusion in a letter of John of Salisbury referred to a proposed alliance between William and Louis VII of France.[106] Yet relations had not deteriorated to such a pass that William refused to attend the coronation of King Henry's designated successor in 1170, and both he and his brother David attended and swore allegiance to the prince.[107] Hence when the young king rebelled against his father in 1173 his invitation to William to join the revolt created a dilemma for the latter, but one that was easily resolved when the young king offered to restore the lost province to the Scots,[108] William joined the rebels against the advice of some of his counsellors, and transferred the earldom of Huntingdon and Lennox to David to bolster the latter's support.[109] David went south and established himself at Leicester whilst William invaded from the north, blockading Wark and Carlisle.[110] William renewed his attack in the following year, and several castles fell to his forces: Liddel, Burgh, Appleby, Harbottle, and Warkworth.[111] It was at this point that fortune favoured Henry II, for William was caught napping whilst besieging Alnwick by forces loyal to Henry, and his capture made further resistance by David useless.

William may have felt he had a reasonable chance of recovering his lost territory, in view of recent Scottish rule there and the many contacts between lay families and religious houses on both sides of the border, but

---

[102] *RRS*, i. 19.

[103] W.L. Warren, *Henry II* (London, 1973), p.183.

[104] Anderson, 'Anglo-Scottish Relations', p.17.

[105] *Materials for the History of Thomas Becket, Archbishop of Canterbury*, ed. J.C. Robertson, 7 vols. (RS, 1875-85), vi. 72.

[106] *Ibid.*, vi. 458.

[107] Benedict of Peterborough, *Gesta Regis Henrici Secundi*, ed. W. Stubbs, 2 vols. (RS), i. 6; Roger of Howden, *Chronica*, ed. W. Stubbs, 4 vols. (RS, 1868-71), ii. 4-5.

[108] *Jordan Fantosme's Chronicle*, ed. R.C. Johnston (Oxford, 1981), lines 263-70.

[109] *Ibid.*, lines 383-406; 1096-1106.

[110] The liveliest account of the campaign is that by Jordan Fantosme, line 1106 ff; see also William of Newburgh, 181-97; Benedict of Peterborough, i. 48-80.

[111] Benedict of Peterborough, i. 65.

Henry had not been idle since 1157 and had taken steps to strengthen his authority in the north. There had been heavy expenditure on key castles: the keep was rebuilt at Newcastle, and after Walter Espec's death the king took over Wark castle and spent a considerable sum there also.[112] Henry also ensured key lordships went to men loyal to himself.

Some were new men, both in terms of their promotion and new to the north. Hubert de Vaux was granted Gilsland in about 1156, previously held by Gille son of Buete.[113] Nothing is known of Hubert's family background, though he had been in Henry's service for a decade or more and witnessed charters both for Henry and the Empress.[114] The heiress to the honour of Papcastle was married to Gilbert Pipard, who came from a family of under-tenants of the honour of Wallingford.[115] Brian FitzCount, lord of Wallingford, had been a staunch supporter of the Angevins during the Anarchy, and Gilbert also may have entered Henry's service before 1154. The heiress to Egremont, also in Cumberland, was bestowed on Reginald de Lucy, a kinsman of the justiciar Richard.[116] Newcastle was committed to Roger FitzRichard in 1157, and at some date also Warkworth, which he held in 1173. Roger was a grandson of Roger Bigod. His career before 1157 is obscure, but he evidently enjoyed the king's favour. In 1163 his service was rewarded with the hand of the widow of Henry of Essex, and by this marriage he secured the honour of Clavering in Essex.[17]

Henry also reinforced the loyalty of established families. First there were the Stutevilles. Robert III de Stuteville had begun before 1154 to recover estates lost to his family earlier in the century; he became sheriff of Yorkshire, his son Nicholas was granted the lordship of Liddel, and his brother Roger became sheriff of Northumberland and keeper of Wark castle.[118] Secondly there were the Umfravilles, a family with particularly close ties to the Scottish royal house. Odinel d'Umfraville, the then lord, continued to witness charters for the Scottish king after 1157.[119] His marriage to a daughter of Richard de Lucy may therefore have been a

---

[112] R.A. Brown, 'Royal Castlebuilding in England, 1154-1216', *EHR*, lxx (1955), 353-98.

[113] Sanders, *Feudal Baronies*, p.124; the lord of Gilsland is possibly to be identified with Gille, son of Boed, one of the *judices* of Cumbria at the inquest into the lands of the bishopric of Glasgow, *Early Scottish Charters*, no.50.

[114] *RRAN*, iii, nos.587, 112, 130, 666, 711, 748, 795, 836, 903.

[115] *Complete Peerage*, x. 527-8.

[116] *Complete Peerage*, viii. 247.

[117] C.T. Clay, 'The Ancestry of the Early Lords of Warkworth', *Archaeologia Aeliana*, 4th series, xxxii (1954), 65-71.

[118] *Early Yorkshire Charters*, ix (ed. C.T. Clay), 5, 13-15.

[119] *RRS*, i, nos.207, 229, 273; ii, nos.78, 80, 143. Keen points out that it is difficult to distinguish Odinel I from his son Odinel II, lord of Prudhoe in 1173: Keen, 'The Umfravilles, the Castle and Barony of Prudhoe', p.171.

measure intended to strengthen his loyalty to the English crown.[120] In the rebellion of 1173-4 he held Harbottle for Henry II, much to the anger of William the Lion.[121] In addition to these families, Henry also initially was well disposed to Hugh II de Morville, whose father had spent a lifetime in King David's service. Hugh held the Yorkshire manors of Aldborough and Knaresborough at farm from the crown, and acted as a royal justice in Cumberland and Northumberland in 1170. In that year he took part in the murder of Becket, but his subsequent loss of lands seems to have had more to do with suspicions about his loyalty than his role in the murder.[122]

Henry's castle-building and his use of patronage help to explain why William made little headway in 1173 and 1174. His capture of the Scottish king gave him the opportunity to impose humiliating terms in the treaty of Falaise.[123] William was to swear fealty for the kingdom of Scotland; the Scottish clergy was to submit to the English church; selected Scots were to do liege homage to Henry; and five key Scottish castles, Roxburgh, Berwick, Jedburgh, Edinburgh, and Stirling, were to be handed over to Henry's castellans. If we are to accept the evidence of the Durham charter of 1095, the treaty of 1174 may not have been the first occasion on which a Scots king recognized English overlordship for his kingdom, yet its significance was greater by the later twelfth century given the way the obligations attendant on homage were more closely defined and more capable of enforcement by the overlord.[124] The other clauses were punitive and in one instance unrealistic: the time was long past when Scots churchmen were prepared to accept subordination to the English church.

Thus the issue that divided Henry and William was essentially the same as that which had set Malcolm Canmore at odds with William the Conqueror, but the circumstances in which it was contested had changed. By the late twelfth century it had become less likely that Scottish kings would be able to advance the frontier of their kingdom southwards than it had been in the days of Canmore. In the mid-eleventh century Edward the Confessor had relatively limited authority in northern England, and it was not inconceivable that a vigorous Scottish monarch, possibly already overlord of Cumbria, would be able to expand into Northumberland. Under David I, one of the greatest kings of medieval Scotland, this indeed occurred, but at a time of civil war in England. Meanwhile under Rufus

---

[120] Keen, p.172.

[121] Jordan Fantosme, lines 591-98.

[122] W. Farrer, 'On the Tenure of Westmorland temp. Henry II and the Date of Creation of the Baronies of Appleby and Kendal', *Cumberland and Westmorland Antiquarian and Archaeological Society*, new series, vii (1907), 100-07.

[123] For the text see *Anglo-Scottish Relations, 1174-1328*, ed. E.L.G. Stones (London, 1965), pp.1-5.

[124] Le Patourel, *Norman Empire*, pp.206-10.

and Henry I Norman settlement had been able to take root in the north and a basis for more effective royal government was established. Yet William the Lion did not abandon hope of ever regaining the northern counties, Scottish claims being finally shelved in 1237. The terms of William the Lion's submission equally were not accepted in Scotland as a definitive statement of subordination to the English crown, and remained central to Anglo-Scottish relations in the thirteenth century.

Chapter 5

England and Iberia in the Middle Ages

Anthony Goodman

The history of diplomatic relations between England and the Iberian powers in the middle ages is a disjointed one. There were periods when the personnel of missions was low-level, and when they were concerned with the conveying of compliments, the settlement of mercantile claims and the renewal of treaties and truces. There were also bursts of intenser activity and more momentous aspiration – which seldom resulted in the making of effective alliances. Throughout the period alliance proposals were normally linked with dynastic marriage proposals. In the Anglo-Iberian diplomatic context, such marriage proposals were more than a means of affirming and strengthening a congruity of aims: they were fragile attempts to create a common bond between powers whose spheres of geographical interest and ambition were difficult to keep aligned. Iberian powers did not traditionally and consistently view an English alliance as important for their regional interests, with the notable exception of Portugal for much of its rule by the House of Aviz. But the English crown had recurrent motives for seeking Iberian alliances. They were a means of helping to safeguard its possession of Gascony. This aim was later subsumed within that of seeking support in the Hundred Years War. Long before its outbreak Castile had been identified in English policy as the most significant Iberian power. The main theme of Anglo-Iberian relations in the thirteenth century was the establishment of an alliance with Castile: their main theme in the fourteenth and first half of the fifteenth centuries was the failure to re-establish it.[1]

Evidence for the development of a variety of social and political contacts between England and the Iberian principalities appears in the twelfth century. Evidence first accumulates then for the popularity in England of the pilgrimage to Santiago de Compostela, and some parties of English crusaders broke their voyages in order to assist the Portuguese

---

[1] I owe thanks on many points in writing this paper to the advice of Professor Angus MacKay. For the betrothal of a daughter of William the Conqueror to a Spanish king, *The Ecclesiastical History of Orderic Vitalis*, ed. M. Chibnall (Oxford, 1972), iii. 114-15 and n.1; D.C. Douglas, *William the Conqueror* (London, 1964), pp.393-5.

against the Muslims.[2] But the Iberian political interest of English kings arose from Henry II's acquisition of Aquitaine: it was not directed primarily at León or Portugal, but at the principalities bordering Gascony – Castile, Navarre and Aragon.[3] In 1159 Henry II allied with Ramon Berenguer IV, count of Barcelona and ruler of Aragon,[4] and in 1170 betrothed his daughter Eleanor to Alfonso VIII of Castile.[5] Six years later Alfonso and Sancho VI of Navarre agreed to refer their territorial disputes to Henry's adjudication: for this purpose they sent distinguished groups to London in 1177, where Henry made an award.[6] His immediate successors preferred to ally with Navarre, still (though not for much longer) a leading Iberian power. In 1191 Richard I married Sancho's sister Berengaria: Sancho was then the ally of other Christian peninsular powers against Alfonso VIII of Castile.[7] Possibly Alfonso had alienated Richard by claiming (as he was later to do against John) that Henry had promised Aquitaine to him as Eleanor's dower. The Navarrese alliance proved useful to Richard in helping to suppress rebellion in Aquitaine in 1192 and to capture Loches in 1194.[8] John allied with Sancho VII of Navarre in 1201: the amplification of the treaty the following year specifically bound them in alliance against Alfonso VIII, and against Pedro II of Aragon.[9] Alfonso took advantage of John's French troubles to claim Gascony and invaded the duchy in 1205. But, though he was welcomed by some nobles, leading communes prepared to resist: he withdrew.[10] In the next few years the Iberian kings tended to sink their differences in order to meet the formidable Almohad challenge: John, concentrating on building predominantly northern European coalitions for the recovery of his lost French lands, could safely downgrade Iberian diplomatic relations.[11]

[2] D.W. Lomax, 'The First English Pilgrims to Santiago de Compostela', *Studies in Medieval History presented to R.H.C. Davis*, ed. H. Mayr-Harting and R.I. Moore (London and Ronceverte, 1985), pp.165-79.

[3] In 1199 John was expecting envoys from Portugal and in 1207 thanked Alfonso IX of León for having allied with him (*Foedera* I, i. 76, 96).

[4] A.L. Poole, *From Domesday Book to Magna Carta, 1087-1216* (Oxford, 1955), p.325; W.L. Warren, *Henry II* (London, 1973), p.85 and n. Henry hoped for Ramon Berenguer's help in gaining the county of Toulouse.

[5] [*Chronicles of the Reigns of Stephen, Henry II, and Richard I, iv. The Chronicle of Robert of*] *Torigni*, ed. R. Howlett (RS, 1889), p.247. Warren argues that Henry's aim was to frustrate any renewal of Louis VII's influence in Castile (*op.cit.*, p.117).

[6] *Foedera*, I, i. 32-4; *Chronica Magistri Rogeri de Houedene*, ed. W. Stubbs (RS, 1869), ii. 122ff.

[7] J.F. O'Callaghan, *A History of Medieval Spain* (Ithaca and London, 1975), pp.242-3.

[8] Houedene, iii. 194, 252-3.

[9] *Foedera*, I, i. 85-6.

[10] F.B. Marsh, *English Rule in Gascony, 1199-1259* (Ann Arbor, Michigan, 1912), pp.5-9.

[11] In 1206 John granted a safe-conduct for his sister Eleanor of Castile to visit him and in 1208 one for the chancellor of Castile (*Foedera*, I, i. 94, 100).

For at least the first two decades of Henry III's reign, Anglo-Iberian diplomacy failed to revive significantly, but in his reign and that of Edward I Iberian political and commercial expansion was to impinge strongly on English consciousness and interests. In particular, contacts between the English and Castilian courts grew, and conflict over Gascony resulted in an attempt to make a close alliance.[12] Realization in England of the growing preeminence of Castile was reflected in the title 'King of Spain' often unofficially conferred there on its rulers.[13] Castile and León were finally united in 1230 under Fernando III: Matthew Paris's accounts of his conquests over the Muslims – and of those of Jaime I of Aragon – suggest that their significance was grasped at Henry III's court.[14] The attachment of much of the economic resources of al-Andalus to Christian Spain, within the context of developing international trade along the sealanes of western Europe, stimulated commercial dealings – and all their characteristic disputes and conflicts – between Henry's subjects and those of the Iberian maritime powers, particularly Castile.[15] So the regulation of commerce and settlement of maritime claims became staples of diplomacy between the English and Castilian courts – and loomed large in English relations with Portugal and Aragon too. In 1234 Henry wrote appreciatively to Fernando III on receiving news from him of the proposed release of his great ship, detained at La Coruña. In 1237, at Fernando's request, Henry licensed the men of San Sebastian to trade in safety in his lands for five years: there had been 'injuries and rancours' between them and the men of the Cinque Ports.[16]

Contacts between the English court and those of Castile and Aragon grew more frequent in the 1240s. In 1241 Henry granted a safe-conduct for Fernando's brother Alfonso to visit him, and in 1242-3, when Henry was campaigning in France, he sought royal cooperation in acquiring

---

[12] Navarre was dwarfed by the enlargement of Castile and Aragon, but long continued to have particular importance for the English crown, because it had the longest Iberian border with Gascony and was to be ruled by French dynasties with important landholdings in France. The succession of the house of Champagne to the crown of Navarre in 1234 ushered in a period of often fraught relations between its rulers and the English crown (*ibid.*, 252, 255, 269-70, 469).

[13] For examples of this usage, Matthew Paris, C[*hronica*] M[*ajora*], ed. H.R. Luard, v.365, 388, 396-7, 399, 416, 449-50, 575-6, 649, 657-8, 694; *The Chronicle of Bury St. Edmunds, 1212-1301*, ed. A. Gransden (London, 1964), pp.56, 57n, 58n, 62, 97. Edward I referred to Alfonso X as king of Spain in his correspondence (*Foedera*, I, i. 594, 607). The imperial pretensions of Castilian kings had been noted in twelfth-century England (*Torigni*, pp.155, 178, 193-4, 247).

[14] *CM*, iii. 334, 384-5, 529, 639-40.

[15] W.R. Childs, *Anglo-Castilian Trade in the Later Middle Ages* (Manchester, 1978), pp. 11 ff.

[16] C[*alendar of*] P[*atent*] R[*olls*], *1232-47*, 68, 192. An envoy from Fernando visited the English court in 1233, C[*alendar of*] L[*iberate*] R[*olls*], *1226-40*, 214.

mounts in Castile.[17] In 1246 he received visits from a messenger of Fernando and a knight of his son and heir, the future Alfonso X;[18] he was exchanging messages with the *infante* in 1247 and 1249.[19] In 1250 Fernando sent a knightly envoy to Henry to propose a joint crusade, a proposal which, according to Matthew Paris, was welcomed but was dashed by Fernando's death (1252).[20] His successor Alfonso X's wide-ranging ambitions – to rule Gascony, to secure English intervention in Spain and Africa, and to become Holy Roman Emperor – produced close and often tense relations beween him and the English Crown for much of his reign. He speedily revived Alfonso VIII's claim to Gascony: Matthew Paris says that he summoned Gaston de Béarn and other Gascon nobles, and that the men of Bordeaux warned Henry that, if he did not act quickly, Alfonso would take over the duchy.[21]

The most probable explanation of Alfonso's policy reversal is that he was tempted to exploit the crisis within Gascony. Prominent Gascons were prepared to recognize his title and may have persuaded him that Henry was not an opponent to be feared.[22] Gaston de Béarn developed a personal relationship with Alfonso.[23] But Henry's energetic diplomatic and military measures in 1253-4 soon resolved the crisis in his favour. In May 1253 he proposed a marriage alliance to Alfonso and announced that he was sending William Bitton, bishop of Bath and John Mansel as envoys to him. They were empowered to agree to a marriage if Alfonso abandoned his claim and allied with Henry against all men.[24] Military successes followed Henry's arrival in Gascony in August 1253: Gaston de

---

[17] *CPR, 1232-47*, 260, 362; *C[alendar of] C[lose] R[olls], 1237-42*, 529. In 1242 the abbot of Garde Dieu went as Henry's messenger to the kings of Castile, Aragon and Portugal, and in 1246 and 1248 he was exchanging messages with Jaime I of Aragon (*CLR, 1240-45*, 156; *CLR, 1245-51*, 26, 55, 57, 177).

[18] *Ibid.*, 36, 73.

[19] *Ibid.*, 117, 120-1, 123, 125, 232.

[20] *CM*, v. 231-2. The envoy provided information about Fernando's conquests in al-Andalus and the wealth of the captured city of Seville.

[21] *Ibid.*, pp.365-6, 370; Marsh, pp.136 ff; J.P. Trabut-Cussac, *L'administration anglaise en Gascogne sous Henri III et Edouard I de 1254 à 1307* (Geneva, 1972), pp.xxvi ff. Alfonso's envoy Lope Fernández de Aín, bishop of Morocco and his messenger G. Perez were at the English court in Oct. 1252 (*CLR, 1251-60*, 79; *CLR, 1267-72*, appendix I, no.2296 A). The probable reason why no text of the Castilian claim to Aquitaine survives is that, as he promised in 1254, Alfonso handed over to Henry or destroyed the charters supporting it (*Dip. Docs. I, 1101-1272*, nos.271, 275).

[22] Powicke suggested that Alfonso put forward the claim as a means of gaining Henry's alliance (*Henry III and the Lord Edward* (Oxford, 1947), i. 232). The suggestion is accepted by J.O. Baylen, 'John Mansell and the Castilian Treaty of 1254. A Study of the Clerical Diplomat', *Traditio*, xvii (1961), 486. This is tortuous reasoning.

[23] Powicke, i. 234 and n.

[24] *Foedera*, I, i. 290; *CPR, 1247-58*, 230; *CCR, 1251-53*, 475-6; *CM*, v. 396-8; Powicke, i. 232.

Béarn fled to Alfonso, who failed to respond to La Réole's plea for relief.[25] Henry announced in February 1254 that he had appointed Peter d'Aigueblanche, bishop of Hereford, and Mansel to negotiate peace with Alfonso. But in March he publicly professed himself fearful of Alfonso's and the Gascon rebels' intentions. Matthew Paris accused Henry of inventing Castilian threats in order to extract subsidies, and alleged that there was scepticism in England about his assertions. But Trabut-Cussac argued that Henry's fears were genuine, if misplaced.[26] However, the situation had in fact been resolved in his favour in March when his envoys at Toledo concerted peace terms with Lope Fernández de Aín, bishop of Morocco and the knight Garcia Martinez. Alfonso agreed that he and his heirs would be *amici et imprisii* of Henry and his heirs against all men. Alfonso gave up for himself and his heirs all claims stemming from Henry II and Eleanor of Aquitaine. Henry promised to be Alfonso's ally on the same terms. His son Edward was to receive knighthood from Alfonso. Henry would seek papal permission to divert his crusade from the Holy Land to *partes Marrochianas vel Affricanas*; there he would campaign jointly with Alfonso, sharing conquests equally. Henry promised to restore Gaston de Béarn's possessions and those of other forfeited Gascons and to remit his charges against them. Alfonso was given a continuing stake in Gascon affairs. He was to counsel Henry on particular cases of forfeiture and to approach him *sicut amicus rogat amicum* on behalf of suitors dissatisfied with the judgements which they had received. Henry agreed to marry a daughter of one of Alfonso's brothers.[27]

By the treaty of Toledo Henry gained the principal points which he had wanted: Alfonso's abandonment of the claim to Aquitaine and of support for rebellion in Gascony. Henry now had a close and possibly advantageous alliance with the leading Iberian power. Alfonso probably abandoned his claim so swiftly because he was impressed by Henry's vigorous reactions, by the degree of support which he received in the duchy and the collapse of opposition to him. No firm basis for Castilian rule in Gascony had appeared. Henry had proved a worthwhile opponent – and therefore a potentially useful ally. In the summer of 1254 terms for the marriage of Edward and Alfonso's half-sister Leonor were finalised: the marriage took place in Burgos on 1 November.[28] But for years Gascon

---

[25] *CM*, v. 388, 396; Trabut-Cussac, pp.xxxi ff.

[26] *CM*, v. 432-5, 440, 445; *CPR, 1247-54*, 279-80; Trabut-Cussac, pp.xxxvii-viii. Paris asserted that peace was made between Henry and Alfonso in 1253 (*CM*, v. 396-8).

[27] *Foedera*, I, i. 297-9; *Dip. Docs. I, 1101-1272*, no.270. On 1 April Alfonso issued a safe-conduct for Edward to visit him (*CCR, 1253-54*, 316) and on 22 April confirmed the treaty, informed his Gascon allies and instructed them to make peace. Henry confirmed the treaty on 20 April (*Foedera*, I, i. 299-301; *Dip. Docs. I, 1101-1272*, nos.271-4).

[28] *CM*, v. 449-50; A. Ballesteros Beretta, *Alfonso X El Sabio* (Murcia, 1963), pp.99 ff; Powicke, i. 232-3. For the marriage and negotiations leading to it, see also Trabut-Cussac, pp.4, 7, and 7n. For Alfonso's grant of all his rights in Gascony to Edward, dated Burgos, 1 Nov., *Foedera*, I, i. 310; *Dip. Docs. I, 1101-1272*, no.275.

restorations were to be a contentious Anglo-Castilian issue: Gascon officials and Henry himself dragged their feet over notable cases. He was unwilling or unable to fulfil other treaty clauses.[29] In March 1255 Alexander IV wrote refusing to commute his crusading vow in favour of an African campaign.[30]

Alfonso put pressure on Henry, announcing before the end of July 1255 that he was sending an important mission. This included his brother Sancho, archbishop-elect of Toledo, and Martinez.[31] The envoys protested at Henry's tardiness in making some Gascon restorations. He accepted Martinez's suggestion that he send Aigueblanche and Mansel to Alfonso. In his instructions to Mansel (January 1256), Henry said that it was to be made clear to Alfonso that he would not make restorations which he considered dangerous to Edward's rule in Gascony until Alfonso threw his full weight behind the ducal government. Henry would not budge over his daughter Beatrice's intended marriage to Alfonso's brother Manuel until he had details of Manuel's endowment. He was prepared to propose to Alexander IV that his crusading vow should be remitted, on condition that he spent six years in establishing his son Edmund on the Sicilian throne. Henry and his counsellors anticipated that Alfonso would be particularly upset by this proposed commitment.[32]

Alfonso, confronted by Henry's failure to fulfil important treaty obligations and by the renewal of discontent in Gascony under Gaston de Béarn's leadership, denounced Henry's perfidy to a new set of English envoys in the summer of 1256 and threatened to invade Gascony and rule it himself. But, as Henry correctly gauged, he was inhibited by the close relationship which he had formed with Edward.[33] Henry and his officials

[29] Garcia Martinez helped to negotiate pardons for principal rebels, which were issued in Edward's name and confirmed by Henry, 4-5 Aug. 1254 (Trabut-Cussac, pp.4-5). But on 30 Aug. Henry wrote to the constables of Bourg, Fronsac and Cusac forbidding the pardoned vicomte of Fronsac from having seisin of his former lands or travelling in arms (*CCR, 1253-54*, 309-10). In December he wrote to Edward permitting him to settle appeals from Alfonso on behalf of Gascons disappointed in local judgements, and ordered the sénéchal of Gascony to give speedy justice in accordance with the terms of the treaty (*CPR, 1247-58*, 389-90). For the activities of Alfonso and his commissioners in procuring pardons, *ibid.*, 319, 325, 337, 352; *CCR, 1253-54*, 264, 272.

[30] *Foedera*, I, i. 316; *CCR, 1254-56*, 389 ff.

[31] *Ibid.*, 114, 132-3, 212, 391; *CLR, 1251-60*, 234, 245-6; *CM*, v. 509-10. For other emissaries of Alfonso in England in 1255, *CLR, 1251-60*, 201; *CPR, 1247-58*, 412, 414.

[32] *CCR, 1254-56*, 389-91. Henry made no mention in his instructions about Alfonso's request for aid against Jaime I of Aragon, made in a letter dated by Chaplais as *c.*1255 (*Dip. Docs. I, 1101-1272*, no.280). For concessions made by Henry in individual cases whilst the envoys were in England, *CPR, 1247-58*, 458, 506. For Henry's replacement of Aigueblanche and Mansel as envoys by men of less distinction, *CCR, 1254-56*, 318.

[33] *CM*, v. 585-6; *Foedera*, I, i. 343. Matthew Paris's account of Alfonso's anger and Henry's appeal to his relationship with Edward may have been derived from one of the envoys, John de Gaddesden, whom the chronicler knew personally, R. Vaughan, *Matthew Paris* (Cambridge, 1958), p.14. He also knew Bitton, and probably Mansel (*ibid.*, pp.14-15).

made cautious moves to defuse Gascon discontent, though he did not go far enough to satisfy the Castilians. In January 1257 Henry was intending to send an envoy to Alfonso with a proposal to set up a joint Anglo-Castilian commission to adjudicate outstanding suits, whose decisions he would consider binding.[34] Alfonso too made efforts to improve relations, enlisting the help of Jaime I of Aragon in a joint embassy. Alfonso's envoy Pascal, bishop of Jaén and Jaime's envoy the prior of Cornellana were in England before June 1257. The prior told Henry that his master hoped that good peace and amity would continue to prevail between Henry and Alfonso, and proposed a conference between the three kings. Henry replied sympathetically, stressing that he would be upset to lose Alfonso's friendship and affirming his adherence to the Treaty of Toledo. He intended to send envoys to Alfonso.[35]

But further complexities arose to bedevil Anglo-Castilian relations in 1256-7. In 1256 Alfonso's brother Enrique, exiled by him, fled to England, hoping that Henry and Edward would reconcile him with Alfonso. This they were unable to do: Henry's continued lavish favour to a brother whom Alfonso regarded implacably may not have improved relations between the two Crowns.[36] The consequences of Richard of Cornwall's election to the Empire in January 1257 and Alfonso's rival election in April were more serious. Alfonso wrote to Henry complaining about Richard's election and the injuries which Richard had done to him, and requesting Henry's aid against Richard in accordance with the treaty of Toledo. In his reply (14 December 1257) Henry attempted to exculpate himself from the imputation of perfidy. He would aid Alfonso against Richard if he established to his own satisfaction that the alleged injuries had taken place.[37] Like Alfonso, he was unwilling to rupture relations.

Henry dispatched the abbot of Shrewsbury to Alfonso to excuse himself from participating in the proposed conference with Jaime I, on the grounds of Scottish and Welsh problems. Alfonso received the abbot and his fellow envoy John de Castello graciously, but all of Henry's unfulfilled

---

[34] *CPR, 1247-58*, 500; *CCR, 1256-59*, 118-20.

[35] *Ibid.*, pp.135-6. Commenting on Gascon cases apparently raised by the bishop of Jaén, Henry maintained that he was not obliged to carry out certain restorations. Preparations for the Castilian envoys' departure from England were being made on 7-8 June (*CPR, 1247-58*, 558-9; *CLR, 1251-60*, 378).

[36] *CM*, v.575-6; *CCR, 1254-56*, 368; *CCR, 1256-59*, 23; *CCR, 1251-60*, 318, 320, 330, 336, 339, 348, 352, 410, 469. In June 1257 Henry wrote to the pope that he had arranged to send Enrique to Italy in connection with the Sicilian business (*CPR, 1247-58*, 567). In 1259 he allowed Enrique to take ships from Bayonne for an African venture provided that he swore not to molest Alfonso's interests (*CPR, 1258-66* 34). For Edward I's acknowledgement to Enrique in 1303 of the latter's benevolence to himself, his children and his kingdom, H. Johnstone, *Edward of Carnarvon, 1284-1307* (Manchester, 1946), pp.88-9.

[37] *CCR, 1256-59*, 284-5; *CM*, v.649, 657-9; N. Denholm-Young, *Richard of Cornwall*, pp.94ff. For Richard's lukewarm attitude towards the Treaty of Toledo in 1255-6, *CCR, 1254-56*, 389-91.

obligations were raised with them. In response, the domestically beleaguered Henry wrote to Alfonso in conciliatory vein, stressing his anxiety to mediate between the latter and Richard of Cornwall (June 1258).[38]

Despite Henry's slipperiness, Alfonso derived some benefits from alliance with him. It gave him influence at the English court and in Gascony, potentially useful leverage when Henry's brother was challenging him in the Empire and when, in 1259, the Treaty of Paris enhanced French royal power, especially in Aquitaine. In January 1260 the bishop of Jaén and Garcia Perez, treasurer of Seville, were granted safe-conducts to come to England. In fact they met Henry in Paris and raised the issues there of Gascony and the Empire. He proposed to Alfonso in May that a conference be held at Bordeaux in October to settle outstanding Gascon claims. He remained evasive in answer to Alfonso's request for aid in the Empire.[39] In 1262 Alfonso made what was apparently his last attempt to breathe life into the alliance with Henry. His envoys Fernando Rodriguez, abbot of Covarrubias and the knight Pedro de Castello raised the question of the Empire, Gascony and Africa. Alfonso offered help to Henry against the English and Welsh rebels. This offer produced a gratifying response. In his reply (dated St. Germain-des-Prés, 15 August) Henry even addressed Alfonso as King of the Romans. He said that he might need Alfonso's help domestically at a future date. The current papal adjudication on the rival claims to the Empire provided him with an excuse not to aid Alfonso there, but he made a significant concession: he would give aid if Richard injured Alfonso's interests. Henry also offered a new conference on Gascony and professed himself willing to fulfil his African obligations once calm was restored to his realm.[40] But, despite Henry's apparently renewed eagerness for the alliance, it fell into abeyance during the last ten years of his reign. He was unwilling to pay Alfonso's price for support against Simon de Montfort – alignment against his own brother.

The deaths of Henry and Richard in 1272 facilitated a revival of the Anglo-Castilian alliance. Edward I took a more active interest in Iberian affairs than his father had done and weighed the policies of Iberian rulers in the context of the affairs of Christendom. The conflicts which arose between both Castile and Aragon and the French Crown appeared to him as grievous setbacks to the Christian unity necessary to confront Islam, and as possible threats to his good relations with Philip III of France and

[38] *CCR, 1256-59*, 290, 310, 314-15; *CPR, 1247-58*, 629, 640. For Henry's reward to Alfonso's messenger John in February 1258, *CLR., 1251-60*, 425.

[39] *CPR, 1258-66*, 115; *CCR, 1259-61*, 207-9. For Henry's orders in September 1260 concerning the meeting at Bordeaux on the articles of the treaty, as covenanted with Alfonso, *CPR, 1258-66*, 94; *cf* p.171.

[40] *Dip. Docs. I, 1107-1272*, no.357; *CCR, 1261-64*, 172-3.

hence to his tenure of Gascony. Edward, moreover, had close Peninsular ties. His correspondence with Alfonso X in the 1270s expresses affection, respect, a sense of the obligations of kinship and alliance: he was concerned with the threats to Castile posed by the new Marinid invasions led by Ya'qub in 1275 and 1278 and by the deterioration of Alfonso's relations with Philip III among other Christian neighbours. In 1277 Edward wrote to Alfonso that he considered them bound by indissoluble links, since his queen was Alfonso's sister and their respective children were cousins german, and also since Edward had received knighthood from him, and Edward's son Alfonso was his godson. The treaty obligations were inviolable.[41] Such sentiments were reciprocated by Alfonso: in 1279 he addressed Edward 'commo a cunuado que muchos amamos, a que tenemos en logar de Hermano'.[42] But Edward's desire to discharge his obligations to an admired but politically fading mentor and to support him against infidels was tempered by a politic caution. His policy is reflected in three letters to Alfonso (May 1275), responses to Alfonso's requests. Edward refused to commit himself to an expedition against the Moors, on the grounds of the papal call for him to aid the Holy Land, but he was willing for his subjects to serve Alfonso against them and for him to procure ships for use against them at Bayonne. He was willing too to support Alfonso's claim to the succession of Navarre against Philip III, though saving his allegiance to Philip. He was prepared to address Alfonso as 'king of the Romans', and, within limits, to back his claim to the Empire.[43] In November he wrote to Alfonso expressing his alarm at Franco-Castilian tension which, he believed, threatened the peace of Christendom and the prospects of recovering the Holy Land. He intended to meet Philip in order to make peace. But his intention to mediate in person on this and on future occasions was to be frustrated – often due to his Welsh involvement.[44] Relations between Alfonso and the French and Aragonese crowns deteriorated because of his recognition of his surviving son Sancho as his heir, in preference to the children of his deceased elder son Fernando de la Cerda (Philip III's nephews). In 1279 Edward's

[41] *Foedera*, I. ii. 540-1. Edward's daughter Joanna was educated in the 1270s in the household of Alfonso's queen (*ibid.*, 559).

[42] *Foedera*, I. ii. 531. Alfonso used similar phrases in an undated letter written to Edward congratulating him on receiving Ponthieu and Montreuil (PRO, Ancient Correspondence, S.C.I/16/12). Queen Eleanor inherited them from her mother in 1279.

[43] *Foedera*, I. ii. 522-3. For Edward's letter to Gregory X in support of Alfonso's imperial claim, *ibid.*, 522. For Edward's orders permitting Alfonso to acquire naval aid at Bayonne for use against the Moors, *ibid.*, 531 (1276), 552, 563 (1278), 580 (1280). Sir Maurice Powicke analysed Edward's relations with Alfonso (*The Thirteenth Century, 1216-1307*, pp.241-5).

[44] *Treaty Rolls, I, 1234-1325*, no.154; *cf. ibid.* no.153. In December Edward wrote eloquently to the pope voicing his concern about the effects on Christendom of the Franco-Castilian quarrel and his intention to mediate in person (*ibid.*, no.139).

envoys succeeded in arranging a truce between Alfonso, on the one hand, and France and Navarre, on the other.[45] Despite Alfonso's repudiation of Edward as a mediator in 1280,[46] he continued to play a leading part in assisting negotiations.[47] In 1282 Alfonso's rule faltered when Sancho headed a revolt against it, supported by Portugal and Aragon. In December 1282, in response to Alfonso's plea for help, Edward promised to send him a Gascon force, and did so in 1283.[48] Thus at the end of Alfonso's reign the English alliance, for so much of the time a disappointing investment, paid some dividends.

Edward I, however, did not gain substantial Iberian help in his struggle with Philip IV: in the new era of Anglo-French conflicts, the fragility of the common interests which he had tried to foster with Castile and Aragon was to be repeatedly exposed by the failure of English attempts to secure effective alliances. Edward's relations with Alfonso's son and successor Sancho IV (reigned 1284-95) and Sancho's son Fernando IV (d.1312) lacked the cordiality which had existed between him and Alfonso. But both courts remained concerned to foster good relations.[49] These were probably strained by Edward's understandings with the crown of Aragon and by commercial conflicts and outrages, worsened by attacks at sea during the Anglo-French war (1294-1303). In 1293 Edward ratified the peace which Sancho made with the men of Bayonne and in 1294 ordered that letters of safe-conduct be granted to Spanish and Portuguese merchants trading in his realm.[50] That year Edward empowered his lieutenant and officials in Gascony to negotiate an alliance with Sancho – presumably against the French crown.[51] But Sancho's death and the troubled minority of Fernando IV undermined hopes of this: the next major English diplomatic initiative occurred in 1303, when Edward proposed the marriage of his son Edward to the *infanta* Isabella.[52]

In the 1290s diplomatic contacts between the English and Portuguese courts grew, multiplied by problems arising from the growth of Portuguese overseas trade.[53] But the principal new development in Anglo-Iberian relations in Edward I's reign was the establishment of

---

[45] *Foedera*, I, ii.576, 580-1.
[46] *Ibid.*, 583-4; *Treaty Rolls, I, 1234-1325*, no.155. Alfonso may have become exasperated and suspicious because of Edward's procrastination. For instance, in an undated letter Edward told him that he was unable to meet him on 1 August following, as arranged by Edward's envoys William de Valence and Jean de Grailly (S.C.I/12/11).
[47] *Foedera*, I, ii. 594, 607.
[48] *Ibid.*, 620, 625, 629, 638.
[49] In 1285 Edward urged Sancho to treat for peace with the French crown (*ibid.*, 662).
[50] *Ibid.*, 789, 797.
[51] *Ibid.*, 805.
[52] *Ibid.*, 951.
[53] A.H. de Oliveria Marques, *History of Portugal* (Columbia and London, 1972), i. 89ff.

closer ties with the ruling dynasty of Aragon. Edward was their kinsman through his mother: he was well qualified to appreciate the significance of the expansion of Aragonese wealth and power in the Mediterranean, and its potential for aiding the recovery of Jersualem. His personal relationships at the Aragonese court were stimulated by his meeting in Gascony with the future Pedro III in 1273. There they agreed that Edward's eldest daughter should marry Pedro's eldest son: in 1275 Pedro suggested that his eldest daughter Isabel should marry Edward's eldest son too.[54] The marriage contract between the future Alfonso III and Edward's daughter Eleanor was negotiated with an Aragonese embassy in London in 1282 – just after Pedro had precipitated a European crisis by his conquest of Sicily and assumption of its Crown, one of whose immediate effects was a papal prohibition of the marriage.[55] Pedro angled for Edward's support: in January 1283 Edward wrote to his wife Constance (whose Hohenstaufen claim to Sicily he was asserting) refusing her request to fight for her interests against Philip III, but undertaking to intercede with the pope on her behalf. Edward was to mediate tirelessly between Pedro (d.1285) and his Angevin, French and papal opponents, and then betweeen them and Alfonso III, ultimately with some success.[56] But Alfonso died in 1291 without the delayed marriage being carried out. Edward's efforts had only produced a fund of goodwill towards him among the Aragonese nobility, from whom came offers to serve him with military retinues in 1293-4, some in the Holy Land, some in Gascony against Philip IV.[57]

The accession of Edward II brought to the throne the only English medieval king with a Spanish parent: he responded with appropriate warmth in 1308 to Fernando IV's hopes that the old bonds between their crowns would continue.[58] But Edward failed to interest and involve himself in Iberian affairs in the ways in which his father had done in the 1270s and 1280s: they were irrelevant to his mainly Scottish and domestic preoccupations, as they had been increasingly to his father's in the preceding years. Besides, the attention of the crown of Aragon was focused on the defence and extension of its mediterranean empire, and Castile after Fernando IV's death in 1312 was weakened for a decade by the minority of Alfonso XI. The attenuation of personal links between the English and Castilian royal houses is reflected by the fact that one of those

---

[54] *Foedera*, I, ii. 506, 521. For letters to Edward from members of the Aragonese royal family, *ibid.*, 541, 606, 725.

[55] *Ibid.*, 613-15.

[56] *Ibid.*, 625. Powicke analysed Edward's role as mediator in the confrontations resulting from Pedro's seizure of Sicily (*The Thirteenth Century*, pp.251-65).

[57] *Foedera*, I, ii. 787, 793, 797-8.

[58] *Ibid.*, 60. In 1311 Edward refused Fernando's request for a loan for an expedition against the Moors (*ibid.*, 144).

alleged to be principally involved in Edward II's murder, Thomas Gourney, considered it safe to take refuge in Castile (mistakenly, as it turned out).[59] The main substance of negotiation between England and the maritime Iberian powers for most of Edward II's reign was provided by commercial matters.[60] However, the War of Saint-Sardos (1323-5) galvanised Edward into more ambitious diplomatic activity. He and his officials looked on the Iberian Peninsula as a likely source of manpower and victuals for the defence of Gascony.[61] He hoped to gain the alliance of Aragon and Castile against Charles IV of France. He proposed a marriage between his son Edward and Jaime II of Aragon's daughter, but when in 1325 he offered Edward's marriage to Alfonso XI of Castile's sister, he suggested instead to Jaime that the latter's son and heir Alfonso should marry his daughter Joanna.[62]

Edward II's reversal of his hitherto negative policy by making strenuous efforts to involve the Iberian powers in the defence of Gascony was the start of a new and lasting interest in Iberian affairs, an anticipation of the policies, stimulated by the Hundred Years War, of repeated diplomatic initiatives, and, eventually, of military interventions, in the vain hope of securing an Anglo-Iberian alliance which would tip the scales against the Valois. After Edward III seized power in 1330, he revived his father's policy of trying to win Iberian allies against the French crown. In 1334 negotiations were in progress for the marriage of his brother John of Eltham (d.1336) to the daughter of Juan late lord of Vizcaya. In 1335 Edward proposed the marriage of his daughter Isabel to Alfonso XI's son and heir Pedro. But the following year Alfonso allied with Philip VI of France, the alliance making provision for requests for military or naval aid when either party was going to war. In the early decades of the Hundred Years War, Castilian ships on occasion assisted the French. Yet Edward and Alfonso continued amicable diplomatic relations.[64] The earls of Derby and Salisbury impressed the Castilian court by the military support which they brought to Alfonso's campaigns

[59] Gourney fled to Castile in 1331. Alfonso XI and the city of Burgos responded favourably to Edward III's request for his detention, but he escaped to Italy (*ibid.*, 819-21; G.P. Cuttino and T.W. Lyman, 'Where is Edward II?', *Speculum* liii (1978), 541-2).

[60] Disputes were mainly with the Castilians and Portuguese; for Majorcan and Aragonese complaints, *Foedera*, I, ii. 523, 534, 568.

[61] *Ibid.*, 572-3, 598; *The War of Saint-Sardos*, ed. P. Chaplais, Camden 3rd ser., lxxxvii (1954), 76, 80, 114.

[62] *Foedera*, I, ii. 548-9, 573.

[63] *Ibid.*, I, ii. 893. This marriage had been proposed in Edward's name in 1328-9 (*ibid.*, 736, 773).

[64] *Ibid.*, 910; G. Daumet, *Etude sur l'alliance de la France et de la Castille au xive et au xve siècles* (Paris, 1898), pp.2-9, 17-18.

against the Marinids in 1342-4.[65] Edward made new efforts (partly through the two earls) to secure a dynastic alliance with Alfonso: in 1345 his persistence was rewarded when Alfonso agreed to his son and heir's marriage to Edward's daughter Joanna, in preference to a French marriage proposal. But Joanna died in 1348 on her way to Castile.[66]

Alfonso's decision in 1336 to opt for a French in preference to an English alliance was doubtless influenced by Castilian perceptions of the relative prestige of the French and English crowns – and of their relative strength, as exhibited in the war of Saint-Sardos. Alfonso was eager for military aid from across the Pyrenees, especially for his projected campaigns against the Marinids – the French seemed best able to provide it. He apparently calculated that Castilian aid for the French crown against Edward was unlikely to be so critical in scale or effect as to induce the latter to add him to his enemies. Why, then, did Alfonso opt for an English marriage treaty in 1345? He is likely to have been impressed by Edward's successful provision for the defence of Gascony, by the ostensibly formidable coalitions which he raised in the Empire and by the enthusiasm which he and his friends displayed for the fight against the Moors. Edward needed to be treated with greater respect and caution.

Though Alfonso's policies towards the Anglo-French conflict were successful in the short term, in a longer perspective it would have been more prudent of him to have reinforced non-intervention, or to have adopted the sort of mediatory role which Edward I had done in Franco-Spanish conflicts. A partisan policy (especially when occasionally effective) encouraged the protagonists to compete for a Castilian alliance, a policy with dangerous repercussions. For the success of Alfonso's Iberian policies helped to create political conditions in Castile and in the Peninsula generally which facilitated French and English military as well as diplomatic interventions in the later fourteenth century. His decisive victory in 1340 over the Marinids at Salado finally destroyed the recurring threats to the Christian Iberian powers from North Africa which had on occasion led to the amelioration or suspension of their domestic and internecine conflicts. Alfonso's son Pedro I (succeeded 1350) faced formidable threats to royal authority from the nobility, headed by his half-brother Enrique of Trastamara: these became intertwined with his disputes with Pere III of Aragon. From 1369 onwards the usurping dynasty of Trastamara, in order to consolidate its rule in Castile, strove to

[65] P.E. Russell, *The English Intervention in Spain and Portugal in the Time of Edward III and Richard II* (Oxford, 1955), pp.7-8. The account below of events in the later fourteenth century is based principally on this work. For the diplomatic side of the two earls' expedition, K. Fowler, *The King's Lieutenant* (London, 1969), pp.46-7.

[66] *Foedera*, III, i. 19-22, 26-7, 46-7, 58-9, 73-4, 153-4, 171; Daumet, pp.9-10, 16-18. In 1344 Edward fulsomely complimented Alfonso on his capture of Algeciras from the Moors (*Foedera*, III, i. 13, 19-20).

impose a pro-French hegemony in the Peninsula. Trastamaran policy, in part a reaction to French and English interventions, provided inducements and opportunities for their continuance.

In 1350 Edward III served notice on the newly installed Pedro, a minor, that he would not treat him with the forbearance which he had shown to his formidable father: Edward led an attack in person on a Castilian merchant fleet off Winchelsea. Nevertheless, negotiations for Pedro's marriage to a French princess were successfully concluded in 1352. These events did not, as might have been expected, herald a major confrontation between England and Castile. Pedro's extraordinary treatment of his queen alienated John II of France: English military success in France undermined French ability to put pressure on Pedro. The Anglo-French peace of 1360 facilitated a revival of Anglo-French competition for influence in Castile and, with the treaties between Charles V and Enrique of Trastamara (1368-69) a reassertion of French influence over Castile. Enrique II bound himself to engage in war against the English, specifying the commitment of large naval forces. The Trastamaran rulers of Castile down to his great-grandson Juan II (d.1454) regarded the alliance as a pillar of their dynastic power and the Valois dynasty continued to attach great importance to it.[67] In fulfilment of the treaty, powerful Castilian fleets operated in Biscay and with the French in the Channel in the 1370s and early 1380s, defeating the English lieutenant in Aquitaine and his retinue off La Rochelle in 1372 and attacking southern coasts.

These offensives reflect the failure of the interventionist policy pursued in the 1360s by the Black Prince as ruler of Aquitaine, a departure from the traditionally cautious approach of the English crown and its lieutenants in Gascony towards Iberian involvements, presumably motivated by the conviction that an anglophile Castile would help to stabilise the prince's rule in a vastly extended English Aquitaine. Intervention was persisted with after Enrique II's triumph over Pedro in 1369, being cemented by the marriage of John of Gaunt, duke of Lancaster in 1371 to Pedro's daughter and heir Constanza, and Edward III's recognition of Gaunt in 1372 as king of Castile. Over the next decade royal and Lancastrian diplomacy worked together to produce a series of Iberian alliances against Enrique (d.1379) and his son Juan I. English forces operated in Portugal in 1372, in Navarre in 1378-79, in Portugal in 1381-82 and 1385: this interventionist phase ended with Gaunt's occupation of much of Galicia in 1386 and a joint campaign with João I of Portugal in León in 1387. By the Treaty of Bayonne with Juan I (1388), Gaunt and Constanza finally relinquished their claims to the crown of Castile and recognized Juan's title. In return they received heavy financial

---

[67] Daumet, pp.30-35. See also below p.254.

compensation and their daughter Catherine (heir to their pretensions) was to marry Juan's son and heir. Though Gaunt had failed in the objective of making peace between Castile and England, and the alarmed French government successfully held Juan to his treaty obligations, a fundamental cause of conflict between England and Castile had been removed.[68]

But the treaty of Bayonne was an admission of the failure of Lancastrian policy. English invasions of Castile had failed either to put an English prince on the Castilian throne or to trade his claim for an Anglo-Castilian peace. In parliament in 1382 it had been claimed that if Gaunt were given sufficient material backing he would within six months or so be king of Spain or have a decisive battle, and that, if he succeeded, the general war would be successfully concluded too.[69] Arguably he never received sufficient aid to test these claims.[70] But the scepticism exhibited in parliament was perhaps justified: even if his campaigns had been successful, it is not self-evident that the French would have made peace on satisfactory terms. The principal stake for which the English fought in Spain was the security of Aquitaine. The Black Prince and his brothers might have done better if they had imitated their father's earlier Iberian policies, relying on diplomatic pressures – a policy which the Lancastrian kings were to be financially constrained to pursue, and pursued with some success.

The English interventions had long-lasting effects on the pattern of Anglo-Iberian relations in the fifteenth century, but their most significant effects were on Iberian internal developments. They encouraged Trastamaran hegemonism which culminated in Juan I's attempts to impose his kingship on Portugal, in right of his wife Beatriz, daughter and heir of Fernando I of Portugal (d.1383). João of Aviz's usurpation of the Portuguese throne in opposition to Juan in 1385 drew its support from expanding overseas commercial interests (especially those of Lisbon) which had benefited from the disruption of Anglo-Castilian trade.[71] The Treaty of Windsor, the alliance with mutual defence provisions which Richard II and João made in 1386, and João's marriage to Gaunt's daughter Philippa in 1387 gave prestige to the dubious Aviz dynasty,

---

[68] J.J.N. Palmer and B.J. Powell, *The Treaty of Bayonne (1388) with the preliminary Treaties of Trancoso (1387)* (Exeter, 1988), establish the texts of these treaties, the importance of the agreements made at Trancoso and their relationship to the treaty of Bayonne.

[69] *Rotuli Parliamentorum*, iii. 133.

[70] Juan I claimed in a letter written to the governors of Seville that Gaunt landed with at most 1,600 lances and 2,000 archers. He also argued that Gaunt's strategy of landing in Galicia, hemmed in by mountains, presented a minimal threat (Archivo Municipal de Carmona, Privilegios y cartas reales, siglos XIII ỳ XIV). I owe thanks to Professor M. Gonzáles Jiménez of the University of Seville for transcribing this document.

[71] H. Livermore, *A New History of Portugal* (Cambridge, 1976), pp.100-3; Childs, p.42.

though in the next decade or so João's rule received scant support from his royal English kinsfolk. However, their reluctant endorsement of the Portuguese revolution helped to check Castilian expansion and assisted the dominance of elements in Portuguese society attuned to maritime ventures.[72]

In the early fifteenth century Anglo-Iberian relations were affected by breakdowns in the Anglo-French truces which had run since 1389 and by the resumption of war between the English and French crowns in 1414. In 1405 Enrique III responded with alacrity to a French request for naval assistance against England.[73] Gutierre Diez de Games, in his chivalrous biography *El Vitorial*, recalled his master Pero Niño's exploits as commander of galleys in 1405-6 in attacks on Bordeaux, the English coasts along the Channel and Jersey.[74] In 1416, though Catalina of Lancaster (d.1418) was joint regent for her son Juan II (succeeded 1406), a Castilian fleet helped the French against the onslaughts of her nephew Henry V.[75] But Castilian ability and will to provide such aid was ebbing. In the 1420s the dauphin sent a number of requests to Juan II for military and naval aid: Juan's domestic problems prevented him from complying.[76] In 1443 Henry VI and his council were alarmed by a report that a Castilian envoy visiting Charles VII's court had concerted a joint attack by land and sea on Calais, naval action against Bordeaux and a siege of Bayonne. Nothing came of all this.[77]

For much of his reign Charles VII was no better placed than Juan II to fulfil the military obligations of the alliance. In 1435 Charles excused himself from acceding to Juan's request for help on the grounds of his realm's weakness.[78] Castilian domestic political stresses were exacerbated by the consequences of the succession of members of a junior branch of the house of Trastamara to the thrones of Aragon and Navarre. Martin I of Aragon had died without lawful issue in 1410, and in 1412 Fernando of

---

[72] Gaunt would probably have preferred in 1386 to rely principally on Aragonese help, which he tried in vain to procure (Archivo de la Corona de Aragón, Cartas Reales y Diplomaticos, Pedro el Ceremonio, nos.7146-47; Russell, pp.410-1). In his will of 1398 Gaunt referred to the late Juan I of Castile as king of Portugal (S.Armitage-Smith, *John of Gaunt* (London, 1904), p.430).

[73] Daumet, pp.66-7.

[74] *El Vitorial. Crónica de Don Pero Niño*, ed. Juan de Mata Carriazo (Madrid, 1940), pp.139-84; *The Unconquered Knight*, ed. and trans. Joan Evans (London, 1928), pp.100-3, 105ff.

[75] Daumet, pp.72-5. The Castilians responded favourably to further French requests for naval help in 1418-19.

[76] *Ibid.*, pp.75-82.

[77] *Proceedings and Ordinances of the Privy Council of England*, ed. N.H. Nicolas, v (London, 1835), 414-18; G. Du Fresne de Beaucourt, *Histoire de Charles VII*, 6 vols. (Paris, 1885-91), iii. 250-2. In July 1442 Henry had forbidden the grant of safe-conducts to Spanish ships for their voyages home from Flanders (*Proceedings and Ordinances*, v. 192-4).

[78] Daumet, pp.84-6.

Antequera (younger son of Juan I of Castile) was accepted as king. His son and heir Alfonso V (reigned 1416-58) was preoccupied with gaining the throne of Naples, but his three younger brothers, the *infantes* of Aragon (one of whom became Juan II of Navarre in 1425) had estates in Castile and aspired to influence its government. Their ambitions exacerbated strife among the Castilian nobility and tensions between the Castilian court and those of Aragon and Navarre. These developments provided opportunities for renewed English intervention, but, since the Valois largely failed to mobilize Castilian military and naval aid, and since Lancastrian resources were mostly concentrated on stabilizing control of northern France, the English crown's Iberian diplomacy was intermittent and of lower priority. The duke of Bedford, Regent for Henry VI in France, continued Henry V's efforts to persuade Iberian powers to adhere to the Treaty of Troyes.[79] English efforts focused at times on Navarre, vulnerable to pressure because of its kings' possession of the French duchy of Nemours.[80] Though truces with Castile were secured, attempts to wean Juan II from the French alliance failed: only in 1429-30, when Castile had faced attacks from Aragon and Navarre, did the Castilian court show a marked interest in improving relations with England.[81] In English governing circles Aragon (especially when it became dynastically linked with Navarre) seemed a more promising field for the exertion of influence than Castile. English princes were accustomed to dabbling in Aragonese affairs. John of Gaunt – whose influence had been firmly excluded from Castile after the succession of his son-in-law Enrique III in 1390 – had proposed in 1397 to Martin I of Aragon that his son Bolingbroke should marry into his family.[82] In 1412 Edward, duke of York tried to enlist Fernando of Antequera's support for his family's claim to the Castilian throne,[83] and in 1413, Thomas, duke of Clarence supported the claims to the Aragonese throne of Jaume count of Urgel against Fernando.[84] In 1415 Henry V proposed that he should marry Fernando's daughter Maria.[85] Alfonso V of Aragon was determined to avoid being sucked into

---

[79] J. Ferguson, *English Diplomacy, 1422-61* (Oxford, 1972), pp.39ff.

[80] *Ibid.*, pp.41-2, 46-7.

[81] *Ibid.*, pp.45-6.

[82] *The Diplomatic Correspondence of Richard II*, ed. E. Perroy, Camden 3rd ser., xlviii (1933), 253-4.

[83] G. Zurita, *Los cinco libros primeros de la Segunda parte de los Anales de la Corona de Aragon* (Zaragoza, 1579), pp.92-3; A. Goodman, and D. Morgan, 'The Yorkist Claim to the Throne of Castile', *Journal of Medieval History*, xi (1985), 61-70.

[84] J.H. Wylie, *The Reign of Henry the Fifth* (Cambridge, 1914), i. 88-9. In 1413 news was received in Seville of the defeat of 'Vasylio ingles capitan de cierta gente de arrmas e de pie que venian para entrar enlos rregnos de aragon para faser mal e danno sy pudieran' (Archivo Municipal de Seville, Mayordomazgo, 1413, núm.47). I owe thanks to Professor A. MacKay for transcribing this document.

[85] Ferguson, pp.37-8.

the Anglo-French conflict, and steadfast in recognizing Charles VII as king of France. However, in 1429-32 Aragonese and Navarrese envoys negotiated for an English alliance, offering a daughter of Alfonso in marriage to Henry VI. These negotiations foundered principally on the English reluctance to make a commitment to prior military intervention in Castile: the Aragonese were wary of being drawn into the Anglo-French war.[86]

England's ally Portugal was even less involved in the fifteenth-century phase of the Hundred Years War than France's ally Castile, though the house of Aviz took their links with the Lancastrian kings as seriously as the Trastamaran rulers of Castile took theirs with the Valois. But neither Portugal nor England were generally concerned about honouring the military obligations of the treaty of Windsor. In 1405, in response to Franco-Castilian attacks, Henry IV ordered the council to write to João I telling him that the French were breaking the truce and asking him to send galleys.[87] In 1414 Henry V sent an embassy requesting aid from João and so did Bedford in 1424. But apparently there were no positive responses to these requests.[88] In 1445 Alvaro Vaz d'Almada, a leading noble partisan of João's son Dom Pedro, regent for Afonso V, was granted the *comté* of Avranches by Henry VI: some Portuguese military help in the future defence of Normandy was envisaged.[89] But the Lancastrians, a family with strong crusading traditions, presumably accepted that after João's capture of Ceuta in 1415 Portuguese resources would be justifiably committed to African ventures. The Houses of Lancaster and Aviz continued to value their alliance, partly because it provided a framework for the regulation of the important commercial relations between their realms, but mainly because of their close kinship and the mutual honour which they derived from it. João and some of his kinsmen were recipients of the Order of the Garter.[90] He complimented his brother-in-law Henry IV 'como a Irmaao e verdadeiro amigo, que muy fielmente e verdadeiramente amamos e precamos sobre todos os Principes do mundo'.[91] In 1445 Henry VI gave full power to Dom Pedro (who had probably known the king in person since the latter's infancy) to negotiate on his behalf with Juan II of Castile, 'considerans la singuliere et grant confidence que Nous avons . . . en le haulte Prudence, grans Sens et noble

    [86] *Ibid.*, pp.47ff.

    [87] *Calendar of Signet Letters of Henry IV and Henry V (1399-1422)*, ed. J. Kirby, no.514.

    [88] Ferguson, pp.39, 45.

    [89] *Foedera* (London, 1710), xi. 95-6; Goodman and Morgan *loc. cit.*, p.66. The grant was made to Almada and his heirs male. At the same time he was retained by Henry with a life annuity of 100 marks.

    [90] Ferguson, pp.53-4 and 53 n.4.

    [91] *Royal and Historical Letters during the Reign of Henry the Fourth*, ed. F.C. Hingeston, ii (RS., 1965), 83. In 1405 Henry arranged the marriage of João's illegitimate daughter Beatriz to his kinsman the earl of Arundel (*ibid.*, 92-5, 99-102).

Experience [of Pedro] . . . et en la synguler Amour, et naturelle Affection, qu'il a nostre Personne, et a nostre Honneur'.[92] In the 1450s relations between Henry and Afonso may have temporarily cooled down as a result of the civil conflict which overthrew Dom Pedro: he and Henry's retainer Vaz d'Almada were killed in the battle of Alfarrobeira (1449) and Pedro's son of the same name was deprived of the Constableship and exiled from Portugal.[93] In 1451-2 Henry was extending his patronage to two other sons of Dom Pedro, Jaime and João, at the request of their aunt Isabel, duchess of Burgundy (Dom Pedro's sister), not at Afonso V's request.[94]

Thus even Henry VI's relations with his one firm Iberian ally ran into the doldrums, concurrently with the debacle in France. It was to be the Yorkist kings who launched a new Anglo-Iberian relationship: they were not overburdened with the traditional English aim of wishing for an alliance which would promote historic aims in France (an obligation which the Spaniards were traditionally expert at avoiding), but were more concerned to promote their dynastic security by foreign alliance. Yet in the early stages of the struggles between York and Lancaster the Iberian rulers are likely to have sympathized with their kinsman Henry VI. After he was driven into exile his supporters tried to capitalize on these relationships. Their hopes of enlisting Iberian support for his cause rested especially on the patronage which they received from the French crown, since it was Enrique IV of Castile's ally, and Afonso V of Portugal had married his sister to Enrique. Margaret of Anjou sent William Joseph, squire to the king's body, to the Portuguese court *c.*1462 to ask for help in restoring Henry: he was well received.[95] There were rumours that year in England that Spanish and Portuguese forces were about to participate in a Lancastrian invasion.[96] But Peninsular developments provided Edward IV with diplomatic opportunities. The Catalan revolt in the summer of 1462 stirred up tensions between Juan II of Aragon and Enrique IV, and between Juan's new ally Louis XI and Enrique. The overtures which Juan made to Edward, and the truce which Louis made with Edward in 1463, far from driving Enrique into the arms of the Lancastrians, convinced him of Edward's worth as an ally. His offer of his sister Isabella

[92] *Foedera*, xi. 96-7. For Dom Pedro's visits to the English court in the 1420s, R.A. Griffiths, *The Reign of Henry VI* (London 1981), pp.76-7, 190.

[93] Livermore, pp.114-9.

[94] *Foedera*, xi. 284; *CPR, 1446-52*, 521; Griffiths, p.524. For the elevation of 'Jacobus Infans de Portugallia' (d.1459) to the cardinalate by Calixtus III in 1456, *Hierarchia Catholica Medii Aevi*, ii. 1431-1503, ed. C. Eubel (Munster, 1914), 12 and n. I owe this reference to Professor Denys Hay.

[95] *The Works of Sir John Fortescue*, ed. Thomas, Lord Clermont (London, 1869), i. 26; C.L. Scofield, *The Life and Reign of Edward the Fourth* (London, 1923), i. 369.

[96] *The Paston Letters*, 1422-1509, ed. J. Gairdner (Edinburgh, 1910), ii. 93-4; C. Ross, *Edward IV* (London, 1974), pp.43-4.

as a bride to Edward has been dated to 1464.[97] The Lancastrians still remained hopeful of Iberian support. In December Margaret of Anjou and her council concerted proposals to be put to Afonso V for a Portuguese army to restore Henry VI. In view of Afonso's closeness to Enrique IV, and the latter's new friendship with the Yorkists, this mission was apparently doomed.[98] In August 1466 Edward sent ambassadors to Enrique with a draft alliance, in which the parties undertook not to support each other's enemies or to receive their rebels and pledged themselves to provide military aid on request. These terms were agreed on and ratified in 1467.[99] Enrique, disillusioned with Louis XI, reversed nearly a century of Trastamaran policy by replacing the French alliance with an English one.[100] Both he and Edward were motivated by the need to safeguard precarious domestic security. In 1465 Enrique faced domestic revolt: the Yorkist regime now appeared stable enough to provide him with military support against it. In 1468 Edward made a similar alliance with Juan II of Aragon, by then allied with Enrique and hostile to Louis.[101] Thus Edward attained – if fleetingly – the goals in Iberian diplomacy which had eluded many of his predecessors: he had peace with the principal rulers and had displaced the French in the Peninsula.

But in November 1469 the Franco-Castilian alliance was renewed. Enrique turned back to Louis as a result of his breach with Juan II over the marriage of the latter's son and heir Fernando to Enrique's sister Isabella. The breakdown of Edward's rule in 1469-70 undermined his worth as an ally. Enrique, like Louis, supported Henry VI's Readeption.[102] Edward IV, after his restoration in 1471, was probably sympathetic to the claims of Isabella and her husband Fernando of Aragon to the Castilian succession, rather than to that of Afonso V and his wife Juana, Enrique's daughter – the claim supported by Enrique. In

[97] Scofield, i. 235-7, 261-2; *Letters and Papers illustrative of the Reigns of Richard III and Henry VII*, ed. J. Gairdner (RS, 1861), i. 32. Scofield connected the marriage offer with the presence of Castilian envoys in England in 1464 (*op. cit.*, i. 320-1 and 32 n.). In October 1464 Edward gave powers to Bernard de la Force to negotiate with Enrique IV (*Foedera*, xi. 534).

[98] *Works of Fortescue*, i. 23-8; Scofield, i. 368-71; Livermore, pp.119-20. The mission was entrusted principally to the earl of Ormond, who had fled from the Yorkists to Oporto.

[99] *Foedera*, xi. 569-72, 583-90; Scofield, i. 408, 414. For an oration addressed to Enrique IV by Edward's envoy John Gunthorpe at Olmedo on 23 October 1466, see Bodleian MS. 587, ff.73ʳ – 67ᵛ (*Eng. Med. Dip. Practice*, I, no.138).

[100] One inducement for Enrique to ally with Edward was that the latter was prepared to give up the Yorkist claim to the throne of Castile, to which considerable prominence had been given in his domestic propaganda in the 1460s. For the text of Edward's recognition of Enrique and his successors as rightful kings of Castile, Scofield, ii. 470; cf *ibid.*, i. 153-4 and 154 n.; Goodman and Morgan, pp.61-70.

[101] *Foedera*, xi. 631-5.

[102] Scofield, i. 508.

1475, within a year of the latter's death, Edward confirmed the treaty of 1467 with Fernando and Isabella.[103] He was keen to supplement the treaty with a marriage alliance: in 1477 he proposed the marriage of his son 'Edward to the Catholic Kings' daughter Isabella, and in 1479 he proposed his daughter Catherine as a bride for the *infante* Juan.[104] The Catholic Kings took the opportunity of Richard III's succession to offer a more specific military alliance. In August 1483 Isabella's envoy Sasiola outlined to Richard's council a scheme by which the English would provide a force to participate in the conquest of Navarre: subsequently the Castilians would help in the recovery of Gascony for the English crown. The response to these proposals was cautious and evasive. Sensibly, Richard opted solely for a renewal of the more general alliance of 1467.[105] The speed with which this confirmation was accomplished suggests that Anglo-Castilian amity and alliance should be regarded as a Yorkist rather than a Tudor achievement. But there are indications that the relationship never became close under the Yorkists. Sasiola's instructions referred to the personal grudge which Isabella nursed against Edward. There is no evidence that after the renewal of the alliance in 1483 Richard made a sustained effort to get on a more personal footing with the Catholic Kings, a failure which contrasts with Henry VII's attempts to ingratiate himself with them from the start of his reign. Indeed, one of their subjects, Salaçar *el pequeno*, fought for Richard at Bosworth, but their retired councillor Diego de Valera wrote an account of the battle to them repeating anti-Ricardian propaganda. His repetition of this and his readiness to brand Richard as a usurper and to recognize Henry's right to the throne suggest that he considered his sovereigns to be indifferent to Richard's fate.[106]

When Isabella offered Richard an alliance concerned partly with Gascony, she was appealing to a traditional aim in English policy towards Spain. A network of diplomatic relations with Iberian principalities had originally been developed by the Angevin Kings as a means of reinforcing their rule in Aquitaine in various ways. Their successors during the Hundred Years War attempted to align Iberian principalities against the French crown and its Castilian ally. They had the defence of Gascony as a principal object, fearing Castilian attacks against Gascon ports and

---

[103] *Foedera*, xii, 2-5, 109. Edward renewed the Treaty of Windsor with Afonso V in 1472 and with his successor João II in 1482 (*ibid.*, xi. 762-3; xii, 145-6).

[104] *Ibid.* 42, 110-1. The proposal for Catherine's marriage was under consideration in 1482 (*ibid.*, 147-8).

[105] *Letters and Papers*, i. 23-5, 31-3, 48-51; *British Library Harleian Manuscript 433*, ed. R. Horrox and P.W. Hammond (Gloucester, 1979), i. 23-5, 35; *Foedera*, xii. 199-201. Richard knighted Sasiola out of regard for his kinswoman Isabella (*Harleian Manuscript*, i. 1-2).

[106] *Epístolas y otros varios tratados de Mosén Diego de Valera*, ed. José A. de Balenchana, La Sociedad de Bibliófilos Españoles (Madrid, 1878), pp.91-6; Mosén Diego de Valera, *Crónica de los Reyes Cátolicos*, ed. Juan de Mata Carriazo (Madrid, 1927), pp.212-3. I owe thanks to Professor A. MacKay for these references.

Anglo-Gascon trade as well as against English interests in the Channel. The establishment of Castile in English policy as the most significant Iberian power had occurred in the second half of the thirteenth century. The Castilian crown had shown itself to be a powerful influence in Gascony and a threat to English control of the duchy. The impression of Castile's pre-eminence was probably reinforced in the minds of English policy-makers by the variety of ways in which it had impinged and continued to impinge on English consciousness. Castile was the principal source of Iberian trade with England: the ports, merchants and sailors of Asturias were familiar to many English folk.[107] By the end of the thirteenth century the Castilian crown was the principal exponent of the Iberian crusading tradition, a role for which it was admired by the English nobility. Because of the popularity of the pilgrimage to Santiago, Galicia was the part of Iberia (and one of the parts of the continent) best known by Englishmen and Englishwomen.

But such commercial links and cultural attachments were not a sufficiently strong basis for political amity. Nor, in the long run, was the treaty of 1254 and the personal ties which it created. Though this treaty produced long-lasting frictions, it had also stimulated a 'golden age' in the second half of the thirteenth century in relations between the English and Castilian courts. Castilian princes were entertained in England and Castilian entertainers performed at the English court.[108] Henry III retained Alfonso X's envoy Garcia Martinez and both Alfonso and Edward I entrusted diplomatic missions to the Englishman Geoffrey de Eversley.[109] There are parallels to some of these sorts of ties in Anglo-Portuguese relations in the first half of the fifteenth century.[110] But curial ties did not develop again between England and Castile before 1485, despite the marriage which linked their dynasties in 1388. The 'hundred years war' between the two realms (1369-1467) produced expressions of national hostility, most elaborately by Diez de Games in his ethnographical disquisition on the origins of unpleasant English behaviour.[111] Even before the war Sir Thomas Gray's remarkable repetition of Trastamaran propaganda against Pedro I shows that the idea that the Castilian crown was losing its crusading virtue was already

---

[107] Childs, pp.2-3.

[108] In December 1255 two of Alfonso X's players (*istrionibus*) were to be paid 20s. each by the English crown. These may have been the players who were said in 1257 to have received robes of camlet and squirrel of Henry's gift (*CLR, 1251-60*, 388).

[109] For Martinez, *ibid.*, 249; for Eversley, N. Denholm-Young, 'The Cursus in England', *Collected Papers in Mediaeval Subjects* (Oxford, 1946), pp.33-4; cf. *Foedera*, I, ii. 569-70; PRO, SC. 1/12/105; *ibid.*, 107.

[110] For links between the English court and the court and nobility of Aragon in the 1430s, *Official Correspondence of Thomas Bekynton*, ed. G. Williams (RS., 1872), i. 198-9, 201-2; *Tirante El Blanco*, ed. Martín de Riquer (Madrid, 1974), i. ix-xxi, liv ff.

[111] *El Vitorial*, pp.142ff.

current among the English nobility.[112] John of Gaunt, as pretender to the Castilian crown, did nothing to revive pro-Castilian sentiment in England. Few Spaniards became his intimates and councillors; he did not set up a chapter of the crusading order of the Banda. The cultural ambience of his household remained Anglo-French. The crusading bulls which he acquired from Urban VI against Castilian schismatics and the preaching of the crusade by the well-respected Carmelites were calculated to stir up indignation against Castilians.[113] The traditional admiration for the Castilian crown and nobility in English courtly circles was only to be fully rekindled by the Catholic Kings' crusade against Granada.[114]

A recurrent aim of English diplomacy in the Peninsula in the later middle ages was to compel the reigning dynasty of Castile to make a treaty modelled on that of 1254.[115] But the English crown did not pursue Iberian aims with the intensity which it applied in France and Scotland. It had no hereditary claims in the Peninsula which might have nourished bureaucratic expertise and conciliar debate on its affairs. Exceptionally, the Black Prince as ruler of Aquitaine reared an interventionalist interest, which was brought to fruition by his brothers John of Gaunt and Edmund of Langley, but was cut short by Gaunt in 1388. Otherwise, no princely or noble interest developed in England capable of putting pressure on the Crown for its fuller involvement in Iberia. The fourteenth-century Englishmen with claims on Spanish lordships or ambitions to gain them were too few for that. The attempts by the dukes of York and Clarence to interfere in the Aragonese succession dispute in the 1410s do not seem to have been backed by the English crown and were short-lived: they were soon once more campaigning in France. The dynastic discontinuities of the House of York in the first half of the fifteenth century prevented it from pursuing its claim to the Castilian crown. Mercantile interests were strong enough to influence but not to dictate royal policies towards Castile. Though the Crown wished to maintain the mechanisms for the regulation

---

[112] *Scalacronica*, ed. H. Maxwell (Glasgow, 1907), p.163. Chandos Herald's account of Pedro I echoes the propaganda of the free companies supporting Enrique of Trastamara against Pedro I in 1366 (*Life of the Black Prince by the Herald of Sir John Chandos*, ed. M.K. Pope and E.C. Lodge [Oxford, 1910], pp.51-4, 149-50). For an anecdote demonstrating that Enrique II's nobles lacked the courage to defend Christian beliefs, *The Anonimalle Chronicle 1333 to 1381*, ed. V.H. Galbraith (Manchester, 1934), pp.115-16, 188.

[113] In 1380 Gaunt sent his daughter Catherine, prospective heir to the Castilian throne, to be educated by an English lady (*John of Gaunt's Register, 1379-83*, i, ed. E.C. Lodge and R. Somerville, Camden 3rd ser., lvi [London, 1937], no.319).

[114] For Sir Edward Wydeville's crusade and part in the capture of Loja in 1486, Eloy Benito Ruano, 'Un Cruzado Ingléz en la Guerra de Granada', *Anuario de Estudios Medievales*, 9 (Barcelona, 1974-9), 585-93.

[115] In 1344 Edward III instructed his envoys to the Castilian court to request a confirmation of the 1254 treaty (*Foedera*, III, i. 22-3). The text of the 1254 treaty is included in a late fourteenth-century English collection of diplomatic documents (British Library, Cotton Nero D VI, f.56ᵛ).

of disputes and claims established in the thirteenth century, it had other diplomatic priorities: Anglo-Castilian trade was adversely affected by the conflicts of the later middle ages.[116] The main determinant of English policy towards Castile – and, indeed, towards other Iberian powers – down to the reign of Henry VI remained their relevance in the eyes of kings and their councillors to the Anglo-French conflict. Consequently the Iberian policies of the English crown tended to be contingent, intermittent, feeble and lacking in realism. At least they had the negative virtue, for the most part, of avoiding burdensome involvement in Peninsular politics.

But such policies were unable to overcome a serious obstacle in the path of reopening the historic friendly relationship with Castile. The interventionist policies of Edward III's sons had solidified the francophile sentiments of the Castilian court and nobility. These blocked the development by the English crown, as a means of influencing royal policy, of patronal relationships with the Castilian elites, such as Edward II had tried to cultivate during the war of Saint-Sardos, or such as could be cultivated in the Lancastrian period in Portugal and at times in Aragon. There was a striking absence of English influence at work in Castile during royal minorities, even when an Englishwoman was queen or one of the regents, and during civil strife. Only in the 1460s did the international perceptions of the Castilian elites start to change, partly as a result of more flexible English diplomacy, but mainly because the growth of French royal power presented new challenges to Castilian interests. Under the Yorkists and Henry VII a new chapter in Anglo-Spanish relations opened: the 1467 treaty marked the formal beginning of this, but 1485 was the start of an intensification of the process of rapprochement.

[116] Childs, pp.3, 32-3, 40-2, 52-3.

Chapter 6

King Henry III, the Crusade and the Mediterranean

Simon Lloyd

Henry III took the Cross on *Laetare Hierusalem* Sunday 1250 (6 March), but Jerusalem would not rejoice. Despite repeated declarations of intent he never sailed for the Holy Land. His vow instead became embroiled in the combined Plantagenet-papal policy to oust the Hohenstaufen from Sicily. In February 1254 Henry appointed proctors to receive the kingdom of Sicily from Pope Innocent IV on behalf of his younger son, Edmund. On 6 March, exactly four years to the day after taking the Cross himself, Henry's wish was fulfilled; in May the grant was confirmed by Pope Innocent.[1] A year later, Alexander IV authorized the commutation of Henry's vow to this Sicilian project, and in October 1255 Edmund was solemnly invested as king.[2]

These developments have inevitably coloured assessments of Henry's commitment to the crusade. Indeed his very intentions in taking the Cross in the first place have been interpreted on the dubious premise that since he never went to the Holy Land he never planned to do so.[3] Nor has Henry's intervention in the volatile politics of the Mediterranean and the wider papal-imperial struggle earned him much credit. It has instead prompted some of the sharpest criticism of the king, especially in view of its bearing upon the collapse of Henry's regime in England in 1258 and the protracted political crisis which followed. Treharne, for one, savaged him: the Sicilian affair was an 'amazing folly', enjoying no support in England; Richard of Cornwall's imperial candidature was 'ludicrous', the whole 'a military and political absurdity' whereby the papacy quite obviously

---

[1] *Les Registres d'Alexandre IV*, ed. C. Bourel de la Roncière *et al.* (B[ibliothèque des] É[coles] f[rançaises d']A[thènes et de] R[ome], 1895-1953), no.3036; T. Rymer, *Foedera* (London, 1816-69), I, i. 297, 301.

[2] Rymer, I, i. 319-20.

[3] See, for example, N. Denholm-Young, *Richard of Cornwall* (Oxford, 1947), p.73; among others, W. Stubbs, *The Constitutional History of England*, 4th edn. (Oxford, 1906), ii. 67. For a more favourable view, and the fullest discussion of Henry's three crusading vows (1216, 1250, 1271), see A.J. Forey, 'The Crusading Vows of the English King Henry III', *Durham University Journal*, lxv (1973), 229-47. This paper is concerned only with the 1250 vow.

manipulated 'England' for its own ends. 'This unforgivable folly stamps Henry as vain, selfish, obstinate, credulous and silly beyond redemption, and in the end it almost cost him his throne.'[4] Henry's failure to secure political support in England was of course fatal to the success of his schemes, but Treharne's strictures, rooted in a narrowly Anglocentric view of Henry's foreign policy, signally fail to allow for the pressures and influences bearing upon Henry at the time, and the way in which international politics were perceived and conducted.[5] He was little more sympathetic towards Henry's attempts to restore his inheritance, the lost Plantagenet lands in France.[6]

Some reassessment is called for. It may not be possible to rescue Henry from all of the charges laid at his door, but at least the attempt can be made to understand the complex interplay of interests, ideals, dynastic tradition, and international competition which governed his conduct of external relations, and which help to explain the emergence of a grandiose foreign policy in the 1250s. To that policy his crusading vow – itself partly a product of these broader considerations, as we shall see – ultimately became tied. Since this has obvious implications for any assessment of Henry's motives in assuming the Cross, and his later preparedness to see the diversion of his vow, it will be well initially to consider the claim that he never intended to sail for the Holy Land before proceeding to the wider context.

The evidence shows that between 1250 and 1254 Henry was entirely sincere in his declarations of intent to depart for the East, but not, it should be noted, before 1256. According to the intelligence report sent from France in April 1250 by the chaplain Philip to Alphonse of Poitiers, his master then on crusade in Egypt, Henry had taken the Cross 'a movoeir a sis ans'.[7] This neglected report of Henry's long-term intentions may be accepted, for Philip was well-connected and well-informed, and his intelligence is confirmed by Henry's own declaration, on 14 April 1252, that he would sail for the Holy Land on 24 June 1256.[8] It is no surprise, then, that Henry took no practical measures against his departure in the two years following his vow,[9] but he did intervene in the

---

[4] R.F. Treharne, *The Baronial Plan of Reform, 1258-1263* (Manchester, 1932), p.50.

[5] F.M. Powicke, *King Henry III and the Lord Edward* (Oxford, 1947), esp. chs. v, vi, ix; and *idem, The Thirteenth Century, 1216-1307*, 2nd edn. (Oxford, 1962), esp. ch. iii, took a wider view.

[6] Treharne, p.50; E.L. Cox, *The Eagles of Savoy. The House of Savoy in Thirteenth Century Europe* (Princeton, 1974); and M.T. Clanchy, *England and Its Rulers, 1066-1272* (Glasgow, 1983), pp.230-40, provide a convincing antidote regarding Henry's external ambitions.

[7] T. Saint-Bris, 'Lettre addressée en Égypte à Alphonse, comte de Poitiers, frère de Saint Louis', B[*ibliothèque de l'*]É[*cole des*] C[*hartes*], i (1839-40), 400.

[8] Rymer, I, i. 282; C[*alendar of*] P[*atent*] R[*olls*], *1247-58*, 157-8.

[9] Compare Forey, pp.235-6.

campaign promoting the crusade in his dominions, and took measures to stimulate recruitment.[10]

If Henry was merely seeking in cynical fashion to raise as many men and as much money as possible, to be applied to enterprises other than the crusade, then only remarkable dissimulation would explain the very practical preparations which Henry began to make in 1252 after his declaration of 14 April. In June 1252 he requested the masters of the Temple, the Hospital, and the Teutonic Knights in the Holy Land to prepare their best ships for his use. They were to send them a year in advance of his passage to take horses and supplies to the Holy Land, before returning in the year following to convey Henry and his force to the East.[11] By September he was preparing to send royal agents to the Holy Land and the Mediterranean ports to make arrangements against his departure – probably the purchase and storage of foodstuffs and other necessaries, and the hire of ships.[12] Certain men of Marseille, the chosen port of embarkation, were summoned to England to discuss the details of his passage; and in the attempt to determine the shipping required, estimates were sought in May 1253 of the number of crusaders from Ireland and Scotland, at least, who would be accompanying him.[13] He also began the process of drawing up contracts for service in the Holy Land.[14] Moreover, in January 1253 Henry requested Innocent IV to cause preaching of the Cross 'per cetera regna Christicolarum', to publicize the king's fixed departure date, and to admonish all crusaders of other realms to sail with him.[15] These were strange measures for a man to take if he had no intention of departing.

There are other signs that Henry most certainly had set his heart upon accomplishing his vow. He apparently sought to reduce expenditure against his passage; according to Paris, this was why he did not distribute robes in the customary way at Christmas 1250.[16] The timing of the important statutes concerning Jewry, promulgated in January 1253, is unlikely to be just coincidence; such measures were entirely consistent with the *mentalité* of a crusader king seriously planning to liberate the Holy Land from other 'enemies of Christ'.[17] Likewise, the selection of crusading

---

[10] See especially *C[lose] R[olls], 1247-51*, 358, 447, 540; Rymer, I, i. 274, 276; *CR, 1251-3*, 69, 97-100, 210, 231, 281, 436; *CPR, 1247-58*, 84, 164, 168, 372, 377.

[11] Rymer, I, i. 282; *CPR, 1247-58*, 158.

[12] Rymer, I, i. 285.

[13] Rymer, I, i. 289; *CPR, 1247-58*, 191.

[14] The terms of that between Henry and Peter of Savoy survive. Rymer, I, i. 288; *CPR, 1247-58*, 188-9.

[15] *CR, 1251-3*, 448; Rymer, I, i. 288.

[16] Matthew Paris, *Chronica majora*, ed. H.R. Luard (RS, 1872-83), v. 199, and 114; further, 'Annales prioratus de Dunstaplia', in *Annales monastici*, ed. H.R. Luard (RS, 1864-9), iii. 184.

[17] *CR, 1251-3*, 312-13. See H.G. Richardson, *The English Jewry under Angevin Kings* (London, 1960), pp.191-2.

subjects for the decoration of certain royal apartments in 1251 suggests a man looking to the past for inspiration and to dynastic models for his own anticipated deeds in the East.[18]

If such deeds were to be duly accomplished then Henry, like all crusaders, would need to ensure the integrity and security of his dominions during his absence. This requirement helps to explain why Henry intended to delay his departure for six years after taking the Cross.[19] His attempts to settle the affairs of Gascony, if not stimulated by his assumption of the Cross, certainly gained a greater urgency as a result.[20] The marriage of his daughter Margaret to Alexander III of Scotland in December 1251 may also have owed something to Henry's wish to stabilize relations with a traditional foe before departure.[21] It cannot be coincidence that on 8 March 1250, just two days after taking the Cross, Henry sought renewal of the truce with Louis IX of France for six years.[22] Significantly, the truce had been extended only a few months at a time since September 1248. Finally, the gold treasure which Henry began to amass after 1248-9 was intended precisely for use on his projected crusade. Henry was extremely reluctant to see it diverted to finance his Gascon expedition of 1253-4.[23]

This body of material also helps to dispose of the view that Henry took the Cross solely as a means of obtaining money.[24] It is an unconvincing argument for other reasons. Henry certainly went to great lengths to secure funds for his passage, but that should be no cause for suspicion.[25] It is difficult to think of a prospective crusade leader of Henry's time who did not make the urgent quest for funds a central part of his preparations, and if Henry sought papal subsidy *before* assuming the Cross that was only

[18] Below, pp.102-3.

[19] He would also need to complete his other arrangements. Long delays prior to departure were common. Richard of Cornwall took the Cross in 1236, departing in 1240; Louis IX spent four years (1244-8) preparing for his first crusade. Edward I took the Cross in 1287; he was to have sailed in 1293.

[20] Powicke, *Henry III*, i. 230-1.

[21] Powicke, *Thirteenth Century*, pp.587-9.

[22] *Dip. Docs. I, 1101-1272*, no.261; *CPR, 1247-58*, 62; *Royal and other Historical Letters illustrative of the Reign of Henry III*, ed. W.W. Shirley (RS, 1862-6), ii. 59-60. Philip the chaplain directly linked Henry's vow with the meeting between Richard of Cornwall and Queen Blanche at Melun to renew the truce. Saint-Bris, *ubi supra*.

[23] D.A. Carpenter, 'The Gold Treasure of King Henry III', in *Thirteenth Century England I*, ed. P.R. Coss and S.D. Lloyd (Woodbridge, 1986), pp.68-73.

[24] See especially L. Dehio, *Innozenz IV und England* (Berlin, 1914), pp.42 ff; E. Berger, *Saint Louis et Innocent IV* (Paris, 1893), pp.222-3.

[25] See the wise words of W.E. Lunt, *The Valuation of Norwich* (Oxford, 1926), pp.55-8; Forey, pp.231-7.

prudent.[26] The Lord Edward, for one, did precisely the same before he took vows in 1268, yet no one has argued that he took the Cross out of avarice.[27] Edward, however, duly fulfilled his vow; Henry did not, and he came to apply much of the monies raised to enterprises other than the crusade. Here is the bone for sceptics to gnaw at. It is almost inconceivable that Henry was so naive and ill-advised that he did not appreciate that the retention of monies granted would depend upon fulfilment of his vow.[28] With regard to Matthew Paris, whose views inform the opinion that Henry took the Cross for financial reasons, it must be remembered that he wrote partly with the benefit of hindsight, interpreting motives in the light of later developments. His notorious antipathy to financial exactions of any kind, by whomsoever, needs no emphasis here.

If Henry was sincere when he took the Cross in 1250, and in the years immediately following had every intention of fulfilling his vow in the Holy Land, that does not mean that he was motivated purely with the fate of the Latin East and his own soul in mind. One cannot pronounce upon the exact reasons lying behind his assumption of the Cross, but it is possible to consider the influences bearing upon his decision.[29] For a Plantagenet who was also a king, acting in the intensely competitive Western political scene, the crusade and the crusading vow possessed wide significance. As a Plantagenet, first, Henry was heir to traditions of pilgrimage and crusade to Jerusalem. The Plantagenet house, narrowly perceived as the counts of Anjou, included that Fulk who became king of Jerusalem in 1131, establishing the line of Angevins who ruled in the Latin kingdom up to the death of Baldwin IV in 1185. They were cousins to Henry II, Henry III's grandfather.[30] There was also an inherited Norman tradition. In

---

[26] Henry's lobbying at the papal curia in 1247 for crusading monies in England has frequently been considered sinister, but as Lunt, p.54, observed, Henry's intention was surely to secure funding for the separate English crusade which, he hoped, his half-brother Guy de Lusignan would lead. The relevant materials in *Les Registres d'Innocent IV*, ed. E. Berger (BEFAR, 1884-1921), nos.4054-6, should be read together. Compare Forey, pp.232-3.

[27] *Les Registres de Clément IV*, ed. E. Jordan (BEFAR, 1893-1945), no.1288; *Thesaurus novus anecdotorum*, ed. E. Martène and U. Durand (Paris, 1717), ii, no.583.

[28] See Forey, pp.236-7 on this point; compare, especially, with Berger, pp.222-3.

[29] I leave aside as given, here, the general motivating force of the crusader's plenary indulgence and other privileges.

[30] A close tie to the ruling house was maintained since Baldwin's sister, Sibyl, married Guy de Lusignan, king of Jerusalem (1186-92) and lord of Cyprus (1192-4). Guy's elder brother, Amalric, succeeded in both states, and from him and the offspring of his wife Isabella's previous marriages descended the lines which ruled in both in the thirteenth century. There were other connections between Henry III and the rulers of the various crusader states. Neither these nor the full past crusading record of his dynasty can be detailed here.

particular, Duke Robert II was the leader of the Norman contingent on the First Crusade. These precedents were somewhat remote by Henry III's time, but the examples of Henry II, the Young Henry, Richard I and John were closer to hand. All had taken the Cross at some point in their reigns, although only Richard duly departed for the East. His illustrious deeds were naturally a source of great pride to his successors, but dynastic precedent was something of a two-edged sword. It added lustre and prestige to the dynasty's name, and inflated the pride of its later members, but it also imposed a certain burden of emulation. Henry III was left in no doubt of this, both popes and Eastern princes seeking unambiguously to engage his honour as a member of the Plantagenet line, and more specifically successor to Richard I, in their attempts to secure his aid.[31]

That Henry was proud of those ancestral crusading deeds, and eager to emphasize the prestige they imparted, is indicated by the works which he commissioned by way of commemoration. On 5 June 1251 he ordered the painting of the 'history of Antioch' in the chamber of the king's chaplains in the Tower of London.[32] Next day, instructions went out for the painting of Rosamund's chamber, Winchester castle, with the same subject.[33] Shortly after, decoration of the king's chamber under the chapel at Clarendon with 'the story of Antioch and the duel of King Richard' was in hand.[34] Yet a fourth Antioch chamber was being painted simultaneously in the palace of Westminster.[35] The 'duel of King Richard' clearly refers to the single combat in which he supposedly fought Saladin, an accretion to the Lionheart's legend which Henry evidently wished to celebrate. Apart from the painting, tiles almost certainly depicting the duel were found *in situ* at Clarendon during excavations in 1936, whilst the famous decorated tiles of Chertsey which illustrate the combat were very probably made under Henry's influence.[36] The 'story of Antioch' is problematical. Borenius, quite reasonably wishing to see a connection with Richard, considered that it concerned events of the Third Crusade, but this is very unlikely since Antioch, as he recognized, 'was not one of the main pivots of action', and Richard went nowhere near Antioch.[37] More probably, Henry had in mind events of the First Crusade and the deeds of Robert Curthose, duke of Normandy. C.W. David showed that Robert rapidly

[31] See especially *Dip. Docs. I, 1101-1272*, no.268; *Reg. Innocent IV*, no.6072; Rymer, I, i. 172-3, 321.

[32] *CR, 1247-51*, 454.

[33] C[alendar of the] L[iberate] R[olls], *1245-51*, 358.

[34] *CLR, 1245-51*, 362.

[35] *CR, 1247-51*, 464.

[36] See E.S. Eames, *Catalogue of Medieval Lead-Glazed Earthenware Tiles* (London, 1980), i. 144-5, 192-3.

[37] T. Borenius, 'The Cycle of Images in the Palaces and Castles of Henry III', *Journal of the Warburg and Courtauld Institutes*, vi (1943), 45. He omits the painting in Rosamund's chamber, Winchester castle.

became a legendary crusading hero in the twelfth century, the memory of his supposed exploits remaining strong throughout the thirteenth.[38] Naturally, he was celebrated most enthusiastically by Anglo-Normans, many writers regarding him as the pre-eminent crusade leader. Here it will suffice to note that Robert emerged as the hero of the battle of Dorylaeum, 1097, and was developed as the triumphant victor over Kerbogha, the crusaders' greatest foe, in single combat at Antioch: in Anglo-Norman eyes the First Crusade equivalent to Richard's legendary duel with Saladin. It was probably this episode which Henry commemorated in his Antioch chambers.[39] Whether Henry sought otherwise to commemorate the crusading deeds of members of his dynasty is not clear.

As a member of a noble dynasty with a reputation to respect and nurture, Henry could not ignore the crusade in an age which regarded combat with the infidel as an admirable means of winning prestige and honour, for his line as well as himself. But he was also a crowned king with a peculiar dignity to uphold, and kings above all men were under a moral prescription to sustain the interests of Christendom. The point was widely aired in the thirteenth century, and even if it was theoretical it was no less influential for that. Moreover, crusading kings could expect to improve their standing in the West, a point frequently stressed by popes in their appeals.[40] Appeals from the Latin East, too, sometimes underlined the contribution of a crusading record to a king's reputation. In 1263, for example, the legate Thomas and his co-respondents vigorously stressed the fame and acclamation which would accrue to Henry, as a king, if he sent aid or, better still, hastened his own departure,[41] whilst in 1261 the bishop of Acre pandered to Henry's sense of his personal standing as well as his regal dignity by holding up the glorious prospect of his being considered a new Godfrey de Bouillon should he provide support in such dark times.[42]

Behind such honeyed words lurked a further compulsion. Matters of honour and prestige, as these petitioners knew well, operated in a comparative framework, and ever since the precedent set by Louis VII

---

[38] C.W. David, *Robert Curthose, Duke of Normandy* (Cambridge, Mass., 1920), pp.190-202.

[39] The Plantagenet kings probably fostered Curthose's legend. Wace, for example, highlights Robert's supposed crusading role in *Le Roman de Rou*, commissioned by Henry II. It is noteworthy, considering his close connections with Edward I's court, that John of Howden refers explicitly to Robert's deeds at Antioch in his *Rossignol*. L. Stone, 'Jean de Howden, poète anglo-normand du XIIIe siècle', *Romania*, lxix (1946-7), 509, lines 3983-4.

[40] None more succinctly than Innocent III in his appeal to King John in 1215. *Selected Letters of Pope Innocent III concerning England (1198-1216)*, ed. C.R. Cheney, trans. W.H. Semple (London, 1953), no.78.

[41] *Dip. Docs. I, 1101-1272*, no.385.

[42] *Dip. Docs. I, 1101-1272*, no.343.

and Conrad III on the Second Crusade it had become conventional for the crusader's badge to be included among the regalia of kings. The trend was given sharper point and political purpose by the rivalries between the royal houses themselves, and for this reason no king could with impunity allow his rivals to steal a march over him in expressions of commitment to the crusade. The point is well-illustrated by the competition between the Plantagenet kings and their especial rivals, the Capetian kings of France. Their struggles took place as much over prestige and status as disputed territory and conflicting political goals, and kings of both dynasties seem to have approached the matter of the crusade with an eye to the potential political capital to be realized.

In one respect Henry III was at a very marked disadvantage in this connection. He could boast of nothing comparable to the Capetians' past crusading record; there was only Richard to set beside Louis VII, Philip II, Louis VIII and then Louis IX before Lord Edward's crusade of 1270-2. Moreover, the Capetians were heirs to the earlier record of the Merovingians and Carolingians in holy war, a point remorselessly pushed home in an interesting panegyric on the *virtù* of French kings up to and including Louis VIII.[43] The anonymous poet was particularly concerned to stress the long and proud tradition of royal participation in holy war: for him, combat with the infidel was an essential ingredient of regal dignity. Yet he passes over the deeds of Charlemagne and ignores the recent past crusades of Louis VII, Philip II and Louis VIII; perhaps he felt they were too well-known to require special mention. He fastens instead upon the triumphs in holy war, historical or legendary, of earlier kings, especially those of Charles Martel and of the Merovingians, notably Clovis, Lothar, Dagobert and Childibert. This emphasis suited well the poet's overt attempt to demonstrate that through time the kings of England were totally eclipsed by their French rivals. The poem begins sharply:

> Honis soit li rois d'ingleterre!
> Rois francois ont faite mainte gerre
> As Sarrasins per lor vertu.

The figure of Charlemagne nevertheless towered over all others in the pantheon of French kings. It is well-known that it was with him and his cult that the Capetians, his heirs, were most closely identified, and from this association that they derived so much of their lustre and prestige. Henry III's enthusiasm for the crusading deeds of Richard I has surely to be seen partly in this context. To whose memory could Henry otherwise appeal? Indeed, it is tempting to think that he positively fostered the cult of Richard partly in the attempt to set him up as a royal Plantagenet

---

[43] British Library, MS Harleian 4333, fos.100ᵛ-101ᵛ, composed shortly after Louis VIII's death, 1226, and copied *c.*1250.

counterpart to the figure of Charlemagne. We may certainly see a connection with Henry's revival of the cult of Edward the Confessor and his veneration of St. Edmund king and martyr, the jewels in a rival pantheon of English royal saints whose names Henry recited on a famous occasion before Matthew Paris in 1257.[44] Here, at least, the king of England could compete with his Capetian rival on very favourable terms.

The honour of the realm and its subjects must also be taken into consideration, since royal crusades and crusading deeds touched the standing of a king's subjects by virtue of the commonly held notion that the holiness of a king reflected upon his kingdom.[45] Richard I himself drew out the point when he sought to take political advantage of Philip Augustus' withdrawal from the Third Crusade. From Jaffa in October 1191 Richard reported his own famous victory over Saladin's forces at Arsuf and then roundly condemned the Capetian for deserting the crusade: he had scandalously forsaken his vow against God's will, and this to the 'eternal shame of himself and his kingdom.'[46] If kings thought thus it is scarcely surprising that popes occasionally linked the prospect of a royal crusade with the honour which would accrue thereby to king and kingdom alike,[47] nor that observers such as Gerald of Wales stressed the inestimable glory and prestige which would rub off on both.[48] Since, moreover, the overall notion was seen to operate comparatively, it must have been extremely irksome for the king of England and his subjects, increasingly conscious of their national identity, to know that the king of France was generally accredited by the mid thirteenth century as 'most Christian king', his people the most devout.[49]

The operation of this compound of dynastic pride, regal dignity and national honour, set within an intensely competitive atmosphere, helps to

---

[44] *CM*, v. 617. For another possible context, see M.T. Clanchy, 'Did Henry III have a Policy?', *History*, liii (1968), esp. p.214. It is of considerable interest in the context of Capetian-Plantagenet rivalry that in 1254 Henry III displayed Richard I's shield at the Temple, Paris. *CM*, v. 480.

[45] See especially J.R. Strayer, 'France: the Holy Land, the Chosen People, and the Most Christian King', in *Action and Conviction in Early Modern Europe*, ed. T.K. Rabb and E. Seigel (Princeton, 1969), pp.3-16. So far as crusading is concerned, the notion may be traced back to the Second Crusade and the expeditions of Louis VII and Conrad III. *R[ecueil des] h[istoriens des] G[aules et de la] F[rance]*, ed. M. Bouquet *et al.* (Paris, 1737-1904), xii. 88; xv. 495-6; *Monumenta Corbeiensia*, ed. P. Jaffé (Bibliotheca Rerum Germanicarum, i. 1864), pp.126, 300-1.

[46] Roger of Howden, *Chronica*, ed. W. Stubbs (RS, 1868-71), iii. 129-30. The sentiment is echoed in the report of Richard's response to Philip's intention to return home. *Gesta Regis Henrici Secundi Benedicti Abbatis*, ed. W. Stubbs (RS, 1867), ii. 182-3.

[47] See, for example, Innocent IV's responses to Henry III on hearing of his crusading vow, 1250. Rymer, I, i. 272.

[48] *The Conquest of Ireland by Giraldus Cambrensis*, ed. A.M. Scott and F.X. Martin (Dublin, 1978), ii. 201.

[49] As Strayer, p.6 observes, even Matthew Paris admitted this.

explain why Henry III, for one, could barely ignore the crusade. It was necessary to match his rivals and to respond to the ideal of participation in the crusade, so deeply embedded in the conventions of his age, regardless of his personal inclinations and enthusiasm.

The unfolding story of Henry's 1250 vow, from its genesis, is fully comprehensible only if it is set firmly within the context of thought briefly outlined above. More specifically, Henry's compulsive urge to match his particular rival, Louis IX, combined with Henry's failure in their long struggle over territory and political ambitions, helps to explain both why he took the Cross in 1250 and why later that vow became merged in wider Plantagenet schemes in the Mediterranean.

The precise timing of Henry's vow requires explanation. Since the fall of Jerusalem to the Khwarismian Turks in 1244, Henry had been under pressure to aid the Holy Land, the object of a diplomatic offensive which began in earnest in 1245.[50] There is no indication, however, that Henry was moved to consider taking the Cross himself; domestic considerations and the security of his dominions weighed more heavily in these years.[51] Yet he would be left out in the cold if he failed entirely to respond to the crusading call. Of his fellow monarchs, Haakon IV of Norway had been signed with the Cross since 1237; Eric XI of Sweden supported the crusade against the Estonians in 1248; the kings of Aragon and Castile were actively engaged in the *Reconquista* in Spain; and Frederick II was declaring by 1250 that he too hoped to depart on crusade, but that papal malice prevented him for the time being. Above all, Louis IX had taken the Cross in 1244. The eyes of all Christendom were focused upon his expedition when it sailed in 1248. Were he to succeed, especially against the background of recent failures in the East, the Capetians' prestige would soar as the Plantagenets' would sink, a royal dynasty apparently incapable or unwilling to succour the Holy Land in its hour of greatest need, following the loss of Jerusalem in 1244.[52]

If such considerations held force at the Plantagenet court in the late 1240s this would help to explain Henry's petitions to Innocent IV in 1247: that the departure of English crusaders be deferred until one year after the passage of Louis and the French; that Guy de Lusignan, Henry's half-

---

[50] It was then that the envoys of the Holy Land, Bishop Waleran of Beirut and the Dominican, Arnulph, came before Henry III beseeching his aid. See especially *CM*, iv. 337-45, 388, 431. Innocent IV added to the pressure. Rymer, I, i. 254-5. A spate of letters and missions from the Latin East followed.

[51] See, for example, *CM*, iv. 489. Henry also continued to oppose taxation for the crusade imposed in 1245. See Forey, p.231.

[52] The powers of the Latin East considered the Plantagenets and Capetians to be their best hope for salvation in this period. See, for example, *Dip. Docs. I, 1101-1272*, no.386; Rymer, I, i. 396.

brother, be appointed their leader; and that the crusading monies raised in England be made available to them.[53] This, surely, was in part an insurance policy. If Louis should score an outstanding success in the East, then at least a distinct English contingent could share in the glory. Henry could claim that he had done his bit. Louis' initial success in Egypt, however, necessitated reconsideration. News of his capture of Damietta and, more, rumours of his conquest of Cairo, had reached the sharp ears of Matthew Paris, for one, by the autumn of 1249.[54] As Lunt suggested, this news was probably responsible for the undoubted revival in England of interest in the crusade. Henry's hand was being forced, and Lunt was most likely correct in further supposing that Henry's vow of 6 March 1250 was the product of jealousy, a consuming wish to emulate Louis.[55] That he should first have sought papal subsidy before assuming the Cross was entirely reasonable.[56] So too was his attempt thereafter to prevent the independent departure of English crusaders, especially since they would be joining and aiding Louis, Henry's 'capitalis inimicus', as Paris puts it.[57]

Henry was doubtless shocked by the news of the disastrous battle of Mansourah and Louis' capture in April 1250. He probably shed many tears, as was his wont, but many may have been crocodile tears. As the full import of the calamity dawned, Henry, it seems, began to regard himself as the only possible saviour of the Latin East. He was egged on by Innocent IV, who also came to appeal in 1251 and 1252 to the memory of Plantagenet crusading deeds, those of Richard I specifically.[58] It was, surely, under the impact of those suggestions and Henry's own dreams that his Antioch chambers were commissioned in 1251. Henry would indeed be a new Lionheart.

Louis' discomfiture in the East provided distinct possibilities for Henry in the context of the Plantagenet-Capetian struggle. Upon his release in May 1250 Louis sailed for Acre, where he remained for nearly four years, attempting to bolster the position of the Latin kingdom. Signed with the Cross, Henry was an obvious source of support, so it is not altogether surprising that, at some point before October 1251, Louis exhorted Henry

---

[53] *Reg. Innocent IV*, nos.4054-6. Carpenter, pp.70-1, plausibly suggests that the build-up of Henry's gold treasure from 1246-7 was intended to support an English crusade.

[54] *CM*, v. 87, 118; vi. no.87.

[55] Lunt, p.55 and n.3.

[56] The long delay between receipt of news of Louis' initial success and Henry's vow is easily explained because Henry had already been negotiating for papal subsidy. Rymer, I, i. 272. He probably delayed taking vows to await Innocent IV's reply. Compare Forey, p.237.

[57] *CM*, v. 135; further, Saint-Bris, pp.400-1; and see Forey, pp.231-2.

[58] '[Annales monasterii de] Burton', in *Annales monastici*, pp.293-5, 298-9; *Reg. Innocent IV*, no.6072; *Dip. Docs. I, 1101-1272*, no.268.

to fulfil his vow, urging that the two act in concert in the Holy Land.[59] Louis' predicament was Henry's opportunity. His reply to Louis' proposal does not survive, but he alluded to it when he informed Louis in June 1252 that his departure on crusade was fixed for 24 June 1256.[60] He went on to observe that he might anticipate that date should Louis restore the lost Plantagenet lands in France. Concurrent letters to Queen Margaret of France and the leaders of Outremer added to the pressure upon Louis in this piece of crude blackmail. Paris reports that Louis indeed offered to meet Henry's territorial demands, should he come to his aid in the east, but that French baronial opposition killed off the plan.[61] Paris further reports that Louis' reputation suffered badly following his failure in Egypt, and here too Henry could hope to score points. In the selfsame letter of June 1252 he brought Louis' esteem directly into play by observing that he might hasten his crusade 'to the increase of the honour of the said king of France'. The crusade of the new Richard, then, would be the means of restoring Louis' tarnished reputation; the Plantagenet would rescue the Capetian and give him back his pride. Who, one wonders, would be entitled in such an event to the accolade 'most Christian king'?

Henry cannot be rescued from the charge of opportunism in the matter of the crusade. He took the Cross only when it became convenient, or necessary, to do so, and his crass attempt to exploit Louis' predicament after Mansourah reveals blatant expediency of a particularly unsavoury type. Indeed, Henry had attempted to take advantage of Louis even before he departed on crusade in 1248 by playing upon the Capetian's anxieties concerning the security of France during his absence. Although the truce of 1243 was renewed at Louis' request in 1246 to run until Michaelmas 1248, it was then extended only until 31 December 1248.[62] In addition, Henry threatened force to regain the Plantagenet lands, his sabre-rattling backed up by diplomatic pressure.[63] He became more conciliatory after taking the Cross in 1250, as we have seen, but by 1253 he was again threatening force, although an attack did not materialize.[64] Opportunism is also to be seen in the parallel negotiations into which Henry entered in 1254, with a view to the commutation of his vow into an

---

[59] The proposal appears in Innocent's letter of October 1251 to Henry. 'Burton', pp.293-5.

[60] Rymer, I, i. 282; *CPR, 1247-58*, 157-8.

[61] *CM*, v. 280-1.

[62] *Layettes du Trésor des Chartes*, ed. A. Teulet *et al.* (Paris, 1863-1909), ii. no.3075; iii. no.3713.

[63] *CM*, iv. 506; v. 71. Alphonse of Poitiers remained behind in 1248 against threats to Capetian security. *RHGF*, xx. 356, 372.

[64] *CM*, v. 434. Louis is said to have returned to France on hearing that attack from England as well as Germany was imminent. *RHGF*, xx. 17, 386. The French feudal host was indeed summoned in September 1253. *RHGF*, xxiii. 730-1.

assault upon North Africa in the company of Alfonso X of Castile, or upon the Hohenstaufen in Sicily.[65] However, the pressures and influences which lay behind Henry's preparedness to allow his crusading vow to become an instrument of his wider foreign policy have not always been sufficiently appreciated. Once again, Plantagenet-Capetian rivalry, albeit in a different form, would appear to provide much of the rationale behind developments.

Like his father John, Henry III refused to accept the loss to the Capetians of Normandy, Brittany, Anjou, Poitou and their satellites in the opening years of the thirteenth century. The attempt to recover them was the central element of Henry's foreign policy until the 1250s, but neither military expeditions (in 1225-6, 1230-1 and 1242-3) nor diplomacy had succeeded in wresting those lands from the Capetians. Indeed, by 1250 the chances of recovery must have seemed slight. Louis IX had already taken considerable strides towards the consolidation of Capetian authority and influence throughout France following the disintegrative tendencies of his long minority. This was complemented by the installation of Louis' brothers in their appanages. So far as the Plantagenet lands are concerned, Charles was invested with Anjou and Maine in 1246, whilst Alphonse of Poitiers' vast appanage was finally assembled in 1249 when he succeeded to the county of Toulouse on the death of Count Raymond VII. Thereby, Plantagenet Gascony was effectively hemmed in to the north and east. Nor had Henry succeeded in his attempts to block Capetian ambitions elsewhere. In particular, he had failed to prevent Provence falling under Capetian influence in the person of Charles of Anjou, who married the heiress in 1246. The terms of the treaty of Beaucaire (1248), an interim settlement between Charles and the dowager countess, Beatrice, underlined that Henry's hopes had been effectively dashed.[66]

Prospects for Gascony, the sole remaining Plantagenet territory in France, had never been bleaker than in the late 1240s. The political situation within the duchy was chaotic, the administration in utter disarray, a circumstance which inevitably encouraged intervention on the part of those with a claim to the lordship or otherwise hostile to the Plantagenet presence. Invasion was considered to be not so much likely as imminent in circles close to Henry III at the time. Amongst the conditions which Earl Simon de Montfort laid down for his appointment as seneschal of Gascony in 1248 was the requirement that Henry accept responsibility

---

[65] Amongst others, Powicke, *Henry III*, i. 241; *idem, Thirteenth Century*, p.120, argued that Henry was guilty of deception in his negotiations with Alfonso. Forey, pp.238-45, presents a strong case for thinking that Henry, far from having set his heart on Sicily, was waiting upon events. The basic charge of opportunism remains. See also above, pp.76-8.

[66] See especially Cox, pp.145-63. A comprehensive settlement was reached only in 1257. Cox, p.282.

for any war over the duchy which might break out against 'the four neighbouring kings'.[67] The reference was to the kings of France, Castile, Navarre, and Aragon. With regard to the Capetians, Earl Simon later declared that he considered Gascony to be in imminent peril in 1248 from that quarter, and in 1249 the viscount of Fronsac was indeed accused before Henry III of plotting with Alphonse of Poitiers to betray the duchy to the Capetian.[68] Of the remaining hostile kings, Theobald I of Navarre certainly lent his support to Gascon rebels in 1248, the latest episode in a long-standing conflict over rival jurisdictional claims, whilst James I of Aragon had inherited a claim to Gascony via the rights of his queen.[69] Above all, Alfonso X of Castile revived his inherited claim to Gascony on his accession in 1252. Considering the close relationship between the royal houses of France and Castile, most obviously personified by the indomitable Blanche of Castile, Louis IX's mother and regent of France, and considering the alienation and turbulence following the despatch of Earl Simon to quell the duchy in 1248, it is scarcely surprising that Alfonso's threat was taken seriously at the Plantagenet court.[70]

A Plantagenet initiative was by now quite essential. Henry decided upon a policy of appeasement towards Alfonso. This was sensible; he could not fight all his opponents at once and it was vital to prevent their combination. He was helped by Alfonso's further claim, in 1252, to the overlordship of Navarre, for this led to an alliance between James of Aragon and Theobald II of Navarre against Castile.[71] Nevertheless, the strife within Gascony remained virulent, the stance of the kings of Aragon and Navarre a cause of anxiety. In short, Henry could not be confident in 1253-4 that Gascony and its borders were secure, nor that the threat of an alliance between his Castilian, Gascon and Capetian foes had been scotched.

These uncertainties, combined with Henry's failure to recover his other French lands, help to explain the emergence of a grandiose Plantagenet foreign policy in the late 1240s and 1250s. Henry apparently considered that if he could not recover his position in France, then he would look further afield in the hope of compensation. If this was the motive, the opportunity was presented by Innocent IV's deposition of Frederick II in 1245 and the prospect of disintegration and collapse of Hohenstaufen

[67] C. Bémont, *Simon de Montfort, Earl of Leicester, 1208-1265*, trans. E.F. Jacob (Oxford, 1930), pp.75-6.

[68] *CR, 1247-51*, 343-4; Bémont, pp.75, 84.

[69] See Powicke, *Henry III*, i. 191-4, 214-15; Bémont, pp.73-4, 81-2.

[70] Powicke, *Henry III*, esp. i. 230-6, considered Alfonso's claim frivolous, intended to force Henry into negotiations, and the scare of Castilian invasion in 1253-4 a sham, which Henry turned to his advantage in England. Forey, pp.237-44, argues convincingly that Alfonso was in earnest, and that there was real fear of invasion. Negotiations were certainly more protracted and difficult than Powicke, and others, have allowed.

[71] Powicke, *Henry III*, i. 235 and n.

power in Germany and the Mediterranean. In the course of the next decade Henry would seek to grasp the constituent parts of the Hohenstaufen inheritance for members of the Plantagenet line, but Henry was not alone in seeking to capitalize on the Hohenstaufens' demise. In particular, the Capetians – more specifically, Charles of Anjou – and Alfonso X of Castile clearly recognized the possibilities. Henry, then, was under some compulsion to act through competition in the extremely volatile international situation which developed.

This is particularly apparent with regard to the kingdom of Sicily. To Richard of Cornwall the papal invitation to become king may have been akin to being offered the moon, to paraphrase Paris's famous words.[72] To Henry, however, the prospect was altogether more enticing, and he was surely aware that in August 1252 Innocent IV offered the throne to Charles of Anjou as well as Richard.[73] In the circumstances facing him, could Henry afford to stand back and watch Charles seek to acquire Sicily, especially as he was now count of Provence, well-placed to launch an invasion? Should Charles accept the offer and take Sicily his dynasty would dramatically extend its power and influence, depressing Plantagenet stock still further. Its proverbial wealth, notwithstanding Frederick II's savage exploitation in recent years, coupled with its strategic position, rendered Sicily a prize of massive potential value to whoever could seize it.[74] In 1252, then, Henry's hand was being forced by the appearance of Sicily on the open market, and he had little option but to press Richard to accept the throne, for if the Plantagenets did not grasp the nettle then the Capetians, it appeared, would. Charles took the offer very seriously and only dropped the project in late 1253, largely as a result of the prospects that opened up for him in Hainault and Flanders in the course of that year.[75]

At this stage Henry's projected crusade to the Holy Land remained apart from the matter of Sicily. The king envisaged two distinct expeditions: he would complete his crusade to the East; his brother would invade Sicily. This is made quite plain in his letter of 28 January 1253 to Innocent IV, in which Henry responded to the pope's request that he afford aid and counsel to Richard in the matter of Sicily. Henry agreed to do what he could, but on condition that the grants he had received, or would receive, to prosecute his crusade should not be compromised. His agreement, in the circumstances, to a grant of monies to Richard from the English clergy is striking evidence of his desire that Richard should

[72] On Richard's reactions, see *CM*, v.346-7, 361, 457.

[73] On the two sets of negotiations, see Berger, esp. pp.398-408.

[74] History demonstrated this, as the citizens of Brindisi impressed upon Lord Edmund in 1257. *Dip. Docs. I, 1101-1272*, no.295.

[75] Charles probably broke off negotiations in September. See R. Sternfeld, *Karl von Anjou als Graf der Provence 1245-1265* (Berlin, 1888), pp.92-6.

proceed with the Sicilian project.[76] On the very same day, as we have seen, he requested Innocent to cause the Cross to be preached throughout the west, and to publicize the date fixed three years' hence for his passage to the Holy Land.[77] However, these plans came to nothing because Richard refused Innocent's offer of Sicily and remained impervious to Henry's pressure: Henry would have to find an alternative candidate. Edmund, his younger son, was the obvious choice from among Henry's immediate kin, and when Charles of Anjou finally withdrew in late 1253, Edmund was left alone in his candidacy. By the following May the negotiations had been completed.[78]

Henry's crusading vow still remained apart from Edmund's elevation at this juncture. The papal envoy, Albert of Parma, had been empowered to commute Henry's vow in support of Edmund in 1253 but, significantly, Henry did not avail himself of the offer judging by the materials which survive.[79] By Spring 1254, however, Henry had come round to the idea: to launch both an invasion of Sicily and a crusade to the Holy Land would place impossible strains on Plantagenet resources. But when Henry accordingly sought commutation he met with an ambivalent response. On 31 May 1254 Innocent replied that Conrad's death (21 May) had removed many of the obstacles to the settlement of Sicily, and very pointedly he further observed that once Sicily had been won the Holy Land could be more easily succoured. Accordingly, he would permit commutation only with the greatest reluctance.[80] Henry should continue with his crusade to the East.

Innocent's change in heart may be explained by his reassessment of the fluid political situation in Italy and Germany. Since Frederick II's death in 1250 he had adjusted his policy to accord with the realities of the moment and the comparative strength of the papal and Hohenstaufen parties. As far as Sicily was concerned, Innocent oscillated between a policy of direct papal overlordship, when the Hohenstaufen cause appeared on the wane (with a rapprochement with Frederick's sons an option), and one which looked to external support when the papacy seemed in peril. Conrad's death in May 1254 brightened the prospects once more for direct papal overlordship; inevitably, Innocent's enthusiasm for Edmund waned as a consequence.[81] Hence, too, he could

[76] *CR, 1251-3*, 449; Rymer, I, i. 284.

[77] *CR, 1251-3*, 448; Rymer, I, i. 288.

[78] *Reg. Alexander IV*, no.3036; Rymer, I, i. 297, 301.

[79] Compare Cox, pp.242-3.

[80] Rymer, I, i. 304, 308. Compare Lunt, *Financial Relations of the Papacy with England to 1327* (Cambridge, Mass., 1939), p.265 and n.3, with Powicke, *Henry III*, i. 370-1; and see Forey, pp.238-9, 241.

[81] E. Jordan, *Les origines de la domination angevine en Italie* (Paris, 1909), remains the best survey of the background to papal policy in this context. Forey, pp.238-41; and Cox, pp.242-5, underline the ambiguity in the papal position even when Sicily was granted to Edmund in 1254.

look again to Henry to fulfil his vow in the Holy Land, and when the next Hohenstaufen, Manfred, surrendered Sicily to Innocent in October 1254, Plantagenet prospects must have seemed bleak indeed. Yet within weeks the situation changed radically again, for the accord between Innocent and Manfred collapsed and the papal forces were in utter disarray by the time of Innocent's death in December. No wonder, then, that Alexander IV turned again to Henry for support in 1255.[82] In May he authorized commutation of Henry's vow to Sicily; in October Edmund was invested as king of Sicily.[83]

The sequence of events which followed with regard to Sicily is well-known, but certain points, insofar as they touch upon Henry's crusading vow, should be stressed. First, as Forey has noticed, the proposal to commute that vow to Sicily appears originally to have been a papal initiative rather than a response to Henry's petition.[84] Second, Henry's interest appears more reasonable, his actions less incoherent, if due weight is given to the wider background of Plantagenet prospects in the west, especially in relation to the Capetians, and the changing directions of papal policy in the 1250s. Henry was not a free agent; he had to react to developments as did the pope. The pressures upon him at this time obliged him to gamble heavily, and once he had begun to play his hand it was not easy to turn back. Third, these considerations help to explain the significant fact, established by Forey, that Henry never formally commuted his vow to Sicily, notwithstanding papal permission. On the contrary, he continued to proclaim his intention of fulfilling his vow in the Holy Land once the affairs of Sicily had been satisfactorily resolved,[85] partly perhaps because it was by no means clear in 1254-5 that Sicily would indeed be granted to Edmund. If the papacy was not yet committed to a single policy, then, it may be argued, Henry also was keeping his options open. If he should be denied Sicily, then the Plantagenet position in the west required that he should look elsewhere in hope of compensation.[86]

When Sicily was put on the market by Innocent IV, and Henry decided to grasp the opportunity, other possibilities came into consideration. The

---

[82] Already, in November 1254, Innocent had sent strong and unambiguous signals to Henry, that he send a representative to take over the government of Sicily. Jordan, esp. p. xiii.

[83] Rymer, I, i. 319-20.

[84] Forey, esp. pp.243-5.

[85] Forey, pp.238-46.

[86] The negotiations with Alfonso X for the commutation of Henry's vow to North Africa may be set partly in this context. See Forey, pp.239-44. The timing of Henry's embassy to Rome in September 1254 to seek that commutation, following upon Innocent's rapprochement with Manfred, is no coincidence. See Rymer, I, i. 308, 331; *CR, 1253-4*, 275, 316.

conquest of Sicily would undoubtedly have expedited Henry's crusade to the Holy Land for logistical and strategic reasons, as Innocent IV impressed upon him in May 1254 and then the citizens of Brindisi in 1257,[87] but Henry's thoughts seemingly stretched further to contemplate the establishment of Plantagenet power in the East Mediterranean as well as Sicily. In itself the idea was not absurd: Charles of Anjou, after all, succeeded initially in his bid for a new mediterranean empire based on Sicily, and with further ambitions in the direction of Byzantium and the Latin kingdom of Jerusalem. In 1277 indeed he assumed the title of king of Jersualem after purchasing the rights of Maria of Antioch, and until the Sicilian Vespers of 1282 the Angevin presence in the Latin kingdom was a very real one. There was logic in Charles' opportunism. The Angevin conquest of Sicily followed upon the crushing defeat inflicted upon Conradin, the last Hohenstaufen ruler, at the astonishing battle of Tagliacozzo in August 1268, but Conradin was also the last of his line to be king of Jerusalem (1254-68). If Charles saw the logic in seeking to supplant the Hohenstaufen in both Sicily and Jerusalem, then so, it appears, did Henry III before him. Indeed, Henry went further in his energetic support of Richard of Cornwall's candidature for the German part of the Hohenstaufen inheritance following the premature death of William of Holland in January 1256. Richard's election as king in January 1257 took place in the face of stiff opposition from his rival, Alfonso X of Castile, backed by Louis IX, and Alfonso further envisaged the conquest of Sicily. He too approached the Hohenstaufen inheritance in Germany and Sicily from a single perspective.[88]

That Henry was at least toying with the idea of extending Plantagenet power into the East Mediterranean is suggested most strongly by the negotiations being conducted in 1256 with a view to a marriage alliance between the Plantagenets and their distant kin, the Lusignans of Cyprus. When those negotiations began is unclear, but there are indications in Henry's reply to the letters of the bishop of Bethlehem in September 1256

[87] Rymer, I, i. 304; *Dip. Docs. I, 1101-1272*, no.295. Alexander IV took the same line, seeking in 1256 to fix a new date for Henry's crusading passage and to extend the term within which Henry should despatch a force to Sicily. Rymer, I, i. 347, 348, 350; *Reg. Alexander IV*, no.1543.

[88] See Powicke, *Henry III*, i. 242-4; Forey, p.244, n.115. The Plantagenet approach to Germany was again shot through with fear concerning the Capetians and Alfonso. See, especially, Henry III's instructions to William Bonquer, his envoy in Rome, in March 1256. *CR, 1254-6*, 408-9. Richard's candidature seemingly emerged from that fear, his intentions first becoming apparent in June 1256. See, now, H-E. Hilpert, 'Richard of Cornwall's Candidature for the German Throne and the Christmas 1256 Parliament', *Journal of Medieval History*, vi (1980), 185-98.

that they had been in progress for some time.[89] They concerned the proposal that the Lord Edmund marry Queen Plaisance of Cyprus, and that her son marry Beatrice, Henry III's daughter.[90] Henry observed that he could not yet make firm reply since such a weighty matter required discussion amongst his counsellors, and as yet he had been unable to consult with all those he wished. He would make a definite response once his deliberations were complete.[91] If Henry indeed took the matter seriously then this is all the more significant because in June 1256 active consideration was being given to the proposal that Edmund marry the daughter of Manfred of Sicily and that Manfred grant the kingdom to Edmund once the union occurred.[92] Since many of the practical and financial obstacles to the Plantagenet take-over of Sicily would have been solved at a stroke, it may be presumed that some glittering prize for the Plantagenets in the East Mediterranean was in prospect.

When Henry I of Cyprus died in 1253, leaving an only child Hugh II as a minor, the regency of the kingdom fell to Plaisance in accordance with the *bailliage* rules.[93] Were Edmund to have married Plaisance he could have expected to enjoy effective exercise of the regency on her behalf, lasting until Hugh II came of age in 1267, and he could also have hoped for children by Plaisance, for she was still young, born sometime in the late 1230s. As half-brothers or half-sisters to the Lusignan king they would have provided the foundations for a lasting Plantagenet influence in Cyprus. The second marriage would have worked in the same direction, for Beatrice would have become queen consort of King Hugh II and any children would have ruled in Cyprus. There was a further possible prospect. Since 1242 the Cypriot Lusignans had acted as regents of the Latin kingdom of Jerusalem on behalf of the absentee Hohenstaufen, beginning with Queen Alice of Cyprus (1242-6) and then her son Henry I (1246-53), but on his death John of Arsur (Ibelin) was chosen as regent since Hugh II's claim was not then pressed. In due course, however, first

---

[89] In August 1255 Alexander IV pronounced against Plaisance's marriage to Balian d'Ibelin. See H.E. Mayer, 'Ibelin *versus* Ibelin: the Struggle for the Regency of Jerusalem, 1253-1258', *Proceedings of the American Philosophical Society*, cxxii (1978), 46. Negotiations with Henry probably began around that time.

[90] *CR, 1254-6*, 445-6. Plaisance's nuncio Roland brought the letters. *CR, 1254-6*, 354; *CLR, 1251-60*, 319. Henry's reply perhaps suggests that Plaisance initiated the proposals, but it is impossible to be sure: no further instruments survive.

[91] A similar reply was sent to 'the white cardinal', apparently Master John Tolet, an English Cistercian then cardinal-priest of S. Lorenzo in Lucina. *CM*, iv. 306, 354, 578-9. This suggests that the negotiations were supported at the highest levels in Rome. Is it coincidence that in September 1256 Alexander IV sought a new date for Henry's crusading passage? Above, n.87.

[92] *Dip. Docs. I, 1101-1272*, nos.282-3; Rymer, I, i. 360.

[93] I am indebted to Dr. Peter Edbury for his information and suggestions regarding what follows concerning Cyprus.

Plaisance and then other kin acted on Hugh's behalf as regent after 1258, and ultimately in 1268-9 the Lusignans inherited the throne of Jerusalem upon the extinction of the Hohenstaufen. In 1256 contemporaries could not have been able to predict many, perhaps any, of these developments. Nevertheless, at the time of the marriage proposals the Cypriot Lusignans had a stake in the Latin kingdom, and Henry III must have known it. He surely knew, too, that there were definite opportunities for a determined outside power following the collapse of the Hohenstaufen administration in 1242 and subsequent developments.[94] Mayer has observed that a power vacuum 'without precedence or parallel in the history of the kingdom' developed after the death of Henry I in 1253, the return to France of Louis IX in 1254, and then the death of Conrad. His heir, Conradin, was aged only two in 1254 and would not come of age until 1267; in any case, Hohenstaufen influence in the east was negligible by the early 1250s.[95] Moreover, the Crown of Jerusalem was immensely prestigious, and in the 1250s it remained lucrative. Richard of Cornwall told Matthew Paris that Acre alone was worth £50,000 of silver per annum.[96] Richard's brother was surely aware of this estimate; it compared well with Henry's ordinary revenue as king of England.

Queen Plaisance's consideration of a marriage alliance in 1256 suggests that she thought it likely that the Plantagenets would indeed seek to become a mediterranean power and that Henry's crusade might shortly occur.[97] Her thinking was echoed by the hopes of others in Outremer concerning Henry's crusade. Following Louis IX's departure for France in April 1254, all turned to Henry as the next prospective crusade leader, their hopes forcefully expressed in the letter sent in the name of the community of Jerusalem in September 1254 imploring Henry to accelerate his passage.[98] But the Cypriot marriage negotiations suggest further that Plaisance had more particular objectives in mind concerning Henry, especially since this is the earliest evidence for the Cypriot Lusignans seeking to intermarry with any Western royal house. Moreover, the fact that the intended partners were Plantagenets was tantamount to a major diplomatic volte-face since Henry I of Cyprus had been a leading member of the party opposed to the Hohenstaufen in the east, and the Plantagenets had been identified with the Hohenstaufen

[94] P. Jackson, 'The End of Hohenstaufen Rule in Syria', *BIHR*, lix (1986), 23-6, establishes 1242 as the most likely date.

[95] Mayer, esp. pp.42-3.

[96] Matthew Paris, 'Itinéraines de Londres à Jérusalem' in *Itinéraires à Jérusalem et Descriptions de la Terre Sainte*, ed. H. Michelant and G. Raynaud (Société de l'Orient Latin, iii, 1882), p.137.

[97] Considering the logistics and distance, it is exceedingly unlikely that Plaisance would have sought to negotiate with Henry unless there was real prospect that he might materially affect the situation in the Mediterranean.

[98] 'Burton', pp.368-9; Rymer, I, i. 308.

because of their connections.[99]

When Henry I died in 1253 the claim of his infant son, Hugh II, to the regency of Jerusalem was not then presented and the Lusignans lost their tenure of the office. Mayer has argued that Hugh was deliberately excluded, first by John of Arsur, who married his son Balian to Queen Plaisance shortly after Easter 1254, it appears, in the hope either of preventing Hugh from pressing his claim or of benefiting otherwise from the relationship, then by his kinsman and supposed rival John of Jaffa, who replaced him as regent in August 1254.[100] According to Mayer, John of Jaffa then sought to undermine the marriage of Plaisance and Balian since that would strike at John of Arsur's position, and Alexander IV duly ruled against the union in August 1255 on the grounds of consanguinity.[101] The political situation remains very unclear and Mayer's arguments in this connection have to be regarded as speculative.[102] Nevertheless, annulment suited Plaisance's purpose of loosening the Ibelin hold upon the regency, but if she was to reassert the Lusignan tenure of the office she would need powerful support to counter the immense Ibelin influence. Her brother, Bohemund VI of Antioch, who sided with her when she sought annulment, duly came to her aid.[103] In February 1258, at Acre, he presented Hugh's claim to be heir to the kingdom and Plaisance's claim to the *bailliage* by virtue of Hugh's minority.[104] But it looks further as if both had previously looked to Henry III's projected crusade as an instrument to be used to their advantage in this business. It cannot be entirely coincidence that Bohemund's only known request for Henry's aid was despatched in May 1255,[105] and within months the Cypriot marriage proposals were formulated. If Henry indeed contemplated the establishment of Plantagenet power in the east Mediterranean then his crusade, in conjunction with the Cypriot marriages, would be crucial. Equally, if Plaisance and Bohemund could secure his support on crusade, then the Lusignan claim to Jerusalem, upon which Plantagenet prospects partially rested, would be altogether

---

[99] In the Holy Land itself, Richard of Cornwall had recently been associated closely with the imperial party during his crusade of 1240-1.

[100] Mayer, esp. pp.43-7.

[101] Mayer, pp.46-7.

[102] See especially P.W. Edbury, 'John of Ibelin's Title to the County of Jaffa and Ascalon', *EHR*, xcviii (1983), 115-33; Mayer's reply, 'John of Jaffa, his Opponents and his Fiefs', *Proc. American Phil. Soc.*, cxxviii (1984), 134-63; J.S.C. Riley-Smith, *The Feudal Nobility and the Kingdom of Jerusalem, 1174-1277* (London, 1973), esp. pp.215-16, on the regency.

[103] Riley-Smith, p.216.

[104] G.F. Hill, *A History of Cyprus* (Cambridge, 1940-52), ii. 150-1. In February 1258, significantly, Alexander IV again pronounced against Plaisance's marriage to Balian.

[105] 'Burton', pp.369-71; Rymer, I, i. 321.

more easily realized. Henry's failure to take up the papal offer to commute his vow to Sicily, at first sight puzzling, and his continuing proclamation of intent to depart for the Holy Land, become more comprehensible. With Edmund duly installed in Sicily, and with Plantagenet influence established in Cyprus too, the Holy Land might indeed be the more easily secured.

In the event the marriage alliance with the Cypriot Lusignans did not materialize, nor did the proposed union between Edmund and Manfred's daughter. Henry did not set out on crusade and Edmund was not enthroned in Sicily. None of Henry's ambitions concerning the Hohenstaufen inheritance was realized, although Richard of Cornwall did what he could to establish himself in Germany, but that, here, is not the point. Out of Henry's failure to restore the Plantagenet inheritance in France was born the perceived necessity to compensate for that failure elsewhere. It is most unlikely that Henry started with the precise intention of supplanting the Hohenstaufen and gathering up their inheritance in Plantagenet hands, but as events unfolded after Frederick II's deposition in 1245, and as opportunities opened up in different directions, something of a grand design appears to have emerged, slowly and piecemeal, under the force of competition from others, notably the Capetians and Alfonso X of Castile. The new Plantagenet empire, so envisaged, would be immeasurably more powerful than that of old. It would dominate both eastern and western Christendom, and the Capetians, to return to the old rivalry, would be totally overshadowed. If Matthew Paris can be credited, Henry even regarded the establishment of this new polity as a means to the restoration of the former Plantagenet greatness in France. He reports, *sub anno* 1255, that Henry considered that his French lands could be regained, by force if necessary, 'because between Apulia and England, France would be crushed as if between two millstones'.[106]

Henry's crusading vow was taken at the point when the question of the fate of the Hohenstaufen inheritance was emerging as the central issue in the power politics of Christendom, both east and west. It may even be that the matter of the crusade was an unwelcome distraction in 1250, partly forced upon the king by his compulsion to match Louis IX. In the course of the next few years, that vow, and Henry's projected crusade, took on a very different complexion, emerging as just one element of an elaborate foreign policy, itself intended both to secure the prize of the Hohenstaufen inheritance and to turn the tables on the Capetians. The feud between John and Philip Augustus over the fate of the Plantagenet inheritance in France, continued under Henry III and Louis IX, did not simply die out in the 1250s, as is sometimes suggested. On the contrary, the stakes were

---

[106] *CM*, v.516.

raised and the frame of reference extended as Henry, or his advisers, conceived a much more ambitious strategy to curb the apparently inexorable growth in Capetian influence, both within and beyond the French kingdom, whilst seeking to secure for the Plantagenets a place in the sun. With regard to these wider schemes Henry found support and encouragement from Pope Alexander IV. He energetically backed Henry's bid to place Edmund on the throne of Sicily, and plainly welcomed the vision of a meaningful Plantagenet presence in Germany, Cyprus, and the Holy Land. It was not just diplomatic niceties which led him to observe in 1255 that 'the royal family of England which we regard with particular affection . . . we wish to exalt above the other kings and princes of the world'.[107]

The stakes were very high indeed, for both parties, but who was the pawn and who the queen on this chessboard? Treharne's decisive declaration that 'everyone except Henry himself could see that the Papacy was merely using England as a catspaw for the overthrow of the Hohenstaufen', is untenable.[108] The relationship between Henry and the papacy in the 1250s was altogether more complex, and so was the conduct as well as substance of Henry III's foreign relations. On hindsight, and with knowledge of the events of 1258, it is easy to denounce Henry's schemes, but we should at least seek to understand what it was that he sought to achieve and why. Whether his goals were attainable is another matter, especially in the light of his circumstances in England, but even then we must remember that Henry was not just a king of England. He was a Plantagenet, with his dynastic honour to protect, a vendetta to settle with the Capetians, and a tarnished reputation to reverse, both his own and his dynasty's. The disasters of 1204, 1214, 1230 and 1242 were painfully fresh in the 1250s, but a new Plantagenet empire in the Mediterranean might yet win the day. Henry's capacity to play for high stakes, yet lose, is truly remarkable.

---

[107] 'Burton', pp.339-40.
[108] Treharne, p.50.

Chapter 7

Anglo-Welsh Relations, 1066-1282

A.D. Carr

Wales is England's oldest neighbour. Anglo-Welsh political relations began when English invaders first made contact with native Britons and even today the presence of members of Plaid Cymru in the house of Commons and the fact that three successive leaders of Her Majesty's Opposition have represented Welsh constituencies reflect their enduring complexity. But the relationship of the crown with Welsh rulers came to an end with the final extinction of Welsh independence at the hands of Edward I in 1282-3. Between 1066 and 1282 this relationship underwent changes which reflected the changing nature of both English kingship and Welsh politics. Unlike relations with Scotland or France, Anglo-Welsh relations were not at first a matter of bilateral dealings between two kings or two kingdoms. By the middle of the tenth century all England lay under a single kingship but this was far from being the case in Wales. When William of Normandy became king of England there were four main kingdoms, Gwynedd in the north, Powys in the centre, Deheubarth in the south-west and Morgannwg in the south-east, each with its own interests and priorities.[1] Wales was not a single political entity; it was, rather, a political world, 'not so much a nation as an association'.[2] There was a legal and linguistic unity but it was not until the thirteenth century that any real sense of national identity was to emerge.[3]

From the time of Alfred Welsh kings had submitted to the overlordship of their West Saxon neighbours and it was this claim to overlordship that William inherited.[4] William regarded himself as the legitimate king of the

---

[1] The development of the political geography of Wales is discussed by Wendy Davies, *Wales in the Early Middle Ages* (Leicester, 1982), pp.102-12.

[2] W.L. Warren, *Henry II* (London, 1973), p.156.

[3] R.R. Davies, 'Law and National Identity in Thirteenth-Century Wales' in R.R. Davies *et al.*, eds., *Welsh Society and Nationhood* (Cardiff, 1984), pp.51-69.

[4] Davies, *Wales in the Early Middle Ages*, pp.112-4; H.R. Loyn, 'Wales and England in the Tenth Century: the Context of the Athelstan Charters', *W[elsh] H[istory] R[eview]* x (1980-1), 283-301; F. Barlow, *Edward the Confessor* (London, 1970), pp.201-11; A.J. Roderick, 'The Feudal Relation between the English Crown and the Welsh princes', *History*, xxxvii (1952), 202-3; M. Chibnall, *Anglo-Norman England, 1066-1166* (Oxford, 1986), p.44; J. Le Patourel, *The Norman Empire* (Oxford, 1976), pp.57-67, 160.

English but there was no intention of extending the sphere of conquest beyond the borders of England. What he sought above all was stability; the only way to secure this was to seek out Welsh rulers with whom agreements could be made and formal relations established. This may explain his visit to St. David's in 1081; here he may have met Rhys ap Tewdwr of Deheubarth, received his submission and come to an agreement with him.[5] *Domesday Book* records that in 1086 a certain 'Riset', almost certainly Rhys ap Tewdwr, was paying an annual farm of £40 for south Wales and this may have been the result of the meeting; for the king this secured stability, while for Rhys it meant that no Norman adventurer would dare threaten him.[6]

Welsh support for English rebels beween 1067 and 1069 may have led William to establish earldoms based on Hereford, Shrewsbury and Chester, the main strategic centres on the border.[7] This led in turn to the extension of Norman power into adjacent parts of Wales and brought them into Welsh politics; in 1072 the Welsh chronicler recorded the death of Maredudd ab Owain of Deheubarth at the hands of Caradog ap Gruffydd of Gwent and the 'French'.[8] This is the first Welsh reference to the Normans and it shows them becoming involved in Welsh politics on Welsh terms, becoming just one more element in an already complicated political pattern. There were similar forward movements from Shrewsbury and Chester; by 1078 the Normans may have reached Degannwy on the Conwy estuary.[9] But the border earls and their followers do not seem to have enjoyed unfettered freedom of action; the immunity which Rhys ap Tewdwr enjoyed during William's lifetime suggests that the presence of a Welsh ruler recognised by the king of England precluded any attempt at conquest by an ambitious Norman. When Bleddyn ap Cynfyn of Gwynedd, who had submitted to Edward the Confessor in 1063, was killed in 1075, there was a struggle for power. In such circumstances, following the death of a ruler recognised by the crown, an outsider might join in and this is what Robert of Rhuddlan, a member of a notable Norman family, may have done. In *Domesday Book* he is described as holding north Wales of the king at a farm of £40, which may indicate that he was recognised by William as ruler of Gwynedd by right of conquest.[10] But such men as Robert could only move into lands where there was no legitimate authority recognised by the crown; although Wales lay outside the kingdom of England, the Norman invader was, in

---

[5] J.E. Lloyd, *History of Wales* (London, 1911), ii. 394; L.H. Nelson, *The Normans in South Wales, 1070-1171* (Austin, 1966), pp.34-41.

[6] *Domesday Book*, i. 179a.

[7] R.R. Davies, *Conquest, Coexistence and Change: Wales 1063-1415* (Oxford, 1987), pp.27-8.

[8] *Brut y Tywysogyon (Pen. 20 version)*, ed. Thomas Jones (Cardiff, 1952), p.16.

[9] Davies, *Conquest, Coexistence and Change*, pp.31-2; Le Patourel, *Norman Empire*, p.64.

[10] *Domesday Book*, i. 269a.

the last resort, the king's subject and his was the ultimate overlordship.[11]

With the death of William the Conqueror in 1087 the understanding with Rhys ap Tewdwr came to an end and Rhys was killed in action in 1093; the result was a rapid Norman advance into Deheubarth.[12] The Norman penetration of Wales which really began in the last decade of the eleventh century was largely a matter of private enterprise and its result was the creation of the March; the term does not lend itself to easy definition but it may be described as that part of Wales which had come into the hands of Anglo-Norman lords by right of conquest.[13] In this activity the king took little direct part, although his authority was always present in the background. William Rufus did lead two abortive campaigns against Gwynedd in 1095 and 1097, following the Welsh revolt of 1094, but the invasion of 1098, which forced the rulers of Gwynedd and Powys to flee to Ireland for a time, was led by the earls of Chester and Shrewsbury.[14] But Rufus's successor Henry I was one of the most successful and masterful of all English kings. In Wales he sought control rather than conquest and had little difficulty in imposing his will.[15] After the fall of Robert of Bellême, earl of Shrewsbury, in 1102 he tried to build up Powys as a strong Welsh client kingdom on the border but its ruler, Cadwgan ap Bleddyn, lacked the strength to keep his ambitious kinsmen under control and Powys collapsed in dynastic struggle.[16] The revolt of Rhys ap Tewdwr's son Gruffydd in Deheubarth in 1116 failed because of his inability to capture castles, while Gruffydd ap Cynan of Gwynedd kept a low profile as he consolidated his power. Nevertheless, Henry found it necessary to lead two expeditions to Wales, against Gruffydd ap Cynan in 1114 and against Maredudd ap Bleddyn of Powys in 1121; the impact made by the first campaign is shown by the fact that, when Gruffydd ap Rhys sought help from Gwynedd, Gruffydd ap Cynan would have handed him over to the king, had he not taken sanctuary in a church.[17]

Henry treated Welsh rulers with generosity when they came to his court but at the same time he emphasised their subordination.[18] And he

[11]   Davies, *Conquest, Coexistence and Change*, pp.93-4.

[12]   Lloyd, *Hist. Wales*, ii. 400-1; Nelson, *Normans in South Wales*, pp.82-94.

[13]   The origin and nature of Marcher lordship have engendered considerable debate; see particularly J.G. Edwards, 'The Normans and the Welsh March', *Proc. British Academy*, xlii (1956), 155-77 and R.R. Davies, 'Kings, Lords and Liberties in the March of Wales, 1066-1272', *TRHS*, 5th ser., xxix (1979), 41-61.

[14]   Lloyd, *Hist. Wales*, ii. 403-11; Nelson, *Normans in South Wales*, pp.113-4.

[15]   R.R. Davies, 'Henry I and Wales' in H. Mayr-Harting and R.I. Moore, eds., *Studies in Medieval History Presented to R.H.C. Davis* (1985), pp.132-47.

[16]   The details may be found in *Brut y Tywysogyon (Pen. 20 version)*, pp.23-37; see also Lloyd, *Hist. Wales*, ii. 415-22.

[17]   Davies, 'Henry I and Wales', pp.141-2; Lloyd, *Hist. Wales*, ii. 463-5; *Brut y Tywysogyon (Pen. 20 version)*, pp.39-40.

[18]   Davies, 'Henry I and Wales', p.139.

acted no differently with Norman lords in the March, where he brought in new men of his own creation.[19] He had his own territorial power-base in the south-west; by 1109 a royal castle had been built at Carmarthen and this became the first centre of English royal authority in Wales. It was not long before revenue was being collected there for the crown.[20] Henry I dominated Wales, both native and Anglo-Norman, as he dominated England and Normandy; his reign shows just how effectively the crown could control native Welsh rulers without resorting to conquest. It is hardly surprising that the Welsh chronicler described him as 'the man . . . against whom no one could be of avail save God himself'.[21] To the Welsh Henry was more than a king; he was a cosmic force.

But the events which followed Henry's death on 1 December 1135 showed very clearly that royal overlordship and control in Wales depended entirely on the skill and personality of the king; there was no kind of institutional framework to sustain it. The new king, Stephen, faced with civil war in England, was in no position to deal with the war which had erupted and after two abortive expeditions he decided, according to one chronicler, that the subjugation of the Welsh would cost too much.[22] His reign, therefore, saw the collapse of that power and authority which had been built up by Henry; to be successful in Welsh politics an English king had to be in complete control of the situation in England.

Stephen was succeeded in 1154 by Henry II. For the new king stability was still of prime importance, particularly since his dominions extended from the Pyrenees to the Cheviots. Because of his preoccupations in France and England he was unable to turn his attention to Wales until 1157 when his intervention was precipitated by the advance of Gruffydd ap Cynan's son Owain Gwynedd into the territory between the Clwyd and the Dee and the consequent threat to Chester whose young earl was a royal ward; it was also necessary to remind Owain that he was subject to the overlordship of the crown. Henry's campaign came near to disaster on more than one occasion but, faced with a major display of royal power, Owain withdrew, gave hostages and did homage.[23] This was the first recorded occasion on which a Welsh ruler actually did homage to the king of England and thus entered into a feudal relationship; the event has been described as 'the beginning of the end of Welsh independence, if not the

---

[19] *Ibid.*, p.146.

[20] *Ibid.*, p.144. Henry's position in south-west Wales is discussed in detail by Ifor Rowlands, 'The Making of the March: Aspects of the Norman Settlement in Dyfed' in R. Allen Brown, ed., *Proceedings of the Battle Conference on Anglo-Norman Studies*, iii (Woodbridge, 1981), 143-56; Lloyd, *Hist. Wales*, ii. 427-8.

[21] *Brut y Tywysogyon (Pen. 20 version)*, p.42.

[22] *Gesta Stephani*, ed. R.C. Sewell (1846), pp.10-13.

[23] Davies, *Conquest, Coexistence and Change*, p.51; Warren, *Henry II*, p.161; Lloyd, *Hist. Wales*, ii. 496-500.

very end itself.[24] Thus Henry II's first campaign in Wales, if inconclusive in military terms, was politically a success.

Henry was equally active in south Wales where Rhys, the youngest son of Gruffydd ap Rhys, had by 1155 gained control of Deheubarth and was pressing hard on his marcher neighbours. Two expeditions were led against him in 1158, one in 1159 and one in 1163; three of these were led by the king himself. Each time Rhys submitted but as soon as the royal armies left he resumed his activities. Eventually, after his submission at Pencader in 1163, he was taken to England as a prisoner, but the removal of the most powerful ruler in south Wales was a recipe for instability and the only answer was to reinstate him; first, however, he was summoned to Woodstock, along with Owain Gwynedd and Malcolm IV of Scotland to do homage.[25] A year later the irrepressible Rhys was active again, joined this time by Owain Gwynedd, and Henry now decided on a campaign to deal with the Welsh once and for all; the stability and order which could not be secured by agreement were to be imposed by force of arms. In the face of this threat the Welsh joined forces under the leadership of Owain Gwynedd and in July 1165 the royal army set out from Oswestry; its fate is well-known.[26] Driven back by summer storms, Henry learned his lesson; the immense campaign which would be required to impose his will on the Welsh was not a practical proposition and he never again sought a military solution.

A drastic reappraisal of royal policy was required, especially in the wake of the king's isolation following the murder of Thomas Becket and the Anglo-Norman invasion of Ireland, largely mounted from south-west Wales. Henry was suspicious of the Norman settlement in Ireland which gave some of the invaders a new power-base independent of his control.[27] This may have led to the cultivation of Rhys, now the leading ruler in Wales following the death of Owain Gwynedd in 1170, and the other Welsh magnates to create a new balance of power. When Henry crossed to Ireland in 1171 he met Rhys twice on the way and again at Laugharne on his return; Rhys had already handed over 24 hostages and paid a tribute of horses and cattle, as well as having his territorial gains confirmed, and at Laugharne he was appointed justiciar or royal representative in south Wales. The appointment may well have involved the delegation to him of the king's authority over native rulers with the addition, perhaps, of a measure of authority over the king's Anglo-Norman subjects.[28] Rhys was

[24] S.B. Chrimes, *King Edward I's Policy for Wales* (Cardiff, 1969), p.6.

[25] Lloyd, *Hist. Wales,* ii. 506-7, 510-14; Warren, *Henry II,* p.162.

[26] Lloyd, *Hist. Wales,* ii. 515-8; *Brut y Tywysogyon (Pen. 20 version),* pp.63-4.

[27] The point was first made by Lloyd, *Hist. Wales,* ii. 537; see also W.L. Warren, 'The Interpretation of Twelfth-Century Irish History', *Historical Studies,* vii (1969),,12-16.

[28] *Brut y Tywysogyon (Pen. 20 version),* pp.66-8; Lloyd, *Hist. Wales,* ii. 540-3; Davies, *Conquest, Coexistence and Change,* p.54; Warren, *Henry II,* pp.164-7; Le Patourel, *Norman Empire,* p.213.

the dominant Welsh ruler; he was also one of the great feudatories of the Angevin empire, moving in a cosmopolitan milieu.

From now on Henry and Rhys worked together. When Henry's sons rebelled in 1173 Rhys sent one of his own sons to his aid. In the summer of 1175 he led several of the southern rulers to Gloucester to make their peace with the king.[29] In May 1177 there was a meeting of all the Welsh rulers at Geddington, where they swore fealty, and in the same month their leaders assembled at Oxford where Rhys and Dafydd ab Owain Gwynedd did homage and were granted fiefs by the king.[30] This reflects that polarisation of political authority in Wales which had by now developed; these assemblies may suggest a new approach to royal supremacy in Wales, best described as overlordship by common consent. Henry needed to reassert his authority after his sons' rebellion and was seeking at the same time to display his overlordship within the British Isles; Rhys, for his part, was able to guarantee stability and keep the peace.[31]

But although this relationship ensured stability it was a personal one which could not survive the death of one of the parties.[32] Rhys had gone out of his way to work with the king, as was shown by the welcome he extended to Archbishop Baldwin of Canterbury in 1188, although he knew very well that Baldwin's purpose was to display the authority of Canterbury over the Welsh church.[33] But once Henry died in 1189 war broke out, caused probably by the insensitive handling of Rhys by the new king, Richard I.[34] Rhys himself died in 1197. He had shown great political skill; peace had depended on trust and personal friendship and he and Henry had shown that equilibrium was possible. But, once again, there was no formal structure to sustain Anglo-Welsh relations at this level, apart from the homage of individual rulers. And new men were emerging. In 1199 John ascended the throne and his reign marks the opening of a new chapter in the relationship. From the early thirteenth century there was an increasing interest in Wales on the part of the crown which was by now the only power strong enough to hold the Welsh in check.[35] Under

[29] *Brut y Tywysogyon (Pen. 20 version)*, pp.70-1; Warren, *Henry II*, p.167; Lloyd, *Hist. Wales*, ii. 544-5; Davies, *Conquest, Coexistence and Change*, p.290.

[30] Lloyd, *Hist. Wales*, ii. 552-4; Warren, *Henry II*, pp. 168-9; Davies, *Conquest, Coexistence and Change*, p.291; M. Richter, 'The Political and Institutional Background to National Consciousness in Medieval Wales', in T.W. Moody, ed., *Nationality and the Pursuit of National Independence* (Belfast, 1978), pp.41-2, 45-6; J. Beverley Smith, *Llywelyn ap Gruffudd, Tywysog Cymru* (Cardiff, 1986), p.22 (an English version of this important book is in preparation).

[31] Davies, *Conquest, Coexistence and Change*, pp.290-1.

[32] *Ibid.*, p. 292.

[33] J. Conway Davies, ed., *Episcopal Acts Relating to Welsh Dioceses, 1066-1272* (Cardiff, 1946-53), i. 210.

[34] Lloyd, *Hist. Wales*, ii. 573-5.

[35] Davies, *Conquest, Coexistence and Change*, p.290.

John it began to take a more positive and more aggressive role in Welsh affairs; the new king knew the country better than any other English ruler, before or after, having been lord of Glamorgan by right of his first wife and having been involved in Wales in the early 1190s.[36]

By 1200 most of Gwynedd was ruled by Llywelyn ab Iorwerth, one of the grandsons of Owain Gwynedd, while southern Powys was in the hands of Gwenwynwyn ab Owain Cyfeiliog. Both rulers were ambitious and John was able to take advantage of their rivalry. In September 1199 he took Llywelyn under his protection but in the following December he confirmed Gwenwynwyn's territorial gains.[37] Then he swung back to Llywelyn and on 11 July 1201 a treaty was made with the prince of north Wales.[38] This was the first written treaty between an English king and a Welsh ruler; in it the prince *venit ad servitium Regis* and he and the magnates of Wales swore fealty to John. He also undertook to do homage on the King's return from France. He would retain his territorial gains and could choose if disputes over land would be settled by English or Welsh law. In 1204 Llywelyn married John's illegitimate daughter Joan; like his uncle Dafydd ab Owain Gwynedd, who had married Henry II's half-sister Emma, he saw the advantage of an alliance with the house of Plantagenet, even on the wrong side of the blanket.[39]

Llywelyn remained in favour although he had invaded Powys while Gwenwynwyn was in royal custody at Shrewsbury in 1208, having tried to take advantage of the fall of the most powerful marcher lord, William de Braose, with an unsuccessful foray into the middle March; the ruler of Powys was not released until he had surrendered hostages and sworn to serve the king for ever.[40] Llywelyn may have done homage to his father-in-law at Woodstock in October 1209 and in the same year he joined John's expedition to Scotland, being probably present when the king and William the Lion made a treaty at Norham.[41] This was an interesting and unique event in Anglo-Welsh relations; it was the only occasion on which a prince of Gwynedd joined the king of England on a military expedition outside Wales and it indicates what John must have hoped to gain by marrying his daughter to a Welsh ruler.

But relations began to deteriorate in 1210, possibly because Llywelyn may have allied himself with the disgraced William de Braose during John's absence in Ireland.[42] On his return John decided to move against

---

[36] *Ibid.*, p.293; Lloyd, *Hist. Wales*, ii. 614.

[37] Lloyd, *Hist. Wales*, ii. 614.

[38] *Foedera*, I, i. 84; Lloyd, *Hist. Wales*, ii. 615.

[39] A.J. Roderick, 'Marriage and Politics in Wales, 1066-1282', *WHR*, iv (1968-9), 14; Lloyd, *Hist. Wales*, ii. 551, 616-7.

[40] *Foedera*, I, i. 101, 102.

[41] Lloyd, *Hist. Wales*, ii. 622-3.

[42] *Ibid.*, 631-2.

the Welsh prince, mobilising the other Welsh rulers, who probably feared his ambitions, against him. In May 1211 the royal army advanced from Chester; it was forced to withdraw because of a lack of supplies, but a lightning campaign in July took the king as far as Bangor and Llywelyn had to submit.[43] The terms were harsh; they included the cession of the lands beween the Conwy and the Dee, the surrender of hostages, including Llywelyn's own son Gruffydd, and a heavy tribute of horses and cattle.[44] The prince also agreed that if he had no son by Joan his lands would escheat to the king. This was royal overlordship with a vengeance; John had gone further than any of his predecessors and had attained the strongest position yet held by the crown in Wales.

John had gone too far. The other rulers had expected him to withdraw, having dealt with Llywelyn, but royal lieutenants were appointed in their territories and castles built.[45] They began to make their peace with the prince and war was soon resumed. John's response was to plan a major campaign to deal with Llywelyn once and for all, probably with a view to the final solution of conquest; this would free his hands for the recovery of Normandy and Anjou. By now the Welsh had papal and French support and John's campaign had to be called off; it was rumoured that Joan had warned her father of a baronial plot to kidnap him.[46] Philip Augustus, threatened by the alliance of John and the Emperor Otto IV, had offered Llywelyn an alliance but papal backing was withdrawn following the king's submission to Innocent III in 1213.[47] The French victory at Bouvines in 1214 led to a baronial revolt in England, supported by Llywelyn, and at Runnymede, on 15 June 1215, John was forced to grant Magna Carta.

Three clauses in the charter related to Wales; they included provision for the settlement of territorial disputes, for the immediate return of all hostages, including Llywelyn's son, and for the return of all the charters delivered to the king in 1211.[48] A series of campaigns in south Wales now brought much of the country under Llywelyn's control and at Aberdyfi in 1216 the other Welsh rulers may have done him homage.[49] In England John's death in the same year was followed by civil war and Llywelyn and Alexander II of Scotland were invited to a meeting at Northampton to

[43] *Ibid.*, 634-6; *Brut y Tywysogyon (Pen. 20 version)*, pp.85-6.

[44] J. Beverley Smith, 'Magna Carta and the Charters of the Welsh princes', *EHR*, xcix (1984), 344-62.

[45] Lloyd, *Hist. Wales*, ii. 636; Davies, *Conquest, Coexistence and Change*, p.296.

[46] W.L. Warren, *King John* (London, 1966), pp.219-20.

[47] Llywelyn's letter to Philip Augustus is printed and discussed by R.F. Treharne, 'The Franco-Welsh Treaty of Alliance in 1212', *B[ulletin of the] B[oard of] C[eltic] S[tudies]*, xviii (1958), 60-75.

[48] For these clauses see Stubbs, *Select Charters*, 9th edn. (Oxford, 1913), p.300.

[49] *Brut y Tywysogyon (Pen. 20 version)*, p.92.

choose a new king.[50] There was no response; both men must have realised that their presence would be tantamount to admitting their subjection to the English crown. The civil war ended with the treaty of Lambeth of 1217; a clause offered inclusion to the Welsh but the terms were unacceptable, including as they did the surrender of all recent territorial gains.[51] However, in March 1218 Llywelyn came to Worcester, did homage and obtained a cessation of hostilities.[52] It is significant that he came on his own; his object was to do homage on behalf of all the Welsh rulers but as far as the crown was concerned they were his allies, not his vassals, and he was their leader, not their lord.[53]

The main aim of the princes of Gwynedd from now on was to secure recognition by the crown in a treaty of the predominance they had achieved in Wales. Llywelyn had imposed his own overlordship on his fellow-rulers; the next step was to have it accepted by the king of England so that he would render homage on behalf of all the Welsh lords and they in turn would do homage to him. On his death a similar position would be held by his successor. Such a treaty would give the single Welsh principality the princes were trying to create a constitutional basis; it would provide a permanent relationship with the crown and put Anglo-Welsh relations on a secure footing. Although he never used the title, Llywelyn ab Iorwerth was, to all intents and purposes, prince of Wales. For its part the crown wished to retain the direct overlordship of individual rulers; nevertheless Henry III was, on a number of occasions, interested in a permanent settlement, although his policy varied according to the strength of his position at any given time.

The Peace of Worcester secured for Llywelyn the position he was to retain for the rest of his life. But his supremacy was only a personal one; he needed a treaty and he also needed to secure the undisputed succession of Dafydd, his son by Joan. At a council held at Shrewsbury in 1220, in the presence of the papal legate and the justiciar, Dafydd was recognised as his heir.[54] Two years later this recognition was confirmed by the pope at Llywelyn's request and in 1226 Dafydd was recognised by the other Welsh rulers.[55] In 1229 he did homage as his father's heir, although Henry III was careful not to commit himself to any acceptance of the permanence of Llywelyn's position.[56] Llywelyn was always punctilious about his status; in 1224, on being told by the king not to receive the fugitive Falkes de Breauté, he replied that, as an independent ruler like the king of Scotland,

[50] A.A.M. Duncan, *Scotland: the Making of the Kingdom* (Edinburgh, 1978), p.523.
[51] J. Beverley Smith, 'The Treaty of Lambeth, 1217', *EHR*, xciv (1979), 578.
[52] *Foedera*, I, i. 150.
[53] Smith, *Llywelyn ap Gruffudd*, pp.22-3.
[54] *Foedera*, I, i. 159.

he could receive whoever he liked (although he had undertaken at Worcester not to receive the king's enemies).[57]

The period after 1218 was not one of uninterrupted peace. There were three royal campaigns in Wales, in 1223, 1228 and 1231, all under the auspices of the justiciar, Hubert de Burgh, who in 1224 began the building of a new castle at Montgomery, the first of the great stone fortresses to be constructed in Wales by the crown.[58] All three campaigns were inconclusive and from 1223 there were successive proposals for negotiations to secure a permanent settlement. The 1231 campaign ended with a truce which was to be renewed regularly for the rest of Llywelyn's life, although the prince was involved in the revolt of Richard Marshal in 1233-4.[59] In March 1234 a truce was agreed at Brocton through the good offices of the archbishop of Canterbury in the hope that a settlement would follow.[60] On 21 June of the same year an agreement was reached at Myddle in Shropshire, but the pact of Myddle was no more than a truce for two years confirming the *status quo ante bellum*.[61] From 1232 onwards there is a substantial body of correspondence relating to Anglo-Welsh relations but Henry seems only to have been interested in negotiations when his own position was weak, while Llywelyn never gave his envoys plenary powers.[62] According to Matthew Paris he offered the king a treaty in 1237, even offering military service; the suggestion is that, because of his age and the stroke he suffered in that year, he could not contain the increasing restlessness of his elder son Gruffydd.[63] There is no other record of this offer.

Early in 1238 the Welsh lords were summoned to the abbey of Strata Florida to do homage to Dafydd; this event may have been intended to mark the abdication of the old and ailing Llywelyn and the investiture of his son.[64] Henry forbade the lords to do homage and wrote to Llywelyn and Dafydd in similar terms.[65] His view was that homage was due only to him; while he was prepared to accept the personal position which Llywelyn had attained, he was not prepared to countenance the unilateral

---

[57] J.G. Edwards, ed., *Calendar of Ancient Correspondence concerning Wales* (Cardiff, 1935), pp. 24-5.

[58] For Hubert's activities in Wales see R.F. Walker, 'Hubert de Burgh and Wales', *EHR*, lxxxvii (1972), 465-94.

[59] *Foedera*, I, i. 201; Lloyd, *Hist. Wales*, ii. 678-80.

[60] *CPR, 1232-1247*, 43.

[61] *Ibid.*, 59.

[62] Smith, *Llywelyn ap Gruffudd*, pp.26-7.

[63] M. Paris, *Chronica Majora*, iii. 385; Gwyn A. Williams, 'The Succession to Gwynedd, 1238-47', *BBCS*, xx (1964), 401-3.

[64] Williams 'Succession to Gwynedd', 403; Smith, *Llywelyn ap Gruffudd*, pp.28-9.

[65] *Close Rolls, 1237-1242*, 124-6; at the same time Llywelyn was invited to send representatives to Oxford to discuss a permanent peace; Williams, 'Succession to Gwynedd', 396.

creation of a permanent principality unconfirmed by treaty. The lords went to Strata Florida but they only swore allegiance.[66] When Llywelyn died on 11 April 1240 Dafydd succeeded him. Henry moved quickly. A month later Dafydd went to Gloucester to do homage, but what he underwent was a public humiliation. He did homage but so did all the other Welsh lords; in the treaty to which he was forced to agree it was stated that the homage of all the Welsh lords should be reserved to the king.[67] This was a treaty, but it was not the treaty which Llywelyn had sought. Henry's trump card was Dafydd's elder brother Gruffydd, whose claim to a share of the inheritance had wide support. He had, so Matthew Paris says, been imprisoned by Dafydd in breach of a safe-conduct and he may have sought royal help.[68]

The treaty of Gloucester meant the surrender of most of Llywelyn's territorial gains. Dafydd did his best to delay its implementation but Henry soon lost patience and in August 1241 he invaded north Wales. An exceptionally dry summer facilitated his advance and on 29 August Dafydd surrendered at Gwern Eigron near St. Asaph.[69] The terms were set out in another treaty; they included further territorial concessions and the handing over of Gruffydd and his eldest son Owain to the king. Dafydd was also to pay the costs of the war. The settlement was confirmed in the treaty of London on 24 October 1241; the war indemnity was replaced by the surrender of Degannwy and on the same day Dafydd agreed that if he died without direct heirs his lands would escheat to the crown.[70] The whole was a major royal victory; Gruffydd was lodged in protective custody in the Tower of London, despite Henry's promise to his wife to secure his freedom. Dafydd knew that one false move would bring a royal army to north Wales to install his brother in his place.[71]

The two treaties also provided that Gruffydd's claim to a share of Gwynedd would be heard by the king; in other words the prince would be justiceable in the king's court. The crown's overlordship was fast developing in the 1240s into something far more positive and the object was the reduction of Gwynedd to the status of an ordinary lordship.[72] On

---

[66] *Brut y Tywysogyon (Pen. 20 version)*, p.104.

[67] J.G. Edwards, ed., *Littere Wallie* (Cardiff, 1940), pp.5-6; Williams, 'Succession to Gwynedd', 397-8; Smith, *Llywelyn ap Gruffudd*, pp.29-32; F.M. Powicke, *King Henry III and the Lord Edward* (Oxford, 1947), ii. 631-2.

[68] *CM*, iv. 8; Williams, 'Succession to Gwynedd', 403-4.

[69] Edwards, *Littere Wallie*, pp.9-10; Lloyd, *Hist. Wales*, ii. 697-8; Powicke, *King Henry III and the Lord Edward*, ii. 633.

[70] Edwards, *Littere Wallie*, pp.10-12, 22-3.

[71] Williams, 'Succesion to Gwynedd', 408; Smith, *Llywelyn ap Gruffudd*, pp.32-3, 45; J. Beverley Smith, 'Dynastic Succession in Medieval Wales', *BBCS*, xxxiii (1986), 221-2.

[72] Williams, 'Succession to Gwynedd', 408; Davies, *Conquest, Coexistence and Change*, pp.302, 305; Ceri W. Lewis, 'The Treaty of Woodstock, 1247: its Background and Significance', *WHR*, ii (1964-5), 37-65.

1 March 1244, Gruffydd was killed in an attempt to escape from the Tower and the political situation changed overnight. In the same year Dafydd seems to have tried to become a papal vassal; this was nothing less than a formal rejection of English overlordship and no other Welsh ruler had gone so far before or would do so later.[73] He failed; Henry had far more influence in Rome and a longer purse. In the meantime, with the threat of Gruffydd removed, Dafydd was again on the march. In August 1245 the king invaded north Wales; his army was forced by logistical problems to withdraw but on 25 February 1246 Dafydd died, leaving no direct heirs.[74] Gruffydd's two elder sons Owain and Llywelyn were persuaded to divide Gwynedd between them, thus avoiding a destructive power-struggle, but a renewed royal offensive penetrated the heart of Snowdonia, forcing them to seek terms. The settlement at Woodstock on 30 April 1247 reflected Henry's victory; the brothers agreed that Gwynedd west of the Conwy should in future be held of the king by royal grant in return for specified military service. If they misbehaved their territory would escheat.[75] As in 1211, the land between the Conwy and the Dee was surrendered and once again the king declared his right to the homage of all the Welsh rulers.

The treaty of Woodstock marked the highest point so far achieved of royal success in Wales. No previous treaty had demanded military service although Dafydd and Gruffydd ap Madog of northern Powys had been invited to send troops to Gascony in 1242.[76] Henry was able to impose his own terms and the division of Gwynedd was confirmed. Later events suggest that further division was intended as Gruffydd's younger sons, Dafydd and Rhodri, came of age. His attitude suggests that Henry, like many later historians, saw partible succession as the immutable rule in Wales, but it is arguable that he misunderstood the usages of Welsh kingship.[77] His whole strategy had been based on the premise that Gruffydd had been unjustly disinherited by his father and that he was therefore able to present himself as the defender of legitimate Welsh tradition. But, even if his policy was based on a false premise, his success between 1240 and 1247 cannot be denied; he had 'lain firm foundations for Edward I to build on later'.[78] If one examines the sequence of treaties from Gloucester to Woodstock one can see the working out of a conscious royal

[73] M. Richter, 'David ap Llywelyn, the First Prince of Wales', *WHR*, v (1970-1), 205-19.

[74] Lloyd, *Hist. Wales*, ii. 700-5; Smith, *Llywelyn ap Gruffudd*, pp.49-50; Davies, *Conquest, Coexistence and Change*, p.302.

[75] Edwards, *Littere Wallie*, pp.7-8; Lewis, 'Treaty of Woodstock', 46-65; Smith, *Llywelyn ap Gruffudd*, pp.56-61; Davies, *Conquest, Coexistence and Change*, pp.303-5.

[76] Williams, 'Succession to Gwynedd', 409; Lewis, 'Treaty of Woodstock', 53.

[77] Smith, *Llywelyn ap Gruffudd*, p.56; Smith, 'Dynastic Succession', 221-32.

[78] Davies, *Conquest, Coexistence and Change*, pp.300-7; Smith, *Llywelyn ap Gruffudd*, pp.58-9, 61.

policy; the aim was not to dispossess the princes of Gwynedd but to break up their principality and reduce them to the status of ordinary tenants-in-chief. In his dealings with Wales Henry III displayed skill and intelligence, along with a capacity for seizing opportunities; he was no less masterful in his dealings with the March, as well as with other Welsh lords.

The success of such a policy depended on the cooperation of the other Welsh rulers. In the 1240s they had learned that the days of independence under a vague royal overlordship were over; the only choice left to them was between the crown and Gwynedd.[79] Even before Woodstock some rulers were beginning to suspect royal motives and it was not long before Owain and Llywelyn began to rebuild their relationships with other lords. Henry continued to insist on strict partibility and in the summer of 1253 he indicated that he was ready to recognize Dafydd ap Gruffydd's rights.[80] This may have contributed to the tensions in Gwynedd which were resolved by Llywelyn's defeat of Owain and Dafydd at Bryn Derwin in 1255. This victory shattered the edifice so carefully constructed by Henry; having consolidated his position in Gwynedd west of the Conwy, Llywelyn, in the autumn of 1256, invaded and overran the north-east, now held by the king's eldest son Edward. His success here was followed by a series of rapid campaigns which, in less than twelve months, restored his grandfather's position.[81] The English barons showed a distinct lack of enthusiasm for the expedition which left Chester on 19 August 1257; it ended in a truce, having achieved nothing.

In 1258 Llywelyn ap Gruffydd assumed the title of prince of Wales and the other lords did him homage; around the same time he and some of these lords made a treaty, aimed at securing a common front against Henry III, with the Comyn faction in Scotland.[82] Llywelyn's priority now was the treaty which would recognize his position and his principality; the political situation in Wales had changed completely and the king would have to come to terms with it. A planned royal campaign in 1258 failed to secure any support and Llywelyn began to state his terms; in June 1259, having already asked for a formal grant of the homage of the Welsh magnates, he is said to have offered 4,500 marks for a permanent treaty and the following autumn he offered £16,500 payable in annual instalments of £200.[83] He also offered to marry one of the king's nieces.

---

[79] Williams, 'Succession to Gwynedd', 408-9.

[80] Smith, *Llywelyn ap Gruffudd*, pp.67-9.

[81] *Ibid.*, pp.82-94. The standard account in English is still Lloyd, *Hist. Wales*, ii. 716-22.

[82] *Brut y Tywysogyon (Red Book of Hergest Version)* (Cardiff, 1955), p.251; Davies, *Conquest, Coexistence and Change*, p.311; Smith, *Llywelyn ap Gruffudd*, pp.97-9; Edwards, *Littere Wallie*, pp.184-6.

[83] Smith, *Llywelyn ap Gruffudd*, pp.98-111; R.F. Treharne, *The Baronial Plan of Reform, 1258-1265* (Manchester, 1932), pp.131, 194.

But the offer was not taken up, although, as in the 1230s, there was frequent talk of negotiations for a permanent settlement. In 1260 he resumed campaigning in the March, not so much, perhaps, to gain territory as to bring Henry to the conference table; the result was a further truce but, even if this proved to be permanent, it was not enough.[84] For all the talk, there were no serious negotiations and Henry would not negotiate unless under pressure. This is shown very clearly by his reaction in 1262 when he heard a rumour that Llywelyn had died; his plan was to lead an army into Wales, release Owain, imprisoned by his brother since 1255, and make him prince, while the other rulers would be ordered to return to the king's allegiance.[85]

Dafydd, Llywelyn's brother and heir, had gone over to the royal camp early in 1263, but civil war now broke out in England. By February 1264 Llywelyn and Simon de Montfort were collaborating and Simon's victory at Lewes gave him control of the kingdom. Edward's subsequent escape to the March transformed the situation but on 19 June 1265, at Pipton, near Glasbury, on the Wye, a treaty was made between Simon, on behalf of the king, and Llywelyn.[86] The treaty of Pipton contained the terms which Llywelyn had been seeking for so long. He was conceded the overlordship of the other Welsh rulers and the title of prince of Wales for himself and his successors. For this he would pay £20,000 over a period of ten years and his territorial gains were confirmed. In the circumstances this was a meaningless settlement and Llywelyn and his advisers must have known it; Simon's position was crumbling almost daily and at Evesham on 4 August he was defeated and killed by Edward. But the agreement had its advantages for Llywelyn since it set out the terms which he hoped to secure from the crown. In October 1265 the papal representative Ottobuono had arrived in England to try and end the civil war by mediation and it was he who finally secured a Welsh settlement. Negotiations under his auspices began at Shrewsbury late in August 1267 and by 21 September agreement had been reached and Ottobuono authorized to arrange the final details. On 29 September at Rhyd Chwima near Montgomery, in the presence of Ottobuono, the king's sons and many others, Llywelyn ap Gruffydd did homage and fealty to Henry III.[87]

The treaty of Montgomery changed the nature of Anglo-Welsh

---

[84] Smith, *Llywelyn ap Gruffudd*, pp.112-7; J. Beverley Smith, 'Llywelyn ap Gruffudd and the March of Wales', *Brycheiniog*, xx (1982-3), 12.

[85] *Foedera*, I, i. 420; Smith, *Llywelyn ap Gruffudd*, pp.117-9.

[86] There are two texts of the treaty, being the royal letters patent (*Foedera*, I, i. 457) and those of Llywelyn (*Dip. Docs. i, 1101-1272*, no.400); Smith, *Llywelyn ap Gruffudd*, pp.138-47; Davies, *Conquest, Coexistence and Change*, pp.312-4; T.F. Tout, 'Wales and the March during the Barons' Wars' in *idem, Collected Papers* (Manchester, 1934), ii. 47-82.

[87] Edwards, *Littere Wallie*, pp.1-4; Smith, *Llywelyn ap Gruffudd*, pp.152-9; Tout, 'Wales and the March', 88-97; Lloyd, *Hist. Wales*, ii. 739-41; Davies, *Conquest, Coexistence and Change*, pp.314-7.

relations. Llywelyn was granted the overlordship of all but one of the Welsh rulers. He was recognized as prince of Wales and his heirs would be princes after him. The treaty defined the territory of the principality and for all this he would pay 25,000 marks. The king of England had at last granted the recognition for which Llywelyn and his grandfather had worked so hard and the principality now existed as a permanent constitutional entity. Anglo-Welsh relations would from henceforth involve the crown and a single Welsh ruler, the prince of Wales. It has often been suggested that Llywelyn's success was due to his ability to take advantage of division and disunity in England; the truth of the matter is that most of his success in Wales had been before English baronial discontent had come to a head. Moreover, to win a settlement he had not only to deal from a position of strength himself; if there was no firm government in England a treaty would be worthless.[88]

With the treaty of Montgomery the final chapter in Anglo-Welsh relations opens. Fifteen years later Llywelyn ap Gruffydd was dead and the remains of his principality annexed to the English crown. The debate about the causes of the Edwardian conquest continues but it is fair to say that the successive crises which led up to it did not, in the first instance, stem from the relationship of the crown with the prince.[89] Disputes had begun before Henry III's death in 1272 but they arose from Llywelyn's uneasy relations with his marcher neighbours, some of whom he had dispossessed, although it is conceivable that Edward I's absence on crusade until 1274 aggravated matters. The turning-point came in 1274 when a major crisis erupted in Wales as a result of the unsuccessful conspiracy by Llywelyn's brother Dafydd and the lord of southern Powys, Gruffydd ap Gwenwynwyn, to assassinate the prince. This did not initially involve the king but by the end of 1274 the plotters had fled to England. It was this, more than anything else, that led to a rapid deterioration in relations. Llywelyn should have done homage to Edward on his return but would not do so until the fugitives were returned; Edward insisted that homage must be rendered before the matter could be discussed. Llywelyn had not paid the annual instalments due for the treaty since before Henry's death; it is very possible that this was the result of the financial problems with which he was increasingly beset, but this, from Edward's point of view, was no excuse.[90] He was in clear breach of a

[88] Smith, *Llywelyn ap Gruffudd*, p.104.

[89] The main contributions to this debate are those in Edwards, *Littere Wallie*, pp. xxxvi-lxix; J. Conway Davies, *The Welsh Assize Roll, 1277-1284* (Cardiff, 1940), pp.1-233; Powicke, *King Henry III and the Lord Edward*, ii. 618-85; Chrimes, *King Edward I's Policy for Wales*, pp.10-14 and more recently Smith, *Llywelyn ap Gruffudd*, pp.238-392 and Davies, *Conquest, Coexistence and Change*, pp.320-54. For a summary see A.D. Carr, *Llywelyn ap Gruffydd* (Cardiff, 1982), pp.37-83.

[90] Keith Williams-Jones, ed., *The Merioneth Lay Subsidy Roll, 1292-3* (Cardiff, 1976), pp. xvii-xx; J. Beverley Smith, 'Llywelyn ap Gruffydd, Prince of Wales and Lord of Snowdon', *Trans. Caerns. Hist. Soc.*, xlv (1984), 29-32.

treaty which he had sought; he had his principality but the king had neither homage nor money.

Tension was heightened by Edward's capture of Llywelyn's bride Eleanor de Montfort when on her way to join him. Negotiations continued but by now Llywelyn was regarded as a contumacious vassal and on 12 November 1276 Edward declared war.[91] In a textbook campaign most of Wales was overrun and the other Welsh lords all made their peace; Llywelyn's principality melted away. The prince had no choice but to come to terms. On 9 November 1277 he accepted the king's terms in the treaty of Aberconwy.[92] In this treaty he relinquished all his territorial gains and once again the north-east was ceded to the crown. He retained the title of prince of Wales for his own lifetime, along with the homage of five lords in what was left of his principality, and he undertook to pay off the arrears under the treaty of Montgomery as well as an indemnity of £50,000 which Edward promptly remitted. The following December he went to London and did homage.

Aberconwy was the last in a sequence of treaties which had begun in 1201. Again Llywelyn was dealing with the king as prince of Gwynedd, despite his title; his vassals had deserted him. In effect it was a return to the situation of 1247, although his principality was larger and he was in a slightly stronger position than he had been in thirty years earlier. Relations do seem to have improved after the treaty and neither party showed any lack of goodwill, but during the next five years tension built up again. Some of this derived from the interpretation of the clauses in the treaty which related to the resolution of territorial disputes. Llywelyn had also other grievances, but these were not incapable of solution. These problems must have preyed on his mind.[93] None of them, not even the dispute with Gruffydd ap Gwenwynwyn over the cantref of Arwystli on the upper Severn and Edward's legalism in dealing with it, was enough to lead to the war which broke out on the night of 21 March 1282, when Dafydd attacked the castle of Hawarden.[94] When exactly Llywelyn became involved is uncertain, but on 12 December he was killed near Builth in mid Wales in circumstances which remain something of a mystery. Dafydd was captured some months later and eventually

[91] For details of the campaign see J.E. Morris, *The Welsh Wars of King Edward the First* (Oxford, 1901), pp.110-48; Smith, *Llywelyn ap Gruffudd*, pp.286-308.

[92] Edwards, *Littere Wallie*, p.118-22; Llywelyn's *inspeximus* and confirmation is *ibid*, pp.113-4; Smith, *Llywelyn ap Gruffudd*, pp.308-18.

[93] See, for example Edwards, *Cal. Anc. Corr.*, pp.90-1; the issues which arose between 1277 and 1282 are considered by Smith, *Llywelyn ap Gruffudd*, pp.308-46, Davies, *Conquest, Coexistence and Change*, pp.336-48 and F.M. Powicke, *The Thirteenth Century*, pp.412-9.

[94] *Brut y Tywysogyon (Pen. 20 version)*, p.120; Morris, *Welsh Wars*, pp.152-97; Smith, *Llywelyn ap Gruffudd*, pp.346-92; Davies; *Conquest, Coexistence and Change*, pp.348-64; D. Stephenson, *The Last Prince of Wales* (Buckingham, 1983), pp.20-71; A.D. Carr, 'The Last Days of Gwynedd', *Trans. Caerns. Hist. Soc.*, xliii (1982), 7-22.

executed at Shrewsbury; at Rhuddlan on 19 March 1284 Edward promulgated his arrangements for the government of his newly-conquered territories in the Statute of Wales.[95]

This account of the last fifteen years of Welsh independence is, of necessity, highly condensed; what is important in this context is the nature of the Anglo-Welsh political relationship during this period. The treaty of Montgomery had transformed the whole of that political relationship, making it clear and unambiguous, defining it in writing and providing for the recognition of the principality of Wales on the one hand and for homage by the prince on behalf of all the Welsh rulers on the other. In future relations would be based on the treaty and not on tradition or precedent. There seemed no reason why it should not endure as long as both sides observed it. The problem was that there were other factors, such as the resentment of the marcher lords who had been dispossessed by Llywelyn and the uneasy nature of his supremacy within Wales; the comment that 'the triumph of 1267 was founded not on a rock but on sand' is in some respects a fair one.[96] And, above all, as far as the political relationship was concerned, the settlement came to mean different things to Edward and to Llywelyn. By 1277 Edward's concept of overlordship could no longer be reconciled with Llywelyn's view of the nature of his principality.[97] To Edward Llywelyn was his vassal: the greatest of his vassals, perhaps, but a vassal none the less. Llywelyn saw himself as an independent prince doing homage for his principality but no more than that.[98] In the thirteenth century political relationships were becoming ever more precise and definite and it was this clarification that contributed to the tension.[99] The issue was pinpointed in the course of the argument over which law should be used to settle the Arwystli dispute in which the two parties had appealed to the king; Llywelyn argued that every province under the king's *imperium* had its own laws and customs and should proceed by them, but this was unacceptable to Edward who saw his prerogative and his authority as overlord as overriding all local usages.[100] Welsh law had its place but the last word was the king's.

Although the treaty of Montgomery had defined a relationship and set out the obligations on both sides, it meant different things to Edward and to Llywelyn. The very fact that relations were being defined and clarified carried with it the seeds of trouble. The question, though, is how far

[95] Ivor Bowen, *The Statutes of Wales* (London, 1908), pp.2-27.

[96] A.J. Roderick, 'The Conquest of Wales' in *idem*, ed., *Wales Through the Ages*, (Llandybie, 1959-60), i. 121.

[97] Davies, *Conquest, Coexistence and Change*, p.330.

[98] The point was made by Llywelyn in the dispute over the building of Dolforwyn castle in 1273, Edwards, *Cal. Anc. Corr.*, p.86.

[99] Chrimes, *King Edward I's Policy for Wales*, p.5.

[100] Conway Davies, *Welsh Assize Roll*, pp.266-7, 138-9; Powicke, *King Henry III and the Lord Edward*, ii. 663-76; Smith, *Llywelyn ap Gruffudd*, pp.337-40.

Edward was consistent in his attitude. Did his dealings with and his attitude towards Llywelyn after 1277 stem from a concept of overlordship which he had held since his accession or had this view developed gradually in the light of his experience during the 1270s? Was there a place for Llywelyn and his principality under Edward's overlordship as he visualized it after Aberconwy? Was it his intention to destroy the prince in 1277 or to teach him a lesson and bring him to submission?[101] Would he have settled for less than unconditional surrender in 1282? Even at the end he does not seem to have wished to destroy Llywelyn completely; when Archbishop Pecham went to Wales in a vain attempt to mediate, the prince was offered an earldom and an estate in England in return for the cession of the principality.[102]

The relationship which came to an end in 1282-3 had developed over three centuries. Individual Welsh rulers had often submitted to Anglo-Saxon and Anglo-Norman kings. Henry I had relied on his power and personality, while Henry II had tried a military solution and had then secured stability through a personal relationship with the most powerful ruler of the time; it was during his reign, too, that the leading rulers had begun to do homage. In the thirteenth century Gwynedd emerged as the predominant power in Wales and in 1201 its relationship with the crown began to be defined by treaty. The treaties of the 1240s were imposed by Henry III from a position of strength but the princes of Gwynedd were seeking a different kind of agreement which would recognize their supremacy in Wales and put their relationship with the crown on a permanent footing; this was eventually secured at Montgomery. But the weakness of the Welsh position may have lain in the fact that these princes had to build up their position under an English overlordship which was becoming ever less passive. Apart from Dafydd ap Llywelyn's brief and unsuccessful flirtation with papal overlordship, they never challenged the suzerainty of the crown; rather did they try to make it work to their advantage. To secure their position they needed a treaty, but this could not be achieved except at a time of royal weakness; at the same time, for such a settlement to work the crown had to be strong enough to guarantee it. This was the dilemma and perhaps it made the 1267 settlement unworkable. The treaty of Aberconwy may be seen as a continuation of the policy of John and Henry III; while the princes sought to interpose themselves between the king and the other Welsh lords, the royal objective was to retain the direct overlordship of each individual ruler. Because of what happened five years later Aberconwy was to be the last formal agreement in a relationship of the English crown with native Welsh rulers in a political world which was, between 1066 and 1282, undergoing rapid and profound change.

[101] Chrimes, *King Edward I's Policy for Wales*, pp.11-12.

[102] *Registrum Epistolarum Johannis Peckham, Archiepiscopi Cantuarensis*, ed. C.T. Martin (1884), ii. 433-7; D.L. Douie, *Archbishop Pecham* (Oxford, 1952), pp.247-8.

Chapter 8

England and Ireland, 1171-1399

Robin Frame

An inquisitive outsider who began to read the political history of medieval England as it is normally written might be struck by a paradox. From the time of King John the title 'lord of Ireland' was a prominent part of the royal style, taking precedence over the French ducal and comital titles used by kings before 1340. The *dominium Hibernie* was thus perpetually conspicuous on royal seals, in the headings of royal documents, and on the coins handled by the king's subjects. Yet if the newcomer turned to modern writings, especially on the period 1216-1360, in the expectation of learning about Ireland, he would be disappointed; for with one or two exceptions, English historians tend to ignore the lordship, or to allot it at best a few uneasy pages.

This state of affairs to some extent reflects the simple fact that Ireland's place on the scale of kings' priorities rarely matched its position in the royal style. But it also has a good deal to do with historiographical traditions. One of these is the reluctance of English medievalists to bring the 'Celtic fringe' in general within their compass, a matter that has perhaps been sufficiently aired of late.[1] The explanation does not, however, lie entirely on the English side of the sea; the conventions of Irish historical writing, which assume that significance must be attributed to things according to their observed position in the unfolding past of the island of Ireland, are themselves partly responsible. This outlook has of course resulted in much distinguished work, for instance on the process by which the descendants of those who colonized Ireland in the late twelfth and early thirteenth centuries identified with the country and became 'Anglo-Irish'. J.F. Lydon has recently devoted an illuminating article to this theme. He begins with some words that Gerald of Wales put into the mouth of his kinsman Maurice fitz Gerald at the siege of Waterford in 1170: 'just as to the Irish we are English, so to the English we are Irish'. Gerald's literary flourish forms a leitmotiv that carries author and reader

---

[1] E.g., R.R. Davies, *Historical Perception: Celts and Saxons*, Aberystwyth Inaugural Lecture (Cardiff, 1979), pp.23-5; G.W.S. Barrow, *The Anglo-Norman Era in Scottish History* (Oxford, 1980), pp.162-3.

unhesitatingly through to Richard Stanihurst and the Old English of the sixteenth century.[2] Under J.C. Beckett's guidance it seems entirely fitting that we should find our way elegantly from the Anglo-Norman invasion, through Swift and Grattan, to Shaw and Yeats.[3] On a less majestic note, the early history of Dublin Castle is more likely to prompt the Irish historian to reflect on the continuity of English administration in Ireland from 1171 to 1922, than on Dublin's place in King John's financial network or its position among the coastal centres that formed part of the sinew of the Angevin empire.[4]

This habit of mind is a way of making sense of the past; for the historian writing in Ireland it is likely to remain the most appropriate way. But it carries a penalty, in that it tends to disconnect things from their own time and circumstances and to draw them instead into a closed system where they refer back and forth down the centuries, with the result that the surface Ireland presents to the outsider is one on which he can find it hard to obtain a grip. It may therefore be worth attempting to sketch some of the political links between England and Ireland and the changes they underwent between the time of Henry II and that of Richard II, concentrating particularly on the reigns of the four kings, from Henry III to Edward III, who never set foot in their other island. In doing so, we may identify certain areas where 'English history' and 'Irish history' intersect, or even merge.

From the time of Henry II's intervention in 1171 the lordship of Ireland seems to present two facets. Henry quickly ordered his relations with the barons and knights who were occupying the south and east, bringing about a definition of tenures along contemporary English lines. In addition, he accepted submissions from the Irish kings who flocked to him. The position is summed up in the agreement of 1175, known to historians as the treaty of Windsor, which he made with Rory O'Connor, king of Connacht and current high king of Ireland. The document distinguishes between the lands of Henry and his men in Leinster and Meath, and those of the Irish in the west and north. The plan that Rory would act as an agent in the latter region, collecting tribute and hostages on Henry's behalf, never fully worked and the agreement soon collapsed, along with any pretence that there was a single over-king of the Irish with

---

[2] *Expugnatio Hibernica*, ed. A.B. Scott and F.X. Martin (Dublin, 1978), p.80; J. Lydon, 'The Middle Nation', in *The English in Medieval Ireland*, ed. Lydon (Dublin, 1984), pp.1-26, at p.2.

[3] *The Anglo-Irish Tradition* (London, 1976).

[4] R. Frame, *Colonial Ireland, 1169-1369* (Dublin, 1981), pp.55, 88; Beckett, p.15. Cf. J.E.A. Jolliffe, 'The Chamber and the Castle Treasuries under John', in *Studies in Medieval History presented to F.M. Powicke*, ed. R.W. Hunt *et al.* (Oxford, 1948), pp.124, 126-7, 139; J. Gillingham, *The Angevin Empire* (London, 1984), Chapter 4.

whom deals could be made.[5] Nonetheless during the early decades of its history the lordship continued to be marked by the existence of two sets of political relationships. Although the importance of the crown's connection with the Irish kings diminished as the proportion of Ireland under baronial occupation expanded, the duality provides a rough and ready framework within which Anglo-Irish relations may be considered.

The story of the original move into Ireland by knights from south Wales associated with Strongbow lays a false trail. The free enterprise ended almost immediately, and from 1171 the lordship was shaped by royal power and the politics of the metropolis. This is graphically shown by the events of 1185, when the young John was sent to take charge of the potential kingdom that had been assigned to him. The expedition was watched over by Rannulf Glanville, who himself acquired property in Ireland, and accompanied by a number of notable figures. John's older companions included Bertram de Verdon and Gilbert Pipard who had regularly served as justices in England and were soon to accompany Richard I on crusade; among the younger group were Theobald Walter, John's butler, a brother of Hubert Walter, and William de Burgh, a brother of Hubert de Burgh. The Verdons and Pipards gained lands on the northern fringes of the expanding royal lordship, towards Ulster where John de Courcy, another figure who had had strong connections with the king's household, was carving out a principality; Theobald and William obtained grants in Tipperary and Limerick, on its south-western outskirts.

Discussion of this and other episodes has concentrated on their significance for Ireland, and elaborate royal policies towards the lordship have been deduced from them.[6] A simpler point has tended to escape attention: the possibilities Ireland offered for the advancement of men close to the court and administration, and this at a time when the availability of major landed patronage in England had shrunk.[7] Gerald of Wales tells us as much in the well-known passages where he condemns the soft and over-rewarded *curiales* introduced to Ireland by the crown at the expense of his own people, the *marchiones*, sturdy but under-valued.[8] This is nonsense inasmuch as the 'courtiers' included some of the toughest

---

[5] *The Chronicles of the Reigns of Henry II and Richard I*, ed. W. Stubbs (RS, 1867), i. 102-3. See W.L. Warren, *Henry II* (London, 1973), pp.201-3.

[6] W.L. Warren, 'John in Ireland, 1185', in *Essays Presented to Michael Roberts*, ed. J. Bossy and P. Jupp (Belfast, 1976), pp.11-23, and 'King John and Ireland', in *England and Ireland in the Later Middle Ages: Essays in Honour of Jocelyn Otway-Ruthven*, ed. J. Lydon (Dublin, 1981), pp.26-42. Cf. R. Mortimer, 'The Family of Rannulf de Glanville', *BIHR*, liv (1981), 1-16.

[7] See J.E. Lally, 'Secular Patronage at the Court of Henry II', *BIHR*, xlix (1976), 159-84, at 181-3.

[8] *Expugn. Hib.*, pp.168-72, 190, 238-40. See R. Bartlett, *Gerald of Wales, 1146-1223* (Oxford, 1982), pp.20-5.

military men around, but as political comment it is revealing. It may be that the dynamic of expansion should be sought partly within the *familia regis* itself, and that the recent tendency to view the Angevin involvement in Ireland as reactive and even reluctant may have gone too far, not least because it rests on an over-simple contrast between royal and aristocratic interests. We soon glimpse rivalry within court circles over lucrative Irish property. The most dramatic instance was the clash during King Richard's reign between the interests of William Marshal and John himself in Leinster.[9] The court-centred competition a decade later between William de Braose, Theobald Walter, William de Burgh and others in the south-west might be viewed from the same angle.[10] Ireland provided some scope for the ambitions of men close to the centre of affairs; those ambitions could be kept within bounds by the king's ability to manipulate rival expectations.

During the thirteenth century the lordship became more congested. Nonetheless forfeitures and escheats allowed some redistribution; the marriage market offered opportunities in a land of very large lordships; and at least until the 1270s there was still room in the west. Under Henry III the lordship provided useful trifles for many of those connected with the court, and the possibility of major enrichment for a few. Amaury de St. Amand, for example, who belonged to the *familia*, served in Ireland in the later 1220s, when he acquired some property near Dublin. In 1230 he had a grant of the rich coastal manor of Gormanston. He went on to become a king's seneschal and godfather to the Lord Edward, before dying on crusade in 1241. The family held Gormanston until 1363, when another Amaury, a banneret of Edward III and former justiciar of Ireland, sold out.[11] More striking is the case of Robert Muscegros, the son of one of King John's judges, who had a long career in royal service, dying in 1254 as steward to Queen Eleanor of Provence. In the last years of his life Robert received important grants in Ireland, a land with which he seems to have had no earlier connection: extensive lands west of Limerick along the northern bank of the Shannon, together with high franchisal justice, free warren, resources to help him build castles, and a fair and market at Bunratty, which was to be the *caput* of the new lordship.[12] His son John,

[9] *Histoire de Guillaume le Maréchal*, ed. P. Meyer (Paris, 1891-1901), ii. 343-7; M.T. Flanagan, 'Strongbow, Henry II and Anglo-Norman Intervention in Ireland', in *War and Government in the Middle Ages: Essays in Honour of J.O. Prestwich*, ed. J. Gillingham and J.C. Holt (Woodbridge, 1984), pp.74-7.

[10] See C.A. Empey, 'The Settlement of the Kingdom of Limerick', in *England and Ireland*, ed. Lydon, pp.1-25.

[11] C[alendar of] D[ocuments Relating to] I[reland], ed. H.S. Sweetman (London, 1875-86), *1171-1251*, nos.1400, 1438, 1523, 1564, 1617, 1772; *Dict. Nat. Biog.*, xvii, 607; R. Frame, *English Lordship in Ireland, 1318-1361* (Oxford, 1982), pp.59, 88.

[12] *CDI, 1171-1251*, nos.2920-1, 3126; *1252-84*, nos.4, 155. See R.V. Turner, *The English Judiciary in the Age of Glanvill and Bracton c.1176-1239* (Cambridge, 1985), pp.169, 188-9.

who acted as sheriff of Limerick and as a royal emissary to Ireland, strove to make all this real; and although after his death the family surrendered their claims, this was so that Edward I could give the embryonic frontier lordship to Thomas de Clare, one of his intimates.[13] The Muscegros grant has a good deal in common with those of the 1170s and 1180s; it involved rewarding somebody from the inner circle with potential riches on the edge of what still appeared to be an expanding dominion. It is not the only sign that during the last phase of his personal rule Henry III regarded Ireland as a place where some of those around him might be enriched; among the beneficiaries, through outright grant or marriage, were Stephen Longespee, Fulk *de Castro Novo*, John fitz Geoffrey, Peter of Geneva, Geoffrey de Geneville and Godfrey de Lusignan.[14]

That contemporaries could perceive Ireland in this way is apparent from a document taken to court by a messenger from one of the king's ministers in Ireland after the fatal wounding of Richard Marshal on the Curragh of Kildare in 1234. His brief was to urge Henry to come to the lordship. The arguments used, though tendentious, differ significantly from the moans and prophecies of collapse that decorate such appeals in the fourteenth century:

> My lord advises and asks you to come to Ireland, for now you will be richer in Ireland, with greater wealth than ever you or your father had . . .
>
> Ask the lord chancellor to come to Ireland with the king if he conveniently can; and also Sir Henry de Trubleville and Sir Ralph fitz Nicholas, the king's seneschal, and Sir John Marshal, for they can be greatly enriched if they come.
>
> Tell Earl Richard, the king's brother, to come to Ireland with the king; and if the king will not come, he should certainly come, for he can have castles and lands in no small measure.[15]

The implication is that the king and those close to him should not miss the chance to benefit in a land where others had absorbed the chief advantages in the past; indeed Henry de Trubleville, Ralph fitz Nicholas and John Marshal were among those who already had minor Irish interests that might be expanded.[16] The lordship's importance should not be exaggerated: the possibilities it offered were, of course, limited. But it was part of the arena where royal patronage operated, and a place where many men of note had a stake.

---

[13] *CDI, 1252–84*, nos.451, 498, 505, 899, 919–20; 'Accounts of the Great Rolls of the Pipe of the Irish Exchequer', in *35th Report of the Deputy Keeper of the Public Records of Ireland*, pp.40-1, and *36th Report*, p.25. See M. Prestwich, 'Royal Patronage under Edward I', *Thirteenth Century England:I*, ed. P.R. Coss and S.D. Lloyd (Woodbridge, 1986), pp.46-7.

[14] E.g., *CDI, 1171–1251*, nos.2121, 2600, 2645, 2662, 2699, 2730, 2807, 2810, 2948; *1252-84*, nos.69, 78, 226, 289, 301-2, 319, 321, 364, 392-3, 410, 415, 434, 447.

[15] [*Documents on the*] *Affairs of Ireland* [*before the King's Council*, ed. G.O. Sayles (Dublin, 1979)], no.3.

[16] *CDI, 1171–1251*, nos.353, 537, 913, 1324, 1541, 1554, 1567, 1675, 1966, 2034, 2038, 2040.

Moreover the court connections of major magnates whose holdings lay chiefly in Ireland did not rapidly fade. William de Burgh (d.1206) married a daughter of the O'Brien king of Thomond, obtained a speculative grant of Connacht in the 1190s, and plunged into a round of wars and alliances in the west of Ireland.[17] Richard, his son and successor (d.1242), may have learnt Irish at his mother's knee as well as at his nurse's breast; but he by no means rode off into a Celtic twilight. His conquest of Connacht during the 1220s and 1230s was achieved largely at court. The first hint that the grant might be renewed for him came within weeks of the appointment of his uncle Hubert de Burgh as justiciar in 1215.[18] His grip on Connacht closed at the height of Hubert's power, and relaxed when he fell in 1232; it tightened again when Richard identified himself with King Henry during his quarrel with the Marshal two years later. And the first English lord of Connacht died, not in some skirmish on the Atlantic coast of Ireland, but serving Henry in Poitou and Gascony. Matthew Paris gave him an obituary, embellished with a drawing of the de Burgh arms.[19] The next generation, which grew up long after Hubert's eclipse, is perhaps even more revealing. Richard II (d.1248) was raised at court, and Matthew tells the chilling news of his marriage to a lady from Provence.[20] His brother Walter (d.1271), who succeeded him, was also brought to England.[21] He developed an association with the Lord Edward, whom he provided with military support during the Barons' Wars, circumstances that probably explain his startling acquisition of the earldom of Ulster in 1263. His marriage to a daughter of John fitz Geoffrey was by the end of the century to bring the 'Irish' de Burghs the firm landed base in England that they had lacked.[22]

In the earlier thirteenth century at least, it is difficult to identify a distinct Irish baronage, and probably misguided to try to do so. It is true that the king frequently employed the phrase 'the barons of Ireland' when sending information or requests for advice to the lordship, and that the term is properly of interest to those studying councils and the prehistory of parliaments – occasions that in the long run did indeed help a community of Ireland to crystallize. But what he meant was those of his greater subjects who were of age, had Irish lands, and were believed to be in Ireland at the time; a significant proportion had property, and the

---

[17] See G.H. Orpen, [*Ireland under the*] *Normans* [*1169-1333*] (Oxford, 1911-20), ii, Chapters 18 and 19.

[18] *CDI, 1171-1251*, no.653.

[19] *Chronica Majora*, iv. 232; *Historia Anglorum*, ed. F. Madden (RS, 1866-9), ii. 468. See Orpen, *Normans*, iii, Chapters 25, 28-31.

[20] *CM*, iv. 628, 655.

[21] *CDI, 1171-1251*, no.3011; *C*[*lose*] *R*[*olls*], *1247-51*, 309.

[22] R. Frame, 'Ireland and the Barons' Wars', in *Thirteenth Century England: I*, pp.161, 164-7, and *English Lordship*, pp.48-9.

majority strong associations, elsewhere.[23] Nor, despite the existence of councils and military musters, is it easy to detect what might be called a 'politics of Ireland'. Often it may be preferable to arrange our thoughts, not so much around England and Ireland, as around the Angevin court, the aristocratic networks that centred on it, and the regions and sub-regions these embraced. Within such a scheme the lordship of Ireland can find a more natural place; moreover the opportunity exists to give content to other phrases, which have been less successful in catching the eye of the historian: 'the barons of Leinster', 'the barons of Meath', 'the barons of Ulster'.[24]

In the early decades of the thirteenth century the more powerful Irish kings of the west and north, particularly the O'Connors of Connacht and the O'Briens of Thomond who lay close to the royal centres at Athlone and Limerick respectively, retained a limited position in the formal structure of the lordship. They might be notified when the king changed his justiciar of Ireland, applied to alongside the baronage when an aid was sought, or even asked for advice on a specific matter.[25] In the time of Henry III direct royal contact with individual Irish kings was not specially common. But communication did take place (we hear, for instance, of Conor O'Brien's clerk Matthew travelling to court in 1251 and 1253[26]); and comings and goings were more frequent than the small handful of surviving letters from Irish rulers might suggest. The letters that remain are mostly from the O'Connors, and are in conventional style; nothing suggests that Gaelic kings were inhibited about addressing their overlord.[27] Felim O'Connor, writing in 1261, was unclear about the implications of the recent treaty of Paris for the royal style: he addresses Henry as 'illustrious king of England by the grace of God, lord of Ireland

[23] See H.G. Richardson and G.O. Sayles, *The Irish Parliament in the Middle Ages* (Philadelphia, 1952), Chapter 2. There are early lists of 'Irish' barons in *ibid.*, pp.285-7 (1212) and *CDI, 1171-1251*, no.1001 (1221).

[24] E.g., *CDI, 1171-1251*, nos.157, 225, 228, 315, 1124. For some preliminary reflections on these matters, see R. Frame, 'Aristocracies and the Political Configuration of the British Isles', in *The British Isles 1100-1500: Comparisons, Contrasts and Connections*, ed. R.R. Davies (Edinburgh, 1988), pp.142-59.

[25] *Rotuli Litterarum Patentium*, ed. T.D. Hardy (Rec[ord] Comm[ission], 1835), p.84; *Rotuli Litterarum Clausarum*, ed. T.D. Hardy (Rec. Comm., 1833-4), i. 224, 375, 390, 476-7; *CR, 1227-31*, 383. The status of the leading Irish rulers is discussed in P.J. Dunning, 'Pope Innocent III and the Irish Kings', *Jnl. Ecclesiastical Hist.*, viii (1957), 26-9.

[26] *CR, 1247-51*, 530; *1251-3*, 496-7.

[27] Three letters from Cathal O'Connor (d.1224) are printed in *Royal [and other Historical] Letters [Illustrative of the Reign of Henry III*, ed. W.W. Shirley (RS, 1862-6)], i. 165, 183-4, 223-4, (respectively PRO, S.C.1/1/86 and S.C.1/47/30, 31); S.C.1/1/11 is another. A letter *c.*1274 from O'Neill and other northern rulers is printed in *Foedera*, I, ii. 520 (= PRO, S.C.1/18/211).

and count of Anjou'.[28] But this lapse is exceptional: a few years later his son wrote a perfectly business-like letter about the restoration of the temporalities of a local bishop.[29] Face-to-face encounters were rare after King John's Irish expedition of 1210, but not unknown. As soon as he emerged as a plausible candidate for the Connacht kingship in 1233, Felim O'Connor, who was anxious to exploit the opportunity presented by the eclipse of the de Burghs, unsuccessfully asked Henry if he might come to see him.[30] Felim did, however, reach court in 1240, when the recovery of de Burgh influence was becoming very serious. Matthew Paris tells us that Henry sent him home 'in good hope', and his misplaced euphoria may be glimpsed in the Connacht chronicle's description of his return 'in safety, happy and cheerful'.[31] He also served Henry in Anglesey in 1245.[32]

The fragmentary character of the evidence bearing on these tenuous relationships makes the identification of attitudes a treacherous business. But the more abundant material from Wales, which has been much more thoroughly studied, can provide helpful analogies. A feature common to the world of Celtic rulership were the constant rivalries and succession struggles within dynasties, which played an important part in shaping relations with outside powers, including the crown. For example, Felim O'Connor's father, King Cathal of Connacht (d.1224), had emerged around 1202 as victor in a long segmentary dispute, when he succeeded in excluding the descendants of his brother, King Rory, from the kingship and in shutting William de Burgh, their backer, out of Connacht. Thereafter Cathal bargained with King John for a territorial settlement. During the last years of his life his mind turned to the succession, and he sought royal recognition for his favoured son, Aedh, who had been established as virtual co-regent within Connacht. Behind this lay justifiable concern about a de Burgh revival; and the episode readily turns into a cautionary tale, to do with the Gaelic king obliged to seek a foreign title to what was his in the first place, only to find himself undone by baronial greed and the duplicity of the English princes in whom he had placed his trust. It is easy to forget that Cathal's activities were directed first and foremost towards outmanoeuvring the other branches of the O'Connor lineage, and that the succession of Aedh would represent the triumph, with external sanction, of one dynastic segment at the expense of

---

[28] PRO, S.C.1/3/51; *Royal Letters*, ii. 199-200. See P. Chaplais, 'The Making of the Treaty of Paris (1259) and the Royal Style', in *Essays*, I, 248-53.

[29] PRO, S.C.1/47/32; *Foedera*, I, i. 464.

[30] *Foedera*, I, i. 209; cf. *CDI, 1171-1251*, no.2644.

[31] *CM.*, iv. 57-8; *The Annals of Connacht*, ed. A.M. Freeman (Dublin, 1944), pp.72-3.

[32] *Annals of Connacht*, pp.84-5.

the rest.[33] There are in this distinct echoes of the contemporary attempts of Llywelyn the Great to have his son Dafydd accepted as his heir. As well as seeking to advance Dafydd's position within native Wales, Llywelyn turned both to Henry III and to the papacy.[34] Cathal O'Connor too invoked Rome as well as England: in 1220 Pope Honorius III extended his protection to the persons, kingdom, rights and status of 'Catholicus, the illustrious king of Connacht, and Odo his son'.[35] The association of father and son in this privilege is striking.

Henry III's regime, like its predecessors, seems to have understood very well the idiom of Welsh dynastic politics. When Dafydd succeeded Llywelyn in 1240, Henry quickly moved to cramp his style, partly by cultivating those among the Welsh who resented him. After Dafydd's death in 1246, the king posed as defender of the custom of partible inheritance, and presided over the dismemberment of Gwynedd.[36] Ireland was a good deal less pressing. But there are clear signs that both John and Henry exploited the rivalry between the brothers Murtough and Donough Cairbrech O'Brien, would-be kings of Thomond.[37] Just occasionally we can see techniques of management being consciously applied. Within the Five Cantreds, a district near Athlone that had been excluded from the renewed grant to the de Burghs, Felim O'Connor had been permitted to rent land from the crown. During the 1250s, at the same time as the Muscegros were being intruded into Thomond, Henry made a speculative grant in the Five Cantreds to his half-brother, Godfrey de Lusignan. When Felim grew agitated a letter was despatched, ostensibly to calm him down. It contains a passage heavy with irony and menace: 'some of your kinsmen . . . who presumably would not in any way detract from your right – if any – to those lands, have frequently asked us for a grant of them, offering us a great sum of money for them'.[38] Felim was being offered a choice between accepting a well-connected Poitevin neighbour and overlord, and seeing the king offer his backing to a dynastic

[33] *Royal Letters*, i. 223-4. See K. Simms, *From Kings to Warlords: The Changing Political Structure of Gaelic Ireland in the Later Middle Ages* (Woodbridge, 1987), pp.52, 55, 71, 97; also more generally, R. Dudley Edwards, 'Anglo-Norman Relations with Connacht, 1169-1224', *I[rish] H[istorical] S[tudies]*, i. (1938-9), 141-53; Frame, *Colonial Ireland*, pp.38-41; and J. Lydon, 'Lordship and Crown: Llywelyn of Wales and O'Connor of Connacht', *The British Isles*, ed. Davies. pp.48-63.

[34] D. Stephenson, *The Governance of Gwynedd* (Cardiff, 1984), pp.1-2, 152-4; M. Richter, 'David ap Llywelyn, the First Prince of Wales', *W[elsh] H[istory] R[eview]*, v (1970-1), 213-4; J. Beverley Smith, 'The Succession to Welsh Princely Inheritance: the Evidence Reconsidered', *The British Isles*, ed. Davies, pp.64-81.

[35] *Pontificia Hibernica*, ed. M.P. Sheehy (Dublin, 1962-5), i, no.147.

[36] G.A. Williams, 'The Succession to Gwynedd, 1238-47', *Bull. Board of Celtic Studies*, xx (1962-4), 393-413.

[37] *CDI, 1171-1251*, no.673; *CR, 1227-31*, 126-7; Orpen, *Normans*, iv. 54-8.

[38] *CR, 1254-6*, 213; Orpen, *Normans*, iii. 232-4.

rival. There can be little doubt that the former would have seemed to him the lesser evil.

There are also indications that in Ireland as in Wales the titles accorded (or withheld) by the royal chancery might repay attention. Aedh O'Connor was called 'king of Connacht' by the king's ministers after he succeeded Cathal in 1224; by 1226, fallen from favour, he had become 'Aedh, son of Cathal, late king of Connacht', a style reminiscent of the humiliating 'son of Llywelyn, former prince of North Wales' with which Dafydd had to make do for most of his brief career.[39] When Felim, also a son of Cathal, recovered the kingship for Cathal's line in 1233, the chancery was slow to respond. Despite his visit to England in 1240, he does not seem to have been accorded his royal title until he served Henry in north Wales five years later; and when friction occurred in the following decade, he found himself demoted to 'Felim O'Connor, an Irishman'.[40] Though both Donough O'Brien (d.1242) and his son Conor (d.1268) themselves employed royal styles, the chancery on the whole denied these to the kings of Thomond after the 1220s.[41] For Irish leaders unambiguous acceptance of their royal status was a goal that mostly lay just over a horizon that was itself receding.

Although the Irish political facet of the lordship had contracted between 1175 and 1250, it was still perceptible. For Henry III it was a variation on a familiar theme. In the same year that Felim O'Connor visited court Henry was attended at Gloucester by Dafydd of Gwynedd, whom he knighted, and who wore 'the small circlet that is called *garlonde*, the insignia of the principality of North Wales, submitting himself moreover in everything to the king of England'.[42] In 1246 Harald Olafsson, king of Man and the Isles, who existed uneasily between the Norwegian and English orbits, 'was knighted, as his father had also been, by Henry, king of England, who bade him farewell with much honour and rich gifts'.[43] Alongside the expanding assertiveness of the 'administrative kingship' of the Angevins, there remained a vestige of the tradition of patriarchal overlordship, associated with the English monarchy since the tenth century, into which dealings with Irish rulers might fit. It was an imperial tradition that contemporaries could still choose to stress, as they did in 1235 when, on the occasion of the marriage of Henry's sister to

[39] *Royal Letters*, i. 292; P[atent] R[olls], *1225-32*, 48-9. Cf. Richter, pp.206-7.

[40] *Foedera*, I, i. 257 (misdated 1244); *CDI, 1252-84*, no.448.

[41] G.H. Orpen, 'Some Irish Cistercian Documents', *EHR*, xxviii (1913), 307, 309. Cf. *PR, 1216-25*, 336 ('*Rex D. regi Tosmunde salutem*'), and *1225-32*, 118 ('*Rex Dunecano Carebrac salutem*'). In 1245 the Pope too referred to Donough merely as *nobilis vir* and *dominus Tuadomonie* (*Pontificia Hibernica*, ii. no.266).

[42] *Annales Monastici*, ed. H.R. Luard (RS, 1864-9), i. 115.

[43] *Chronica Regum Manniae et Insularum*, ed. P.A. Munch (Christiana, 1860), p.23; cf. *CM*, iv. 551.

Frederick II, it was a question of keeping up with the Hohenstaufen.[44]

By the fourteenth century Ireland's political connections with England present a sharply different appearance. For one thing, the direct link between the crown and native Irish leaders has faded to the point where anybody who attempts to write about Anglo-Irish relations is left with the uncomfortable feeling of producing an Irish history without the Irish. One of the last recorded examples of contact dates from 1285, when Donal Rua MacCarthy *dominus Hybernicorum Desmonie* sent a letter to Edward I and obtained a safe-conduct to visit him.[45] Thereafter the only obvious area of interaction was provided by the Anglo-Scottish war. On several occasions before 1335 the English chancery acquired lists of those currently powerful among the Irish and summoned them alongside a host of Anglo-Irish knights and esquires. There was now no question of conceding royal titles to the Irish as there might still have been in the 1240s; they are referred to as *duces, principales*, or merely by family name in the manner of clan chiefs.[46] When in rare instances royal records do employ phrases such as *rex hibernicorum* or *reguli hibernici*, there is a palpable implication that these were not kings in any sense that a reasonable man would recognize.[47]

One explanation of the virtual extrusion of the Irish rulers from the high political scene was the progressive crumbling that afflicted the provincial kingships themselves in the course of the thirteenth century. As baronial power expanded, their wealth declined and their dynastic instability was exploited and intensified; this instability was to ensure that no O'Connor or O'Brien would be in a position to deliver the backing of Gaelic Connacht or Thomond to Edward Bruce during the Scottish invasion in the years 1315-18.[48] By 1300 the more distant parts of Ireland contained a large number of small Irish powers that had scarcely any direct contact with England. Where major overlordships existed, they tended to be in baronial hands, the grandest example being that of the de Burghs.[49] If they collapsed, as the de Burgh supremacy in Ulster and Connacht did after the murder of the last earl in 1333, they could not readily be replaced.

[44] *The Flowers of History by Roger of Wendover*, ed. H.G. Hewlett (RS, 1886-9), iii. 113; *CM*, iii. 325. Cf. G.W.S. Barrow, 'Das Mittelalterliche Englische und Schottische Königtum: Ein Vergleich', *Historisches Jahrbuch*, cii (1982), 364-71.

[45] PRO, S.C.1/16/115 (*CDI, 1252-84*, no.2362); *CDI, 1285-92*, no.61.

[46] *CDI, 1302-7*, no.47; *Rotuli Scotiae*, i. 118, 343. Territorial arrangements made with the O'Connors of Connacht in 1325 and the O'Neills of Ulster in 1338 do seem to have been referred to England (PRO Dublin, R.C.8/14, p.309; *CCR 1337-9*, p.329).

[47] E.g., PRO, C.260/57, no.28; E.101/28/21, m.10ᵛ.

[48] R. Frame, 'The Bruces in Ireland, 1315-18', *IHS*, xix (1974-5), 16-25.

[49] Simms, *From Kings to Warlords*, pp.13-15, and 'The O Hanlons, the O Neills and the Anglo-Normans in Thirteenth-Century Armagh', *Seanchas Ardmhacha*, ix (1978-9), 82-93.

The shrinkage and demotion of Irish kingship might also be seen in a broader context. By the later years of Edward I, when kings of Man were a thing of the past and the apparatus of English government had spread into north Wales, there existed scarcely a remnant of the old western arc of *'reges* and *principes* in which Irish rulers had found a place: if Edward had imperial pretensions, they were along very different lines from those of Athelstan, or Henry II.[50] Under Edward II and Edward III the crown remained skilled at manipulating segmentary conflicts and maintaining an Irish style of lordship over the minor Gaelic lineages that occupied the uplands and bogs of the south and east, but it did so almost entirely at one remove, through the justiciar of Ireland and his colleagues.[51] The decay of Irish kingship, the spread of baronial power, and the enlargement of the sphere of English government are all visible as early as 1253 in Conor O'Brien's complaint that he was 'much vexed on account of the suit that he owes at the county [court] of Limerick', words that recall contemporary Welsh grievances, which were likewise sparked by the expansion of royal jurisdiction.[52] This background adds interest to Richard II's visit to Ireland in 1394-5. As in the time of Henry II, Irish leaders, who by this stage rarely assumed royal titles, came in to submit to a king of England. Among Richard's problems there seems to have been the lack of familiar conventions for the type of lordship over ethnic rulers that had come so naturally two centuries earlier. His response was to grope towards the idea of redefining the position of the Irish in English terms, and even – if Froissart is to be believed – re-educating them socially.[53] The attempt to accommodate them within the structure of the lordship at once encountered the obstacle that the claims of Irish and English to land and lordship were incompatible. The game was a new one, and the players did not stay on the field long enough to discover whether workable rules could have been devised.

The other striking difference from the time of John or Henry III is less negative: the presence of a more clearly-etched political world bounded by English Ireland itself. This is not to say that there was the sort of disconnection from England sometimes suggested in older writings on the period. It is true that the dispersal of the vast unitary lordships of Leinster and Meath among successive generations of heiresses from the 1240s onwards produced a class of English landholders for whom Irish interests

---

[50] Cf. L.B. Smith, 'The Statute of Wales, 1284', *WHR*, x (1980-1), 137-8.

[51] R. Frame, 'English Officials and Irish Chiefs in the Fourteenth Century', *EHR*, xc (1975), 748-77.

[52] *CR, 1251-3*, 496. Cf. R.A. Griffiths, 'The Revolt of Rhys ap Maredudd, 1287-8', *WHR*, iii (1966-7), 122-9; R.R. Davies, *Conquest, Coexistence, and Change: Wales 1063-1415* (Oxford, 1987), pp.305-7.

[53] See D. Johnston, 'Richard II and the Submissions of Gaelic Ireland', *IHS*, xxii (1980-1), 1-14, 20; J.L. Gillespie, 'Richard II's Knights: Chivalry and Patronage', *Jnl. Medieval Hist.*, xiii (1987), 148-9.

were distinctly subsidiary; but despite this the web of property-holding was still closely woven and important, and for the king the management of Ireland remained in part an extension of aristocratic court politics.[54] Nonetheless the fourteenth-century sources seem to invite us to speak of a political community which identified itself with the lordship.

The label usually affixed by historians to that community and its members is 'Anglo-Irish'; possibly their characteristic traits are better caught by the contemporary term 'the English of Ireland'. Their identity was defined, on the one hand, by a contrast with the Irish. This had special point in the fourteenth century because the military and other problems of the lordship encouraged a defensive outlook which is visible not least in petitions reaching Westminster. In 1334, for example, we have a Kildare knight asking Edward III 'to take note of the great labours, losses and costs which [he] has sustained and laid out in the service of our lord the king in going in the armies of various justiciars against the enemy Irish, in which he lost his brother and many of his men'.[55] The calculated phrases become so hackneyed that we almost cease to notice them; yet as well as reflecting a view of the lordship they helped to create one. These sentiments were put to work in a grander way in 1342, when a parliamentary assembly meeting at Kilkenny addressed the king about the alleged misdeeds of his ministers in Ireland. Writing a generation after their defeat of Edward Bruce, and stung by an ill-considered revocation of grants, 'the prelates, earls, barons and commons of [the] land of Ireland' reminded Edward III of the loyalty of his 'English liege people of Ireland', who had held the lordship for him 'as well against the Scots as the Irish, [his] enemies; and this, moreover, at their own costs'.[56] The function of the English of Ireland was self-consciously a garrison one, and it demanded a firm contrast between themselves, the king's subjects, and the Irish, his enemies.

Their political identity had another, less straightforward, ingredient. For the English of Ireland their Englishness was crucial; the establishment to which they belonged rested on grants made by English kings from 1171 onwards, and held by English common law. Yet the difficulties that attended the relationship with England made the designation 'English' an awkward one. Unlike the modern Ulster loyalist, who claims a 'British' identity and may even reserve 'English' for the aspects of the British connection that offend him, the English of Ireland had to do the best they could with one word. The results were by turns clumsy and curiously stylized. The royal servants reviled in 1342 were not

---

[54] Frame, *English Lordship*, Chapters 5-9.

[55] PRO, C.81/217/8187.

[56] *Statutes [and Ordinances and Acts of the Parliament] of Ireland, [King John to Henry V]*, ed. H.F. Berry (Dublin, 1907), pp.342-5. See R. Frame, 'English Policies and Anglo-Irish Attitudes in the Crisis of 1341-2', in *England and Ireland*, ed. Lydon, pp.86-103.

'English' ministers but ministers 'sent from England'.[57] An annalist writing in Dublin describes the clash as between 'English of English origin' and 'English of Irish origin'.[58] During the 1350s and 1360s we are told of recurrent tensions between 'the English born in England' and 'the English born in Ireland'. Such episodes were transient and tended to be associated with the arrival of English governors accompanied by large retinues; they reflect the hostility of a provincial elite to the invasion of their world by acquisitive outsiders; and indeed the line between the two varieties of English proves very difficult to draw in individual cases.[59] The whole phenomenon may have been invested with too much solemnity by historians in search of a nascent colonial nationalism. Yet it would be a mistake to dismiss it; as with the outcry against 'aliens' in thirteenth-century England (which raises not dissimilar problems of definition), the choice of terms to express political resentment is revealing. The uneasiness of their connection with England was another defining characteristic of the English of Ireland.

Those English had in addition a sense of their own past and historical role, which was articulated and sharpened during the Scottish invasion. In 1317 the Gaelic Irish supporters of Edward Bruce sent a defence of their actions to the pope. The original papal grant of Ireland to Henry II placed them in a difficulty which they tried to meet by arguing at length that their actions were justified by the failure of English kings, their ministers and subjects in Ireland to observe the terms of *Laudabiliter*, which had obliged Henry to protect and extend the church and to give the Irish a stiff dose of twelfth-century law and morals. John XXII did not accept the case that the lordship should be transferred to Bruce, but he was sufficiently impressed by the litany of complaint to urge Edward II to look into it.[60]

There survives, in a petition sent to Edward *c.*1318 by 'the ordinary [English] people of Ireland', an alternative reading of the past, penned by somebody who may well have been acquainted with the facts if not the detailed contents of the Irish case. The preamble runs:

> When St. Patrick discovered only heretics in the land, he founded churches all around and planted Christianity there; this remained good and healthy for a long time afterwards and was obedient to the Church of Rome. Later, because the land was shared between various kings . . . there arose wars . . . amongst

[57] *Statutes of Ireland*, p.344.

[58] *Chartularies of St Mary's Abbey, Dublin*, ed. J.T. Gilbert (RS, 1884-6), ii. 383: 'inter Anglicos in Anglia oriundos et Anglicos in terra Hibernie oriundos'.

[59] Frame, *English Lordship*, pp.105-6, 121-2, 246-7; Lydon, 'The Middle Nation', pp.10-11.

[60] *Irish Historical Documents, 1172-1922*, ed. E. Curtis and R.B. McDowell (London, 1943), pp.38-46, at pp.42-4. See J.A. Watt, 'Negotiations between Edward II and John XXII concerning Ireland', *IHS*, x (1956-7), 1-5.

them. Hence MacMurrough, king of Leinster, who was driven out, came to King Henry in the time of St. Thomas of Canterbury and begged him to undertake the conquest of the land with his help . . . The king informed Pope Adrian of MacMurrough's suggestion and asked for permission to enter that land . . . And when the pope had been informed by his representatives of the wickedness of the Irish, he permitted the king by his bull to enter the island to subject the Irish to law and instruct them in virtue, and extend the boundaries of Holy Church . . . Since the Irish would not obey him voluntarily, [Henry] sent force and learning there to conquer the land, in the shape of troops and lawyers, who imposed English law: to wit, that if a man kills another, he should be hanged . . . Through this law, so long as the conquerors and their heirs upheld it, the English multiplied and the boundaries of Holy Church expanded.

The document goes on to complain about judges who take fines for homicide, together with other things that, in the view of its authors, have caused the decay of the lordship, but returns to generalities with the remark that 'the foundation of the king's right is true and good . . . and the continuance of the conquest was guided by law, and through law came peace, and through peace the English multiplied and the church expanded'. This is one of a number of signs that the English of Ireland possessed the awareness of themselves in space and time that characterizes a political community.[61] Edward II and Edward III were faced by a land where there was a vocal ruling group who claimed to be English and to speak for Ireland – an Ireland that by definition excluded the Irish.

The appearance of collective political awareness among the English of the lordship may have had something to do with emotional identification with Ireland and protracted cultural shifts. But the growth of English government in Ireland forms a less elusive background that has been oddly neglected. In midland and southern Ireland the trend in the thirteenth century was towards a greater number of smaller administrative units, a process that was facilitated by the fractioning of Leinster and Meath. By 1300 a close mesh of counties and well-supervised liberties occupied a swathe of territory from the borders of Ulster round to Cork, Limerick and even Kerry; in pockets within it were substantial gentry societies whose members manned a system of local institutions that derived from England.[62] The significance of the expansion and greater intrusiveness of government can be seen above all in the military sphere.

---

[61] *Affairs of Ireland*, no.136; this petition (PRO, S.C.8/177/8820) may possibly have been accompanied by a copy of *Laudabiliter* (S.C.8/177/8818). Cf. J.A. Watt, '*Laudabiliter* in Medieval Diplomacy and Propaganda', *Irish Ecclesiastical Record*, 5th ser., lxxxvii (1957), 425-32.

[62] A.J. Otway-Ruthven, 'Anglo-Irish Shire Government in the Thirteenth Century', *IHS*, v (1946-7), 1-28.

The century of the three Edwards was marked by the organization of the lordship for war, both to defend itself against the Irish threat in Leinster and Munster, and to support the wider war-effort against the Scots from 1296 onwards. The royal records are packed with evidence of military recruitment, the requisitioning of supplies, local taxation for local emergencies and, increasingly, general taxation too; there was, besides, much legislation on matters of defence and order.[63]

We seem to be faced by the Irish version of a familiar late medieval story, concerned with the shaping of a political community through the demands of its ruler, and the interaction of ruler and ruled this entailed. If in the reign of Edward III there was an English politics, to do in part with the management of a community that periodically manifested itself in parliament, so too there was a politics of Ireland. The community of the lordship had its characteristic concerns and attitudes. On the one hand there were matters that arose from the existence of the Irish and the condition of Ireland: taxation, and problems of order and defence of a distinctive type. On the other might be set the areas of friction in relation to England: neglect (whether actual or imagined) by absentee landholders; greed and stupidity (whether real or invented) on the part of ministers sent from England; the insensitivity of English regimes in handling patronage. On all these questions leaders of the English of Ireland had their say in councils and parliaments and in the last resort expected to address the king directly.[64]

For Edward III dealings with his Irish subjects were, needless to say, far less frequent and insistent than with their equivalents in England. But the form of the relationship was familiar. Consciousness of it is apparent in 1350, when the king assented to a suggestion made by ministers who had recently arrived in the lordship,

> that the magnates and commons should be specially commended by the king, in parliament and also in council, for their good and loyal bearing towards him, and for the labour they have undergone and the expenses they have sustained in the king's absence for the protection of the king's land and people against the enemies.[65]

Its significance is visible ten years later when Edward, now resting on his Continental laurels, was induced to spend money on Ireland after a case was made in a Great Council at Kilkenny and forced home in England

---

[63] See A.J. Otway-Ruthven, *A History of Medieval Ireland* (London, 1968), pp.200-308; and, on the Scottish wars, J.F. Lydon in *A New History of Ireland, ii: Medieval Ireland, 1169-1534*, ed. A. Cosgrove (Oxford, 1987), 195-204.

[64] See in general, A. Cosgrove, 'Parliament and the Anglo-Irish Community: the Declaration of 1460', in *Parliament and Community: Historical Studies, XIV*, ed. Cosgrove and J.I. McGuire (Belfast, 1983), 32-7.

[65] *Affairs of Ireland*, no.217 (p.193).

when representatives from the lordship travelled to court.[66] It is particularly clear in the 1370s when Edward was anxious, with the renewal of the French war, to stem the haemorrhage of funds and push the burden of financing Irish wars back on to the community of the lordship. When the governor failed to get the Irish parliament to swallow the medicine, instructions were given to hold another parliament in the presence of a persuader who was to be specially sent from England; and there was even an attempt to bring the recalcitrant representatives of the Irish counties, boroughs and lower clergy over to England for a scolding.[67]

All this suggests one way in which Ireland might find a natural place in the political history of the later Plantagenet world. In the fourteenth century the British Isles contained two 'English' political communities, markedly unequal, it is true, in size and wealth, and moulded by experiences that were not exactly parallel, but nonetheless sharing a great deal besides their allegiance and the appellation 'English': a common law, a full set of English regnal institutions ranging from parliament to commissions of the peace, and not totally dissimilar preoccupations (for both, military service, taxation, and the enforcement of law were central). Among England's neighbours, Ireland had the distinction of being overseas, and yet not foreign (or indeed wholly English); historiographically it may have suffered from the difficulty of finding a category to which to assign it. Thus the English of medieval Ireland have tended to be discussed almost entirely within the confines of Irish historical discourse.[68] Its long perspectives have been richly illuminating: and yet the king's subjects of Ireland, more than most groups, possessed two dimensions, one of which asks to be understood in a different context, that of English history, to which the *Anglici in Hibernia nati* also have a strong claim to belong. Just as the development of English government in England and Ireland in the thirteenth century is – or ought to be – one subject, so the political consequences on both sides of St George's Channel might profitably be drawn within a single story.

---

[66] Frame, *English Lordship*, pp.318-26; P. Connolly, 'The Financing of English Expeditions to Ireland, 1361-76', in *England and Ireland*, ed. Lydon, pp.104-21.

[67] J.F. Lydon, 'William of Windsor and the Irish Parliament', *EHR*, lxxx (1965), 262-7.

[68] These points seem as appropriate to this as to the later period considered in S.G. Ellis's thought-provoking 'Crown, Community and Government in the English Territories, 1450-1575', *History*, lxxi (1986), 187-204.

Chapter 9

The Decoration and Illumination of Royal Charters in England, 1250-1509: An Introduction

Elizabeth Danbury

On 6 April 1796 Thomas Hall, then mayor of Northampton, returned from London bearing with him George III's newly issued letters patent confirming to the borough privileges granted to it by previous monarchs. On the arrival in Northampton of the carriage containing the mayor, with Lord Compton, Mr. John Markham and the Honourable Spencer Perceval, the horses were removed from the traces and the men of the town drew the carriage through the streets. That night the chief inhabitants were feasted by the mayor and corporation at no small expense. The account for the banquet, together with a Ladies' Assembly and the erection and lighting of a transparency, came to nearly £160. This was not the end of the celebrations. Another triumphal banquet (costing just under £100), was held on 16 May. In addition, 100 guineas were voted to the deputy recorder and five guineas to his clerk for their work in furthering Northampton's petition for a new royal grant. The total expenditure for the new letters patent was much more; in 1795 and 1796 the corporation borrowed £1,600 for this purpose.[1] The Northampton celebrations in 1796 help to explain why individuals and corporate bodies in earlier centuries went to such trouble and expense to obtain royal grants and have them decorated or illuminated: such documents were treasured and displayed as valuable evidence of royal favour and enhanced status.

The study of decorated documents (royal and others) presents many problems.[2] First, decorated documents are extremely hard to identify. They are scattered throughout the country in national, local authority and private repositories and, for the most part, there is no indication in catalogues and lists of which documents are decorated. In the second place, many documents which may have been decorated, have disappeared. Some have been destroyed by fire,

---

[1] C.A. Markham, and J.C. Cox, *The Records of the Borough of Northampton*, 2 vols., (Northampton, 1898), i. 152-4.

[2] I am deeply indebted to the many archivists who have discussed charters with me, to the late Professor T. Julian Brown and to James Campbell for advice, criticism and encouragement.

accident or deliberate vandalism,[3] some lost or misplaced, some stolen or sold with no record kept of the buyers. Paradoxically, some losses may be accounted for by steps taken for greater security. In the fifteenth century the most important charters which had been granted to Queenborough, Kent, were distributed among various corporation officials and members. In 1476 an entry in the Statute Book reported that the mayor held in his possession a papal bull and the common seal of Queenborough, John Raynet had a leather-covered box containing two charters, while three other dignitaries had in their safekeeping one charter each.[4] Documents could too easily stray and, if recovered, it was often only by accident or after sustained searching. Martyn Cotes, a sixteenth-century town clerk of Rochester, endorsed a royal charter of 6 February 1266 to the city with the observation: 'Memorandum that thys Charter was found at Norton anno 1578 by reason of a Serche I ther made amonge the wrytinges of myne Aunte Finches at which tyme upon my Requeste she gave yt to me and so I Restoryd yt to the Cyttye agayne. Martyn Cotes'.[5] Martyn Cotes was an antiquary. Not all town clerks took such trouble: documents therefore remained with 'Aunt Finches' across the land and were dispersed or destroyed in the course of time.

The subject of this essay is the decoration and illumination of documents between 1250 and 1509, and its discussion will concentrate on royal charters and letters patent, which were the documents most likely to be decorated in England during this period. Other types of documents occasionally embellished with ornamentation included non-royal charters endowing or supporting the foundation by others of religious and educational institutions, episcopal indulgences, grants of arms, letters of confraternity, mortuary rolls and (very rarely) private deeds of title.[6] There is no general study of the palaeography, diplomatic and embellishment of decorated royal charters, or of other decorated documents in England. The secondary sources are limited both in number

[3] In 1800 or 1801, Thomas Hall, who had led Northampton's rejoicings when the letters patent of 1796 were obtained, was discovered by Theophilus Jeyes, the town clerk, in the Guildhall. He was cutting the seals and signatures from leases, charters and other documents taken from an old wooden chest in the Guildhall. When challenged, Alderman Hall laughed and said that the old documents were totally useless, and should be destroyed. Markham and Cox, ii. 5.

[4] C.E. Woodruff, 'Notes on the Municipal Records of Queenborough', *Archaeologia Cantiana*, xxii (1897), 173.

[5] Rochester City Council, second charter of Henry III, granted 6 February 1266, P.H. Bartlett, *The City of Rochester Charters* (Rochester, 1961), p.21.

[6] Victoria and Albert Museum, *The Common Chronicle: Archival Treasures from the County Record Offices of England and Wales* (London, 1983) includes some examples of decorated documents, pp.19, 45, 47.

and in scope.[7] The importance to art historians of dated examples of decoration and illumination has long been recognized,[8] but much work remains to be done on the contribution of decorated documents to the study of palaeography, diplomatic and administrative practice and procedure, as well as to those of heraldry, ceremonial, personal and institutional imagery. The practice of decorating royal charters and letters patent appears to have begun in England in the mid thirteenth century. During the 1240s and 1250s the initial letter 'H' of the king's name *Henricus* began to be omitted in certain royal charters and letters patent.[9] Usually the resulting space was left blank, but occasionally it was filled in with an elaborate capital letter. This letter could be executed in pen and ink, using ordinary (brown/black) writing ink or coloured inks (almost invariably red or blue) or alternatively, an illuminated initial letter 'H' could be inserted in the space. The earliest examples of such illuminated initials so far discovered date from the 1250s and 1260s and are all on grants to East Anglian beneficiaries.[10]

The reasons for the origin in England of the practice of decorating grants of lands and privileges are hard to discover. There is no obvious evidence of continental influence: indeed the prima facie most likely source for any such influence, the French chancery, did not produce documents with any form of decoration until the late thirteenth century.[11] The practice of illuminating collective indulgences also postdates the

---

[7] The most useful secondary sources are: British Records Association, *Catalogue of an Exhibition of Borough Charters on the Occasion of the Annual Conference 1959* (London, 1959); H.C. Maxwell-Lyte, *Historical Notes on the Use of the Great Seal of England* (London, 1926), pp.266-7; C.T. Clay, 'An Illuminated Charter of Free Warren, dated 1291', *The Antiquaries' Journal*, xi (1931), 129-32; Erna Auerbach, *Tudor Artists* (London, 1954).

[8] Illuminated charters have been cited in studies of the portraiture of Richard II: F. Wormald, 'The Wilton Diptych', *Journal of the Warburg and Courtauld Institutes*, xvii (1954), 191-203; J.H. Harvey, 'The Wilton Diptych: A Reexamination', *Archaeologia*, xcvii (1961), 1-28; S. Whittingham, 'The Chronology of the Portraits of Richard II', *The Burlington Magazine*, cxiii (1971), 12-21.

[9] St. John's College, Cambridge, Archives 12/3 (Charter of Henry III to St. Mary's Hospital, Ospringe [co. Kent], 15 April 1258); *ibid.*, Archives 12/4 (Charter of Henry III to Ospringe, 27 January 1267); Corporation of London Record Office, City Charter 18 (Letters Patent of Henry III to City of London, 11 January 1266); *ibid.*, City Charter 19 (Charter of Henry III to City of London, 26 March 1268).

[10] King's Lynn Borough Records, KL/C2/5, 7 and 8 (old references Aa3, Aa4a, Aa4b); H. Grieve and F. Roberts, *Ornament and Decoration in Essex Records* (Essex County Council, 1950), p.1.

[11] E.A. Danbury, 'English and French Artistic Propaganda during the period of the Hundred Years War: some Evidence from Royal Charters', *Power, Culture, and Religion in France c.1350-c.1500*, ed. C.T. Allmand (Woodbridge, 1989), pp.76-7.

1a St. John the Baptist: letters patent granting Robert de Conyers permission to endow a chantry in honour of St. John the Baptist at Hutton Conyers, Yorkshire, 27 Oct. 1286.

(West Yorkshire Archive Service, Leeds District Archives, Vyner Mss., VR 1652)

1b 'Figure initial' incorporating human and animal representations: letters patent confirming an agreement made between the mayor, bailiffs and burgesses of Oxford on the one part, and William de Wykeham and the warden and fellows of New College on the other part, 13 Jul. 1389.

(New College, Oxford, Archives Ms. 5361)

1c The arms of Warenne, with hawking and fox-hunting scenes: letters patent granting lands to John de Warenne, earl of Surrey, 4 Aug. 1316. *(Public Record Office E 41/495A)*

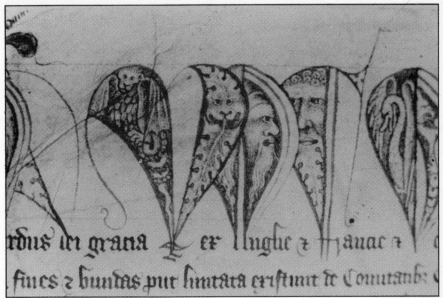

2a Decorated looped ascenders: letters patent confirming grants made to the newly created county of Bristol, 20 Dec. 1373. *(City of Bristol Record Office, 01210)*

2b Standardised pen and ink charter decoration of the 1440s: Henry VI in majesty within an initial letter composed of strapwork or cadels; above is a crown with one of Henry VI's mottoes 'Dieu et mon droit' on the rim, and, to the left, an angel holds a shield left blank for the arms of the grantee: charter of incorporation of Ipswich, 28 Mar. 1446. *(Suffolk Record Office [Ipswich Branch] C3/13)*

earliest English illuminated charter,[12] while a very early illuminated grant from Scotland, Malcolm IV's charter of 1159 to Kelso Abbey, appears to be a unique and isolated survival.[13] Not only is there a lack of any obvious stimulus from outside England, but also there is as yet no evidence that the origin of the practice of decorating the most formal products of the royal chancery was in any way influenced by contemporary English decorated documents such as mortuary rolls.[14] Finally, it is not at present possible to link the new developments in charter decoration to administrative or personnel changes in the mid thirteenth-century chancery. All that can be said is that the appearance of this practice must tell one something about the attitude of beneficiaries to documents recording grants and that it may in some way be connected with the rising demand for an increasing number of such documents.

There is little doubt that, other than in exceptional circumstances, it was the beneficiaries, not the king, who paid for any decoration added to the document. Accounts (admittedly later than the beginning of this practice of decoration) survive to support this likelihood. The audit roll of Eton college for 1447-8 includes a payment of 26s. 8d. to William Abel for the illumination of Henry VI's consolidation charter of 5 March 1446 to the college.[15] The Winchester college accounts of 1442-3 include a payment of 5s. 4d. 'clerico Kirkeby' for writing various documents and for illuminating the letters patent of 9 February 1443, which permitted Winchester to acquire lands to the yearly value of 100 marks.[16] There is no reason to suppose that this fifteenth-century evidence refers to other than established practice. For example, the decoration of charters often has

---

[12] H. Delehaye, 'Les lettres d'indulgence collectives', *Analecta Bollandiana*, xliv (1926), 342-379; xlv (1927), 97-123, 323-344; xlvi (1928), 149-57, 287-343. The existence of ornamental initials in collective indulgences is noted in xliv (1926), 363, 365, 367, 371-2, 374, 377 and the subject discussed in xlvi (1928), 287-343; E.M. Donkin, 'A Collective Letter of Indulgence for an English Beneficiary', *Scriptorium*, xvii (1963), 316-23; C.R. Cheney, 'Some Features of Surviving Original Papal Letters in England', *Annali della Scuola Speciale per Archivisti e Bibliotecari dell' Universita di Roma*, Anno XII, 1972 (1973), 1-25.

[13] National Library of Scotland, Edinburgh, Duke of Roxburghe Mss: Kelso charter (G.W.S. Barrow *Regesta Regum Scottorum, Volume I. The Acts of Malcolm IV King of Scots 1153-1165* [Edinburgh, 1960], no.131); G.W.S. Barrow, 'Das Mittelalterliche Englische und Schottische Königtum: ein Vergleich', *Historisches Jahrbuch*, 102 (1982), 387.

[14] The practice of decorating mortuary rolls in England antedates the decoration of charters; for example BL, Egerton Charter 2849 is the mortuary roll of Lucy (de Vere?) foundress and first prioress of Hengham (Hedingham, Co. Essex) and is dated *circa* 1230. A recent example of the use of mortuary rolls in an art historical study is P. Binski and D. Park, 'A Ducciesque Episode at Ely: the Mural Decorations of Prior Crauden's Chapel', *England in the Fourteenth Century: Proceedings of the 1985 Harlaxton Symposium*, ed. W.M. Ormrod (Woodbridge, 1986), p.37. The subject of mortuary rolls is studied in L.V. Delisle, *Rouleaux des Morts du ixe au xve siècle* (Paris, 1866).

[15] Eton College, ECR EA.3, m.9.

[16] Winchester College, Bursar's Accounts 1442-3.

very strong personal and local significance and connections and this suggests local commissioning. The charter of Edward II to the city of Carlisle dated 12 May 1316 has, in its initial letter 'E', a representation of the siege of Carlisle by the Scots in July 1315, and its defence by English troops, led by Sir Andrew de Harcla, sheriff of Cumberland.[17]

There are two separate letters patent of Edward II to John de Warenne, Earl Warenne and of Surrey, both dated 4 August 1316, by which certain lands formerly given to the king by the earl were regranted to him, with remainder to Matilda de Nerford (Warenne's mistress) for her life, and then with successive remainder to John and Thomas de Warenne, his illegitimate children by her. Both these documents are decorated in pen and ink with hunting scenes, almost certainly intended as a pun on 'Warenne', and the more elaborate of the two also has, within the initial letter E, a shield of the Warenne arms (chequy or and azure).[18] The style of the decoration is close to that of early fourteenth-century manuscripts of the East Anglian school, and it is certainly possible that these letters patent could have been decorated in East Anglia; for Warenne held large estates in Norfolk, centred on the honour of Castle Acre. The style and practice of decorating royal documents altered significantly after 1399, but it is still possible to find local themes and legends illustrated in charters. Henry V's letters patent of 7 July 1413 confirming earlier grants to the borough of Colchester contain, within the illuminated initial letter 'H', a representation of St. Helena. She, according to Geoffrey of Monmouth, was the daughter of Coel, the king who supposedly gave his name to Colchester. The arms of Colchester (gules, two ragged staves vert joined in the form of a cross, its arms and foot pierced by Passion Nails and three golden crowns, the bottom one encircling the foot of the cross)[19] are represented below the initial letter, while the Emperor Constantine, St. Helena's son, is shown standing to the right of the initial letter, holding the horizontal bar of a cross. Around the saint is an inscription which associates her, and her real and legendary achievements, with the borough: 'Sancta Elena nata fuit in Colcestria. Mater Constantini fuit et sanctam crucem invenit. Elena.' Civic, personal and institutional pride could thus be enhanced by the payment of artists to illustrate it.

[17] Cumbria Record Office (Carlisle) Ca/1/2, *CCR, 1300-26*, 211; R.S. Ferguson, 'Notes on the Initial Letter of a Charter of Edward II to the City of Carlisle', *Transactions of the Cumberland and Westmorland Antiquarian and Archaeological Society*, vi (1881-2), 319-27; British Records Association, *Catalogue*, p.34.

[18] PRO,E41/495A2 *CPR, 1313-17*, 528-9. The other decorated letters patent of 4 August 1316 in favour of Earl Warenne are PRO, E41/495B; *CPR, 1313-17*, 528. See plate 1c.

[19] Colchester Borough Council, Colchester charters 7 July 1413 (Henry V); *CPR, 1413-16*, 63; British Records Association, *Catalogue*, p.37. The current arms of Colchester are those illustrated in the letters patent of 1413, but the staves are argent, not vert (Geoffrey Briggs, *Civic and Corporate Heraldry* [London, 1971], pp.114, 117).

It is difficult to prove, other than on stylistic grounds, exactly when the royal and other grants were decorated. It does seem most likely, however, that decoration was added very soon after the document was written in the vast majority of cases. A few decorated documents exist or are known to have existed which were cancelled or invalidated soon after they were written. On 8 September 1385, Michael de la Pole, who had been created earl of Suffolk on 6 August, was granted the reversion of the lands of William de Ufford, late earl of Suffolk, to the yearly value of £500.[20] De la Pole was impeached in October 1386, and it was ordered that lands and revenues previously granted to him by Richard II should be taken back into the king's hands.[21] The initial letter 'R' of the original letters patent of 8 September 1385 is elaborately decorated in pen and ink with Michael de la Pole's name and arms. Similarly a royal charter to the prior and convent of the Blessed Mary of Chester, dated 16 November 1383, had an illuminated initial letter 'R'. It was endorsed with the statement that the grant had been superseded by a later award, made before 28 May 1392 allowing the convent lands to the value of 20 marks *per annum*, and the document itself was cancelled by three knife cuts.[22] In both cases it is obvious that the decoration must have been added soon after the document was written: it would have been a waste of time and money to embellish invalid grants. Some documents must have been decorated even before the great seal was attached. On 26 July 1466 Edward IV confirmed Henry VI's charter to the Drapers Company of London and, notwithstanding the statute of Mortmain, allowed the Drapers to acquire property from any person to the value of £20 a year.[23] In the original charter, Edward IV's arms supported by the white lion of March and the black bull of Clarence appear within the initial letter 'E', and all four borders – above, to either side and below the text – are elaborately illuminated by a very fine artist or artists, probably Flemish.[24] The lower border is under the turn-up of the charter, so the illumination must have taken place before the foot of the document was folded back to allow the

[20] PRO E156/29/41; *CPR, 1385-9*, 18.

[21] *Rot. Parl.*, ii. 219.

[22] Royal Commission on Historical Manuscripts, National Register of Archives typescript list 4738 no.18. The present location of this document is not known; *CPR, 1391-96*, 62.

[23] Drapers' Company of London, charter xiii; *CPR, 1461-7*, 537.

[24] If the decoration of this charter is indeed Flemish, it predates the arrival of Flemish manuscripts and painters in England after Edward IV's return from Flanders in 1471 (M. Rickert, *Painting in Britain: The Middle Ages*; 2nd ed. [London, 1965], p.181); J. Backhouse, 'Founders of the Royal Library: Edward IV and Henry VII as Collectors of Illuminated Manuscripts', *England in the Fifteenth Century: Proceedings of the 1986 Harlaxton Symposium* (Woodbridge, 1987), pp.23-32; J.J.G. Alexander, 'Painting and Manuscript Illumination for Royal Patrons in the Later Middle Ages, *English Court Culture in the Later Middle Ages*, ed. V.J. Scattergood and J.W. Sherborne (London, 1983), pp.152-3.

great seal to be attached. It is, of course, possible that when a previously undecorated charter written many years earlier came into new ownership, it would be embellished at the new owner's expense, or that the successors of the original grantees of a charter would decide to have it decorated. On 1 January 1359 Thomas Beauchamp, earl of Warwick, made a grant to the townspeople of Warwick by which he renounced in perpetuity his claims to tolls from alien merchants visiting or trading there.[25] From the style of the illumination it has been argued that the charter was decorated at some date between 1400 and 1420, probably in Warwick 'as a monument to the first grant of free trade to the city and a cornerstone of the city's prosperity'.[26] If this was indeed the case, this document represents a departure from the apparent normal practice. For the evidence of the few relevant medieval accounts supports the physical evidence of the charters themselves and the stylistic evidence of the decoration: all link the decoration or illumination on the document very closely to the date given in the dating clause.

During the period 1250-1509 the amount of space on the document which could be set aside for embellishment was gradually and deliberately increased. Up until about 1340 only one letter, the initial letter of the king's name, was omitted from the undecorated, but otherwise completed, charter or letters patent. Occasionally the chancery clerk followed the practice customarily used by writers of books intended for illumination and inserted a very small guide letter in the space to the left of the remaining letters of the king's name.[27] This indicated to the illuminator the letter which should be embellished in the space provided. In the late thirteenth and early fourteenth century the chancery clerks displayed their own calligraphic skills by lengthening, thickening, exaggerating and decorating certain of the ascenders and capital letters in the king's style and title on the top line of the document. Letters which commonly received such attention were the first 'd' and the 'w' of *Edwardus*, the 'd' of *dei*, 'R' of *Rex*, 'A' of *Anglie*, 'D' of *Dominus*, 'H' of *Hibernie*, 'D' of *Dux* and 'A' of *Aquitannie*. Other ascenders in letters of the address were often similarly treated, as was the first letter of the dispositive clause. Very occasionally, other letters at the beginning of clauses were also embellished. This decoration was almost invariably the work of the clerk who wrote the text. The style of the work on the ascenders and the colour

[25] Warwick County Record Office, CR, 2389.

[26] Sotheby's *Catalogue of Western Manuscripts and Miniatures to be Sold on 11 December 1984* (London, 1984), no.26.

[27] Charter of Edward II granting the castle and manor of Tutbury to his younger son, John of Eltham, 9 July 1322 (PRO, E40/3265); letters patent of Edward II confirming the liberties of the abbey of Cartmel, 12 November 1323 (BL, Harley Charter 51 H 2); letters patent of Edward III confirming the grant of the county of Cornwall to his mother Isabella, 1 March 1327 (PRO, E40/222).

of the ink are identical to those employed in the main text. A document which illustrates the skill of the clerk as penman is the charter of 6 August 1307 by which Edward II bestowed on Piers Gaveston the earldom of Cornwall.[28] Capitals and ascenders on the top line and throughout the text are embellished by the hand of the clerk who wrote the document. The name at the foot of the document is also decorated. Unusually, it is that of the writer of the document, not the supervising chancery official, and this is clearly stated: 'T. de Newehagh' scripsit'. Among many examples of royal grants incorporating elaborately embellished ascenders on the top line are the two letters patent of 4 August 1316 in favour of the Earl Warenne, the Carlisle charter of 12 May 1316, a charter confirming previous royal grants to Hull, dated 25 May 1330,[29] another confirmation charter to Maldon of 4 December 1330[30] and letters patent dated 28 February 1331, the form of an exemplification of proceedings in parliament whereby Richard fitz Alan, earl of Arundel, had restored to him the lands and titles forfeited by his father at his execution.[31] The elaborate ascenders which appear on these grants are a hallmark of early fourteenth-century charters and letters patent, whether illuminated or not.

Between the late 1330s and early 1340s, this particular form of decorated ascender disappeared from the top line of royal charters and letters patent. During this period, chancery clerks began to leave gaps instead of writing certain capitals in the king's style and title. The purpose of this was, presumably, to allow additional space for decoration and illumination in the top margin. It is not at present possible to identify an exact date for the start of this practice or to link it with a specific senior chancery official. Apart from the initial letter of the king's name, the capitals and ascenders most commonly omitted were the 'R' of *Rex*, the 'A' of *Anglie*, the double 'ff' of *Francie*,[32] the 'D' of *Dominus*, 'H' of *Hibernie*, the initial letters of the groups of the addressees listed in charters, and in

[28] PRO, E41/460; *CChR, 1300-26*, 108; Maxwell-Lyte, p.267. The charter and letters patent relating to the conferral of the earldom of Cornwall on Piers Gaveston (*CPR, 1307-13*, 9) were two of the first documents issued under the great seal after Edward II's accession. The initial letter and all four borders of the charter are decorated in pen and coloured inks with Cornish choughs, displayed eagles, which are the charges on Gaveston's own arms, and with shields containing the arms of England, Gaveston and Clare (Gaveston's wife was Margaret de Clare). The decoration of the charter is, as opposed to the sophisticated writing of the text, crude in style and execution.

[29] Kingston upon Hull City Record Office, BRC5; *CChR, 1327-41*, 175. The initial letter 'E' has a simple pen and ink design of trefoil leaves.

[30] Essex Record Office, D/B/3/13/3; *CChR, 1327-41*, 195.

[31] BL, Harley Charter 83 c 13; *CPR, 1330-4*, 84; Maxwell-Lyte, pp.197, 267.

[32] After Edward claimed the throne of France, his style and title altered to *Edwardus dei gratia Rex Anglie et Francie et Dominus Hibernie*. Before the claim, his style and title were *Edwardus dei gratia Rex Anglie Dominus Hibernie et Dux Aquitannie*, A.B. and A. Wyon, *The Great Seals of England* (London, 1887), pp.29-32.

letters patent the 'O' of *Omnibus* and the 'L' of *Littere* as well as letters in the greeting and the initial letter of the first word of the dispositive clause. When the charter or letter patent took the form of an *inspeximus* the initial letter of this word was often omitted whenever it occurred in the course of the document.

Different artists used the resulting spaces in different ways. In some charters and letters patent, notably those produced during the reigns of Edward III and Richard II, the ascenders on the top line were made into exaggerated loops and adorned with human and animal heads, grotesques and a huge variety of leaf, flower and abstract ornament. Some of the most spectacular examples of this decoration of ascenders are to be found in the top lines of two of the grants awarded by Edward III to the city of Bristol, when it was created a county in its own right in 1373. The charter of 8 August and the letters patent of 20 December not only possess illuminated initial letters, executed by a very fine artist or artists, whose work may possibly be associated with the Bohun group of manuscripts, but the ascenders on the top line of both documents are ornately elaborated in pen and ink, those in the charter of 8 August in blue-black and red inks, those of the letters patent of 20 December in ordinary writing ink.[33]. Other elaborated ascenders may be found in Richard II's letters patent of 9 March 1382 to Bath[34] and in his charter of 22 November 1389 to Shrewsbury.[35] In the Bristol, Bath and Shrewsbury documents the style of decoration of the pen and ink ascenders is very different to that of the initial letters and the other illuminated areas. The illuminator of the Bath letters patent, when executing the border above the top line of the text, had to move the border up nearer the top of the document, in order to avoid the ascenders. Some ascenders were illuminated and formed part of the illuminator's total design, as in the instrument of 19 July 1362 by which Edward, the Black Prince was granted the newly created principality of Aquitaine and Gascony.[36] Capitals and ascenders were often left uncompleted, even when money and labour was expended in the decoration of the initial letter of a royal grant. The initial letter of Richard II's charter to Norwich of 26 February 1378 is an impressive piece of penmanship.[37] The strokes forming the letter 'R' are made up of

[33] Bristol Archives Office, 01208 (*CChR, 1341-1417*, 228) and 01210 (*CPR, 1370-4*, 371); N. Dermott Harding, 'Bristol Charters, 1155-1373', *Bristol Record Society*, i, (1930), 170-3. See plate 2a.

[34] Bath City Record Office, Bath City charters, 9 March, 1382; *CPR, 1381-5*, 101.

[35] Shrewsbury and Atcham Borough Council, Guildhall, Shrewsbury, Muniments 1.24; *CChR, 1341-1417*, 315-6; J.J.G. Alexander and P. Binski (eds.), *Age of Chivalry: Art in Plantagenet England, 1200-1400* (London, 1987), no.716. The costumes and figures in this illumination are very close to those in the *Liber Regalis* (Westminster Abbey Library, London, Ms. Book 38).

[36] PRO, E30/1105. The document is discussed in R. Barber, *Edward, Prince of Wales and Aquitaine* (London, 1978), pp.177-8, and pl.4.

[37] Norfolk Record Office, Norwich Charter No.13; *CChR, 1341-1417*, 238.

grotesques, while in the spaces in between are five-petalled flowers. The document itself has a distinctly odd and unfinished appearance, for there is no 'R' in *Rex* and the other ascenders in the king's titles are stunted or lacking. If, rather than leaving a blank space where the ascenders should have been, it was decided to complete the letters, then the most common practice in the late fourteenth and early fifteenth centuries seems to have been to fill the space with enlarged unornamented letters and add to the attenuated ascenders simple enlarged shapes resembling elongated geometric forms.

The last change in the treatment of ascenders, a change which is paralleled in the decoration of the initial letter of the king's name, appears in the mid 1430s and early 1440s. It coincides exactly with the introduction into English usage of strapwork, or cadels, as a means of embellishing individual letters or groups of letters in documents.[38] Strapwork is composed of interlacing strokes and is particularly well suited to the skilful penman. Probably originating in Northern Europe,[39] it was first used in England to embellish two apparently unrelated classes of documents; the Plea Rolls of King's Bench on the one hand, and charters and letters patent on the other. In the Plea Rolls, the only letter usually decorated with strapwork before 1509 was the initial letter 'P' of the first word *Placita* on the first membrane of the roll.[40] On charters and letters patent, strapwork was used to decorate not only the initial letter of the king's name, but also capital letters and ascenders in the royal style and title. Occasionally other letters and ascenders on the top line and elsewhere in the document were also embellished. The earliest Plea Roll on which strapwork decoration appears is that of Easter 1439.[41] The earliest examples so far discovered of its use on royal charters and letters patent date from the late 1430s and early 1440s. They include letters

[38] There is no study of the use of strapwork or cadels in English documents. Strapwork is not found in England before 1430. After its introduction, it became immensely popular. The skilful penman could embellish his work without needing recourse to an illuminator. As a result, it became one of the chief forms of decoration recommended by writing masters (J. Backhouse, *John Scottowe's Alphabet Books*, Roxburghe Club, London, 1974). Strapwork was used to embellish a wide variety of legal, financial and ecclesiastical records in the sixteenth and seventeenth centuries (Victoria and Albert Museum, *ubi supra*, pp.22, 31, 38, 51). It is still used to embellish the initial letters of *pro forma* legal documents: *Oyez Forms, 1988* (Oyez Stationery Group, 1988).

[39] The use of strapwork in Northern Europe predates its first use in England. In the early fifteenth century, Jean Flamel, librarian of the duke of Berry, inserted ownership inscriptions ornamented with strapwork into the duke's manuscripts (J.J.G. Alexander, *The Decorated Letter* (London, 1978), pp.27, 32). Jan Van Eyck's painting *The Arnolfini Marriage* (National Gallery, London) has the artist's signature *Johannes de eyck fuit hic 1434*. The initial letter 'J' of *Johannes* is finely embellished with strapwork.

[40] M. Post, *Royal Portraits from the Plea Rolls, Henry VIII to Charles II* (London, 1974); Auerbach, pp.17-25, pls.1-4.

[41] PRO, K.B. 27/712.

patent from Henry VI, dated 18 March 1439, granting the alien priory of Ravendale to the dean and chapter of Southwell Minster,[42] several of the royal grants relating to the foundation and endowment of Eton College,[43] and individual letters patent issued after 1441 granting or confirming privileges to boroughs.[44] Strapwork as an embellishment for the top line of royal grants was an immediate and lasting success. Its use became standard practice in most decorated charters and letters patent after 1440, and continued not only until 1509 but throughout the Tudor and Stuart periods.[45] Moreover, the layout and design of royal grants decorated with strapwork in pen and ink were followed almost exactly by some of the major artists who illuminated royal grants in and after the fourth decade of the fifteenth century. William Abel illuminated two grants for Eton College in 1442 and 1446 and one for King's College, Cambridge in 1446.[46] Although his workmanship and iconography are infinitely more brilliant and complex, the basic strokes elaborating the capitals and ascenders in the top line of the text of all three documents, and the initial letters themselves, are based by Abel on the interlacing strokes of the pen and ink strapwork employed on decorated royal grants. After 1440 the shapes of the embellished letters, and therefore the entire appearance of decorated charters and letters patent, were to a considerable extent dictated by strapwork.

Although the embellishment of the top line of the document was an important feature of the whole decorative programme, the highest quality of artistic work, and the most important symbolic statements, were normally centred on the initial letter of the king's name. The development of the decoration of the initial letter can be divided into two stages; from its origins up to the end of Richard II's reign in 1399, and thereafter until 1509. These two stages display contrasting characteristics. Before 1399 there seems to have been a distinct preference for illuminated rather than pen and ink initials. A wide variety of style and approach to the

---

[42] Lincolnshire Archives Office, Cragg 4/22; *CPR, 1436-41*, 261.

[43] Eton College, ECR 39/3 (Foundation Charter of Eton College, 1 October 1440); ECR 39/4 (duplicate, sealed with the Great Seal in natural wax); ECR 39/7 (Letters patent to Alice Houseworth and Margaret Water, relating to lands in Eton, 20 December 1441); ECR 39/11 (Grant in frankalmoign of lands in Eton to Provost and College of Eton, 31 January 1441).

[44] King's Lynn Borough Records, KL/C2/35 (old reference Ba 1) (letters patent to King's Lynn, 1 December 1441); Kingston upon Hull City Record Office, BRC 16 (letters patent granting a licence in mortmain to Hull, 25 June 1443); Suffolk Record Office, Ipswich branch, C3/13 (charter of incorporation of Ipswich, 28 March 1446).

[45] Auerbach, plates 4-51; British Records Association, *Catalogue*, pp.23-5, 39-48.

[46] Eton College, ECR 39/8, ECR 39/57; King's College, Cambridge, muniments A20. J.J.G. Alexander includes the two latter documents in his study of William Abel: 'William Abell "Lymnour" and Fifteenth-Century English Illumination', *Kunsthistorische Forschungen Otto Pächt zu ehren*, eds. A. Rosenauer and G. Weber (Salzburg, 1972), pp.166-72.

embellishment of charters during this period is also apparent: initials were decorated, probably in many cases locally, by artists whose individual approach to their work suggests a lack of knowledge of charter decoration elsewhere. It is not possible to suggest a centre for the decoration of documents. After 1399, the characteristics of charter decoration undergo a total change. Many initials seem to have been added at a specific centre, almost certainly in London and near the chancery. Most of the initials are in pen and ink and have a uniform content and style. From the reign of Henry IV onwards, the sovereign's mottoes, badges and supporters, together with the royal arms and the arms or emblems of the grantees, feature with increasing dominance in the decorative content of royal grants: this dominance reaches its apogee under the Tudors and Stuarts. There are, of course, exceptions to these general rules, but most documents so far discovered appear to conform to them.

Until 1399 most charters which were embellished were illuminated, rather than decorated in pen and ink. The choice of subject for the illumination varied, but a considerable number include a representation of the king, either seated in majesty or with saints associated with the grantee. The initial letter of Edward III's charter of 25 June 1338 to the dean and chapter of St. Paul's cathedral shows the king handing the charter to St. Paul, who is represented bearing a sword, his usual attribute.[47] Within the initial letter of Richard II's letters patent of 7 July 1393 to Crowland abbey confirming two Anglo-Saxon royal charters, Richard himself is depicted together with St. Guthlac and another king, probably Aethelbald of Mercia, whose charter founding the abbey was one of those confirmed.[48] Richard II, St. Guthlac and Aethelbald are shown seated together. Richard II is depicted as rather more than a patron of the abbey, for while with his left hand he holds his letters patent, with his right he presents the kneeling abbot to St. Guthlac, rather in the manner of a saint presenting a donor to the Deity. Kings could also be depicted together with the beneficiaries and without the presence of saints. Four of the royal grants received by the university of Cambridge between 1291 and 1343 were illuminated: all four illuminations underline the association of king and university by depicting the king, either handing the charter to scholars or university officials or simply standing with them.[49]

One of the most popular ways of representing the king between 1250 and 1399 was to show him seated alone in majesty. The earliest example of this type of illumination dates from 26 June 1280 in letters patent to the

[47] Guildhall Library, London, Ms.8762; *CChR, 1327-41*, 451-2.

[48] Bodleian Library, Oxford, Ms. Ashmole 1831; *CPR, 1391-6*, 300. P. Lasko and N.J. Morgan, *Medieval Art in East Anglia* (Norwich, 1973), no.39.

[49] Cambridge University Archives, Luard *7, Luard *11, Luard 15, Luard *33a.

abbey of Glastonbury.[50] Although the document is damaged, it is possible to identify the king, crowned, holding in his left hand the letters patent sealed with the great seal in green wax. The great seal may have played a considerable role in forming the artist's image of the king. Many people who would never have had the chance to see the king in person may well have formed their idea of majesty from the only representation widely circulated; namely the great seal which authenticated royal orders and grants. Thus the charter of Richard II to Great Yarmouth, dated 28 November 1386,[51] confirming earlier grants and awarding new privileges to the borough, has within the initial letter a representation of the king crowned and enthroned, with the sceptre in his right hand and the orb in his left. The image of the king in majesty had been portrayed in this way on the obverse of all great seals since the first use of the second great seal of Henry III in 1259.[52] The initial letters of Richard II's letters patent allowing Nicholas Cristisham to alienate property in Wells to the guild of the borough of Wells, dated 17 November 1394,[53] and of his charter to Oswestry of 14 August 1398,[54] confirming it as a borough, both illustrate the same subject as the Great Yarmouth charter; the styles of illumination of the three initials are so different that it seems most likely that a common factor must have been the artists' knowledge of the great seal. The relationship between the design of seals and of the illumination of initial letters of royal grants is also underlined in a charter of 18 November 1347, to the Queen's Hall, Oxford.[55] This charter, awarded at the request of Queen Philippa, declared that the king's hospital of St. Julian (also known as God's House) in Southampton, which had lately been granted to Queen's Hall, should henceforth be held in frankalmoign, free of tolls, purveyance and taxation. The initial letter 'E' of *Edwardus* contains within it a representation of a standing crowned figure with long hair holding in its right hand a sceptre. Although this illumination is described in the typescript catalogue of the Queen's College archives as representing Edward III,[56] it is far more likely that it is intended to be Queen Philippa,

[50] Society of Antiquaries of London, Ms.607; *CChR, 1257-1300*, 226.

[51] Great Yarmouth Borough Council, Y/C2/4; *CChR, 1341-1417*, 305-6.

[52] A.B. and A. Wyon, *The Great Seals of England*, p.24. Before 1259 the king had been depicted with a sword in his right hand and an orb in his left; thereafter he was represented with a sceptre in his right hand and an orb in his left hand.

[53] Wells City Council, charter 13; *CPR, 1391-6*, 515; D.O. Shilton and R. Holworthy, 'Wells City Charters', *Somerset Record Society*, xlvi (1932), 13-14.

[54] Oswestry Town Council; A20 no.2. *CChR, 1341-1417*, 373-5; S.Leighton, *The Records of the Corporation of Oswestry* (Oswestry n.d. [1879-83]), pp.8-16.

[55] Queen's College, Oxford, charter 318; *CChR, 1341-1417*, 70. The style of decoration is similar to that in the initial letter of letters patent of 22 March 1344 granting God's House, Southampton, to the queen's new foundation of scholars in Oxford (Queen's College, Oxford, charter 316).

[56] N. Denholm Young, *Archives of the Queen's College, Oxford, a Calendar* (1930-1), i. 148.

for the whole design of the figure is based on the seal of a queen: namely a standing crowned female form, holding a sceptre in her right hand.[57] Within the initial letter of the Queen's College charter the shields of arms surrounding the figure confirm that it is Philippa: to the left are the arms of her husband Edward III (quarterly, France ancient and England), to the right are her paternal arms (quarterly, Hainault and Holland) and below her feet are the arms of Robert de Eglesfield, royal clerk and founder of the college. The payment for the elaborate and finely executed illumination may have been made by Eglesfield, in order to associate Philippa even more closely with the college which was named after her.

Decorative schemes for charter illumination could be derived directly from the content of the grant. Edward I's charter of 10 June 1291 granting Roger de Pilkington free warren in his demesne lands in Pilkington and elsewhere in Lancashire, was decorated on all four borders with animals which could be hunted or farmed within the limits specified by the charter.[58] The animals include roe and fallow deer, boar and fox, woodcock and quail, rabbit and hare. In contrast, the letters patent of 24 April 1347, by which Edward III gave the mayor and bailiffs of Bristol licence both to make a cage for the imprisonment of malefactors and to punish bakers who had broken the assize of bread by drawing them through the streets on hurdles, has representations of both these punishments in the intial letter.[59] The upper half of the 'E' shows two evildoers being driven into the cage and the lower half depicts a fraudulent baker, his short-weight loaf suspended above his head in uneven scales, being dragged on a hurdle drawn by two horses. The whole effect is both exuberant and eye catching. Dramatic effect could be obtained without historiated initials, though not without cost. Several charters and letters patent incorporate extensive use of gold leaf in initials and borders featuring leaves and flowers or abstract designs. The illumination is of extremely high quality and indicates the value placed on royal grants by the beneficiaries. The cities of Canterbury and Norwich were prepared to pay for such elaborate initials, and for borders above and to each side of the text, to decorate charters granted by Richard II on 3 February 1380[60] and 15 February 1380.[61] The appearance of the charters is very impressive

[57] W. de Gray Birch, *Catalogue of Seals in the Department of Manuscripts in the British Museum* 6 vols. (London, 1887-1900), i. 99-101.

[58] Fitzwilliam Museum, Cambridge, Bradfer-Lawrence Ms. B 1/51; *CChR, 1257-1300*, 390; C.T. Clay, 'An Illuminated Charter of Free Warren, dated 1291', *The Antiquaries' Journal*, xi (1931), 129-32; 'A Charter of Edward I – Enchantingly Adorned with Birds and Beasts', *Illustrated London News* (colour supplement, March 1957), p.iv.

[59] Bristol Archives Office, 01250 (1-2); *CPR, 1345-8*, 281; N. Dermott Harding, *ubi supra* pp.108-9; British Records Association, *Catalogue*, p.35.

[60] Canterbury City and Cathedral Archives, AA12; *CChR, 1341-1417*, 263.

[61] Norfolk Record Office, Norwich Charter no.14; *CChR, 1341-1417*, 264. British Records Association, *Catalogue*, p.36.

and suggests the possibility that, from time to time, they may have been taken out to be admired by those who had paid for the decoration and benefited from the privileges recorded in them.

It is, of course, impossible to know how many people saw the completed embellished charter, but the amount of care expended on the devising of the decorative programmes is notable. The relatively few documents dated before 1399 decorated in pen and ink, demonstrate the same forethought and skill as were employed on illuminated charters. By letters patent dated 27 October 1286, Robert de Conyers was given permission to endow a chantry at Hutton Conyers in Yorkshire.[62] The initial letter of the letters patent contains a pen and ink representation of St. John the Baptist, in whose honour the chantry was dedicated. The artist's work is of very high quality, as is that in the Carlisle charter of 1316 and the letters patent to John de Warenne of the same year. The choice of subject is, in almost all cases, either directed specifically to the purpose of the grant or has particular relevance to the beneficiary. The initial letter of a charter of 14 March 1316 granting the abbot and convent of Suleby in Northamptonshire free warren in all their demesne lands within that county has a deer hunting scene,[63] while another charter dated 30 May 1317, inspecting and confirming earlier royal grants to Ipswich, contains within the initial letter the representation of a citizen, the town walls of Ipswich and a ship: the design of this initial seems to have been based on the Ipswich borough seal.[64]

It is among grants embellished with pen and ink that one of the most significant changes in the treatment of initial letters in decorated royal and non-royal documents may be found. In England, until the end of the fourteenth century, the strokes making up the initial letters acted as frames which supported or enclosed the representational or abstract designs. The letter forms themselves were not important other than as supports or frames. In other countries the practice was different. In France, for example, the strokes which formed the letter were an integral part of the decorative design.[65] In January 1372 Charles V formally confirmed his gift of a portion of the True Cross to his brother John, duke of Berry.[66] The document has an elaborate initial' K' (the initial letter of *Karolus*). Charles V is represented standing and crowned in the vertical upright of the 'K'. Within the right-hand downwards stroke the duke kneels to receive the relic, while the right hand upwards stroke is occupied

---

[62] Leeds District Archives, Vyner Mss., VR 1652. See plate 1a.

[63] University of London Library, Fuller Collection 1/21/4; *CChR, 1300-26*, 306.

[64] Suffolk Record Office, Ipswich branch, C3/4; *CChR, 1300-26*, 344-5; W. de Gray Birch, ii. 95-6; G. Pedrick, *Borough Seals of the Gothic Period* (London, 1904), pp.77-8 and plate iv.

[65] E.A. Danbury, *ubi supra*, p.79.

[66] Archives Nationales, Paris, J 185, no.6 [Musée AE II 393].

by an angel playing the viol. The action and figures are contained inside the strokes of the letter. These 'figure initials' are first found in England during the reign of Richard II. The vertical upright of the initial letter 'R' of Richard II's letters patent of 5 October 1380 granting lands in Oxford to the fellows of Merton College contains a representation of the king.[67] The fellows are shown kneeling at the king's feet, outside and to the left of the initial letter, to receive the charter from him. Among several documents incorporating figure initials in the archives of New College, Oxford, are the letters patent of 13 July 1389 confirming an agreement between the mayor, bailiffs and burgesses of Oxford on the one part and William de Wykeham (the founder), Nicholas de Wykeham (the Warden) and the fellows of New College, on the other, concerning lands to be given to the college by William de Wykeham.[68] The initial letter 'R' is decorated in pen and coloured inks with a representation of a bearded man standing beneath an oak tree within the horizontal upright, while the loop of the 'R' and the down-stroke are each inhabited by an animal; a bear within the loop and a cat within the down-stroke. The incomplete text: 'ecce agnus dei qui tollit peccata' links the horizontal upright to the loop of the 'R'. These pen and ink figure initials are an important development in England. After 1399 the decoration of initials on royal documents was, in the main, closely linked to the forms of the letters themselves and most royal charters and letters patent were not illuminated but decorated in pen and ink.

The change of medium from illumination to pen and ink after 1399 is striking, and its impact is heightened by the appearance at the same date, of a uniform style and content in much royal charter decoration. Though some documents including the letters patent to Colchester of July 1413 and the Drapers' Company charter of July 1466 are not only illuminated but individual in style and content, nevertheless the great variety of charter decoration which exists between 1250 and 1399 is not found thereafter. The uniformity, which emerges at the beginning of Henry IV's reign and continues throughout the following centuries, suggests very strongly that after 1399 decorated initials were added to royal grants at a specific workshop or group of workshops. It seems likely that such workshops would have been in London, for there would have been no point in sending the newly written documents to another city or centre to

---

[67] Merton College, Oxford, charter 370; *CPR, 1377-81*, 550; J.J.G. Alexander, *The Decorated Letter*, p.23.

[68] New College, Oxford, Archives Ms. 5361. F.W. Steer, *The Archives of New College, Oxford* (Chichester, 1974), p.79. The agreement of 18 November 1388 confirmed by these letters patent also has a pen and ink figure initial. The initial 'H' (*Hec indentura*) is composed of two fighting beasts and an oak tree. A bishop's crozier is thrust horizontally through the upright stroke of the 'H' (New College Archives, Ms. 12186). I owe this reference to Mrs. Caroline Dalton. See plate 1b.

be decorated. Surviving accounts indicate that municipal officials came to London to press for the issue of a new charter or letters patent in favour of their community, and, if necessary, to 'oil the wheels' of government.[69] If they were successful, they returned home with the new royal grant. Any decoration added to the document could most conveniently be added in London. It has not yet been discovered if the artists responsible for the decoration worked within the chancery itself. This may have been the case. The title, 'Master of the Decorated Documents', has been applied to the artist or artists who embellished the initial letters of royal grants and of plea rolls during the reigns of Edward IV and Richard III,[70] and certainly artists who worked on these two apparently unrelated classes of documents could be argued to have had some form of privileged access to the royal writing offices. It is also possible that such artists were attached to workshops close by, and received their commissions for charter decoration through recommendations made to grantees or their representatives by the clerks of the chancery.

Most artists working on charter decoration after 1399 emphasized the king's personal connection with the privileges or liberties granted, and with the grantees, by incorporating into the initial letter the royal mottoes, badges, arms, supporters or image. Charters of Henry V in favour of the Cinque Ports (16 October 1413),[71] Bristol (12 January 1414),[72] Canterbury (10 October 1414)[73] and Gloucester (5 February 1415)[74] and letters patent to Hull (10 December 1414)[75] have almost identical decoration, obviously by the same artist or group of artists, based on an enlarged initial letter 'H'. The Canterbury, Hull and Gloucester charters incorporate one of Henry V's mottoes 'In deo salutare meum'[76] on the vertical stroke and bow of the 'H'. In addition, in the Bristol, Cinque Ports, Canterbury and Hull documents, the initial letter is surmounted by a crown of fleurs de lis with Henry IV's motto 'Soverain'[77] inscribed on the rim.

[69] J.R. Boyle, *Charters and Letters Patent Granted to Kingston upon Hull* (Hull, 1905), pp.47-9, 66-7; Maxwell-Lyte, pp.358-9.

[70] P. Tudor-Craig (ed.), *Richard III* (National Portrait Gallery, 1973), pp.33, 48-9, pls.20-3.

[71] Fitzwilliam Museum, Cambridge, Henderson deeds no.22; *CChR, 1341-1417*, 456.

[72] Bristol City Record Office, 01216; *CChR, 1341-1417*, 466; H.A. Cronne, 'Bristol Charters, 1378-1499', *Bristol Record Society*, xi (1946), 102-17.

[73] Canterbury City and Cathedral Archives, AA26; *CChR, 1341-1417*, 477.

[74] Gloucester City Guildhall, GBR I 1/16; *CChR, 1341-1417*, 477.

[75] Kingston upon Hull City Record Office, BRC 11; *CPR, 1413-16*, 290.

[76] 'In deo salutare meum (et gloria mea)', Psalm 61 verse 8 (Vulgate text).

[77] 'Sovereyne' appears on the scabbard and hilt of the great Dublin civic sword. In 1403 Henry IV granted the mayor of Dublin and his successors the right to have a sword borne before them: it is suggested that he gave this sword to Dublin from his own armoury. Alexander and Binski, no.730.

Royal mottoes figure prominently in charter decoration after 1399. The appearance of 'Soverain' in charters and letters patent of Henry V's reign demonstrate that the use of a particular motto did not end with the death of the king with whom it was first associated. Some mottoes were used by more than one king. 'Dieu et mon droit'[78] and 'Domine salvum fac regem'[79] were first employed on charters of Henry VI's reign but were adopted by his successors. 'Dieu et mon droit' appears twice on scrolls attached to the initial letter of letters patent of 12 February 1441, founding King's College, Cambridge.[80] The pen and ink 'H' itself is made to appear as if it is created from the 'SS' collar of Lancaster. The use of strapwork as the chief means of embellishing letters in royal grants after 1440 resulted in the decoration of many charters and letters patent having an almost identical appearance, based on a strapwork initial letter 'H' surmounted by a crown. Inscribed on the rim of the crown or on a scroll around the crown was the motto 'Dieu et mon droit'. The earliest use of the motto 'Domine salvum fac regem' so far discovered is on letters patent to Hull dated 17 July 1431,[81] and it is used thereafter throughout Henry VI's reign, occasionally in conjunction with 'Dieu et mon droit', as in the charter creating Southampton a county in its own right, dated 9 March 1447,[82] or on its own, as in letters patent of 30 October 1449 in favour of Eton College, granting it the reversion of the wardenship and of the hospital of St. James by Westminster.[83] On these letters patent, which have no crown above the initial letter, an extended variation on the motto: 'Domine salvum fac Regem Henricum fundatorem nostrum' is on a scroll round the vertical stroke of the 'H'. When William Abel illuminated the charter of *inspeximus* of 25 January 1442 confirming, with the authority of parliament, the foundation and endowment charters of Eton college, he incorporated twice into his design the motto 'Domine salvum fac Regem', as well as the motto of the Order of the Garter and the last two lines of the *Te Deum Laudamus*: a canticle of thanks and praise and one closely linked with the consecration and coronation of kings.[84] Edward IV's letters patent to Gloucester of 6 April 1473,[85] continued the use of Henry VI's

[78] Thomas Willement, *Royal Heraldry: The Armorial Insignia of the Kings and Queens of England, from Coeval Authorities* (London, 1821), p.35.

[79] 'Domine salvum fac regem (et exaudi nos in die qua invocaverimus te)', Psalm 19 verse 10 (Vulgate text); Willement, pp.35-9.

[80] King's College, Cambridge, muniments A1; *CPR, 1436-41*, 521-3.

[81] Kingston upon Hull City Record Office BRC12; *CPR, 1429-36*, 141.

[82] Southampton City Record Office SC1/1/8; *CChR, 1427-1516*, 76. H.W. Gidden, 'The Charters of the Borough of Southampton, Vol.I', *Southampton Record Society*, vii (1909), 70-81.

[83] Eton College, ECR 39/100; *CPR, 1446-52*, 296.

[84] The *Te Deum Laudamus* has a place in every English coronation order from the eleventh century onwards. L.G. Wickham Legg, *English Coronation Records* (London 1901).

[85] Gloucester City Guildhall, GBR I 1/21; W.H. Stevenson, pp.19-20.

motto, extending it to refer to Edward IV, his queen and his eldest son Edward: the words 'Domine salvum fac Regem Reginam et Principem' are on a scroll round the outside of the initial letter 'E'. The motto was finally given an English form: 'God save the king' in the reign of Henry VII.[86] The motto 'Dieu et mon droit' is inscribed on the rim of the crown above the strapwork initial letter 'R' in Richard III's letters patent of 28 November 1484 confirming Edward IV's grants to Bristol,[87] and the use of this motto continued under the Tudors. In contrast, mottoes connected only with the house of York were not employed after 1485. A charter of 2 August 1461 to Canterbury,[88] letters patent of 1 July 1462 to Hull[89] and the charter of incorporation of Doncaster of 30 October 1467[90] all feature a strapwork initial letter 'E' surmounted by a crown. Inscribed on the rim of the crown is the motto 'Comfort et liesse'. This motto was adopted as its own by Doncaster, but it is not found on any royal document postdating the reign of Edward IV.

In addition to mottoes, badges play an increasingly important role in charter decoration during the course of the fifteenth century. The grants of Edward IV to Canterbury, Hull and Doncaster cited above all feature different Yorkist badges in the decoration of the initial letter 'E': the Canterbury charter has three crowns, the Hull letters patent feature double white roses and the Doncaster charter has sunbursts as well as one of Edward IV's heraldic supporters, the white lion of March, holding a banner. Heraldic supporters begin to appear in charter decoration in the mid-fifteenth century. They are shown supporting either the crown above the strapwork initial letter or shields of the royal arms. Two antelopes, which were Henry VI's heraldic supporters appear,[91] one on each side of the crown above the initial letters 'H', in the 1447 charter creating the city of Southampton into a county and in the charter of January 1442 confirming the foundation and endowment of Eton. The decoration of the

---

[86] It is used in Latin on the rim of the crown surmounting the initial letter of letters patent of 10 November 1490, allowing Robert (Stillington), bishop of Bath and Wells, with others, to alienate lands in Somerset and Devon (St. John's College, Cambridge, Archives D56.194). In English it is found in extended form on a scroll surrounding the arms of Henry VII in the statutes of Christ's College, Cambridge: 'God save our noble king harry the vij and preserve Margaret his moder Also preserve harry arturis broder' (Christ's College, Cambridge, Lady Margaret Beaufort's copy of the statutes, f.11ᵛ).

[87] Bristol Record Office 01226, enrolled on the confirmation rolls, PRO, C56/2 no.7; H.A. Cronne, Bristol Charters, 1348-1499, p.153.

[88] Canterbury City and Cathedral Archives, AA34; *CChR, 1427-1516*, 138-41.

[89] Kingston upon Hull City Record Office, BRC 18; *CPR, 1461-7*, 237.

[90] Doncaster Archives Department, AB1/1/4; *CChR, 1427-1516*, 218-20. British Records Association, *Catalogue*, p.38.

[91] It has been argued that the visual evidence for the personal use of supporters by Henry VI postdates his death (J.H. and R.V. Pinches, *The Royal Heraldry of England* [London, 1974], pp.97-8.) The charter does not postdate his death and supports the evidence in Willement, pp.35-6.

incorporation charter of Gloucester, dated 2 September 1483, includes the arms of Richard III supported by the white lion of March and a boar[92] and the letters patent of 30 August 1507, granting fishery rights to Eton College, has within the initial letter the arms of Henry VII supported by a dragon and a greyhound.[93] The combination of royal arms, supporters and badges is given its most forceful expression under Henry VII. Illuminated letters patent of 1 May 1505 granting permission to Lady Margaret Beaufort to found Christ's College, Cambridge,[94] contain within the initial letter 'H' the arms of Henry VII surmounted by an imperial closed crown and supported by a dragon and a greyhound. All four borders contain Tudor and Beaufort badges: the double red rose, the portcullis and the daisy (this last being the personal badge of Lady Margaret Beaufort). The use of mottoes, badges and shields of arms with heraldic supporters in charter decoration in the fifteenth century gives us, in miniature, some evidence for the likely embellishment of tents, wallhangings, horsetrappers, surcoats, liveries, standards and banners. These, which now chiefly survive as individual rarities, or are known from depictions in heraldic and illuminated manuscripts or from descriptions in wills and chronicles, acted as vehicles for artistic propaganda promoting factions or causes. Documents could do the same. The decorative content of documents can be identical to that of objects made of cloth, stone, glass or metal.[95] The letters patent granting permission for the foundation of Christ's College, Cambridge and the entrance gates to Henry VII's chapel at Westminster abbey both incorporate the royal arms, surmounted by a crown and supported by a dragon and a greyhound. Both have the double rose[96] and the portcullis. The chapel entrance features the motto 'Dieu et mon droit', which the charter does not, although 'Dieu et mon droit' was frequently employed in charter decoration. By studying the decoration of charters, it may be possible to learn more about the use of heraldry, badges and mottoes in artistic propaganda in later medieval England.

One of the most skilful exploiters of such artistic propaganda was Henry VII. It was in his reign that the pattern for the embellishment of royal grants for the following two hundred years was established. The essential elements of Tudor and Stuart charter decoration were, firstly, a

---

[92] Gloucester City Guildhall, GBR I 1/22, enrolled on the confirmation rolls, PRO, C56/1 no.20: W.H. Stevenson, pp.16-19. N.M. Herbert, R.A. Griffiths, S. Reynolds, P. Clark, *The 1483 Gloucester Charter in History* (Gloucester, 1983).

[93] Eton College, ECR 39/149; *CPR, 1494-1509*, 523.

[94] Christ's College, Cambridge; *CPR, 1494-1509*, 415.

[95] R. Marks and A. Payne, *British Heraldry from its Origins to c.1800* (British Museum and British Library, 1978).

[96] Henry VII's own badge was the double red rose. The double red rose may be found on his hearse cloth (Fitzwilliam Museum, Cambridge, on loan to Great St. Mary's Church, Cambridge).

portrait of the sovereign seated in majesty within the initial letter, and secondly, a series of royal badges and mottoes in the margins. The representation of the king in majesty in charters of Henry VII's reign was probably derived from exemplars of the reign of Henry VI. Letters patent of 25 June 1443 granting a licence in mortmain to Hull,[97] the charter of incorporation of Ipswich dated 28 March 1446,[98] and William Abel's illumination of the Eton confirmation charter of 25 January 1442, all show Henry VI seated in majesty within the bow of the strapwork initial letter 'H'. As yet, no royal charter portraits of Edward IV or Richard III have been found, but the image of majesty was reaffirmed in Henry VII's reign. The charter of 17 December 1499 granting additional privileges to the mayor and aldermen of Bristol, includes an illuminated portrait of Henry VII, with a tiny figure, representing the mayor, kneeling at his feet.[99] The illuminated letters patent of 20 November 1506, confirming earlier grants to Denbigh, contain within the initial letter a representation of Henry VII seated in majesty, with his courtiers about him.[100] In the left-hand margin of the document are two of Henry VII's badges: the double red rose and the portcullis. The loyalty of the subject is directed to the monarch whose image and emblems dominate the written evidence of his beneficence.

Although the decorative content of royal charters in the fifteenth century emphasized, above all else, the attributes of the sovereign, nevertheless badges, heraldic arms and symbols of local significance could be incorporated into the design. The letters patent of 1443 to Hull and the charter of incorporation of Ipswich of 1446 each have an angel standing to the left of the initial letter. The angel holds a shield: it was probably intended that the arms of the beneficiary should be depicted there. In the case of Hull, this was done, albeit incorrectly,[101] but the shield in the Ipswich charter remains blank. Letters patent of 1 December 1441 to King's Lynn include, to the left of the initial letter, a ship with 'lenn' inscribed on one of its sails, while, below the ship, an angel holds a shield bearing the arms of the town.[102] The inclusion of the written name of the town in the decoration is not unique to King's Lynn. The banner held by the white lion of March in the Doncaster incorporation charter of 1467 is inscribed with 'don': there was no room for the full name on the banner. A tiny minority of documents have decoration of purely local significance and lack any direct reference to the monarch in their decorative content.

[97] Kingston upon Hull City Record Office, BRC 16; *CPR, 1441-6*, 180-1.

[98] Suffolk Record Office, Ipswich branch, C3/13; *CChR, 1427-1516*, 54-5. See plate 2b.

[99] Bristol City Record Office, 01230; *CChR, 1427-1516*, 273; H.A. Cronne, Bristol Charters, 1378-1499, pp.163-88.

[100] Clwyd Record Office (Ruthin), BD/A/806; *CPR, 1494-1509*, 496.

[101] The arms of Kingston upon Hull are azure, three ducal coronets in pale or (G. Briggs, pp.219-20). In the letters patent to Hull the three coronets are depicted two and one, rather than in pale.

[102] King's Lynn Borough Records, KL/C2/35 (old reference Ba 1); *CPR, 1441-6*, 74.

The letters patent granting the alien priory of Ravendale to Southwell Minster have a representation of the Annunciation within the bow of the initial letter, while letters patent of 16 January 1454 granting a licence in mortmain to the guild of the Holy Trinity in the parish church of Louth have a representation of the Holy Trinity.[103] The strapwork initial letter 'H' which frames the Trinity is surmounted by a crown with the words 'Sancta Trinitas unus Deus miserere nobis' on the rim. However, in spite of the specific local relevance of the decoration of the Southwell and Louth documents, their style and workmanship clearly indicate that they, like so many other charters and letters patent, were decorated in one locality and within one workshop or group of workshops.

Although the vast majority of charter decoration in England between 1399 and 1509 does appear to have been executed in one style, in pen and ink, and at central workshops, there are a few documents which do not conform to this pattern. Those who wished to do so could arrange for charters to be embellished by a craftsman of their choice. Thus, the Colchester letters patent of July 1413 are illuminated by a sophisticated and skilful hand, and one apparently uninfluenced by contemporary pen and ink charter decoration. Two letters patent to Maldon, of 5 November 1416 and 8 April 1454, have illuminated initial letters and borders based on abstract or leaf and flower designs.[104] These illuminations include no figures, heraldry, badges or local imagery, although they may have been executed in a local workshop. Other examples of royal grants featuring elaborate and finely illuminated initial letters and borders, include letters patent of 20 June 1428 confirming a licence of Henry IV to merchants living in the ports of Prussia, Denmark, Norway, the Hansa and Sweden to elect their own governors,[105] a charter of 7 June 1445 in favour of Shrewsbury,[106] and a charter of Henry VII inspecting and confirming earlier royal grants to Exeter.[107] All these illuminations are of high quality, and bear testimony to the willingness of beneficiaries to pay to enhance the appearance of the physical evidence of new privilege, increased status and royal favour.

This is still the case. The decoration of the most formal products of the

---

[103] Louth Naturalists' Antiquarian and Literary Society, 'Letters Patent of Henry VI to the Guild of the Holy Trinity'. R.W. Goulding, *Louth Old Corporation Records* (Louth, 1891), pp.171-2.

[104] Essex Record Office, D/B 3/13/7; *CPR, 1416-22*, 52; Essex Record Office, D/B 3/13/8; *CPR, 1452-61*, 156.

[105] King's Lynn Borough Records, KL/C2/32 (old reference Ae 6); *CPR, 1422-9*, 488.

[106] Shrewsbury and Atcham Borough Council, Guildhall, Shrewsbury, Muniments 1.32; *CChR, 1427-1516*, 45-6; W. Phillips, E. Calvert, T. Auden, W.G.D. Fletcher, H.M. Auden, *Calendar of the Muniments and Records of the Borough of Shrewsbury* (Shrewsbury, 1896), p.4.

[107] Devon Record Office, ECA charter xxix.

English royal chancery continues to this day.[108] The purpose of this essay
has been to investigate the origins and early development of this practice
and to suggest certain guidelines and avenues for further research. There
is much to be done. Even though the contents of formal royal grants issued
between 1250 and 1509 are enrolled and calendared, nevertheless the
originals have much to add to our knowledge of art, society and
administrative practice in later medieval England. Charters and letters
patent survive as a vivid link between the crown and the community: they
can provide unique illustrations of both.

[108] M. Angel, *Painting for Calligraphers* (London, 1984), pp.92, 109. The City of
Chester's most recently awarded letters patent are dated 15 and 28 May 1974. Both have
illuminated initial letters (Chester City Record Office, CH/44, CH/45).

Chapter 10

England and Scotland during the Wars of Independence

Michael Prestwich

Many elements go to make up a successful system of international relations, but a very important one is mutual recognition of the relevant status of the countries concerned. Independent sovereign states can approach each other on an equal footing, treating each other's ambassadors alike, and in the event of conflict, applying the same conventions to the conduct of war. Matters become more difficult if one country denies another's right to nationhood. Thomas Aquinas implied that a true state of war could exist only between sovereign princes: many acts of what appear to have been war were, for him, no more than seditious rebellions.[1] In reality, medieval rulers rarely regarded each other as being on fully equal terms. Sometimes, an acknowledgement of another's superior status mattered little. Henry II, in an embarassingly fulsome letter, made much of Frederick Barbarossa's imperial authority, but at the same time made it clear that this was of little practical importance as far as England was concerned.[2] The situation was much more serious with regard to relations between England and France. After the treaty of Paris of 1259, English kings could not deny that they were vassals of the king of France, as it was from him that they held the duchy of Aquitaine. As a result, when war broke out between the two countries in 1294, a formal *diffidatio*, or renunciation of homage, had to be made.[3] One of the reasons for Edward III's assumption of the title of king of France in 1340 was that this enabled him to appear, at least in theory, as the equal in status of Philip VI, rather than as a rebellious vassal. Boniface VIII had criticized Edward I for fighting in Flanders against the French, when the issue at stake was the English position in Gascony: such criticisms could not be levelled against Edward III when he was claiming the French throne.[4]

---

[1] F.H. Russell, *The Just War in the Middle Ages* (Cambridge, 1975), p.270.

[2] K. Leyser, 'Frederick I, Henry II and the Hand of St. James', *EHR*, xc (1975), 482-3.

[3] P. Chaplais, *English Medieval Diplomatic Practice*, I, ii. 417-9; *Foedera*, I, ii. 807. Edward sent an embassy composed purely of friars to withdraw his homage. It was presumably considered that Philip IV was unlikely to retaliate against such envoys.

[4] Chaplais, *Eng. Med. Dip. Practice*, I, ii. 269-75.

In the mid fourteenth century, Geoffrey le Baker stated that in wars between the English and Scots, the same laws applied as in the conflict between England and France.[5] The implication is that the Anglo-Scottish war was being fought between two independent nations. The laws of war comprised various elements: the *jus gentium*, the law of nations; canon and civil law; and the *jus militare*, the 'special law' concerned with military matters. If the laws of war were to apply, then a conflict should be a just war. A situation in which rebels were fighting against their lawful sovereign lord would not fit the category of a just war, and the laws of war would not be applicable.[6] It might, nevertheless, be the case that some of the practical considerations which had led to the formulation of the laws of war were still applicable. If one side disregarded the usual conventions, then it might suffer itself in due course, should the fortunes of war be reversed. In 1215 the mercenary captain Savaric de Mauleon argued against King John's intention of hanging the garrison of Rochester castle, on the grounds that if the course of the war turned against the king, then he and John's other supporters might themselves be hanged in turn.[7]

Under Edward I and Edward II, there was no agreement between the English and the Scots as to the relative standing of their countries, and consequently, as to the character of the war they were fighting. For the majority of the Scots the situation was clear. Scotland was an independent country, over which only the pope might claim any form of lordship. The Declaration of Arbroath of 1320 expressed in ringing tones the fact that the Scots were an independent, free people, and stated that the realm of Scotland should never be subjected to English lordship. The rightful king was Robert Bruce. The argument was buttressed by the historical myth which placed the origins of the Scots in Egypt, from where they had migrated via Spain to the British Isles.[8] A war fought in support of this position was, for the Scots, clearly just. The English view of the position was very different.

On the tragic death of the child Margaret of Norway in the Orkneys in 1290, the Scots were faced with an extremely difficult succession dispute as the late king, Alexander III, who had died in 1286, had left no other descendant. Edward I intervened, not as an impartial, independent arbitrator, but in the role he claimed for himself of feudal lord of Scotland. He failed to obtain recognition of this status from the representatives of the community of the Scottish realm, but the various claimants to the

---

[5] *Chronicon Galfridi le Baker*, ed. E.M. Thompson (Oxford, 1886), p.86.

[6] For fuller explanation, see M.H. Keen, *The Laws of War in the Late Middle Ages* (1965), pp.7-22.

[7] *Chronica Rogeri de Wendover* ed. H.G. Hewlett, (RS, 1887), ii. 150.

[8] *Acts of the Parliament of Scotland*, ed. T. Thomson and C. Innes (Edinburgh, 1814-75), i. 114-5; for a convenient translation, see A.A.M. Duncan, *The Nation of Scots and the Declaration of Arbroath (1320)* (Historical Association, 1970), 34-7.

throne, who eventually numbered thirteen, were ready to acknowledge
Edward's claims. Without doing so, they would have stood little chance.[9]
There were considerable technical and practical difficulties involved in
Edward's obtaining seisin of Scotland, and so putting his claim to
overlordship into effect. How could the competitors to the throne, who did
not themselves have seisin, grant it to Edward? The keepers of the royal
castles in Scotland, or at least some of them, raised this problem, which
was solved by an ingenious legal fiction. The castles were handed over to
Edward in his role as one of the competitors: the other competitors then
entrusted them to him in his capacity as feudal lord.[10] It is very clear that
Edward's position was not fully accepted by the Scots. However, once the
hearings of the Great Cause, as the succession dispute has become known,
were concluded, Edward was in a position to exact the terms he wanted
from the new king, John Balliol. Homage was performed by Balliol, and
Edward was acknowledged to be the sovereign lord of the realm of
Scotland.[11]

It is likely that throughout the succession dispute, the English intended
to use the situation to bring Scotland under their control. The Waverley
Annals reported Edward I announcing in 1291 that he intended to
subjugate Scotland, just as he had done Wales.[12] In July that year, a royal
writ announced that the realms of England and Scotland were now
conjoined by reason of Edward's superior lordship, and that as a result,
writs issued by the king in Scotland would be fully valid in England.[13]
Great care was taken to ensure that the facts, as the English saw them,
were properly known. Edward had sought historical evidence from
monasteries to justify his claims, and he made certain that any future
inquiries of this sort would be productive, by circulating copies of the
letters acknowledging his rights which had been issued by the claimants to
the throne.[14]

Once John Balliol had been enthroned, Edward I made his position
abundantly clear. As his vassal, Balliol might be summoned to English
parliaments to answer cases brought before Edward on appeal from
Scottish courts. When Balliol offered defiance, he was brought to heel by
the threat that three of his most important castles and towns would be
forfeited. In 1294 Edward went so far as to summon Balliol and various

---

[9] The Great Cause has been fully discussed, and the relevant records printed in *Edward
I and the Throne of Scotland, 1290-1296*, ed. E.L.G. Stones and G.G. Simpson (Oxford, 1978).
The refusal of the Scots to accept Edward's demands is given *ibid.*, ii. 30-1.

[10] *Ibid.*, i. 119; ii. 112.

[11] *Ibid.*, ii, 260-3.

[12] *Annales Monastici*, ed. W. Stubbs (RS, 1864-9), ii. 409.

[13] *Foedera*, I, ii. 757; *Edward I and the Throne of Scotland*, ii. 119.

[14] *Ibid.*, ii. 120. An original of this text is to be found in the muniments of the Dean and
Chapter of Durham, 2.2. Reg. 9.

Scottish magnates to perform military service in Gascony, although the muster was subsequently cancelled. The Scots were driven to take the government of their realm out of Balliol's hands, and a council of twelve was set up. They made a treaty with Edward's enemy, Philip IV of France. This provided one reason for Edward's invasion of Scotland in 1296. At the same time, his action can also be seen as the culmination of the legal disputes, and in particular the appeal by Macduff, younger son of the earl of Fife, which had bedevilled Anglo-Scottish relations since Balliol's accession.[15]

There is some ambiguity about Edward I's attitude towards Scotland following his successful invasion in 1296. On the one hand, Balliol was forced to resign his throne, and no steps were taken to replace him. The seizure of the Scottish muniments, and above all of the Coronation Stone, strongly implied that the kingdom was no more. Edward I assumed the rule of Scotland himself, as superior lord. On the other hand, no addition was made to Edward's title, and no formal document was issued to announce the change in Scotland's status. The special seal made for Scottish affairs was merely a version of Edward's normal seal. Edward's authority was, at least in part, established when he obtained fealty from a large number of individual Scots. There was no recognition of his position by the community as a whole.[16] Scotland was apparently a realm in abeyance, with little careful consideration given to its precise status.

The conquest of 1296 did not last. William Wallace rebelled in 1297, and in a further invasion in 1298 Edward won the major victory of Falkirk. Although there were some who accepted English rule, resistance continued, and an important part of this took the form of diplomatic pressure at the French court and at the papal curia. Philip IV of France maintained his support for the unfortunate John Balliol, who was released into papal custody in 1299.[17] Scottish envoys at the curia persuaded Boniface VIII in the same year to draw up a powerful indictment of Edward's actions. The pope argued that Scotland was rightfully subject to the Roman curia – a claim not supported by any real evidence – and provided historical arguments to show that Alexander III's fealty to Edward I had been performed solely in respect of the lands he held in

[15] These events are fully described by G.W.S. Barrow, *Robert Bruce and the Community of the Realm of Scotland* (1965), pp.74-96. For the view of the 1296 campaign as the culmination of legal process, see the contemporary official narrative in *Edward I and the Throne of Scotland*, ii. 284-7, and see also W.C. Dickinson, *Scotland from the Earliest Times to 1603*, 3rd edn., revised by A.A.M. Duncan (Oxford, 1977), pp.151-2.

[16] Barrow, *Robert Bruce*, pp.102-9. Barrow notes, on p.102, that 'Constitutionally or legally, Edward I was in a curious position'. For the seal used by Edward for Scottish matters, see H. Jenkinson, 'A Seal of Edward II for Scottish Affairs', *Antiquaries Journal*, xi (1931), 229-35. Rather than making an addition to the royal title, the words *ad regimen regni Scocie deputatum* were added after the normal royal style.

[17] Barrow, *Robert Bruce*, pp.134-5.

England. Boniface laid no emphasis on John Balliol's position as king: he was merely referred to as 'the man to whom you are said to have committed the kingdom'. The question of who should be king in Scotland was carefully sidestepped, and it seems likely that the Scottish envoys in Rome belonged to a different faction from those in Paris, who had been working strenuously to achieve Balliol's release.[18]

Boniface's bull was presented to Edward by Archbishop Winchelsey in the summer of 1300. The arguments that were developed to counter it rested in large part upon history, mostly of a questionable nature, and on the fact that Balliol had been Edward's vassal. As he had rebelled, Edward had proceeded against him as a notorious and contumacious traitor, and as an open enemy. The realm of Scotland had then been 'subjected by right of ownership to our power'. The fact that the Scots had performed fealty and homage to Edward had fully established the English king's right to rule in Scotland. The question of the status of the Scottish crown was not mentioned.[19] It may be that Edward thought it might become necessary, if circumstances changed, to revive the Scottish throne. The highly ambiguous document recording Robert Bruce's surrender early in 1302 mentioned the fear that the realm of Scotland might be removed from Edward's hands, 'which God forbid', and the possibility that 'the right might be put in question, or reversed, and repealed in a new judgement'. Whether this 'right' meant, or included, the right to the throne has been hotly debated: it could be that it suited Edward to leave the position vague.[20] The way in which the king was greeted by a small choir, as used to be done in King Alexander III's day, when he was travelling in Scotland in 1303, was no doubt stage-managed, and suggests that Edward was deliberately beginning to take on the attributes of a Scottish monarch.[21] No formal steps were taken, however, to clarify the position of the Scottish crown.

In 1304, after the negotiated surrender of John Comyn of Badenoch and other magnates early in the year, and the subsequent capture of Stirling castle, Edward appeared to have conquered Scotland. In the next year, 1305, an ordinance for the future government of the country was produced. Interestingly, the document nowhere refers to Scotland as a realm. Throughout, the country is termed a land. Edward made no claim

---

[18] *Anglo-Scottish Relations 1174-1328*, ed. E.L.G. Stones (1965), pp.81-7. The lack of emphasis placed on Balliol contrasts strikingly with Philip IV's stress on his position as illustrious king of Scotland, in *C[alender of] D[ocuments relating to] S[cotland]*, ed. J. Bain (Edinburgh, 1881-8), ii. 531-6. For the dating of this document, see Barrow, *Robert Bruce*, pp.96-109.

[19] *Anglo-Scottish Relations*, pp.96-109.

[20] *Ibid.*, pp.118-9. For alternative interpretations of this difficult document, see Barrow, *Robert Bruce*, pp.172-4, and A.A.M. Duncan, 'The Community of the Realm of Scotland and Robert Bruce', *Scottish Historical Review*, xlv (1966), 195-8.

[21] BL. Add. MS. 8835, f.42[r] and [v].

to the Scottish throne, and the document reads as if there never had been any kings in Scotland. Where the phrase 'community of the realm' would have been used for English circumstances, in a Scottish context, the 'community of the land' was referred to. Edward, it seems, was to exercise lordship over a land in the north, and Scotland was in consequence to be treated in much the same way as the land of Ireland, though rule was to be by a royal lieutenant rather than a justiciar.[22] Robert Bruce's assumption of the Scottish throne in 1306 made no difference to the formal position as far as the English were concerned. He was a traitor to his feudal lord, Edward I, and an enemy. There could be no question of recognizing his royal style.

The position remained the same, in formal terms, throughout Edward II's reign. The English were not prepared to acknowledge Robert Bruce as king, or to address him as such. Letters would refer, at most, to 'Sir Robert de Bruce and the Scottish people'.[23] Bruce, on the other hand, with the sensitivity of a usurper, laid great stress on his royal title. The fundamental disagreement made diplomatic communication difficult. Papal envoys discovered this in 1317, when Bruce refused to open letters addressed to him by the pope, as they made no use of his royal title. In 1323 he took offence when Edward II announced that he had granted a truce to the Scottish people, but made no reference to their ruler.[24] For the English, this was not a war between equal powers. Summonses for military service issued by Edward II referred to the Scots as traitors and public enemies. In 1323 the recently appointed earl of Carlisle, Andrew Harcla, negotiated with the Scots without proper authority, and recognized Robert Bruce as king. The fact that he had done so was the first of the charges brought against him when he was accused of treason. When a truce was made with the Scots after Harcla had been executed, there was no concession made on the question of the recognition of Bruce as king.[25] Disastrous military defeat at Bannockburn in 1314, the failure of the siege of Berwick, the near-disaster at Byland in 1322 when Edward II was almost captured by the Scots, all made no difference. The English would not acknowledge Robert Bruce as king of Scots. The only time when Edward II appears to have conceived of the possibility was when he suggested recognizing the Scottish king, in return for Bruce's providing his favourite Piers Gaveston with a safe refuge.[26]

It was not until the accession of Edward III, and the rule of Queen Isabella and Roger Mortimer, that the English were able to swallow their

---

[22] *Anglo-Scottish Relations*, pp.120-9. It should be noted that the translation fails to take account of the fact that Scotland is not referred to as a realm in this text.

[23] See for example *Rotuli Scotiae*, ed. D. Macpherson and others (1814-19), i. 132-3.

[24] Barrow, *Robert Bruce*, pp.346-7, 349-50.

[25] *Foedera*, II, i. 509; Barrow, *Robert Bruce*, pp.351-3.

[26] *Vita Edwardi Secundi*, ed. N. Denholm-Young (1957), p.22.

pride, and accept that Bruce was king of an independent Scottish realm. On 1 March 1328 formal letters patent were issued in which Edward III formally renounced 'any right in the realm of Scotland which we or our ancestors have sought in past times, in any manner'.[27] A treaty was drawn up and concluded at Edinburgh, and then confirmed at Northampton. This 'shameful peace' did not, of course, end Anglo-Scottish conflict, but it shifted its ground. Edward III could not use the same justification as his father and grandfather for fighting the Scots, but he juggled skilfully with a number of different balls, and would not recognize the position of Bruce's successor David II, as king of Scots.

The initial opportunity for Edward III to intervene following the treaty of 1328 was provided by the ambitions of Edward Balliol, son of the unfortunate King John, and by the grievance of the 'Disinherited', those Englishmen who had lost lands in Scotland as a result of the peace. Edward III turned a blind eye to Edward Balliol's expedition of 1332, which culminated in an astonishing victory at Dupplin Moor. His subsequent support for Balliol led to victory at Halidon Hill in 1333. In the next year, Balliol granted him much of southern Scotland, and did homage for the rest of the country. The English, however, were unable to follow up these initial successes, partly as a result of French support for the child David II.[28] English clerks began to examine the precedents of Edward I's reign, and to consider the claims to superior lordship. One of the memoranda produced in the 1330s interestingly referred to England as a nation, but to the Scots as merely a people (*gens*) inhabiting a land.[29] David II and his supporters were regarded as enemies, and Edward Balliol as the rightful king, under English superior lordship. Ironically, it was the capture of David II at the battle of Neville's Cross in 1346 that changed the situation. If the Scots were to pay a substantial ransom for David, then they would expect him to be recognized as king by Edward. The English conceived a plan whereby part of the terms for David's release involved the acceptance by the Scots of English feudal rights over Scotland, and agreement that Edward, or one of his sons, should succeed David on the Scottish throne. Negotiations were not easy, but in 1356 Edward Balliol was persuaded to relinquish his claims to the Scottish throne, and in the following year David II was at long last released from custody, with a ransom of 100,000 marks to be paid. There was, however,

[27] *Anglo-Scottish Relations*, p.162.

[28] R. Nicholson, *Edward III and the Scots* (Oxford, 1965), provides an excellent full account of these events. J. Campbell, 'England, Scotland and the Hundred Years War', *Europe in the Late Middle Ages*, ed. J.R. Hale, R. Highfield, B. Smalley (1965), pp.184-216, usefully puts the Anglo-Scottish conflict into a wider European setting.

[29] W. Prynne, *The History of King John, King Henry III and the most illustrious King Edward the I*... (1670), iii. 893-4, prints PRO, C 47/30/4, 9. At one point in the text, the clerk did refer to the *regnum Scocie*, but he was careful when he described the Franco-Scottish alliance of 1295 as being between the French king and the people of the land of Scotland.

no agreement reached over the succession to the Scottish throne, and although David was termed king in the document, his position was not formally recognized by the English. Much remained to be negotiated. In 1363, when the ransom payments were substantially in arrears, Edward III agreed peace terms with David, under which the childless king of Scots agreed that either Edward or one of his sons should succeed him. The terms, however, were rejected by the Scottish parliament, and the ransom payments were resumed, a situation which probably did not displease David II. Edward III maintained his refusal to call David king. The old claims and arguments were not forgotten, but for twenty years following David's release in 1357, England and Scotland were in practice at peace.[30] With the accession of the Steward, Robert II, in 1371, English hopes of gaining the Scottish throne were effectively ended.

How did the situation in which the English claimed the right of superior lordship over Scotland, and the Scots claimed independence, affect the conduct of war? In theory, the English were dealing with a rebellion against their authority, as they saw it, whereas the Scots considered that they were conducting a just war. The Declaration of Arbroath stressed that the Scots were led by 'a most valiant prince, king and lord'. This was important, as 'wars which are not declared by a prince are not properly wars', as one Italian lawyer put it. There could be no doubting Scottish motives: 'We fight not for glory, nor riches, nor honours, but for freedom alone, which no good man gives up except with his life'.[31] The English, according to the theories of the day, were not bound by the laws of war, whereas the Scots surely were.

It is usually considered, with some justification, that in the Wars of Independence it was the English who fought by the book, and the Scots who broke the rules. The English relied on sending impressively large armies north, backed by a well-organized system of supply. In 1298 Edward I led a force of perhaps some 3,000 or more cavalry, and 25,700 infantry into Scotland. The army his son took to Scotland on the abortive 1322 campaign numbered well over 20,000. Food supplies were collected on a huge scale, and taken north by sea: permanent victualling bases at Berwick and Carlisle were set up to facilitate the complex business of ensuring that the troops had enough to eat.[32] It was not easy for such large armies to force the Scots to fight: no major battles took place between that

---

[30] In addition to the article by Campbell cited above, n.28, see B. Webster, 'David II and the government of Fourteenth-Century Scotland', *TRHS*, 5th ser., xvi (1966), 115-30; R. Nicholson, *Scotland: the Later Middle Ages* (Edinburgh, 1973), pp.157-74.

[31] Duncan, *Nation of Scots and the Declaration of Arbroath*, pp.35-6. The quotation from Nicholas of Tudeschi is taken from Keen, *Laws of War*, p.69.

[32] M.C. Prestwich, *War, Politics and Finance under Edward I* (1972), pp.68-9, 95, 114-36; N.M. Fryde, *The Tyranny and Fall of Edward II* (Cambridge, 1979), 128.

of Falkirk in 1298, and the Scottish triumph at Bannockburn in 1314. Little tactical originality was shown by the English commanders before Edward III's reign: the battles of Dupplin Moor and Halidon Hill then proved the value of dismounted cavalry fighting with proper support from archers. In siege warfare, the English relied on traditional methods of encirclement, with the use of massive stone-throwing engines and battering rams, as at Stirling castle in 1304.[33]

The Scots, in contrast, did not fight in an orthodox fashion. At the very outset of the conflict, in 1296, they surprised a small English force on its way to Wark, attacking by night, and using a password system to distinguish friend from foe. There was no question of any conventional declaration of hostilities, or use of normal battlecries.[34] The Scots invaded England on Easter Monday, before John Balliol had formally renounced his homage to Edward I. At Dunbar, the Scottish feudal host advanced during a brief period of truce against the English who were besieging the castle. In the great battles of Stirling Bridge in 1297, Falkirk in 1298, and Bannockburn in 1314, the Scots were compelled to rely on their infantry forces, employing tactics which the English found difficult to deal with. In particular, the defensive formation of the schiltrom was one which the English cavalry found hard to break up. Further, the English alleged that numerous atrocities were committed by the Scots. The war as fought by William Wallace was hardly in the best chivalric tradition, with such incidents taking place as the skinning of the cleric Hugh Cressingham's corpse after the battle of Stirling Bridge. There were tales of how Wallace forced men and women to sing naked in front of him, as well as more conventional horror stories.[35] Rather than relying on orthodox sieges, the Scots won castles and towns by surprise attacks, notably in the early years of Edward II's reign, when such places as Perth, Roxburgh and Edinburgh fell in rapid succession.[36] There was no question of issuing the conventional challenges and requests for surrender. Robert Bruce was angered when his brother Edward, who was besieging Stirling castle in 1313, agreed to terms of a standard, if generous type, which provided for the surrender of the castle if it was not relieved by the following midsummer.

---

[33] For a fuller discussion of the military lessons of the Scottish wars, see M.C. Prestwich, *The Three Edwards: War and State, 1272-1377* (1980), pp.42-78.

[34] *The Chronicle of Walter of Guisborough*, ed. H. Rothwell (Camden Soc., lxxxix, 1957), pp.271-2.

[35] Balliol, perhaps taking his cue from Edward I when he renounced his homage to the French king in 1294, used friars to take his *diffidatio* to the English ruler: *Anglo-Scottish Relations*, pp.70-2. For the Scots approaching Dunbar during a truce, see the Hagnaby Chronicle, B.L. Cotton Vesp. B. xi, ff.40ᵛ-41.

[36] *Walter of Guisborough*, p.303; *Flores Historiarum*, ed. H.R. Luard (RS, 1890), iii. 321. The most frequently cited atrocities were those which allegedly took place in the course of the Scottish invasion of 1296: see *Edward I and the Throne of Scotland*, ii. 288-9.

To fight in an unconventional manner was not, however, necessarily the same thing as flouting the accepted laws of war. It would, too, be wrong to expect the participants in the Anglo-Scottish wars under Edward I and Edward II to show the same awareness of those laws as was present later, during the Hundred Years War. In their propaganda, the English did not condemn the Scots for failing to observe international conventions on the field of battle. The laws and customs according to which Edward had, as he saw it, declared war upon the Scots were those of his realm, not those of the canonists and civil lawyers who theorized about the nature of the just war. Unfortunately, only one army plea roll survives for this period. It covers the campaign of 1296, and most of the cases were concerned with relatively minor thefts, and occasional disputes about booty. Save for the fact that the jurisdiction being exercised was that of the marshal, there is little to suggest that anything other than the normal legal system was in operation.[37]

A different set of problems, and one to which it was much easier to apply the conventions of the law of arms, were those presented by the question of the treatment of prisoners taken in the wars. The legal theorists, reliant as they were to a great extent on Roman law, did not find the matter an easy one, but feudal custom was clear. Those taken in war entered into a contract with their captor. They might be kept in prison, even in irons, but they could not be killed. Release might be obtained by payment of a ransom.[38] That was the position in a normal war, but from the English point of view, the Scots they were fighting were rebels, guilty of treason, and liable to the most extreme penalty. Edward I had shown with the execution of Prince Dafydd of Gwynedd at Shrewsbury in 1283 how he thought those who rebelled against his authority should be treated. At the same time, there were political and military realities to be considered, which could modify the way in which the English approached the problem. As far as the Scots were concerned, as in their view they were an independent people fighting to maintain that independence, there was no question of their applying laws of treason to any Englishmen they captured.

The English took many prisoners in the first years of the conflict, notably in the 1296 campaign, and their treatment does not seem to have been unreasonable. The major prize was the capture after the battle of Dunbar of the earls of Atholl, Ross and Menteith, along with about thirty-five knights and a hundred squires.[39] These men were distributed between twenty-four English and Welsh castles, the most important being sent to the Tower of London. They were given a daily allowance for their

[37] PRO, E 39/93/15, calendared in part in *CDS*, ii, no.822.
[38] Keen, *Laws of War*, pp.156-64.
[39] *CDS*, ii, no.742; *Barthomaei de Cotton, Historia Anglicana*, ed. H.R. Luard (RS, 1859), p.312. The agreement between the record source and the chronicle is unusual and striking.

subsistence, the earls receiving 6*d*., the knights 4*d*., and the squires 3*d*. To judge from the fact that it was only when Richard Siward's father was serving Edward I in Flanders in 1297 that he was assigned a chamber to himself, with a privy, their conditions were not particularly comfortable.[40] Service in Flanders was one way of obtaining release. Edward was desperately short of men for his campaign, and was within his rights to ask his prisoners to fight for him in lieu of paying ransoms.[41] Some of the Scots who agreed to serve in this way made use of the opportunity to try to escape, but when they made their way to Philip IV of France, he refused to give them refuge, as a truce was in operation.[42] Some Scots were released when they were exchanged for English prisoners held in Scotland. In April 1299 a high-powered delegation, consisting of the bishop of Durham, John of Brittany and William Latimer the Elder, was appointed to negotiate the exchange, body for body, of ten prisoners from each side.[43] Some prisoners were granted by Edward to favoured magnates and captains, such as Thomas of Lancaster, Robert Clifford, and Thomas Paynel. They could then profit from the ransom paid for their release. There might be trade the other way, as when John of Weardale sold a Scot he had captured to Edward, in exchange for £5 worth of food and wine.[44] A few men were obviously regarded as too dangerous to be released. Robert Keith and Robert Barde were moved from Carlisle in 1300, as it was so close to the border, and sent to the safety of Nottingham.[45]

Many Scots must have remained in custody until 1304, when the release of all prisoners was one of the first conditions laid down by John Comyn in his surrender negotiations early in that year at Strathord. The one exception that Edward I insisted on was that neither Herbert de Morham nor his father should be freed.[46] The reason for this could lie in Herbert's role in besieging Stirling castle in 1299, or in his abduction of the countess of Fife in the same year, but it is much more likely that Edward regarded the Morhams with particular hatred, as both had been enrolled as royal household knights, and had been in receipt of fees and robes from the king. As household knights, they would have been under a

---

[40] *Accounts of the Constables of Bristol Castle*, ed. M. Sharp (Bristol Record Soc., 1982), pp.44, 62. The deaths of a number of Scots while they were held in custody suggests that their conditions were poor. See for example *CDS*, iii, nos.1, 188.

[41] Keen, *Laws of War*, p.161.

[42] *The Chronicle of Pierre de Langtoft*, ed. T. Wright (RS, 1868), ii. 310. See also for the Scots serving Edward in Flanders, N.B. Lewis, 'The English Forces in Flanders, August-November 1297', *Studies in Medieval History presented to F.M. Powicke*, ed. R.W. Hunt, W.A. Pantin, R.W. Southern (Oxford, 1948), p.313.

[43] *CDS*, ii, no.1062.

[44] *Ibid.*, ii, nos.1326, 1585.

[45] *Ibid.*, ii, no.1147. They were later moved again, to Bristol and Gloucester: *ibid.*, ii, no.1159. See also *Accounts of the Constables of Bristol Castle*, pp.66-7.

[46] *Documents and Records Illustrating the History of Scotland*, ed. F. Palgrave (1837), i. 281.

special obligation to Edward, breach of which deserved severe punishment.[47]

The major contrast between the way in which the English and the Scots treated prisoners at this stage of the war was probably the manner in which they treated castle garrisons after surrender. When the Scots took Stirling after a long siege in 1299, they permitted the garrison to leave unharmed, and to make their way to Berwick and safety. Many of them were then retained by Edward in his household, to form what appears to have been a kind of bodyguard.[48] Yet when the English retook Stirling in 1304, the situation was very different. Edward had refused to allow the Scottish constable, William Oliphant, to consult his superior, John de Soules – as de Soules was in France, this was understandable – and insisted on totally unconditional surrender. He would not allow the Scots to come out of the castle until he had tried out his latest and grandest siege engine, the Warwolf, and he threatened them with hanging and dismemberment. Oliphant and twenty-five others eventually emerged, in full penitential garb, and only after they had submitted themselves most abjectly did Edward relent, and send them off to imprisonment in various English castles.[49] Earlier, at Caerlaverock in 1300, some of the garrison had been executed on Edward's instructions, although the constable and eleven others were sent to prison at Newcastle upon Tyne. Ten were imprisoned at Appleby.[50] Edward's conduct, however, was not out of keeping with the laws of war as they developed: the 'unusual and savage severity' of those laws as they applied to sieges was noteworthy. If a garrison did not agree to terms, then the king was entitled to do with them as he chose.

In the early stages of the war, up to 1304, there was little to suggest that the English view of the Scots as rebels against their lawful feudal superior affected the way in which prisoners were treated. In 1305, however, the English chancery began denying Scotland the status of a kingdom. The case of William Wallace, finally captured in that year, shows that Edward's attitude had changed, now that Scotland appeared to be fully conquered. Wallace was brought to London and tried. His judges were, in formal terms, commissioners of gaol delivery, and employed 'the law and custom of England'. This was not a case heard under the law of arms. The

---

[47] *CDS*, ii, nos.1066, 1108, 1949; *Liber Quotidianus Contrarotulatoris Garderobae*, ed. J. Topham (Soc. of Antiquaries, 1787), p.190.

[48] *Willelmi Rishanger, Chronica et Annales*, ed. H.T. Riley (RS, 1865), p.402; *Flores Historiarum*, iii. 113. See also *CDS*, ii, no.1119. Gifts to some of the garrison are recorded in *Liber Quotidianus*, pp.160, 163.

[49] *CDS*, ii, nos.1560, 1668; *Foedera*, I, ii. 965-6.

[50] *CDS*, ii, nos.1162, 1196; *Chronicon de Lanercost*, ed. J. Stevenson (Maitland Club, 1836), p.164. It should be noted that, in contrast to this account, the poet who described the siege suggested that the king was most generous to the defeated Scots: *The Siege of Carlaverock*, ed. N.H. Nicolas (1828), p.86.

core of the accusation was that Wallace had risen against the king, unmindful of the homage and fealty he owed him. He was guilty of treason, according to the royal record, as he had borne a banner against his liege lord in war, but this did not mean that he was tried according to military law. In his defence, Wallace appears to have been prepared to concede the charges against him, all save that of treason against the king of England. He had not sworn an oath of fealty to Edward, or performed homage to him. This argument was ignored, and Wallace was executed with hideous thoroughness, being hanged, decapitated, eviscerated (his heart and bowels then being burned), and quartered. Throughout the sentence Scotland was consistently referred to as a land: Wallace was simply treated as a rebellious subject of the king.[51]

The reopening of the war, the result of the murder of John Comyn at Dumfries and Robert Bruce's seizure of the throne, saw Edward hold to the doctrines set out at Wallace's trial. The English were very successful in the campaigns of 1306, notably with Aymer de Valence's victory at the battle of Methven, when a number of prisoners were taken. Not long afterwards, Simon Fraser, who like the Morhams had been a royal household knight, but who had then changed sides, was captured. The earl of Atholl was another notable prize, as was Nigel Bruce. The king's initial order was for all prisoners to be slain, but he then asked for the major figures to be kept in custody, until he had decided what should be done with them. He does not seem to have been in much doubt. Similar procedures to those employed against Wallace were adopted, with justices of gaol delivery and charges of treason. The record of the trial of a number of Scots taken at Methven makes it clear that as the offences were considered notorious, the Scots could simply be convicted on the king's record. No opportunity was allowed for them to answer their accusers.[52] In the case of the earl of Atholl, the queen and various magnates begged Edward to show mercy, as the earl was related to the royal family, but the king's response was to order that he be hanged from a higher gallows than the rest.[53] In the case of Herbert de Morham, Edward was particularly vindictive. He had sworn, it was said, that the English would never take Simon Fraser, and wagered his head on it. Accordingly, on the day after Fraser's execution, he and his squire suffered the same dismal fate.[54]

Even Edward I could not order the deaths of the bishops of Glasgow and St. Andrews, or of the ladies of Bruce's court, his queen, sister,

---

[51] 'Annales Londonienses', in *Chronicles of the Reigns of Edward I and Edward II*, ed. W. Stubbs (RS, 1882), i. 139-42. See also Barrow, *Robert Bruce*, p.194, where the argument that Wallace was tried under the law of arms is rightly dismissed.

[52] *CDS*, ii, nos.1790, 1811.

[53] *Walter of Guisborough*, p.369.

[54] *The Political Songs of England*, ed. T. Wright (Camden Soc., 1839), pp.218-9; Barrow, *Robert Bruce*, p.218n.

daughter and the countess of Buchan. The king was, however, remarkably savage in his treatment of these prisoners. The bishops were to be kept in irons, in Winchester and Porchester castles. They were imprisoned in the keeps, which were locked, with drawbridges raised.[55] Bruce's queen, who was fortunate to be a daughter of the earl of Ulster, was simply sent off to custody at the royal manor of Burstwick. Orders were issued for the other three women to be put in substantial wooden cages, well reinforced. The countess of Buchan's was at Berwick, and Bruce's sister Mary was held at Roxburgh. In the case of Bruce's daughter Marjorie, who was to have been caged in the Tower of London, Edward relented, no doubt because she was only a child. There has been much controversy regarding these cages. Edward I's defenders have justified him by pointing out that they were not small affairs, such as a parrot might be placed in, but that they were equipped with privies. On the other hand, the chronicle evidence is clear that the cages at Berwick and Roxburgh were in full public view, and the fact that Edward had the countess of Buchan and Mary Bruce imprisoned in this way in Scotland strongly suggests that he fully intended to make a spectacle of them. Even by contemporary standards, the treatment of these noble ladies was surely cruel and unusual.[56]

Edward I could not have behaved towards his Scottish captives as he did, if it had been recognized that a true state of war existed between the two countries of Scotland and England. On the other hand, horrific executions were quite usual where rebels, or men regarded as rebels, were concerned. The example of the appalling treatment meted out by the emperor Henry VI to the Sicilian rebels towards the end of his reign or of that accorded to the conspirators led by Tibaldo Francesco by the emperor Frederick II in 1246, provides a parallel to Edward's conduct. There was certainly no revulsion among Edward's own subjects. He was, indeed, rebuked by the chronicler Pierre Langtoft for showing too much clemency towards the Scots at a slightly earlier point, and the death of Simon Fraser met with great rejoicing, being celebrated in a popular song of the day.[57]

Although Edward II did not alter his father's policy as far as recognition of the Scots was concerned, he did not continue Edward I's vindictiveness towards Scottish prisoners. In 1308 the bishop of St. Andrews was released, admittedly under severe financial terms, and with the proviso that he should remain within the bounds of the diocese of

[55] *Foedera*, I, ii. 996. It is interesting to note that when the bishops were taken south, along with the abbot of Scone, their escort was strengthened by 20 men when they passed through Barnsdale, one of the legendary homes of Robin Hood: E 101/13/5.

[56] *Documents and Records*, ed. Palgrave, i. 357-9. This matter has been extensively discussed: see E.L.G. Stones in *SHR*, lii (1973), 84, and Barrow, *Robert Bruce*, p.230, with an additional note in the second edition of this book (Edinburgh, 1976), p.233.

[57] *Pierre de Langtoft*, ii. 326; *Political Songs*, pp.212-3.

Durham. His colleague of Glasgow was handed over to the pope. William Oliphant was freed from the Tower, having provided guarantors of good conduct, and after he promised to accompany Edward II to Scotland. In 1310 negotiations for the release of Mary Bruce began, though these were not successful. The countess of Buchan was released from her cage.[58] The major change in policy, however, came about not as a result of Edward II's accession, but because of the changing fortunes of war. By 1311, Robert Bruce was in a sufficiently strong position for him to take the war to the English, raiding across the border, as well as capturing English-held castles in Scotland. The battle of Bannockburn in 1314 did not provide him with final victory, but it proved that English ascendancy was over. As far as the question of prisoners was concerned, the problem for the English was no longer how to deal with the Scots that they captured, but how to obtain the release of Englishmen held by the Scots. In such circumstances, practical realities meant that Edward II had to observe the conventions of military law which his father had ignored in the last years of his reign.

The capture of Humphrey de Bohun, earl of Hereford, at Bannockburn, was a major coup for the Scots. His release was obtained only by exchanging him for Bruce's queen, sister, daughter, and the bishop of Glasgow.[59] In other cases, however, the demands made by the Scots were relatively moderate. The sums demanded as ransoms were low in contrast to the inflated figures of the Hundred Years War. Ralph Neville had to pay 2,000 marks for his release, and John de Segrave was probably charged a similar figure. At a lower level of society, John of Hesilrigg, who was held in prison for two years after Bannockburn, was ransomed for 200 marks. Luke de Wharton, a former member of the Berwick garrison, was taken by the Scots in Northumberland, and had to pay 44 marks for his release. He lost his lands as a result of mortgaging them to raise the money.[60] In some cases, the king was prepared to contribute towards the cost of ransoms, but this was usually only when notable men, or members of his household, were involved. The earl of Hereford received 1,000 marks to recompense him for the losses he incurred as a result of his capture in 1314, and John de Segrave received a grant of £1,000. Andrew Harcla was promised 1,000 marks towards his ransom after he was taken prisoner, and Henry de Sully, a French banneret captured at Byland in 1322 was given the same sum. When Andrew Tang, the notary employed to make a copy of the proceedings of the Great Cause, was taken prisoner, the arrears of wages due to him were paid over, so that the ransom demand could be met. Henry de Bois, a

[58] *CDS*, iii, nos.44, 50, 58, 131; *Rotuli Scotiae*, i. 61, 85.
[59] *CDS*, iii, no.393.
[60] *Ibid.*, iii, nos.527, 611, 676; *Ancient Petitions relating to Northumberland*, ed. C.M. Fraser (Surtees Soc., 1966), p.160.

household knight, was given £50 towards his ransom, and Wardino de Bois £40.[61] Robert Bruce did not demand ransoms in all cases: Marmaduke Tweng and Ralph de Monthermer, both notable men, were allowed to return home after Bannockburn without making any payments at all.[62]

Robert Bruce's humanity and chivalrousness do not in themselves provide a sufficient explanation for his clemency towards his English captives.[63] The legal position in which he was placed, whereby in fighting what he considered to be a just war, he was under an obligation to adhere to the laws and conventions of war, meant that he could not easily have behaved in the way in which Edward I had done. He may also have calculated that if he treated his prisoners well, then it was more likely that the English would treat Scottish captives better in the future, should the war once again turn in their favour.

Under Edward III, there were moments when the days of Edward I seemed to be returning. The hanging of the young hostage, Thomas Seton, outside the walls of Berwick in 1333 was one such. Another was the sentence of death passed on the earls of Menteith and Fife in 1347. Although the latter's life was spared because he was related to the king, Menteith was hanged, drawn and quartered. The Scots, too, executed the Englishman Walter of Selby in 1346, in what was widely regarded as an atrocity: Walter had surrendered on the assumption that he would be ransomed. In all these cases, however, there were exceptional circumstances. Edward III was fully entitled to execute the hostages at Berwick under the terms of the agreement he had made with the defenders of the town.[64] The earl of Menteith had been a sworn member of Edward III's council, and was therefore guilty of treason for going against the oath he had taken. Duncan, earl of Fife, had done fealty and homage to Edward Balliol, and in supporting David II's cause he was technically guilty of treason.[65] As for Walter of Selby, he had fought with the Scots in Edward II's day, and there is therefore no difficulty in explaining why David II should have regarded him as a traitor.[66]

In general, under Edward III the war against the Scots was fought following similar conventions to those which applied when fighting in France, as Geoffrey le Baker pointed out. There were some special arrangements which applied to the border regions, but it would not have

---

[61] *CDS*, iii, nos.515, 611, 676, 680; Society of Antiquaries MS. 120, pp.59-60; MS. 121, p.63; B.L. MS. Stowe 553, f.69.

[62] Barrow, *Robert Bruce*, pp.330-1.

[63] *Ibid.*, p.331, refers, quite rightly, to Bruce's humane behaviour in the aftermath of Bannockburn.

[64] Nicholson, *Edward III and the Scots*, p.126.

[65] *Rotuli Scotiae*, i. 687-8; *CDS*, iii, no.1486.

[66] *Ibid.*, iii, no.1356. Walter's treason towards the Scots was, however, a mystery to Geoffrey le Baker, *Chronicon*, p.86, and to Keen, *Laws of War*, pp.46-8.

been easy to fight two simultaneous wars under different codes of conduct. The fact that the French and Scots were allies was also a factor. It even proved possible to exchange the earl of Moray, captured in Scotland by the English, for the earl of Salisbury, taken prisoner on the continent.[67] If the English had behaved harshly toward the Scots, the French might have responded in kind. In addition, during the period of David II's captivity, Edward needed to behave with due propriety towards the Scots, if he was to obtain the much-needed ransom payments.

The relationship between theory and practice is never easy to elucidate. The situation in which the English saw the war in the north as a rebellion against their rightful authority, and the Scots viewed it as a justified struggle to maintain national independence against unwarranted claims, led to a situation where the English could consider that the laws of war were not applicable. At the same time, this might conflict with the practical needs of those who fought, with their desires to profit from ransom payments, and their fears of what might happen to them if they were captured. It was only for a short period, after Edward I considered that conquest had finally been achieved with the capture of Stirling castle in 1304, that he was able to put into full effect his view that those who opposed him were traitors and rebels, liable to the full rigours not of the law of arms, but of the English common law. The executions of many Scots in the last years of Edward's reign were not simply the vindictive actions of a malevolent and unsympathetic king: they were also the logical development of the English view of the nature of the conflict. Edward I was a believer in the law, as long as it lent support to his position, and he was acting according to the law as he saw it. Yet when the war began to go against the English, under Edward II's incompetent leadership, it was no longer possible to apply the full logic of the theoretical position, even though there was no recognition of Scotland's independence, or of Robert Bruce's right to be king. As the conflict dragged on into Edward III's reign, it was inevitable that the combatants would regard it increasingly as a normal war, subject to the usual conventions. The English justification for the war changed, and the old arguments about English suzerainty were only one weapon in the king's diplomatic armoury. There were some acts of brutality against the Scots, but there were specific reasons for these, and they should not be explained in terms of the nature of the war as a whole. The Anglo-Scottish conflict became, increasingly, a part of the wider struggle of the Hundred Years War, and it became accordingly more difficult to pretend that it was no more than a rebellion against the authority of the English crown.

[67] *CDS*, iii, no.1343.

Chapter 11

England, France and the Origins of the Hundred Years War

Malcolm Vale

The conflict which, as K.B. McFarlane remarked, 'we have agreed to miscall the *Hundred* Years War' is often viewed as one phase in a much larger and longer dispute between the kingdoms of England and France in the middle ages and beyond.[1] Whether one dates the beginnings of that conflict to 1066, 1152, or 1294, and its end to 1453, 1492, 1558 or even 1802, is probably immaterial. The point at issue is that some form of hostile relationship existed between England and France throughout the middle ages. Such an interpretation of Anglo-French relations has had the salutary effect of forcing us to think in terms of broad patterns and long-term developments, but it can also distort the realities of political, economic, social and cultural contacts between England and its nearest continental neighbour. To see Anglo-French connections in a consistently hostile light, of course, does less than justice to the evidence. As long ago as 1922, T.F. Tout spoke of the century or so before the Hundred Years War (1216-1340) as a 'century of approximation', by which he meant close and generally fruitful contact between the two realms.[2] 'From one point of view', wrote Tout, 'it is a period of increasing division between [them] . . . marked by a rising tide of national sentiment which, more mighty than the separating sea, was to divide the two nations for the rest of their history.' 'From another equally legitimate standpoint', he went on, 'it represents a new wave of common impulse, an increasing share in a common heritage, and a time of the greatest likeness of the two lands . . . in temperament, character and institutions that history was ever to witness.'[3]

Tout's views on the institutional similarities of the two countries have

[1] K.B. McFarlane, *The Nobility of Later Medieval England* (Oxford, 1973), p.5: McFarlane spoke of the war as having been 'fought from the time of Edward I to that of Henry VIII and Wolsey'. See, most recently, S.J. Gunn, 'The French Wars of Henry VIII' in *The Origins of War in Early Modern Europe*, ed. J. Black (Edinburgh, 1987), pp.28-51.

[2] T.F. Tout, *France and England in the Middle Ages: their relations in the Middle Ages and now* (Manchester, 1922), p.78.

[3] *Ibid* p.77. See also his *Chapters in the Administrative History of England*, 2nd edn. (Manchester, 1937), i. 7-8.

not worn very well – indeed, they have never really been followed up – but his writing was a reaction against an interpretation of English medieval history which had dominated the historical literature of the late nineteenth and early twentieth centuries. This was that expounded by those whom Tout called the 'Germanists' – those English scholars who had not only applauded and emulated the great advances made by German historians in the study of the middle ages, but had indulged in what seemed to be a kind of historical Pan-Germanism.[4] Although (or possibly because) he was a pupil of Stubbs, it was against Stubbs and, to a lesser extent, Freeman that Tout directed his most withering fire. Their anti-French prejudice, their pontifical statements about the Germanic origins of English institutions, and their denial of French influences upon English constitutional development clearly dismayed him. A few examples, drawn at random from Stubbs' great *Constitutional History of England* (1874) may suffice to explain the force of Tout's reaction. 'The English', wrote Stubbs, 'are a people of German descent in the main constituents of blood, character and language, but most especially . . . in the possession of the elements of primitive German civilization and the common germ of German institutions.'[5] Or, a little later, 'if [England's] history is not the perfectly pure development of Germanic principles, it is the nearest existing approach to such a development'.[6] The bishop of Oxford was as scathing in his dismissal of French constitutional history as he was eulogistic in his admiration for Germanic institutions: 'the system', he declared, 'which has for the last twelve centuries formed the history of France . . . was originally little more than a simple adaptation of the old German polity to the government of a conquered race'.[7] Stubbs' views are perhaps best summed up in his assertion that 'the German element is the paternal element in our system . . . and the chain of proof is to be found in the progressive persistent development of English constitutional history from the primeval polity of the common fatherland'.[8] English parliamentary democracy was born deep in the Teutonic forests.

Criticism of Stubbs' views soon came from both sides of the English Channel. The French responded through the work of Charles Petit-Dutaillis and C.-V. Langlois; in England the task of *critique* and modification was largely assumed by Tout. For him, the study of Anglo-French relations in the middle ages was not to be simply an examination of political, diplomatic, and military history. 'The shiftings day by day', he

---

[4] Tout, *France and England*, pp.96-98, where Tout observed that Stubbs's teaching was 'not so much wrong as out of focus'. See also M.T. Clanchy, *England and its Rulers, 1066-1272. Foreign Lordship and National Identity* (London, 1983), pp.32-4.

[5] W. Stubbs, *The Constitutional History of England* (Oxford, 1874), i. 2.

[6] *Ibid.*, i. 6.

[7] *Ibid.*, i. 3; cf. Tout, *France and England*, p.97.

[8] Stubbs, *Constitutional History*, i. 11.

wrote, 'of the diplomatic game give very little enlightenment as to permanent conditions'.[9] His theme was therefore the 'undercurrent of affinity' which flowed beneath the surface waves of hostility. From 1066 to 1340 (if not beyond), English and French medieval history were to be treated as one subject, and his ideas clearly owed something to an article which Langlois had written in the *English Historical Review* for 1890 entitled 'The Comparative History of England and France during the Middle Ages'.[10] In that paper, Langlois had suggested that the comparative method, as practised by early anthropologists, might be applied to the study of Anglo-French history in the medieval period. An 'easy and legitimate application' was, he believed, possible and he spoke not only of the parallel histories of the two nations but of their common origins.[11] Stubbs had perhaps forgotten (or chosen to forget) that there was a common basis for Anglo-French civilization in the Celtic foundations of the two countries, overlaid by Roman, Germanic and Christian cultures. There was also the fact of the Norman Conquest. Langlois urged a study of interactions and cross-influence between England and France within an essentially institutional frame of reference. 'Under the Capetians and Plantagenets', he asserted, 'nearly all elements of French and English society are commensurate' and a comparative treatment of English and French institutions was desirable.[12] What fruitful results might stem from a comparison of the *curia regis* in both kingdoms, between exchequer and *chambre des comptes, parlement* and the courts of king's bench and common pleas, the *grand conseil* and the privy council, sheriffs and *baillis* and *sénéchaux*, justices in eyre and *enquêteurs-reformateurs* and, above all, parliament and states-general?

The work of Robert Fawtier on English parliament and French Estates, and of Edward Miller on 'The State and Landed Interests in Thirteenth-Century England and France' took Langlois' suggestions a little further. But Tout's approach was taken up most notably by John Le Patourel.[13] If one follows Tout in his argument that the underlying theme of Anglo-French relations before 1340 was one of harmonious and productive interaction, then it is necessary to explain how, when and why this gave way to hostility and divergence. Tout's conclusions in 1922 about the reasons which lay behind Edward III and his successors' wars with France were fundamentally two-fold: first, that the basis of the quarrel

[9] Tout, *France and England*, p.2.
[10] C.-V. Langlois, 'The Comparative History of England and France during the Middle Ages', *EHR*, v (1890), 259-63.
[11] Langlois, 259-60.
[12] Langlois, 261.
[13] R. Fawtier, 'Parlement d'Angleterre et Etats généraux de France au Moyen Age', *Comptes rendus à l'Académie des Inscriptions et Belles-Lettres*, (1953), 275-84: E. Miller, 'The State and Landed Interests in Thirteenth-Century England and France', *TRHS*, 5th ser. ii (1952), 109-22; J. Le Patourel, *Feudal Empires. Norman and Plantagenet* (London, 1984).

that led to the so-called Hundred Years War which broke out in 1337 and effectively ended in 1453 was 'the impossible position of an English king who was also duke of Gascony'.[14] In 1945, Edouard Perroy echoed Tout's words when he wrote that 'nowadays it is established that the primary cause of the conflict is to be sought in the disturbing question of Guyenne'.[15] Tout's secondary conclusion was that there was really very little difference between the aims of the major protagonists in the Anglo-French negotiations and occasional armed clashes of the eighty years' peace before the Hundred Years War (i.e. from 1259 to 1340). Both Edward I (1272-1307) and Philip the Fair (1285-1314), for instance, were essentially similar: they were both 'centralising monarchs', attempting to exercise an authority superior to that of their barons. Even in his continental possessions – Aquitaine and Ponthieu – Edward I, thought Tout, was trying to construct a 'centralised state', to act as sovereign de facto, and (ironically) thereby enabled a subsequent Valois monarch of France to incorporate those lands more easily into the French kingdom after the English debacle in 1453. This is a theme which more recent scholars, such as Pierre Chaplais, have also developed.[16]

The notion that not merely the behaviour of two rival kings, but the interactions and collisions of two 'state-building enterprises' should be the concern of Anglo-French historians was born from Tout's analysis. But is this an accurate picture of the realities of thirteenth- and early fourteenth-century politics? Tout cautioned his readers: 'We must begin by clearing away from our minds the modern doctrine of nationality as the normal basis of the political state'.[17] Perhaps we should also be wary of the concept of 'centralised states' and 'state-building enterprises' in an age in which the sovereign political unit was still in its infancy. Tout nevertheless saw a connection between the emergence of the sovereign state and the 'rising tide of national sentiment', but national feeling was always modified, he claimed, by common influence. However great the political and military animosity between the two kingdoms, they were still united by cultural, intellectual and social assumptions. In other words, they spoke the same language (or versions of it), admired the same cultural models, and played the political and diplomatic game by the same rules. It is therefore to the area of 'mentalities' that more recent work has been directed.

In 1952 Geoffrey Templeman concluded, as Tout had done, that 'the French possessions of the English kings were the real root of the trouble'

---

[14] Tout, *France and England*, p.114.

[15] E. Perroy, *The Hundred Years War*, tr. W.B. Wells (London, 1954), p.69.

[16] P. Chaplais, 'La souveraineté du roi de France et le pouvoir législatif en Guyenne au début du XIVe siècle', *Le Moyen Age* (1963), 449-69.

[17] Tout, *France and England*, p.8.

which led to the Hundred Years' War.[18] But he also looked beyond the diplomatic game of chess to the assumptions which underlay the behaviour of both sides. Their concern, he argued, was with rights: the protracted series of legal wrangles which constituted so much of Anglo-French diplomacy was the accepted and acceptable norm. If the Capetian kings of France had wished to raise the quarrel above the level of a dispute over feudal rights then, he claimed, they could easily have ended English (or rather Plantagenet) rule within France. This was in fact by no means so easy a task: and was it in fact even desirable for the French kings to attempt it? The Anglo-French wars of 1294-1303 and 1324-5 had ended in the restoration of Aquitaine to the Plantagenets.[19] A tenacious grip in Gascony and elsewhere upon ancient (and more recent) regional privileges meant that Capetian *démarches* had to overcome very considerable stumbling-blocks before real inroads could be driven into the Plantagenet domains. Templeman, however, summed up his views on the origins of the war by, first, shifting the emphasis away from Gascony towards other areas of tension: Flanders, the German Empire and, above all, Scotland. By refusing to isolate the Gascon issue, Templeman claimed, the importance of other factors in making the war of 1337-1453 a 'Hundred Years War' could be brought out in sharper relief. Scottish affairs between 1333 and 1337 were, he asserted, crucial to the outbreak of war, and one comes away from his article with the feeling that there was some novelty and innovation here.[20] But had not Edward I and Philip IV faced very similar issues in 1294-7, when both Scottish and Welsh affairs were brought into play?[21] War and rebellion in Wales and Scotland had been exploited by the French at previous periods of crisis – why should Philip VI have acted in an essentially different manner in the 1330s? The origin of the Franco-Scottish alliance against England can, after all, be traced to 1295.[22] Secondly, Templeman adduced what is perhaps the weakest argument of all to explain why the conflict which broke out in 1337 became a Hundred Years' War. The men of 1337, he concluded, were 'not of the same stature' as those of the 1290s.[23] The introduction of personalities into the argument only blurs the issues. What does 'stature'

[18] G. Templeman, 'Edward III and the Beginnings of the Hundred Years War', *TRHS*, 5th ser., ii (1952), 71.

[19] P. Chaplais, 'Le duché-pairie de Guyenne: l'hommage et les services féodaux de 1259 à 1303', *Annales du Midi*, lxix (1957), 37-8; 'Le duché-pairie de Guyenne: l'hommage et les services féodaux de 1303 à 1337', *Annales du Midi*, lxx (1958), 155-60.

[20] Templeman, 86-7.

[21] F.M. Powicke, *The Thirteenth Century* (Oxford, 1954), pp.612-14; J.G. Edwards, 'The Treason of Thomas Turberville, 1295', *Studies in Medieval History Presented to F.M. Powicke*, ed. R.W. Hunt, W.A. Pantin, R.W. Southern (Oxford, 1948), pp.296-309.

[22] *Foedera*, I, ii. 822.

[23] Templeman, 88. The same point is made by G. Cuttino, *English Medieval Diplomacy* (Bloomington, Ind., 1985), p.83.

in this context mean? One reason why the crises of 1294-7 did not lead to a 'Hundred Years War' was that Philip IV met greater resistance than he had bargained for in Flanders, and was soundly defeated by the Flemings at Courtrai in 1302, while the animosity of Pope Boniface VIII towards him tended to play very much into Edward I's hands. There was nothing about the relative stature of rulers in the 1290s and early 1300s which was essentially different from that of the 1330s. Perhaps there lies behind Templeman's belief the Huizinga-esque notion of fourteenth- and fifteenth-century cultural and moral decay.[24] Edward III, Philip VI and Benedict XII could not be as great and as statesmanlike as Edward I, Philip IV and Boniface VIII (given that they were) simply because they lived after them – they were infected by the decadence of their times.

A more convincing argument was proposed shortly after Templeman's essay appeared. Professor Philippe Wolff paid homage to Lucien Fèbvre with an essay on 'Un problème d'origines: la Guerre de Cent Ans'.[25] Wolff took a 'meridional' view of the issues. His emphasis lay firmly upon regional particularism – especially Gascon particularism – in rendering the Anglo-French problem insoluble: he summed up the political behaviour of the Gascons by arguing that they were 'skilful in playing one power off against another . . . so that they were not pressed by either; they were accustomed to a high degree of autonomy, nourished by it, and full of vivacity'.[26] The shift away from the conference table, where the Anglo-French diplomats met, to the castles and communes of south-west France was highly desirable. It has not yet been taken far enough in discussions of the origins of the Hundred Years War. Diplomatic historians tend often to become absorbed in the minutiae of negotiations (which were in any case artificial) to the virtual exclusion of the interests and attitudes of those who lived in the territories pushed back and forth across the diplomatic chess-board. No treaty between England and France could ever have been fully implemented without the consent and co-operation of those independently-minded and often turbulent people for whom English ducal authority might be a useful weapon to wield against the French crown, their neighbours, or their traditional enemies.[27] Vice versa, French royal authority could similarly be exploited by them against the English king-duke and his officers. Without a closer attention to the assumptions and behaviour of such interest-groups, discussion of

[24] J. Huizinga, *The Waning of the Middle Ages* (Harmondsworth, 1965), p.7: Huizinga saw the period as 'an epoch of fading and decay'.

[25] P. Wolff, 'Un problème d'origines: la Guerre de Cent Ans', *Eventail de l'histoire vivante: Hommage à Lucien Fèbvre* (Paris, 1953), ii. 141-8.

[26] Wolff, 143.

[27] See, for example, P. Chaplais, 'Some Documents Regarding the Fulfilment and Interpretation of the Treaty of Brétigny, 1361-69', *Camden Miscellany*, xix (1952), 1-78; P. Wolff, 'The Armagnacs of Southern France (14th-15th centuries)', *BIHR*, xx (1945), 186-91.

diplomatic proceedings at the highest level can often be sterile and unilluminating. Wolff also introduced the importance of Flemish affairs into his account: indeed, he saw Gascon and Flemish issues together, possessing certain striking affinities. As a student of medieval commerce and of the merchant class in Toulouse, he rightly pointed to the similarities between Flanders and Gascony – to their common dependence upon England: the one as a market for its wine; the other as a source of wool for its cloth industry.[28] This could only have had the effect of strengthening regional sentiment and of hindering French intervention. The significance of urban and communal developments in both areas needed to be considered, and a much broader dimension introduced into the study of Anglo-French relations. Yet Wolff's final conclusion was perhaps rather less original: he accounted for the outbreak of the Anglo-French war by citing the degree to which the feudal relationship of 1259 between Henry III, as duke of Aquitaine, and Louis IX, as king of France, had become an 'unnatural' one by 1337, if not by 1294.[29] He supported this assertion by emphasizing the retardation of 'feudal' concepts behind 'non-feudal' realities by the early fourteenth century. The feudal forms of the past, he alleged, could no longer contain the new non-feudal sovereignties. The mental framework of the time lagged behind the actual nature of things, and the origins of the Hundred Years' War lay in 'the liquidation of the feudal world'.[30] How solid that world had ever been (outside the pages of the law books, the political treatises and the works of more recent historians) is a matter for debate. But Wolff's focus upon the changing nature of royal power in France, especially under Philip IV (1285-1314) and the reaction of the English king-dukes to it at a regional level, deserves to be taken very seriously. How, in the conditions of the 1330s and 1340s, could two rulers who regarded themselves as sovereigns with equal authority play the old game of lord and vassal?

Hard on the heels of Wolff's questioning of received impressions came Professor George Cuttino's article of 1956 and his subsequent books.[31] Cuttino wrote from the standpoint of a student of English diplomatic administration. He pointed to the fundamental mistake made by English diplomacy in 1259, claimed that French policy 'reflects a doctrine synonymous with modern sovereignty', and put the blame for the outbreak of war in 1337 squarely on the shoulders of the French. The confiscation of Gascony by Philip VI in that year was, he wrote, 'the

---

[28] Wolff, 'Problème d'origines', 144-5; also F. Funck-Brentano, *Les origines de la Guerre de Cent Ans. Philippe le Bel en Flandre* (Paris, 1897), pp.678-9.

[29] Wolff, 'Problème d'origines', 147-8.

[30] Wolff, 'Problème d'origines', 148.

[31] G. Cuttino, 'Historical Revision: the Causes of the Hundred Years War', *Speculum* (1956), 463-77; *English Diplomatic Administration, 1259-1339*, 2nd edn. (Oxford, 1971); *English Medieval Diplomacy* (1985).

inevitable result of French attempts to exercise sovereignty and *ressort* in Aquitaine', and English policy accordingly changed from an honest attempt to work within the terms of the 1259 agreement to a 'conscious effort to achieve unchallenged sovereignty over Gascony by assuming the title king of France' and by going to war.[32] 'Feudal and national claims', he argued, 'were incompatible'.[33] Cuttino's final conclusion was that 'the cosmopolitanism and suzerainty of 1259 had become the nationalism and sovereignty of 1339': abstractions were, for him, also the key to the Hundred Years' War.[34] Theoretical concepts of power, however, can be misleading guides to the actual nature of politics. One must always question the extent to which ideas of 'nationalism' or 'nationhood' had developed by 1340, and the readiness with which compromise over the definition and exercise of 'sovereignty' could be achieved needs always to be taken into the reckoning. In any case, what *was* 'sovereignty' in the context of Anglo-French affairs by 1340?

The most recent contribution to the debate about the Hundred Years' War has been the work of the late John Le Patourel. Like Tout, Le Patourel saw the issues more in institutional, than political or diplomatic, terms. In his articles (published 1958-84) he provided analysis of the administrative developments which tended towards the creation of those two rival 'centralisations' of which Tout spoke.[35] Le Patourel's work, in one sense, forms a postscript to his study of the Norman Empire, because much of his argument is informed by the belief that a coherent 'political and administrative complex [consisting] of England and its overseas dominions' was the real political entity of the period after the Norman Conquest.[36] To some extent, his views upon the origins of the Hundred Years' War are an extension of his thesis that the meaningful units of medieval government were not so much the kingdoms of England and France but the 'empires' of the Normans, Plantagenets and Capetians which constantly overlapped and interpenetrated. He wrote: 'the political edifice which the Plantagenet king-dukes were constructing was as valid for its day as the Capetians' kingdom: and no one could then have said whether the future lay with one or the other'.[37] The major difference between the Angevin empire and the truncated political conglomeration

---

[32] Cuttino, 'Historical Revision', 472.

[33] Cuttino, *English Diplomatic Administration*, p.111.

[34] Cuttino, 'Historical revision', 472.

[35] See especially, 'The King and the Princes in Fourteenth-Century France', in *Europe in the late Middle Ages*, ed. J.R. Hale, J.R.L. Highfield and B. Smalley (London, 1965), pp.155-83; 'The Origins of the Hundred Years War', in *The Hundred Years War*, ed. K. Fowler (London, 1971), pp.28-50 and 'France and England in the Middle Ages', in *Feudal Empires*, XVIII, 1-14. (All of these are reprinted in his *Feudal Empires, Norman and Plantagenet*, see n.13 above.)

[36] Le Patourel, 'The Plantagenet Dominions', *History*, l (1965), 290.

[37] Le Patourel, 'Origins of the Hundred Years War', 44.

which replaced it after the loss of Normandy by the Plantagenets in 1204 was, he claimed, the creation of an assemblage of territories which were far more dependent upon England than the continental lands of the Normans and Angevins had ever been. The centre of gravity of this conglomeration after 1204 was the English kingdom, and he argued that 'the administration of Gascony was subordinated to what were primarily English institutions' – i.e. exchequer accounting procedures and parliamentary petitions by the later thirteenth century – although the internal administrative developments there were 'characteristically French in form'.[38] As the connection between Aquitaine and England grew closer, so the possibilities for independent action there by the king-duke through his officers increased. When this reached intolerable levels for the crown of France, conflict broke out. The feudal relationship could no longer accommodate the facts of the situation, and so Edward III ended it once and for all by assuming the crown of France. 'A feudal dispute', Le Patourel concludes, 'was converted into a long conflict in which the old feudal overlapping and interlocking gave way to the autonomous and self-contained national kingdoms of France and England.'[39]

It can hardly be claimed that the implications of Le Patourel's hypothesis have yet been fully worked out. Nor can it be said that there is as yet a consensus among historians about the origins of the Hundred Years' War which is notably different from Tout's position of 1922. We are faced with at least two kinds of methodological approach to the problems of Anglo-French relations: a standpoint from which ideas and abstractions (e.g. Tout's 'rising tide of national sentiment') are seen as fundamental to the changes which took place between 1259 and 1340; or an approach which centres on the interpretation of concrete political and diplomatic facts. The two views are, of course, not irreconcilable. Abstract theories can, after all, be expressed (or distorted) in the sphere of political action, thereby providing concrete facts provable by evidence. As Pierre Chaplais has shown, arguments about the feudal or allodial status of Aquitaine, for instance, did have a certain influence upon pragmatic politics, especially after 1298.[40]

Yet we are not in a political world in which ideologies were uppermost, when just causes were elevated to the level of high principle from which there could be no retreat and no compromise. Perhaps rulers were simply not powerful enough to put such notions into practice. To comprehend the relationship between abstract theory and political practice it is necessary to know far more about the personnel engaged in formulating policies and

[38] Le Patourel, 'Plantagenet Dominions', 303.
[39] Le Patourel, 'Origins of the Hundred Years War', 46.
[40] P. Chaplais, 'English Arguments Concerning the Feudal Status of Aquitaine in the Fourteenth Century', *BIHR*, xxi (1948), 203-13.

carrying them out. Who made the decisions? Who executed them? What
was their professional and intellectual formation? What was the nature of
the relationship between the diplomats, advocates, nobles and knights on
either side? Secondly, an attempt has to be made to recreate the attitudes
and assumptions which lay behind Anglo-French dealings before the
Hundred Years War. This is in part related to my previous point: Tout
wrote in 1929 that the administrative and diplomatic personnel of the
English crown in the fourteenth century had to be re-animated by the
historian. 'We need', he argued, 'to picture to ourselves what manner of
men they were . . . their ideals, ambitions, characters, personalities,
education, habits and amusements.'[41] French historical writing has
perhaps succeeded better in this respect than English: work on the *légistes
et gens de finance*, or any other socio-professional group, has become
common.[42] But Tout's point was an important one: how can we study the
determinants of Anglo-French affairs without some knowledge not only of
the often-obscure aims of kings, but of the mental habits and assumptions
of those who advised, influenced and served them? One means of
establishing the prevailing ethos of Anglo-French sentiments at this time
is to look at the presence of Englishmen in France and of Frenchmen in
England. How (if at all) did the recorded views of each change by 1340?
Furthermore, the administrators, legal counsellors and diplomats formed
a permanent group, which tended not to change drastically at changes of
king or even of ministers. This clearly gave a certain continuity to political
and diplomatic practice.

One result of the Anglo-French treaty of 1259 was that the king-duke of
Aquitaine was obliged to maintain a presence by proxy at the 'court of
France' (i.e. at the nascent supreme court of appeals emerging as the
parlement of Paris). Constant vigilance was necessary to tackle the problem
of appellants from the ducal courts in Aquitaine to the higher jurisdiction
of the French crown. Le Patourel indeed claims that, at least between 1272
and 1292, Edward I saw this vigilance over appeals to the Paris *parlement*
as 'the natural order of things', and Henry III had accepted this aspect of
St. Louis' lordship as the price of peace with France.[43] The
representatives of the king-dukes at Paris fall broadly into two groups:
first, the English-born clerks and lawyers sent either on ad hoc or on more
permanent missions to the French court; secondly, the nobles who acted

---

[41] Tout, 'Literature and Learning in the English Civil Service in the Fourteenth
Century', *Speculum*, iv (1929), 367.
[42] See, for example, R. Fédou, *Les hommes de loi lyonnais à la fin du Moyen Age* (Paris, 1964);
B. Guenée, *Tribunaux et gens de justice dans le bailliage de Senlis à la fin du Moyen Age (vers 1380-
vers 1550)* (Paris, 1963); J. Bartier, *Légistes et gens de finance au XVᵉ siècle. Les conseillers des ducs
de Bourgogne Philippe le Bon et Charles le Téméraire* (Brussels, 1955); for England, now see R.A.
Griffiths, 'Public and Private Bureaucracies in England and Wales in the Fifteenth
Century', *TRHS*, 5th ser., xxx (1980), 109-30.
[43] Le Patourel, 'Plantagenet Dominions', 305.

as intermediaries between the two sides. The first were members of
Cuttino's embryonic 'Foreign Office': men such as Philip Martel, Elias
Joneston, Henry of Canterbury, Thomas Cobham, Roger Sheffield, or
Andrew Ufford, all of them king's clerks.[44] These men are not to be
confused with the French advocates hired by the English to defend them
and plead cases for them in *parlement*. It is perhaps paradoxical that
Edward I, Edward II and Edward III were in effect paying subjects of the
French crown to defend their interests, as dukes of Aquitaine, against that
crown. Practitioners such as the great and avaricious Guillaume du
Breuil, author of the *Stilus Curie Parliamenti*, or Eudes de Sens, advocate, or
Pierre Dubois himself were retained by Edward I and Edward II to plead
against their French colleagues.[45] Gascons were also used: men such as
Guillaume de Cazes or Austence Jourdain, learned and skilled in the laws
and customs of Aquitaine, members of the king-duke's council at
Bordeaux, often represented English interests at Paris.[46] But this was
normal practice among the peers and great magnates of France. The
development of the *parlement's* appellate jurisdiction after 1259 meant that
certain days of legal business were reserved for cases from a given area:
thus the 'days of Burgundy', or Artois, or Champagne were as frequent as
the 'days of Aquitaine'. In the early fourteenth century, for example,
Mahaut, countess of Artois, was permanently retaining no less than seven
advocates at Paris to handle cases from Artois.[47] The services even of the
best French and Gascon lawyers, however, were not always effective in the
defence of the English king-dukes' authority. In 1332 Edward III was
advised not to use French and Gascon advocates and proctors at a
particularly delicate phase of negotiations, because it was thought that
they were more easily coerced and frightened by the French. Threats of
disinheritance, even of death, were made (it was claimed) at that time
against them if they dared to proceed.[48] Yet until that date, French and
Gascon lawyers served amicably beside Englishmen such as Martel and
Joneston, or alongside greater and more ambitious clerks such as John de
Hildesley, Thomas Cobham or Richard de Bury.

As early as October 1262, only three years after the treaty of Paris,
Henry III was retaining Englishmen as proctors before the court of
France. A letter dated 11 October 1262 from Roger de Doncaster, king's
clerk, to John de Kirkby, tells us what the incidental, non-legal functions

---

[44] Cuttino, *English Diplomatic Administration*, pp. 143-4.
[45] R. Delachenal, *Histoire des avocats au Parlement de Paris, 1300-1600* (Paris, 1885), pp.338,
340-1; G. du Breuil, *Stilus Curie Parliamenti*, ed. F. Aubert, (Paris, 1909), pp.i-vi, 99, 179; F.
Aubert, *Histoire du Parlement de Paris de l'origine à Francois Ier* (Paris, 1894), i. 207; P. Dubois,
De recuperatione terre sancte, ed. C.-V. Langlois (Paris, 1891), p.1.
[46] Cuttino, *English Diplomatic Administration*, pp.144-6.
[47] Aubert, *Histoire du Parlement*, i. 207.
[48] Cuttino, 'A Memorandum book of Elias Joneston', *Speculum*, xxvii (1942), 57.

of these men were. Doncaster had arrived in Paris on Michaelmas Day, where he found Roger de Missenden and Thomas de la Ley, king's clerks, seated at dinner 'jocose, sanos et hillares'.[49] He waited until the festive meal had ended before giving them Kirkby's letters – this rather cooled their spirits, because Missenden's failure to do what was required of him about some case of ecclesiastical preferment was criticised. However, Doncaster absorbed the rumours and news of the court from them: Henry III, then in Paris, was still convalescent, and would not move before Christmas. These men provided a useful intelligence service for the English at home. More private matters were then attended to by Doncaster: he reported his search for a tapestry at Paris, to cover the walls of the chancellor's hall at Westminster, but he had not yet found one suitable.[50] All kinds of business – from the lobbying of cardinals who happened to be at the court of France to the purchase of fine saddles for palfreys – could be conducted as a by-product of the Anglo-French connection. Indeed, diplomacy provided the great bibliophile Richard de Bury, later bishop of Durham, with unparalleled opportunites to buy and exchange books. He had been a member of diplomatic missions (which he found tedious) to the court of France in 1325-6, 1331, and 1336.[51] A better diplomat than he was a bureaucrat, he used his position as envoy and representative of Edward III to further his book-collecting activities on the continent. In the *Philobiblon* (his treatise on the love of books), which he wrote in his last year (1344-5), he tells us that his entry into the royal household was crucial to his career, and that at Paris 'opening our treasuries and unfastening our purse-strings we scattered money with joyous heart and purchased inestimable books with mud and sand'.[52] What one might call 'cultural' connections of a productive kind were a normal accompaniment of Anglo-French relations in the century before the Hundred Years War. The fact that Paris was so rich a source of books – from de luxe manuscripts to 'soiled tracts and battered codices'[53] – was in part a product of its position as the greatest European centre of learning. Richard de Bury, in his eulogy of the city, spoke of its 'academic meadows shaken by the tramp of scholars'.[54] Some of these scholars, moreover, were Englishmen, and some of them certainly served as proctors and representatives for the English at Paris.

Tout illustrated the affinity between France and England at this time by remarking that 'in the early fourteenth century English diplomatists

---

[49] *Diplomatic Documents, 1101-1272*, ed. P. Chaplais (London, 1964), i. no.370.

[50] *Diplomatic Documents*, i. no.370; 'Tapetum quesivi necdum aliquod michi placens inveni, quia tale quero cujus finbrie aulam cancell' possint cum mendacio cooperire'.

[51] N. Denholm-Young, 'Richard de Bury (1287-1345), *TRHS*, xx (1937), 135-68; *CPR, 1324-7*, 166-71; Bodleian Library, Oxford, MS Bodley 751, fo.4ᵛ (August 1325).

[52] Richard de Bury, *Philobiblon*, ed. M. Maclagan (Oxford, 1960), p.87.

[53] *Philobiblon*, p.83.

[54] *Philobiblon*, p.84.

must have been college friends of the diplomatic representatives of the enemy'.[55] This, if true, must surely have influenced the manner in which legal and diplomatic business was transacted. We know that king's clerks such as John de Hildesley and Thomas Cobham (who became bishop of Worcester in 1317) had studied at Paris.[56] In 1309 and 1311, Hildesley was granted licence to study there for two-year periods. He was an Oxford bachelor of canon law by 1317 and served Edward II and Edward III in Gascony, France and Aragon. His most important assignment was his appointment as proctor for Edward III at the court of France in 1330 and 1331 to discuss Edward's homage for Aquitaine and Ponthieu, and he was still employed on missions to France after the outbreak of war, in 1343.[57] His knowledge, and his training at Paris, must have served him well. Master Henry of Canterbury, responsible for many of the diplomatic memoranda of Edward II's reign, had also studied law at Paris, and his professional judgement upon Anglo-French affairs must have been valuable.[58] 'Foreign policy' (if such it can be called at this time) was partly determined by the appreciation of possibilities, based upon precedent, formed by these experts. Canterbury's job was, in essence, to advise both Edward II and Edward III on the best means of sustaining their interests before the Paris *parlement*, and he was still doing this on the eve of war in 1336. If these men were Paris graduates as well as graduates of Oxford or Cambridge, their relationship to their opposite numbers must have been nothing if not ambiguous. The fact that they sometimes pleaded beside Guillaume de Breuil or Eudes de Sens in the *parlement* was surely significant. In the conduct of the extended lawsuit that Anglo-French relations became between 1259 and 1340, the professional connections which bound the representatives of both sides together deserve further study.

The second group which mediated between England and France in the thirteenth and early fourteenth centuries were nobles and knights in the service of the Plantagenents. Since the loss of Normandy by King John in 1204, the 'cross-channel' nobility of England had been radically reduced in numbers. Some magnates, however, such as William Marshal, continued to hold their French lands, and this practice was continued by Simon de Montfort and William de Valence in the mid and later thirteenth-century.[59] Montfort was indeed purely 'French' in origin – the

---

[55] Tout, *France and England*, p.28.

[56] A.B. Emden, *A Biographical Register of the University of Oxford to 1500*, 3 vols. (Oxford, 1957-9), ii. 933-4 (Hildesley); i. 450-1 (Cobham).

[57] Emden, *Biographical Register*, ii. 934; Cuttino, *English Diplomatic Administration*, pp.143-4.

[58] Cuttino, 'Henry of Canterbury', *EHR*, lvii (1942), 298-311.

[59] Powicke, *The Loss of Normandy*, 2nd edn. (Manchester, 1961), pp.294-6; C. Bémont, *Simon de Montfort*, tr. E.F. Jacob (Oxford, 1930), pp.35-7; J.R.S. Phillips, *Aymer de Valence, earl of Pembroke, 1307-24* (Oxford, 1972), pp.2-5.

so-called defender of English liberties was in no way a true-born patriot. The influx of Savoyards, Poitevins and Provençals into England under Henry III did not end with the king's death in 1272.[60] Edward I employed and endowed men such as the Lusignan William de Valence, earl of Pembroke, Odo de Grandson, knight, and Jean de Grilly, knight (both Savoyards) using them both in Anglo-French and Gascon affairs throughout the reign.[61] As knights of his household, these 'aliens' played a vital part in dealing with France. Grandson was among Edward's most trusted lieutenants, accompanying him on his visit to France and Gascony in 1286-9, and was constantly employed in business at the courts of France and Aragon during those years.[62] The closest kinsmen of the king also played important 'cross-channel' roles. As a result of his marriage to Blanche of Artois, Edmund of Lancaster (Edward's brother) became governor of the Northern French *comté* of Champagne on her behalf.[63] The heiress to Champagne, Jeanne, was a minor, and until she married Philip IV of France in 1284 the *comté* was effectively held by Edmund bearing the courtesy title of count of Champagne. To have his brother in so central a position, adjacent to the demesne of the Capetians, was very beneficial to Edward. A letter survives from Edmund to his brother the king which must date from 1282.[64] In it, Edmund tells the king that he has heard of the outbreak of the Welsh war while in the process of 'ordering and attending to the state of my affairs in Champagne'. He did not yet know whether Edward wished him to bring to Wales any of his nobles of Champagne to serve there. He had warned many Champenois that they were to be ready to go after him when so commanded and, he went on, 'they willingly agreed'.[65] He was just about to go to Paris in order to take leave of Philip III of France and arrange for the passage of his horses to England. He would bring news of his dealings with Philip when he arrived, and hoped that his English retinue would suffice for Edward's needs until he knew his brother's wishes about the nobles of Champagne. Here an English magnate was in effect offering the services of men who were technically subjects of the crown of France to the king of England in his capacity as king, rather than as duke of Aquitaine.

Examples could be multiplied, especially from among the nobility of Western France. One more will perhaps suffice. It is that of a French-born nobleman who served all his life in England. In 1261, Henry III's

---

[60] For a recent study of their role, see Clanchy, *England and its Rulers*, pp.210-35, 241-4, 261-2.

[61] Powicke, *Thirteenth Century*, pp.287-9, 319-21, 435-6, 514; 292-3, 289.

[62] C.L. Kingsford, 'Sir Otho de Grandison', *TRHS*, 3rd ser., iii (1909), 125-95.

[63] Powicke, *Thirteenth Century*, pp.239, 241-3.

[64] PRO S.C.1/16, no.138; dated at La Ferté-Milon on the Wednesday before Pentecost.

[65] *Ibid.*, 'quar je ai bien garni pluseurs de Champagne quil soient prestz de venir apres moi quelque oure que je leur mande, et eus voluntiers le ferent'.

daughter Béatrix had married Jean, eldest son of the duke of Brittany.[66] A son, aptly named Arthur, was born to them in 1262, described in a familiar and affectionate letter from Blanche, duchess of Brittany to Henry III as 'mout bon enffant e mout beil, le Deu merci'.[67] In 1266, a second son, Jean, was born. Béatrix died in 1275, and Jean was brought up in England, apparently in Edward I's household. After a career of service to Edward in Wales, Scotland, France, Ponthieu and Gascony, Jean was given the earldom of Richmond by a king who was notoriously mean in his endowment of earls. Jean survived into the reign of Edward III, returning to Brittany shortly before his death in 1334.[68] His talents were apparently for diplomacy rather than warfare (although he served against Philip IV in Gascony, 1294-7) and his connections in France (like those of Aymer de Valence) clearly helped to ease diplomatic tension at periods of crisis.[69] He was a valuable go-between. His father and grandfather had also held Richmond and, from their autonomous position in Brittany vis-à-vis the Capetians, had few inhibitions about serving the English crown as vassals. In August 1261, for instance, the future Jean II of Brittany, betrothed to Béatrix, wrote to his prospective father-in-law (Henry III) offering him military aid whenever it was requested.[70] The bonds between some of the great magnates of France and the Capetian monarchy were as yet too slender and too fragile to allow the crown anything like a total monopoly of their service or loyalty. There is no reason to suppose that the Valois accession of 1328 made an appreciable difference.

The fact that the language in which these nobles wrote to each other was French comes as no surprise, yet it is nonetheless significant. Edmund of Lancaster's letter to Edward I of 1282 is in excellent French – there is little to suggest that 'English' magnates were ignorant of the best written French. The books (especially the romances) in their libraries, and their letter collections, bear witness to that.[71] Yet a consciousness of Anglo-French differences was already apparent – it was based upon irrational prejudices and linguistic dissimilarities, and had existed since the mid to late twelfth century. In his verse romance *Jean de Dammartin et Blonde d'Oxford*, for example, written in the 1270s or 80s, Philippe de Beaumanoir, knight, author of *Coutumes de Beauvaisis*, reveals the attitudes

[66] Powicke, *Henry III and the Lord Edward* (Oxford, 1947), pp.257, 412.

[67] *Diplomatic Documents*, i. no.368, datable to late summer, 1262. See also nos.360, 396.

[68] I. Lubimenko, *Jean de Bretagne, comte de Richmond (1266-1334)* (Lille, 1908), pp.2-3, 135-6.

[69] Lubimenko, *Jean de Bretagne*, pp.12-26, 135-6.

[70] *Diplomatic Documents*, i. no.326.

[71] H. Suggett, 'The Use of French in England in the Later Middle Ages', *TRHS*, 4th ser., xxviii (1946), 60-83; Clanchy, *From Memory to Written Record. England 1066-1307* (London, 1979), pp.151-4, 197-201; M.B. Parkes, 'The Literacy of the Laity', in *The Medieval World*, ed. D. Daiches and A. Thorlby (London, 1973), pp.555-62.

of a representative thirteenth-century French nobleman towards England and his English contemporaries.[72] There is no inherent ill-will in it towards Englishmen. Indeed, the hero of the tale, Jean, son of the count of Dammartin, not only inherits his father's French lordships but the earldom of Oxford as well. The tale revolves around Jean's career as a young *gentilhomme* who seeks his fortune in England. Parallels with Simon de Montfort are not entirely inappropriate.[73] Beaumanoir may indeed have visited England shortly before 1270, and the settings of his romances are in Scotland and England. Jean de Dammartin, in Beaumanoir's story, meets the earl of Oxford's retinue on the road from Dover to London on their way to parliament. His appearance attracted the earl's attention, and Jean

> greeted him in French
> And the earl replied fluently
> (Because he understood French very well,
> and had learnt it in France . . .)[74]

Oxford's linguistic ability is sharply contrasted with that of Jean's rival for the hand of Blonde, Oxford's daughter. This is the blustering earl of Gloucester, whom Jean again meets on the road. Gloucester recognises Jean as a Frenchman because of his tunic, which he thinks means that he was born near Pontoise. The poem goes on:

> [Gloucester] tried to talk to him in French
> But his tongue turned into English [i.e. Anglo-Norman]
> (Gloucester): 'Amis, bien fustes vous veneé!
>   Coment fu vostre non pelé?' [i.e. for 'appellé'][75]

Gloucester offers to buy Jean's riding horse (palfrey) but, with heavy irony, Jean demands what he most desires from the earl in payment. Gloucester expostulates.

> 'Nai [for 'non'], par la goiffre biu, nai, nai!'
> [i.e. 'la coiffe Dieu' or crown of thorns]
> Quo deble! [=Provençal] Ce sera trop chère . . .'[76]

Much amusement was no doubt derived by Beaumanoir's audience from the villain's massacre of the best Ile-de-France French through solecisms and Anglo-Norman constructions. Yet this was not so very

---

[72] *Oeuvres poétiques de Philippe de Rémi, sire de Beaumanoir*, ed. H. Suchier (Paris, 1884), i. x-xii; ii. *passim*; P. Rickard, *Britain in Medieval French Literature* (Cambridge, 1956), pp.124-9.

[73] *Oeuvres poétiques*, i. x-xi.

[74] *Oeuvres poétiques*, ii. lines 129-32: 'En son Franchois l'a salué,/Et li quens n'i a delué/(Que le Franchois seut bien entendre,/En France eust este pour apprendre).'

[75] *Oeuvres poétiques*, ii. lines 2635-6, 2639-40: 'Si vaut a lui parler franchois,/Mais sa langue torne en Englois'. . ./"Amis, bien fustes vous veneé!/Coment fu vostre non pelé?!"

[76] *Oeuvres poétiques*, ii. lines 2658-9.

different from the linguistic parodies found in other French narrative verse of the period. In the *Tournoi de Chauvency* (1285) there are jokes about Picard French, and very funny and elaborate parodies of Alsatian speech.[77] The practice of linguistic comedy was not confined to stories which involved the English: all kinds of foreigners were the butt of linguistic satire. In *Jean et Blonde*, the hero's beloved, although English, is described in terms of perfection, and the fact that

> There was just a suspicion in her speech
> That she had not been born at Pontoise[78]

is a very minor and venial offence against *courtoisie*. Jean then set about teaching her the finest French 'Par quoi ele mout chier le tint' ('for which she held him very dear'). There are also in the poem a number of jokes by English characters at Jean's expense. Gloucester and his retinue describe him as 'ce sot français' ('this French ninny'), but his *sottises* are clearly misunderstood by them.[80] Their reaction is partly linguistically determined – they simply do not appreciate the word-play of courtly French and, as a result, Gloucester is worsted in his courtship of Blanche. All ends happily, of course, and there is a splendid scene of Anglo-French entente where the old earl of Oxford decides to pass his remaining time in the company of his English daughter and French son-in-law, spending two years at Dammartin and two years in England by turns.[81] On his death, the earl leaves Oxford to Jean, and he is therefore created earl of Oxford and count of Dammartin – a fictitious, though significant, 'cross-channel' nobleman.

It is sometimes forgotten that Anglo-French relations in the thirteenth and early fourteenth centuries possessed many of the qualities of a family history. Sir Maurice Powicke was quite right to emphasise the domestic quality of high politics, when so much depended upon dynastic marriages, connections and alliances within an enlarged family circle.[82] Henry III and Louis IX, Richard of Cornwall and Charles of Anjou were all kinsmen, French-speaking and French-cultured. 'It was this cordiality' wrote Tout, 'that made easy the mutual renunciations of the treaty of Paris of 1259.'[83] It is important to discover when, and how, this relative harmony was broken. One important step towards the later rift between

---

[77] See J. Vale, *Edward III and Chivalry. Chivalric society and its Context, 1270-1350* (Woodbridge, 1982), p.9, n.62.

[78] *Oeuvres poétiques*, ii. lines 358-9. 'Un peu paroit a son langage/Que ne fu pas nee a Pontoise'.

[79] *Oeuvres poétiques*, ii. line 404.

[80] *Oeuvres poétiques*, ii. lines 2685-6.

[81] *Oeuvres poétiques*, ii. lines 6135-9, 6144-7.

[82] Powicke, *Thirteenth Century*, pp.234-7; and see the observations of R.W. Southern, 'Sir Maurice Powicke, 1879-1963', *Proceedings of the British Academy*, L (1965), 293-4.

[83] Tout, *France and England*, p.90.

the ruling houses of England and France was surely taken in 1326, when the future Edward III was betrothed, not to a princess of the French royal house, but to the daughter of the count of Hainault. The effect of his subsequent marriage to Philippa turned Edward towards the Low Countries, rather than towards France, and the Valois succession of 1328 added weight to a process of estrangement which was to end in war.[84] If the relative harmony of Anglo-French relations was shattered by 1340, then we can be fairly sure, moreover, that it was not as a result of 'national sentiment'. Tout concluded his contribution to Anglo-French understanding in 1922 with a view that: 'Nations grow not only when the men of a country become conscious of national identity one with another, but also when they bring home from their travels a strong feeling that they were not like the men they had seen abroad, and a hatred of foreigners because their manners were not like their own'.[85] Richard de Bury, bishop of Durham, writing in 1344-5, seven years after the outbreak of the Hundred Years War, displayed no overt prejudice against the French, although he had travelled in that kingdom widely. He still wrote of Paris as a 'worldly paradise' (*paradisium mundi*) and his only criticisms of France were that philosophy was lukewarm there, and so 'her soldiery are unmanned and languishing'[86] But there was no nationalistic ill-will or chauvinistic animus behind his words. If the 'rising tide of national sentiment' had not engulfed Anglo-French understanding at the level of the politically powerful and articulate by 1340, then we shall have to look elsewhere for the origins of the Hundred Years War. National sentiment was perhaps a result, rather than a cause, of that conflict.[87]

[84] *Ibid.*, 112-13. For the marriage agreement see Archives départementales du Nord, B.415, no.5766 (dated at Mons, 24 August 1326).

[85] Tout, *France and England*, p.119.

[86] *Philobiblon*, pp.84, 107.

[87] I hope to develop some of the themes of this essay in a forthcoming book on *The Angevin Legacy and the Hundred Years War, 1250-1340*.

Chapter 12

The Dissemination of Manuscripts Relating to English Political Thought in the Fourteenth Century

Jean-Philippe Genet

The present location of manuscripts is the result of a long and complicated history: given to friends or heirs, bequeathed to colleges or churches, sold, stolen, damaged, destroyed, manuscripts have through the centuries disappeared or migrated. In most cases their history cannot be reconstructed: if the manuscript is undated, if the script is uncharacteristic, it is even difficult to make a guess at its origins; without marks of ownership or pressmarks, it is hardly possible to determine the intermediate stages of the 'career' of a given volume. Nonetheless, and without forgetting these considerations, it remains that the present location of manuscripts, which is a known fact, may have a certain amount of significance, which I should like to test in the case of four English theologians of the fourteenth century: William of Ockham, Walter Burley, Richard Fitzralph and John Wyclif.

The contribution of the British Isles to the intellectual life of the later middle ages is certainly out of proportion to their size and population, and most textbooks have a tendency to describe the fourteenth century as a struggle between two British giants, Duns Scotus on the one hand, and William of Ockham on the other. Though Gordon Leff among others has shown that there was much in common between the different philosophical schools of the fourteenth century,[1] the basic opposition between 'realism' and 'nominalism' has some significance, especially since it played an important part in the internal struggles of most European universities; this can be substantiated by the well-known examples of Paris or Prague, for instance. It is indeed noteworthy that the two best exponents (and Ockham at least was quickly recognized as such) of these two opposite tendencies were men trained at Oxford University, or, more exactly, at both Paris and Oxford Universities: a feature which they shared with both Burley and Fitzralph, but not with Wyclif, a pure Oxford product. The recognized importance of these authors is obviously partly a result of the tremendous vitality and fertility of Oxford in the first half of the fourteenth century.[2]

---

[1] G. Leff, *The Dissolution of the Mediaeval Outlook* (New York, 1976).
[2] *The History of Oxford University*, i, ed. J.I. Catto (Oxford, 1984).

At the time, England was asserting itself, albeit hesitatingly, as a national kingdom, and beginning to play on the European stage an essential part, best epitomized by what we call the Hundred Years War. But did this political self-assertion and this intellectual blossoming combine to produce a specific English school of political philosophy? And was this supposedly English political philosophy influential in fourteenth-century Europe? The European dissemination of the political works of the most important English thinkers has been selected here as a possible element to answer such questions.

This however raises several preliminary questions which would require a more careful and detailed examination than they can get here. For instance, what is a political work, since 'political science' (or political philosophy) cannot be considered as an autonomous science before Thomas Hobbes and the seventeenth century? This I intend to discuss elsewhere: suffice it to say that I have here used the word political in the broadest way, and dubbed as political works texts dealing with matters recognized as such in the medieval classification of science – that is as parts of practical theology – as well as texts which were used and quoted in contemporary political debates, even if the declared subject is not at first glance political (this is especially true of works by Fitzralph and even Wyclif). However this is enough to exclude Duns Scotus from such a survey, since his rich and influential political theories are not to be found in an isolated political text. Another difficult question is that of the relation of text and manuscript, especially in the case of a quantitative survey: an undoubtedly political tract may very well be included in a manuscript which is predominantly non-political. But it must be remembered that if it is possible to delineate what a political text is, a 'political' manuscript is in most cases but a conventional description, and nothing else.

We may now sum up briefly the relevant facts of the careers of these four authors and recall the circumstances and nature of their political works.[3] Burley, a Yorkshireman – as Wyclif – got his master's degree at Oxford before 1301, and his doctorate at Paris before 1324; a fellow of Merton at Oxford and of the Sorbonne at Paris, he remained a predominantly academic figure, a distinguished professor of Paris University, invited to take part in disputations at Toulouse and Bologna. After 1326 he began to collect ecclesiastical preferments (canonries at Chichester, Wells, Chester-le-Street and Salisbury) and rose in the civil service: king's clerk, close to Richard de Bury, he was entrusted with the conduct of difficult negotiations at Avignon for the canonisation of Thomas, earl of Lancaster and may have been picked as tutor to the Black

---

[3] These four authors have a full notice in A.B. Emden, *A Biographical Register of the University of Oxford*, 3 vols. (Oxford, 1957-9).

Prince. He died in 1345. Most of his extant works are tracts on logic or commentaries on Aristotle (at least 59 manuscripts of his *Expositio super artem veterem* and 35 of his *Expositio librorum Physicorum* are still extant), but his most popular work is the *De vita et moribus philosophorum*, with 273 manuscripts scattered through continental Europe: to judge by the number of manuscripts which are still extant today, Burley was indeed the most widely read of our four authors. His works on politics are two commentaries on Aristotle's works, *Expositio super libros Ethicorum* and *Expositio super libros Politicorum*. Both commentaries are dedicated to his patron, Richard de Bury, bishop of Durham, but the commentary on *Politics* was written at the request of the bishop of London, Richard Bentworth, and presented with a new dedication to Pope Clement VI.[4]

The life of William of Ockham and the circumstances which prompted him to write his political works are so well known that only the barest outline will be necessary here:[5] a Franciscan, also an 'Oxparis' man, bachelor in divinity in 1318, he never had time to complete his doctorate (hence his title of *Venerabilis Inceptor*) since he had to go to Avignon, summoned by John XXII to clear himself on dangerous propositions detected in his works by John Luttrell, the chancellor of Oxford,[6] who edited them in a *Libellus contra doctrinam G. Occam*. In Avignon he met the general of his order, Michael of Cesena, deeply involved in a raging battle with John XXII about the nature of Franciscan poverty, threw in his lot with him, and fled with him from the papal court, escaping first to Pisa and then to Munich where he worked for the Emperor Lewis of Bavaria: whereas before 1325 his works are entirely devoted to theology (32 manuscripts of his Sentences Commentary), logic (56 manuscripts of his *Summa totius logice*) and commentaries on Aristotle, his many political works (16 tracts, excluding the *Allegationes de potestate imperiali* now ascribed to Bonagratia de Bergamo,[7] but including the *Allegationes religiosorum virorum*, written with at least three other authors) were compiled in the later part of his life, chiefly after 1329.

The Anglo-Irish Richard Fitzralph has an altogether different profile,

---

[4] S.H. Thomson, 'Walter Burley's Commentary on the Politics of Aristotle', *Mélanges Auguste Pelzer* (Louvain, 1947), pp.557-78, and A. Maier, 'Zu Burleys Politik Kommentar', *Recherches de Théologie Ancienne et Médiévale*, xiv (1947), 322-6, reprinted in A. Maier, *Ausgehendes Mittelalter: Gesammelte Aufsätze zur Geistesgeschichte des 14. Jahrhunderts* (Rome, 1964).

[5] See L. Baudry, *Guillaume d'Occam, sa vie, ses oeuvres, ses idées sociales et politiques* (Paris, 1950) and J. Miethke, *Ockhams Weg zur Sozialphilosophie* (Berlin, 1969).

[6] F.E. Kelley, 'Ockham: Avignon, Before and After', in A. Hudson and M. Wilks, *From Ockham to Wyclif*, Studies in Church History, Subsidia v (Oxford, 1987), pp.1-18.

[7] H.S. Offler, 'Zum Verfasser der *Allegaciones de potestate imperiali* (1338)', *Deutsches Archiv für Erforschung des Mittelalters*, xlii (1986), 555-619.

now well delineated by Aubrey Gwynn[8] and Katherine Walsh.[9] A student at both Oxford and Paris (in 1329), he was protected in his early career by the bishop of Exeter, John Grandisson; chancellor of Oxford University in 1332-4, he was selected by the curia to give advice on the beatific vision at the request of John XXII. His connection with Avignon was kept alive by frequent stays there on a variety of errands, and he was commissioned as an expert by the papacy to examine the tenets of the Armenian catholics. He therefore duly wrote his *Summa de questionibus Armenorum* (27 manuscripts at least) between 1347 and 1352. At the same time ecclesiastical preferments brought him back to his native Ireland as archbishop of Armagh: there he was soon drawn into conflict with local Franciscans, who were predominantly of native Irish stock. From his sermon diary, an exceptional document, we know that his first official attack was launched at Avignon in 1350 (*Proposicio 'Unusquisque'*) and that he repeatedly came back to the matter, especially in four sermons preached at London from January to March 1357. Though the conflict covered all aspects of anti-mendicant controversy, ranging from auricular confession to the position of the bishops as conservators of the privileges of the mendicants, it broadened into a larger issue, clearly political, the problem of the nature of Christ's poverty and the theory of dominion: to this Fitzralph devoted his last large work, the *De paupertate Christi*,[10] composed in the midst of difficulties of all kinds, since the Franciscans retaliated furiously, both in England and at Avignon, whereas the English government, greatly annoyed by the strife, tried to impose silence on him. But his best-known work remains the *Defensio curatorum* (*Proposicio 'Nolite judicare'*) of which at least 75 manuscripts are extant, to which the qualification of 'political' may be applied if only in a loose sense. Fitzralph died in November 1360 at Avignon, while defending himself at the curia against his enemies.

John Wyclif has much in common with Fitzralph, though he did not study at Paris:[11] a Balliol man, deeply impressed by the theology of

---

[8] A. Gwynn, 'The Sermon Diary of Richard Fitzralph of Armagh', *Proceedings of the Royal Irish Academy*, xliv, sect.C (1937), 1-57; 'Richard Fitzralph, Archbishop of Armagh', *Studies, an Irish Quarterly Review*, xxii (1933), 389-405 and 591-607, and *Studies*, xxxiii (1934), 395-411.

[9] K. Walsh, *A Fourteenth-Century Scholar and Primate: Richard Fitzralph in Oxford, Avignon and Armagh* (Oxford, 1981).

[10] The *De pauperie Salvatoris* is edited in J. Wycliff, *De Dominio Divino*, ed. R.L. Poole (London, 1890) – books i-iv – and by R. Brock, *An Edition of Richard FitzRalph's De Pauperie salvatoris*, University of Colorado Diss. (Boulder, 1954), – books v-vii; on the *Defensio*, J. Coleman, 'Fitzralph's Antimendicant *proposicio (1350)* and the Politics at the Papal Court at Avignon', *Journal of Ecclesiastical History*, xxxv (1984), 376-90.

[11] The standard biography is still H.M. Workman, *John Wyclif: a Study of the English Medieval Church*, 2 vols. (Oxford, 1926); but K.B. McFarlane, *John Wycliffe and the Beginnings of English Nonconformity* (London, 1952) is indispensable.

Augustine, he turned to politics (and to anti-mendicant controversy as well) rather late in life: he wrote several works on logic, the *Summa de ente* comprising thirteen tracts, and a commentary upon the whole Bible, before accepting a new start for a second *summa*, this time a *Summa Theologie*, *c*.1373-4, with a preliminary if fundamental tract, his *De dominio divino*. Eleven tracts of the *Summa* were more or less completed, and they have all been considered here as political because of the general design of the *Summa*, though this applies more adequately to some of the tracts (*De officio regis, De potestate Pape, De civili dominio*) than to some others (*De apostasia, De veritate Sacrae Scripturae, De blasfemia, De symonia*). Written between 1375 and 1381, these tracts were accompanied, beside a dozen other theological or pastoral works and a complete cycle of sermons extant both in Latin and English, by a flood of polemical letters, petitions, protestations and short tracts which fill the last sections of Williel R. Thomson's catalogue.[12] Many of them deserve to be considered as political. But even before his death in 1384, the opinions of Wyclif had been condemned as heretical and the suppression of his work began at the beginning of the fifteenth century, being systematically carried out at Archbishop Thomas Arundel's command after 1411: in this Wyclif is exceptional and we must bear in mind this obviously distorting factor when examining the dissemination of manuscripts.

It is now time to look at the present geographical location of the manuscripts. This has been tabulated in Table 1, where only towns are mentioned, not individual libraries (Rome includes therefore the Vatican Library, and the manuscripts of Lambeth Library have been added to those of other London libraries).

The prestige and wealth of the greatest European libraries gives clear prominence in such a table to certain cities: the libraries in Vienna, Paris, Rome, London, Oxford (Bodleian and colleges), and Cambridge have between them more than half the total number of manuscripts. Prague libraries are also in a class of their own, but their position is wholly dependant upon their Wycliffite collections. Some other cities (Munich, Wolfenbuttel, Dublin, Florence, Venice, even Basle) may also be considered as centres of secondary importance. The remaining manuscripts are scattered among 49 towns, especially in German-speaking countries.

The evidence is summed up in Table 2, where the data is arranged by country, though it must be kept in mind that Cambrai or Trento do not fit well with modern borders, and that the category 'other countries' has no significance. There are 300 manuscripts in Table 1, but this total grows to 306 in Table 2 as six manuscripts contain texts by two of our authors.

---

[12] W.R. Thomson, *The Latin Writings of John Wyclif*, Pontifical Institute of Mediaeval Studies, Subsidia Medievalia, xiv (Toronto, 1983).

Table 1: Present Location of Manuscripts

BRITISH ISLES	Ockham	Burley	Fitzralph	Wyclif	*Total*
Oxford	1 (–1)	8 (–1)	9	8 /–1/	26
London–Lambeth	5 (–2)	3 (–1)	4	9 /–3/	20
Cambridge	—	6	4	7	16
Dublin	—	—	3	3	6
Durham	—	—	1	1	2
Hereford	—	—	1	—	1
Manchester	—	—	—	1	1
Total	6	17	22	29	72

FRANCE					
Paris	9	2	8 /–1/	2	21
Avignon	2 (–1)	1	—	—	3
Dijon	1	—	1	—	2
Aix-en-Provence	1	—	—	—	1
Cambrai	1	—	—	—	1
Auxerre	1	—	—	—	1
Toulouse	1	—	—	—	1
Tours	—	1	—	—	1
Total	16	4	9	2	31

ITALY					
Rome	14 (–5)	7 (–1)	6 (–3)	1 (–1)	26
Florence	1 (–1)	3 (–1)	—	2 (–2)	6
Venice	2	3	—	—	5
Padua	1	1	—	—	2
Milan	—	2	—	—	2
Belluno	—	1	—	—	1
Cesena	1	—	—	—	1
Mantua	—	—	1	—	1
Naples	1	—	—	—	1
Trento	1	—	—	—	1
Total	21	17	7	3	46

GERMANIC COUNTRIES					
Vienna	–	1	11 (–3)	31 (–31)	41
Munich	—	1	5	1	7
Wolfenbuttel	—	—	4	3	7
Basle	3	—	—	1	4
Eichstatt	1	—	2	—	3
Erfurt	—	1	2 (–1)	—	3
Berlin	—	2	1	—	3
Leipzig	–1	—	2	—	2
Danzig	—	—	2	—	2
Bautzen	—	—	—	1	1

Bremen	1	—	—	—	1
Frankfurt	1	—	—	—	1
Graz	—	—	1	—	1
Innsbruck	—	—	1	—	1
Karlsruhe	—	—	—	1 (–1)	1
Koblenz	1	—	—	—	1
Cologne	1	—	—	—	1
Magdeburg	—	—	1	—	1
Merseburg	—	—	1	—	1
Michaelbeuren	—	—	1	—	1
Pommersfelden	—	—	1	—	1
Stuttgart	—	—	1	—	1
Tubingen	1	—	—	—	1
Ulm	1	—	—	—	1
Total	10	5	36	38	87

BOHEMIA

Prague	—	1	5	39	45
Olomouc	—	—	—	3 (–1)	3
Brno	1	—	—	2	3
Total	1	1	5	44	51

OTHER COUNTRIES:

Bruges	—	1	1	—	2
Bruxelles	—	—	1	—	1
Liège	—	1	—	—	1
Deventer	1	—	—	—	1
Copenhagen	—	1	—	—	1
Upsala	—	—	1	—	1
Madrid	—	1 (–1)	—	—	1
Krakow	—	2	1	—	3
Wroclaw	—	1	—	—	1
Dubrovnik	—	1	—	—	1
Total	1	8	4	—	13
TOTAL	55	52	83	114	300

Manuscripts with Works by Two Authors:

Cambridge Peterhouse 223 (Wyclif and Fitzralph); Lambeth 121 (Wyclif and Fitzralph); Vat. Palat. 378 (Ockham and Fitzralph); Vat. Reg. Lat. 297 (Ockham and Fitzralph); Vienna 3935 (Wyclif and Fitzralph); Vienna 3937 (Wyclif and Fitzralph).

Non-Medieval Manuscripts:

Wyclif: Lambeth 537; Lambeth B 1058; London B.L. Additional 5902; Oxford B.L. James 3. Fitzralph: Paris B.N. Lat. 13079.

Numbers between slashes / / are for modern manuscripts.
Numbers in parentheses ( ) are for manuscripts of foreign origin.

Table 2: Summary of the Actual Distribution

	Ockham	Burley	Fitzralph	Wyclif	*Total*	St.D	V.C.
Great Britain	6	17	22	29	74	8.4	45.3
France	16	4	9	2	31	5.4	69.7
Italy	21	17	7	3	48	7.3	60.6
Vienna	—	1	11	31	43	12.5	116.0
Germanic countries	10	4	25	7	46	8.1	76.2
Bohemia	1	1	5	44	51	17.7	138.8
Others	1	8	4	—	13	3.1	95.7
Total	55	52	83	116	306		
Standard deviation	7.6	6.3	7.7	16.4			
Variation Coeff.	95.6	84.9	65	98.9			

Vienna has been kept apart, since at least 34 of its manuscripts (from a total of 41) had originally nothing to do with it.

What is the significance of such a table? It would be useless to apply sophisticated statistics to such a matrix, since the data, to say the least, is of very uncertain nature: as noted earlier, the fact that a manuscript is today in a French library is not a proof that the manuscript was in France in the middle ages. Some statistics may however help us to interpret the data with more safety. It is for instance possible to compute the standard deviation, which is the square root of the sum of the squares of the deviations from the means in each row and each column (this sum being divided by the number of cells). It is an indication of the dispersal of the data, derived from the amplitude of the deviation from the mean value, for each 'country' and for each author. But since the value of the standard deviation also depends upon sheer numbers, comparison is difficult: we have therefore to compute the variation coefficients, which may safely be compared and which are to be read as percentages (it is the standard deviation divided by the mean of each row or each column and multiplied by 100).[13]

Another very simple statistical device will help us to single out the most important features of Table 2. By multiplying the margins of the matrix by themselves, and dividing them by the total number of manuscripts, we get the 'independence' matrix, which shows how manuscripts would be distributed, if no other elements than the total quantity of manuscripts per author and per country were involved. To identify the anomalous features of the actual distribution, it is then necessary to subtract Table 3 from Table 2: the result is Table 4 (with some slight discrepancies, due to the rounding of numbers).

[13] A clear description of these methods is available in Roderick Floud, *An Introduction to Quantitative Methods for Historians* (London, 1973).

Table 3: Independent Matrix

	Ockham	Burley	Fitzralph	Wyclif	*Total*
Great Britain	13	13	20	28	74
France	6	5	8	12	31
Italy	9	8	13	18	48
Vienna	8	7	12	16	43
Germanic countries	8	8	12	18	46
Bohemia	9	9	14	19	51
Others	2	2	4	5	13
Total	55	52	83	116	306

Table 4: Difference between the two matrices

	Ockham	Burley	Fitzralph	Wyclif	*Total*
Great Britain	−7	+4	+2	+1	0
France	+10	−1	+1	−10	0
Italy	+12	+9	−6	−15	0
Vienna	−8	−6	−1	+15	0
Germanic countries	+2	−4	+13	−11	0
Bohemia	−8	−8	−9	+25	0
Others	−1	+6	0	−5	0
Total	0	0	0	0	0

We can trace the migration of nearly sixty manuscripts, that is one fifth of this particular collection of manuscripts. The vast majority of manuscripts transferred from their original location to a 'foreign' library are to be found today in Vienna (32 manuscripts out of 41) and in the pontifical library of the Vatican, where nearly half of the manuscripts may be traced back to a country other than Italy, and more especially to France. As regards Rome, the lack of adequate descriptions implies an underestimate of these transfers.[14] Besides, there are at least five 'modern' manuscripts in the collection: predominantly Wyclif manuscripts copied in England after the Reformation. The numbers involved are such that is worth computing three tables, Tables 5 to 7, which are modified versions of Tables 2 to 4. Since all the Wyclif manuscripts from Vienna come from

[14] Cf. S.H. Thomson, *Walter Burley's Commentary*, p.565, who reports the loss of his notes on more than 200 manuscripts in the Vatican Library and, while refusing to give precise information, admits that the manuscripts of the *Expositio* which he examined 'were predominantly of French provenance, almost certainly from Paris'; Anneliese Maier does not resolve this matter, but she dismisses two of the Vatican manuscripts mentioned by Thomson: Vat. reg. lat. 1030 is in fact Vat. Pal. Lat. 1030, whereas Ottoboni Lat. 1350 does not contain the *Expositio*: A.Maier, *Ausgehendes Mittelalter*, i. 94 and 464.

Table 5: Summary of the Corrected Distribution

	Ockham	Burley	Fitzralph	Wyclif	*Total*	St.D	V.C.
Great Britain	3	15	23	28	69	9.4	54.7
France	20	7	11	3	41	6.3	61.5
Italy	17	17	4	0	38	7.6	80.3
Germanic countries	13	5	33	4	55	11.6	84.7
Bohemia	1	1	7	75	84	31.4	167.2
Others	1	7	4	2	14	2.3	65.4
Total	55	52	82	112	301		
Standard deviation	8.5	5.6	10.8	26.9			
Variation Coeff.	93.3	64.5	79	144.2			

Table 6: Independent Corrected Matrix

	Ockham	Burley	Fitzralph	Wyclif	*Total*
Great Britain	13	12	19	25	69
France	7	7	11	16	41
Italy	7	6	11	14	38
Germanic countries	10	9	15	21	55
Bohemia	15	15	23	31	84
Others	3	3	4	4	14
Total	55	52	83	116	301

Table 7: Difference between the two matrices

	Ockham	Burley	Fitzralph	Wyclif	*Total*
Great Britain	−10	+3	+4	+3	0
France	+13	0	0	−13	0
Italy	+10	+11	−7	−14	0
Germanic countries	+3	−4	+18	−17	0
Bohemia	−14	−14	−16	+44	0
Others	−2	+5	0	−3	0
Total	0	0	0	0	0

Bohemia – with the exception of one English volume – Vienna has been merged in these three new tables with the German-speaking countries.

It is now possible to attempt an interpretation of these figures. Let us start by the global results. First, if we compare Table 2 and Table 5, we find that the standard deviations have all been increased, with only two exceptions: one is 'other countries' (which, as noted above, has no significance as a category), the other one is Burley. It means that the present distribution of manuscripts is more regular than it was in the middle ages: the effect of time has been to erase, sometimes to a large extent, the medieval details; it is obvious in the case of Wyclif, but the same phenomenon may be detected for Ockham – though the variation coefficient contradicts this view – and even more for Fitzralph (but here largely as a result of the merging of Vienna with the Germanic countries). At the other end of the spectrum, Walter Burley is the author whose manuscripts are the most evenly distributed throughout Europe, both today and in medieval times. The distribution of Burley's manuscripts seems to confer upon him the status of a non-controversial standard author, which is well attuned to the somewhat dry and neutral manner of his commentaries on Aristotle's works, primarily designed as text-books for university students.[15]

The five geographical gatherings exhibit the same tendencies, and here too both standard deviation and variation coefficient have increased between Table 2 and Table 5, with the important exception of France: in fact, this is related to the important migration of French manuscripts to Italy (that is, to the Vatican Library) which has introduced an element of irregularity in the modern distribution of French manuscripts. There may also be a relationship with the ambiguous status of the Avignonese manuscripts, which have been considered as French, a highly questionable move indeed (for instance, Burley's presentation copy to Clement VI). The five 'countries' fall into three groups: in England, and to a lesser degree in France, the distribution of manuscripts is relatively even, which means that the distribution of manuscripts is not too different from what could have been expected, *ceteris paribus*. This conclusion seems an obvious reflection of the fact that these four authors are English, and that three of them had French university connections. Germany and Italy have much more contrasted distributions, splitting the group of authors into two distinct categories: Italy has Ockham and Burley on the positive side, Germany Ockham and Fitzralph. Bohemia is an altogether exceptional case, with a complete polarization on Wyclif. We cannot escape the conclusion that university career and nationality both had an influence on the present as well as the medieval distribution of manuscripts.

But the distribution of each author has distinct features which require a closer examination. John Wyclif is the clearest case. His works are in fact to be found either in England or in Bohemia, where roughly two thirds of

---

[15] L.J. Daly, 'Walter Burley and John Wyclif on some Aspects of Kingship', *Mélanges Eugène Tisserant* (Città del Vaticano, 1964), iv, 163-84; 'The Conclusion of Walter Burley's Commentary on the Politics Books I to IV', *Manuscripta*, xii (1968), 79-92; 'Walter Burley and the Teaching Techniques of a Medieval Professor', *Studies in Medieval Culture*, vi (1971).

the manuscripts containing political works are to be found.[16] At the root of this extraordinary distribution lies the well-known fact that Wyclif's works were relentlessly destroyed by the ecclesiastical authorities, especially after 1410: in that year a great pile of manuscripts was burnt at Carfax in Oxford. And Thomas Arundel also issued orders for having the rooms of students and masters of Oxford searched, in direct violation of the privileges of the university.[17] It ought nevertheless to be stressed that the number of English Wyclif manuscripts is slightly above the mean, even without taking into account the modern manuscripts. And if Wycliffite tracts were scribbled on endleaves, presumably to escape detection,[18] there are also in quasi-official archives surprisingly frank admissions of interest in the work of that arch-heretic, as for instance at Oriel College.[19] A look at the English manuscript shows that some of them at least had a very mixed content: St. Augustine is often found as an appropriate companion, but there are also anti-Wycliffite authors, as in Bodley 703 which shelters works by William of Woodford, or authors with a very different background (Bodley 52 and 333 for instance). The existence of a systematic enterprise of 'edition' does not seem therefore as obvious in the case of the latin works of John Wyclif as it is for the Bible, the sermons, or the English works.[20] Wyclif's political tracts were collected by academics and by opponents, and not only by his followers and by Lollards, more interested by the English adaptations which were soon circulated.

The status of Wyclif's works is quite different elsewhere. In Bohemia, we find what we could call a sectarian diffusion. The Czechs became acquainted with Wyclif's realism in the latter part of the fourteenth century, though the reasons for this are far from clear.[21] The copying of the latin tracts appears to have been systematic, and eased by the help and

---

[16] Cf. Ann Hudson: 'Of the 132 separate works that can reasonably be assigned to Wyclif, considerably less than half survive at all in English manuscripts, whilst only sixteen are found in more than one English copy; so efficient was ecclesiastical eradication of Wyclif's writing', *Selections from English Wycliffite Writings* (Cambridge, 1978), p.3.

[17] G. Leff, *Heresy in the Later Middle Ages* (Manchester, 1967) ii. 570ff.

[18] See Cambridge, Trinity College MS. O 4 43.

[19] N.R. Ker, 'Wyclif Manuscripts in Oxford in the Fifteenth Century', *Bodleian Library Record*, iv (1952-1953) 292-3 and L. Minio-Paluello, 'Two Erasures in MS. Oriel College 15', *ibid.*, 205-7.

[20] J. Catto, 'Some English Manuscripts of Wyclif's Latin Works', in A. Hudson and M. Wilks, *From Ockham to Wyclif*, pp.353-9.

[21] K. Walsh, 'Wyclif's Legacy in Central Europe in the Late Fourteenth and Early Fifteenth Centuries', *ibid.*, pp.397-417.

assistance offered by prominent Lollards.[22] A second impulse seems to have been given by the coming of Peter Payne to Prague, since he may have brought with him some works hitherto unknown and wrote a register of significant extracts from many works of Wyclif.[23] The vast majority of the Bohemian manuscripts were produced in a short period between 1410 and 1450, and most of them do not share the diversity in content of their English counterparts: with those patristic authorities annexed by Lollards and Hussites alike, such as St. Augustine and Chrysostom, we find mostly texts written by members of the Hussite movement, authors such as Stanislas of Znojma, Peter Payne, Stephen of Palec or Jacobus de Misa. A noticeable exception is Prague University Library 1567: but this is a relatively late manuscript, ascribed by the catalogue to the years around 1470.

This sectarian diffusion is totally different from the very small French diffusion: here, Wyclif is simply considered as a controversial theologian, in the classical academic way. Paris B.N. Lat. 15881, a Sorbonne manuscript, links the *De civili dominio* with the *Defensor Pacis* of Marsilius and includes a barely legible *Quaestio disputata* which proves that in 1381 Wyclif's opinions were a matter for normal academic discussion in Paris; and Paris B.N. Lat. 3657, also a fourteenth-century manuscript, is rather a mixed bag, where Wyclif is associated with Pierre Roger and Baldus of Perugia! The traditional university-councils mode of text-diffusion did work at first in Wyclif's case: but its duration was apparently very short in the case of the political texts, whereas the logical works of Wyclif retained a certain amount of popularity, especially as they were considered as useful weapons against Ockhamism.[24]

Ockham, according to the variation coefficient, is surprisingly close to Wyclif, though it would be a rash assumption to speak in his case of a sectarian diffusion: it is true that we are here concerned with his political writings only, and that it may seem understandable at first sight that these polemical tracts, whatever their internal coherence with the philosophical thought of the *Venerabilis Inceptor*,[25] would not have gained the same kind of widespread recognition as his logical or theological texts. It remains

---

[22] The best-known example is that of the manuscript (Vienna O.N.B. 1294) written by Nicholas Faulfis and George Kneyhnicz in which they wrote when and where they had copied the different texts. Dr. Anne Hudson suggests that the link between the different places mentioned (Oxford, Kemerton in Gloucestershire, and Braybrook in Northamptonshire) was Robert Lychlade; see A. Hudson, 'Contributions to a History of Wycliffite Writings', reprinted in her *Lollards and Their Books* (London, 1985), p.3.

[23] See for instance MS. Prague University Library 1912.

[24] See the comments of Jeremy Catto, *op. cit. supra*, pp.354-6 on MSS. Harvard Houghton L.338, Escorial E II 6, Salamanca B.U. 2356 and Assisi 662.

[25] I refer here to the paper read by Dr. Janet Coleman on 'The Relation Between Intuitive Cognition and his Political Science': to be published in J.-P. Genet and J.-Y. Tilliette, *Théologie et droit dans la Science Politique de l'Etat Moderne* (Rome, 1989).

surprising, since Ockham did not write works narrowly focused on the defence of Lewis of Bavaria: the problem with which he was struggling (among many others) was the real extent of the power of the papacy, and this was indeed a European problem.[26] In Lewis's court, there were other scholars, such as Jean de Jandun and Marsilius of Padua, whose works seems to have been better known and in more countries than those of Ockham, though an important feature must be stressed at once: Ockham's texts were practically all written in Munich, whereas the *Defensor* was produced in Paris University itself in 1324; there is evidence to show that Paris may have been one of the early sources for copies of the most important Ockham texts: see for instance the Florence (Santa Croce) copy, bought in Paris in 1372.

We have to acknowledge the fact that Ockham is exceptionally well represented in France and in Italy. If his absence from ultra-realist Bohemia does not come as a surprise, he does not score that well in Germany where he was writing, and the scarcity of his English manuscripts is conspicuous. He himself sent to England one work only *An Rex Angliae pro suo succursu, scilicet guerrae, possit recipere bona ecclesiarum etiam invito papa*,[27] when, at the end of his life, the diplomatic alliance between Lewis of Bavaria and Edward III brought him back to the political problems of his fatherland. There are hints of confusion between his works and that of Marsilius of Padua. Thomas Gascoigne, who owned a copy of the *Defensor Pacis*,[28] apparently thought it to be by Ockham. The English manuscripts are on the whole rather late manuscripts or, at least, they cannot be traced in England earlier than the mid fifteenth century. This is especially true of the manuscripts given by William Gray, Duke Humphrey of Gloucester or the already quoted Gascoigne's manuscript. The 'political Ockham' seems to be quite a late discovery in England. The diffusion of the political writings of Ockham has been thoroughly studied by Jürgen Miethke[29] and the early owners of the manuscripts belonged principally to academic circles, but there are also proofs that Ockham's work was known in the courtly and administrative milieu, especially in Paris. Among other points emphasised by Miethke, the importance of conciliar gatherings for the fifteenth-century diffusion of texts[30] may

[26] On the fundamental problems of Ockham's political theology, see F.E. Kelley, *op. cit.*, pp.11-16 and his comments on Ph. Boehner, 'Ockham's Political Ideas', reprinted in Ph. Boehner, *Collected Articles on Ockham* (New York, 1958); and A.S. McGrade, *The Political Thought of William of Ockham* (Cambridge, 1974).

[27] C. Nederman, 'Royal Taxation and the English Church. The Origins of William of Ockham's *An Princeps*', *Journal of Ecclesiastical History*, xxxvii (1986), 377-88.

[28] On Gascoigne, see Emden, ii, 745-8.

[29] J. Miethke, 'Marsilius und Ockham: Publikum und Leser ihrer politischen Schriften im späteren Mittelalter', *Medio Evo*, vi (1980), 543-67.

[30] J. Miethke, 'Die Konzilien als Forum der öffentlichen Meinung im 15. Jahrhundert', *Deutsches Archiv für Erforschung des Mittelalters*, xxxvii (1981), 736-73.

explain the late appearance of Ockham's political works in England. Franciscans and even more Dominicans seem to have been prominent among the owners of Ockham's manuscripts.[31] The part played by these two orders in English intellectual life in the later middle ages seems surprisingly limited, Carmelite and Austin Friars being much more to the forefront.[32]

Ockham's works were clearly perceived as political and controversial and they are usually found associated with other theoretical works on the questions of the papal and imperial powers. Only one of Ockham's 'political' manuscripts might be described as a miscellany: it is Paris B.N. Lat. 14603 which contains, besides the *Octo Quaestiones*, a collection of tables of works by Anselm, Boethius, Vegetius, St. Augustine, and Aquinas. Another exceptional manuscript in this respect is Vatican Regin. Lat. 1059, which contains the *Commentarium super Valerium Maximum* by Dyonisius de Borgo San Sepolcro, though it also has the *Disputatio inter Clericum et Militem*; and even Avignon 1087 offers a suitable context, canon law (Henri Bohic's *Repertorium*).

The list of the texts found in association with Ockham's political tracts reads like a bibliography of the political controversial literature of the later middle ages. There is an obviously privileged association with Marsilius of Padua, both the *Defensor Pacis* in Ulm St.B. 6706-6708, Paris B.N. Lat. 14619, London B.L. Royal 10 A 15 and Bremen St.B. Lat. b 35 (extracts only with the *Tractatus de juribus regni Franciae et imperii* by Lupold von Bebenburg), and the *De Translatione Imperii*,[33] in Trento B.C. 37 and Koblenz Stadtsarchiv Abt. 701 n.230 (which also has the *Memoriale de prerogative Imperii* of Alexander von Roes). But there are other authors as well: *An princeps* and *Dialogus III* are part in Vatican Lat. 4115 of a collection in which we find works by Ptolemeo de Lucca (*Determinatio compendiosa de iurisdictione imperii*), the bull *Unam Sanctam* of Boniface VIII and the *Tractatus de preheminencia spiritualis imperii* of Oppicius de Canistris (perhaps added later). The *Octo Quaestiones* are in Vatican Palat. Lat. 378 associated with Fitzralph's works, including the *De pauperie salvatoris*, together with the bull *Unam Sanctam*, and in Vatican Regin. Lat. 1123 accompanied by John of Paris, *De potestate regia et papali*, the pseudo-bull *Deum Time*, a *Quaestio* ascribed to Giles of Rome and the *Libellus* of Pierre Bertrand. Extracts of *Dialogus I* are combined in Venice San Marco Lat. IV 70 with the *Summa de potestate ecclesiastica* of Augustinus of Ancona and

---

[31] See for instance the Avignon, Basle and Florence manuscripts of Ockham's works.

[32] See for preliminary statistics on the literary output of English medieval authors in the fields of history and politics, J.-Ph. Genet, 'La mesure et les champs culturels', *Histoire et Mesure*, ii (1987), 137-69, esp. 146-7.

[33] There is a good codicological study in the edition by C. Jeudy and J. Quillet of Marsilius of Padua, *Oeuvres Mineures: Defensor minor, De translatione Imperii* (Paris, 1979), pp.80-138.

the *Tractatus 'Quia nonnulli os suum'* of Jean de Mauroux. The very complete collection in Paris Mazarine 3522 is bound with the *Somnium viridarii*. Auxerre 252 contains the *De potestate regia et papali* of John of Paris (once again), the *De ecclesiastica potestate* of Alexander of Sancto-Elpidio, and the *De causa immediatae ecclesiasticae potestatis* by Pierre de Palude is in Basel B 2 24.

A last point ought to be mentioned about Ockham: a third of the 'political' manuscripts which may be ascribed to a given period are from the fifteenth century: his work remains alive, though these 'late' manuscripts, as we have seen, are predominantly English; but at least one French – or Avignonese: that is Vatican Lat. 4115 – manuscript written in 1411 belongs to the fifteenth century, as do both Vatican Latin 4001 and the Koblenz manuscript, written at the council of Basel in 1437.

Both Walter Burley and Richard Fitzralph enjoyed a much wider and more even distribution throughout Europe. Walter Burley certainly enjoyed a European academic fame; and he was probably better known as a 'moderate realist'[34] than as an 'Averroist':[35] his *Expositio* became in eastern Europe and especially in Poland[36] a textbook in a way which even minimizes the number of manuscripts of this work. It was buried under glosses and commentaries which made it barely recognizable. The Italian popularity of both Expositions points to another reason. As Anneliese Maier has demonstrated, while he dedicated his work to Richard de Bury, bishop of Durham, he presented it to Pope Clement VI, and the pontifical library secured for Burley the southern market, so to speak. The same is true for one of the undoubted best-sellers of the times, the *De vita et moribus philosophorum*, known principally from Avignon and thence copies in Italy and in Germany,[37] while remaining practically unknown in England,[38] until some copies were apparently imported from Flanders.[39]

The academic nature of Burley's *Expositiones* is further demonstrated by the other works found with them, and they are often associated with other Aristotelian commentaries, as in Venice San Marco Lat. XI 1 with the

[34] This is the description of his philosophical position in N. Kretzmann, A. Kenny and J. Pinborg, ed., *The Cambridge History of Later Medieval Philosophy* (Cambridge, 1982).

[35] A. Maier, 'Ein Unbeachteter "Averroist" des 14. Jahrhunderts: Walter Burley', reprinted in *Ausgehendes Mittelalter*, pp.101-21.

[36] P. Czartoryski, 'Gloses et commentaires inconnus sur la Politique d'Aristote d'après les manuscrits de la Bibliothèque Jagellonne de Cracovie', *Medievalia Philosophica Polonorum*, v (1957), 3-44.

[37] Cf. J.O. Stigall, 'The Manuscript Tradition of the *De Vitis et Moribus Philosophorum* of Burley', *Medievalia et Humanistica*, xi (1957), 49-57 and R. Wedler, *Walter Burleys 'Liber de Vita et Moribus Philosophorum' in zwei deutsche Bearbeitungen des Spätmittelalters* (Heidelberg, 1969).

[38] J. Prelog, 'Die Handschriften und Drucke von Walter Burley's *Liber de Vita et Moribus Philosophorum*', *Codices Manuscripti*, ix (1983), 1-18.

[39] H. Silvestre, 'Enfin un manuscrit anglais du *De Vita et Moribus Philosophorum* de Walter Burley', *Scriptorium*, xiii (1959), 255-9.

Expositio in Aristotelis Rhetorica by Giles of Rome (also in Paris Mazarine 3496, where it is bound with another commentary on the *Ethics*) and in Erfurt B. Amploniana Q 319 (commentaries on *Ethics* and *Economics* by Albert of Saxony). Other academic works ascribed to Burley himself are also found in Oxford, Corpus Christi College 230 (*Notabilia* on Porphyry, on the *Sex principia*, and on Aristotle's Physics) and Paris Mazarine 3496 has also Burley's *Tractatus de comparatione*. The most telling assocation is with Giles of Rome's *De regimine principum*, as in Cambridge, Peterhouse 93 and in Cambridge U.L. Ii II 8 (Richard de Bury's copy, which might even suggest that this association was approved, or even intended by the author himself). Another appropriate combination is with Aristotle's texts: the *Expositio super libros Ethicorum* in London B.L. Harley 3413 is accompanied by Aretino's version of the *Ethics*.

We are confronted with the best-seller problem with Fitzralph's *Defensio*: a text gaining so much popularity that, so to speak, it acquired a life of its own, independent from the original intentions of the author, and from the precise circumstances surrounding its writing. This explains why the text remained popular: there are apparently more fifteenth-century manuscripts than fourteenth-century ones of the short tracts of Fitzralph. As Katherine Walsh has shown,[40] other works of Fitzralph, and especially his *Summa de questionibus Armenorum*, were disseminated from Avignon,[41] and everything points to the same kind of diffusion for the *Defensio*.[42] This diffusion may also have been helped by the fact that these texts are sermons and could therefore easily find their way to miscellanies of all kinds. The shorter texts of Fitzralph did gain such a popularity that they are most often found associated with texts bearing no obvious relation to them.

This 'general interest' qualification is for instance exemplified by seemingly strange associations, such as with the *Vade mecum in tribulationis* of J. de Rupescissa in Vatican Lat. 4253 or, even more strikingly, with the miscellaneous collections of the two Prague MSS, Univ. L. 826 (with, for instance, *De re rustica* of Palladius!) and Univ. L. 1714; on the other hand, some of these associations are clearly academic, as in Oxford, Magdalen College 38 (devoted to the *libros Boecii*, including *Quaestiones* by Duns Scotus) and in Erfurt B. Amploniana Q 118 (with a commentary on the Sentences by John Clencock) and F 77 (Bede and the commentary *Super*

---

[40] See the Appendix to her *Richard Fitzralph*.

[41] *Ibid.*, pp.469-71.

[42] *Ibid.*; and, for a work 'edited' by Fitzralph, the *Visiones Georgii*, which has also a strong Germanic diffusion especially in Bavaria and Austria, see A. Gwynn, 'Archbishop Fitzralph and George of Hungary', *Studies*, xxiv (1935), 528-72 and L.L. Hammerich, ed., *Visiones Georgii: Visiones quas in purgatorio sancti Patricii vidit Georgius miles de Ungeria A.D. MCCCLIII*, Kgl. Danske Videnskabernes Sleskab. Hist. filo. Meddel., xxvi (Kobenhavn, 1938).

Cantica Canticorum of Giles of Rome); and there is also some evidence of a relation with canon law, as in Bruges Stadtsbibliotheek 388 (with the *Summa Pisana Bartholomei*) and in Gdansk Mar. F 220 (with the *Summa super IIII lib. Decretalium* of Johannes Andreae and the *Margarida Martinianae*). The wide circulation of these texts may be explained by their association – especially found in German manuscripts – with collections of sermons and with various religious tracts: as in Wolfenbuttel Helmst. 840, Munich Clm. 5861 (sermons by Gerson), 11882, 15567 (works by Aquinas, Gerson, Lyra, Escobar, Nider) and 16208 (works by Aquinas, Albertus Magnus, Joh. de Legnano, Johannes Auerspach), and Gdansk Mar. F 294 (Engelschalk's Sermons and the *Contra errores Waldensium* of Peter of Pilichsdorf) and Leipzig 940 (Capistrano's letters).

These texts are also frequently found in two well-focused neighbourhoods: first, they are associated with texts on the mendicant controversy as in Wolfenbuttel Helmst. 680 (with works by St. Bonaventure), Lambeth 357 (Thomas de Wilton's *De Validis Mendicantibus*) and in Paris Arsenal 465; most usual is the association with Roger Conway's tracts (Wolfenbuttel Helmst. 300 and 311, Berlin St. B. Lat. f.244, Oxford, Corpus Christi College 182 which also has texts by Peckham and John Walsingham). They are also found in a more clearly political setting; this is especially true of French manuscripts: for instance they are associated with the *De Ecclesiastica Potestate* of Alexander de Sancto-Elpidio in Paris B.N. Lat. 14580 (together with works by Pierre d'Ailly, Oresme, Henricus de Hassia, Nicholas de Lyre and Johannes de Ripa) and with the *Defensor Pacis* of Marsilius of Padua in Paris B.N. Lat. 15690.

These two kinds of associations are also characteristic of the *De pauperie Salvatoris*, which is associated with texts on the mendicant controversy, as in Paris B.N. Lat. 3222, and which is also found in a more obviously political context with the *De abusibus Curiae Romanae* of Mathew of Cracow in Dijon 235 and with Ockham's *Octo Quaestiones* and the ubiquitous bull *Unam Sanctam* in Vatican Reg. Lat. 1123. But it is also found in a more general religious setting, for instance with the *Defensio curatorum* and the four London sermons in Oxford B.L. Auct. F infra 1-2 with a collection of 48 sermons, and with the *Notabilia . . . in libro Sancti Johannis Chrysostomi super Matheum* in Oxford B.L. Bodley 784.

This survey shows therefore that Burley enjoyed an academic diffusion; and there was nothing national about academic texts. Ockham, on the other hand, had little to do with England, and the diffusion of his political works shows him to have been more popular – if that word may be applied to such a difficult author – in France than anywhere else. If therefore we look for a specifically English political philosophy, it is to be found in Fitzralph's and Wyclif's works, but only with serious reservations. Much of Fitzralph's political theology has an Avignonese origin, and his debt to the Augustine theologians of the papal court has already been pointed out.[43] Besides, his works were known from Avignon, though not ignored in England, as Ockham's output. In perhaps half of the manuscripts in which his shorter (by far the best known) sermon-tracts have come to us, there is no political or even simply anti-mendicant association. Fitzralph was the best-known of our four English 'political' philosophers in Europe: but neither for his politics, nor because he was English. In one place, however, English he was, as well as Oxonian and Realist: that was Bohemia, and there is some evidence that there at least he paved the way for Wyclif, though not securing for his own works a lasting celebrity. The affiliation between Fitzralph and Wyclif is indeed what comes closest to an English school of political philosophy in the fourteenth century, and the subsequent eradication of Wyclif's doctrines made its ruin unavoidable. Ockham and Burley were – more or less, as the statistics demonstrate – known throughout Europe: but there was nothing English in the least about their political works.

Appendix

It is not possible to print here a complete list of the manuscripts relevant to this paper. I have personally consulted only those located in Paris and London. To date, scholars have systematically searched most major European libraries for the works of only two of the authors mentioned above: Ockham and Wyclif. These two have also benefited from the advantage of modern editions of a majority of their political works (including critical studies of the manuscript tradition). For Wyclif the authoritative catalogue of Williel R. Thomson is now indispensable and supersedes previous lists by W.W.Shirley and J. Loserth. The situation is more difficult for Walter Burley, though thanks to S.H. Thomson we are probably on firmer ground for the political works than for some others, whereas Fitzralph's case is tantalizing, since the excellent book by Katherine Walsh is to be supplemented by a study of his manuscripts which has not yet apparently been published. Here an account of the Viennese manuscripts provides a most useful foretaste, but it is clear that a wealth of information will come to light very soon and certainly alter the present picture. It is also a pleasure for me to thank the Section Latine de l'Institut de Recherche et d'Histoire des

---

[43] To the works of A. Gwynn and K. Walsh already quoted, add G. Leff, *Richard Fitzralph: Commentator on the Sentences* (Manchester, 1940), and A. Gwynn, *The Austin Friars in Medieval England* (Cambridge, 1940), pp.35-73.

Textes, for use of its extensive files, especially on Ockham and Burley, and Professor Jürgen Miethke, who drew my attention to some important bibliographical items. The figures in this paper have therefore been computed from the following works:

1. William of Ockham

L. Baudry, *Guillaume d'Occam, sa vie, ses oeuvres, ses idées sociales et politiques* (Paris, 1950).
J. Miethke, 'Marsilius und Ockham: Publikum und Leser ihrer politischen Schriften im späteren Mittelalter', *Medio Evo*, vi (1980), 543-68.
William of Ockham, *Opera politica*, ed. H.S. Offler & R.E. Bennett, 3 vols. (Manchester, 1956-74).
J.A. Weisheipl, 'Ockham and some Mertonians', *Medieval Studies*, xxx (1968), 163-213.

2. Walter Burley

C.H. Lohr, 'Medieval Latin Aristotle Commentaries', *Traditio*, xxx (1968), 171-87.
A. Maier, *Ausgehendes Mittelalter. Gessamelte Aufsatze zur Geistesgeschichte des 14. Jahrhunderts* (Rome, 1964).
S.H. Thomson, 'Walter Burley's Commentary on the Politics of Aristotle', *Mélanges Auguste Pelzer* (Louvain, 1947), pp. 557-78.
J.A. Weisheipl, 'Repertorium Mertonense', *Medieval Studies*, xxxi (1969), 174-224.
Z. Wlodek, 'Les Traités de Walter Burleigh dans les manuscrits des bibliothèques en Pologne', *Mediaevalia Philosophica Polonorum*, xi (1963), 152-6.

3. Richard FitzRalph

A. Gwynn, 'The Sermon Diary of Richard Fitzralph of Armagh', *Proceedings of the Royal Irish Academy*, xliv section C (1937), 1-57.
K. Walsh, *A Fourteenth-Century Scholar and Primate: Richard Fitzralph in Oxford, Avignon and Armagh* (Oxford, 1981).
K. Walsh, 'Archbishop Fitzralph and the Friars at the Papal Court in Avignon, 1357-1360', *Traditio*, xxxi (1975), 223-45.
K. Walsh, 'The Manuscripts of Archbishop Richard FitzRalph in the Osterreichische Nationalbibliothek, Vienna', *Römische Historische Mitteilungen*, xviii (1976), 67-75.

4. John Wyclif

J. Catto, 'Some English Manuscripts of Wyclif's Latin Works', *From Ockham to Wyclif*, ed. A. Hudson & M. Wilks, Studies in Church History, Subsidia, v (Oxford, 1987), pp.353-9.
A. Hudson, *Lollards and Their Books* (London, 1985).
N.R. Ker, 'Wyclif Manuscripts in Oxford in the Fifteenth Century', *Bodleian Library Record*, iv (1952-3), 292-3.
H. Kuhn-Steinhausen, 'Wyclif Handschriften in Deutschland', *Zentralblatt für Bibliothekwesen*, xlvii (1930), 625-8.
L. Minio-Paluello, 'Two Erasures in MS. Oriel College 15', *Bodleian Library Record*, iv (1952-3), 205-7.

J.H. Stein, 'The Wyclif Manuscript in Florence', *Speculum*, vi (1930), 95-7.

S.H. Thomson, 'A Gonville and Caius MS', *Speculum*, viii (1933), 197-204.

W.R. Thomson, *The Latin Writings of John Wyclif* (Pontifical Institute of Mediaeval Studies, Subsidia Medievalia, xiv, Toronto, 1983).

W.R. Thompson, 'Manuscripts Wyclifiana Desiderata: the Potential Contribution of Missing Latin Texts to our Image of Wyclif's Life and Works', *From Ockham to Wyclif*, ed. Hudson and Wilks, pp. 343-51.

A. Hudson, *The Premature Reformation. Wycliffite texts and Lollard History* (Oxford, 1988) appeared too late for use here.

Chapter 13

Relations with France, 1337-1399

Michael Jones

After the Conquest the king of England was a vassal of the king of France. From time to time this feudal relationship was strained to breaking point by war. With the important exception of Philip Augustus's campaigns against Richard I and John, such wars down to the early fourteenth century were generally brief. After them the traditional relationship was re-established, entailing homage by the king of England for his lands in France. It was dynastic accident rather than war that chiefly modified territorial disposition. While a wise ruler involved many others in promoting a particular line of conduct – his nobility, clergy and leading townsmen most especially – it was above all his own individual or family interests and honour that came first. They determined whether he led his state into war or pursued more peaceful measures. The means usually chosen for territorial aggrandisement (it was lands that mainly attracted princely attention) was marriage and the subsequent exploitation of the complexities of successional law. It was seldom through acts of outright aggression or conquest. In this respect Edward I's wars against Wales and Scotland marked a new beginning in English affairs as Philip II's had in France.

As a result international relations were primarily relations between ruling dynasties and these often took the form of prolonged family litigation arising from intermarriage, a habit particularly fruitful in creating conflicting claims. The importance of such issues in fomenting the Anglo-French war from 1337 and extending it into new theatres hardly requires emphasis once the succession problems affecting France, Brittany, Flanders, Burgundy, Navarre and Castile after 1328 are considered. From the twelfth century uniform diplomatic practices, heavily influenced by traditions of Christian kingship and a common inheritance of Roman law, had been developed to allow princes to conduct those affairs that were both personal and public in a formal and rational manner.[1] It was in this way that Henry III recognized as a fait accompli

[1] P. Chaplais, 'English Diplomatic Documents, 1377-99', *The Reign of Richard II: Essays in Honour of May McKisack*, ed. F.R.H. Du Boulay and Caroline M. Barron (London, 1971), pp.21-3.

the loss of the greater part of the former Angevin empire to Capetian France and accepted the restoration of feudal bonds with Louis IX in the treaty of Paris (1259). Unfortunately interpretation of that treaty, and the concurrent development of a more thorough-going doctrine of sovereignty, soured the normally friendly relations between Louis IX and Henry III and their respective successors.[2]

The king of England as duke of Guyenne expected to provide an administration for his men but the actions of his officials, in carrying out his orders in the duchy, were daily scrutinized by French officials anxious to extend the authority of their master in accord with the maxim *rex in regno suo imperator est*. This placed practical limitations on the English king's administration before 1337. The centralizing tendencies of Capetian and early Valois rule created similar friction in many other regions of France. A reaction was signalled in the movement for provincial charters in 1314-15. Although exaggeration must be avoided – conventions sprang up so that royal and provincial administrations could cooperate over routine matters – Le Patourel's view that the conflict which began in 1337 was in a sense a civil war waged by the princes of France, led by the duke of Guyenne against the crown, nevertheless contains an important truth.[3] It partly explains why the war that broke out on this occasion was not soon ended like earlier Anglo-French conflicts. At the same time this war became the concern not just of the kings and their armies but of two emerging nations, conditioning all aspects of life for the rest of the century and beyond.

The description of the conflict as The Hundred Years Wars is a nineteenth-century one, although fifteenth-century commentators already recognized its validity.[4] Its long-term causes are now fairly well understood. As long ago as 1902 Eugène Déprez could write, 'La guerre de Cent Ans a donc eu pour origine véritable la question de Guyenne'.[5] Modern investigation of the problem of sovereignty has reinforced that view, since shared sovereignty was not then admitted. If the king of France continued to exert his claims and the king of England refused to admit them, conflict was inevitable. That so many conferences were held, so many embassies despatched and so little force used prior to 1337, in efforts to solve this intractable problem, reflects creditably upon respect for the laws governing international relations. From 1300 there were those around the king of England who saw that the only escape from this

---

[2] Above pp.205-6. M. Gavrilovitch, *Etude sur le traité de Paris* (Paris, 1899) first explored this theme.

[3] J. Le Patourel in *Europe in the Late Middle Ages*, ed. J.R. Hale *et al* (London, 1965), pp.155-83 [reprinted in his *Feudal Empires: Norman and Plantagenet* (London, 1984), Chapter XV].

[4] K.A. Fowler, *The Age of Plantagenet and Valois* (London, 1967), pp.13-14.

[5] E. Déprez, *Les préliminaires de la guerre de Cent Ans* (Paris, 1902), p.400.

dilemma would be to obtain recognition of Guyenne as sovereign in its own right.[6] This was to become a principal, perhaps the principal, aim of Edward III and his government after 1337. Guyenne lay not merely at the heart of the dispute between the kings of England and France in the early fourteenth century but remained there until the duchy was lost by the English in 1453.

The other more immediate causes of the war that gradually flared up may be briefly listed: the question of the Capetian succession in 1328 and the dynastic claims of Edward III to the French throne; French intervention in Scotland in support of Robert Bruce and his son; diplomatic and economic rivalry in the Low Countries; the role of Robert of Artois; English fears over Philip VI's crusading intentions; the use to which he might put a formidable fleet; and failure to implement more recent treaties than that of Paris. These must all receive attention in an explanation of why Philip VI confiscated the duchy of Guyenne on 24 May 1337, an action usually taken as heralding the war.[7] In the years immediately preceding this, as mutual distrust mounted and a 'war psychosis' developed (to borrow Fritz Trautz's phrase), both kings had built up ambitious alliances along the whole eastern frontier of France from the North Sea to the Dauphiné. Edward's marriage to Philippa of Hainault (1328) had given him a considerable advantage here by linking him to a powerful family network spreading through the Netherlands and into the Empire where the emperor was his brother-in-law.[8] But both kings lavishly promised financial rewards and granted *fief-rentes* to potential allies.[9] In August 1337 a formal Anglo-Imperial alliance was sealed. Soon afterwards Edward was appointed vicar-general of the Empire, enabling him to strengthen his hold over the princes, many of whom were already in his pay. Advances for diplomatic or other assistance were also made in many other directions. Later in the century even wider geographical horizons would be touched in the search for allies, troops and supplies.[10]

Even if the disputants had wished, it proved impossible to isolate the Anglo-French war from other important political issues. These affected the interests of the papacy and secular powers in Spain, Italy and even

---

[6] P. Chaplais, 'English Arguments Concerning the Feudal Status of Aquitaine in the Fourteenth Century', *BIHR*, xxi (1948), 206-11.

[7] J.R.L. Maddicott, 'The Origins of the Hundred Years War', *History Today* (May, 1986), pp.31-7 is a recent concise summary; see also above pp.199-216 and C. Allmand, *The Hundred Years War* (Cambridge, 1988), pp.7-12.

[8] F. Trautz, *Die Könige von England und das Reich 1272-1377* (Heidelberg, 1961), pp.192ff; W.M. Ormrod, 'Edward III and his family', *Journal of British Studies*, 26 (1987), 398-422 provides a fresh discussion of the dynastic interests of Edward's immediate family.

[9] Bryce D. Lyon, *From Fief to Indenture* (Cambridge, Mass., 1957), pp.214ff.

[10] PRO, E 101, E 364 and E 372 contain the main series of particulars and enrolled accounts for envoys, of which there is no comprehensive study to date.

further afield in Scandinavia and central Europe. Both in the 1330s and later a succession of popes worked with more or less enthusiasm and sincerity for peace, managing to bring the protagonists or their representatives together on a number of occasions – at Avignon in 1344, Guines and Avignon in 1354, Bruges in 1375. Papal legates and *nuntii* tirelessly criss-crossed Europe in the interests of peace. They even followed closely in the wake of royal armies, turning up at critical moments to propose a truce, in Brittany in 1342, for example, or before the battle of Poitiers in 1356. For much of this period the English feared the partiality of the popes to the French cause, justifiably it seems in the case of Benedict XII, Clement VI and Urban V, less so in that of Innocent VI and Gregory XI. The popes did have some success in restricting warfare, promoting peace and alleviating suffering. There is the well-known case of the distribution of charity to war victims in the Cambrèsis in 1340.[11] Yet papal mediation was always limited. The beginnings of the Great Schism in 1378 and war between rival popes and their supporters removed a moderating influence, and in the end it was lay rulers who moved to impose a settlement of the Schism on rival popes.[12]

As for the many schemes for mounting crusades against the Ottomans and Mamluks that came to be linked with plans to end the Anglo-French war, recent work confirms that they preoccupied not only visionaries but also professional diplomats more fully than was previously suspected in almost every decade of the century.[13] This ceaseless activity explains the orientation of papal policy at particular points and it occasionally had an impact on those of the main protagonists, though the only expeditions of any importance in which English and French knights took part jointly ended inconsequentially, as at Mahdia in 1390, or disastrously, as at Nicopolis in 1396. For individual combatants the crusade in Spain, the Mediterranean or the Baltic during the fourteenth century remained for the majority a minor concern, something to be undertaken in the interludes between more serious bouts of fighting, or when it was expedient to withdraw for a time from domestic intrigue.[14] Some of the

[11] L. Carolus-Barré, 'Benoît XII et la mission charitable de Bertrand de Carit', *Mélanges d'archéologie et d'histoire publié par l'Ecole française de Rome* (1950); Diana Wood, 'Omnino partialitate cessante: Clement VI and the Hundred Years War', *Studies in Church History*, xx (1983), *The Church and War*, ed. W.J. Sheils, pp.179-89; N.P. Zacour, 'Talleyrand: The Cardinal of Périgord (1301-1364)', *Trans. American Philosophical Soc.*, new series 1, Part 7 (1960), 45ff; P. Jugié, 'L'activité diplomatique du Cardinal Guy de Boulogne en France au milieu du XIVᵉ siècle', *BEC*, 145 (1987), 99-127.

[12] E. Perroy, *L'Angleterre et le Grand Schisme d'Occident* (Paris, 1933) remains fundamental. See also below pp.265-6.

[13] Norman Housley, *The Avignon Papacy and the Crusades, 1305-1378* (Oxford, 1986); J.J.N. Palmer, *England, France and Christendom, 1377-99* (London, 1972).

[14] Maurice Keen, 'Chaucer's Knight, the English Aristocracy and the Crusade', *English Court Culture in the Later Middle Ages*, ed. V.J. Scattergood and J.W. Sherborne (London, 1983), pp.45-61.

wider territorial ramifications of the Anglo-French war as reflected in these events are discussed elsewhere in this volume. They are mentioned here to underline that from the start any armed clash between the 'only two countries in Western Europe counted as political forces' (in the rather exaggerated words of Edouard Perroy) [15] was likely to involve many more powers and private interests than those of the two principals. Necessarily what is offered here must be highly selective, even on the narrower question of Anglo-French relations strictly-speaking. There can be no discussion of the broader institutional, financial, social or cultural changes that the war wrought on the two societies facing each other across the Channel, about which so much has been written recently. This account simply highlights how the war developed and sustained a momentum of its own, distinguishing it from earlier Anglo-French wars; it concentrates on the issues at stake and the apparent aims of the two protagonists.

It is perhaps easier to deal with those of Philip VI first, for although it was never explicitly spelled out, there is a fair measure of agreement over the drift of royal policy. Certainly Edward III was under no illusions by 1339. The king of France, he reported, did not intend to leave him *une palme de terre el roialme de France*, an inch of ground in the kingdom of France.[16] Though exaggerated for propagandist purposes, this appeared at the time and has subsequently been accepted as a valid construction to place on French policies. It represents a logical solution to the problems over Guyenne, by then of historic standing, since it would have eliminated the major cause of dispute: the king of England holding lands as a vassal on whatever terms. In practice, although some headway was made in driving the English from Guyenne in the early years of the war, implementing the confiscation announced in 1337 proved to be less simple than on two previous occasions. It was an empty title that Philip VI conferred on his son John when he created him duke of Guyenne in 1345. Moreover, a majority of Gascons remained loyal to their king/duke, despite their richly deserved reputation for unruliness and particularism, both now and later.[17] Whether this was because of genuine affection for the Plantagenets rather than attachment to their local customs is more difficult to determine; perhaps it does not matter much since the political results were the same. Moreover, within a few years the Anglo-Gascon administration, reinforced by troops sent from England, was able to move onto the offensive, forcing the French to reconsider their position.

[15] E. Perroy, *The Hundred Years War*, p.xxvii.

[16] *Oeuvres de Froissart*, ed. Kervyn de Lettenhove, 26 vols., (Brussels, 1867-77), xviii. 93.

[17] P. Capra, 'Les bases sociales du pouvoir anglo-gascon au milieu du XIVe siècle', *Le Moyen Age*, lxxxi (1975), 273-99, 447-73; M.G.A. Vale, *English Gascony, 1399-1453* (Oxford, 1970), pp.154-215.

In subsequent negotiations the most that Philip VI would concede, even after the crushing defeat of Crécy (26 August 1346) and with Calais about to fall, was a return to the terms agreed in 1327 after the war of St. Sardos, reinforced by the demand for *superioritas et ressortum* that the French crown now naturally expected from its great vassals in conformity with royal notions on sovereignty. But, as Dr. Palmer has written, 'for most of his reign he felt strong enough to hold out for an English surrender of Aquitaine'.[18] Indeed, the English professed to fear that this was simply a step towards a yet more ambitious plan. For when in 1340 Edward III informed Benedict XII, who had been wrestling with the problem of inducing the two kings to make peace, 'All will not be well until a single king rules over both France and England', these were the reported words of Philip himself.[19] The long-term objectives of Philip VI thus seem to have been both clear and consistent.

They were pursued by his successors, except for a brief lapse in John II's reign, until the last stages of the war brought complete victory. When, later in the century, Charles V and Charles VI found that the final expulsion of the English from Guyenne was still beyond them, despite a considerable military recovery after 1369, they were forced to offer terms. But they insisted on preserving 'the theoretical integrity of the kingdom by retaining rights of sovereignty over the lost provinces'.[20] In this sense the war for them retained its feudal character of a lord in dispute with a rebellious vassal, seeking to discipline or dispossess him. All the solutions proposed in a long series of negotiations, which recommenced under the papal aegis in 1373, foundered on the issue of sovereignty and the terms on which the king of England would hold his lands in France. In the 1330s the English blamed Philip VI for the outbreak of the war because of his obduracy in defence of his rights. Despite some clever schemes to circumvent the problem, a final peace, debated on numerous occasions, in the end proved elusive.[21] After 1369 the French would not seriously contemplate, any more than had Philip VI, relaxing their demands for sovereignty. The English refused to consider any solution that did not give

---

[18] J.J.N. Palmer, 'The War Aims of the Protagonists and the Negotiations for Peace', *The Hundred Years War*, ed. K.A. Fowler (London, 1971), p.62. The implications of the battle for allegiance is well-exemplified in one highly sensitive frontier region immediately prior to 1337 in Y. Dossat, 'L'Agenais vers 1325, après la campagne de Charles de Valois', *Actes du 101ᵉ Congrès national des sociétés savantes, Lille, 1976, Section de philologie et d'histoire jusqu'à 1610, La Guerre et la Paix* (Paris, 1978), 143-54.

[19] Déprez, *op.cit.*, p.424. The propaganda use Edward III made of captured French invasion plans in 1346 is well-known (Robert of Avesbury, *De gestis mirabilibus*, ed. E.M. Thompson [London, 1889], pp.363-7).

[20] E. Perroy, 'Franco-English Relations, 1350-1400', *History*, xxi (1936), 154 [reprinted in his *Etudes d'histoire médiévale* (Paris, 1970)].

[21] Palmer, 'War Aims' and *England, France and Christendom* though his findings have not been universally accepted (see below pp.257-8).

them at least sovereign rights in whatever lands they then held. From this stalemate resulted a series of face-saving truces. Both sides preserved their position, but the conflict was temporarily halted.

A first truce was agreed as early as the autumn of 1337. In the next 60 years general truces were in force for 29 years, local truces for an additional seven and there were about eight years of unratified peace following negotiations in 1360. Major campaigns occurred on average in less than one year in three.[22] For the most part the truces were of short duration, often a year at a time. They were ill-kept, but frequently renewed. In 1376 the idea of a long truce of 40 years was discussed but not agreed. In 1389 a three-year truce was sealed and renewed in 1392 and 1394. In 1396, after several years in which a definitive peace treaty was seriously discussed, the longest truce to date was negotiated. It extended one then in force for a further 28 years from 1398. To mark this semi-permanent cessation of the war, Richard II took as his second wife, Isabelle, the six-year-old daughter of Charles VI, in a marriage celebrated with great pomp on 4 November 1396. For a few years there was respite from a war, which between 1369-89 had 'covered a wider area and was more dangerous and burdensome to England than any she was to fight again until the Anglo-Spanish war of 1585-1604'.[23] What led Edward III and Richard II to call upon their subjects to make such sacrifices must now be considered.

Put in the simplest terms the issue is whether Edward's claim to the crown of France raised in 1328, then left in abeyance till 1337 and only permanently proclaimed from 1340, was at any time intended as a genuine statement of his real objective or whether it was a bargaining counter to be negotiated away for some lesser but tangible concessions. This was certainly Perroy's view over fifty years ago:

> In England, neither Edward III or Richard II allowed themselves to be sidetracked by the upholding of their preposterous claims to the French throne. War had been waged in order to free the Gascon fief from French interference. Thus the goal was the formation of a principality of Aquitaine in which the king of England would rule with full sovereignty.[24]

More recently, whilst changing the perspective a little, Michael Prestwich has expressed a similar opinion, stressing that Edward was prepared ultimately to give up his claim to the French throne 'in return for major territorial concessions'.[25] Opportunism is thus seen by many as the

---

[22] K.A. Fowler, 'Truces', *The Hundred Years War*, ed. Fowler, p.184.
[23] J. Campbell, 'England, Scotland and the Hundred Years War in the Fourteenth Century', *Europe in the Late Middle Ages*, ed. Hale, p.211.
[24] Perroy, 'Franco-English Relations', p.154.
[25] Michael Prestwich, *The Three Edwards* (London, 1980), p.186.

fundamental characteristic of Edward's French policy. His dynastic claims, it is pointed out, were pressed only tentatively before the Flemings gave him an excuse to assume the style 'king of France' in 1340.[26] After the failure of his initial strategy based on a grandiose coalition of princes which only produced bankruptcy, it was the fortuitous chance to open up a new front in Brittany in 1341 that marked a fresh beginning to the war.[27] Once the conflict began to favour him with victories, further demands might be expected. His envoys speaking before Clement VI in October 1344 revealed their full extent:

> Holy father, you know well that our demand is widely understood to be for the kingdom of France as the right of our lord, the king.[28]

As already mentioned, Philip VI was not prepared to countenance this. There were no further discussions seriously aimed at resolving the conflict in his reign.

It was at Guines in April 1354 that John II admitted for the first time the possibility of a partition of his kingdom. A satisfactory explanation of this remarkable volte face has not been produced despite close modern scrutiny.[29] Since 1347 the French had suffered a number of reverses but they had redressed the balance in regions like the marches of Poitou. There seems to be no adequate military explanation for the French offer. The tangled skein of diplomacy and internal political intrigue offer a better hope of understanding John's action, though surviving documents leave many questions unanswered. In 1350 Edward allied with the young and ambitious Louis de Male, count of Flanders.[30] In 1351 a further alliance was arranged with Charles II of Navarre, whose claim to the French throne could be considered superior to Edward's. Then on 1 March 1353 Edward also came to terms with Charles de Blois, the

---

[26] H.S. Lucas, *The Low Countries and the Hundred Years War 1326-1347* (Ann Arbor, 1929), pp.259-67; J. van Herwaarden, 'The War in the Low Countries', *Froissart: Historian*, ed. J.J.N. Palmer (Woodbridge, 1981), pp.101-17.

[27] Prestwich, *op.cit.*, p.174; Allmand, *op.cit.*, p.14; Michael Jones, 'The Breton Civil War', *Froissart: Historian*, ed. Palmer, pp.64-81 [reprinted in *The Creation of Brittany: A Late Medieval State* (London, 1988), pp.197-218].

[28] *Oeuvres de Froissart*, xviii. 221 (cf. E. Deprez, 'La conférence d'Avignon [1344]', *Essays in Mediaeval History presented to Thomas Frederick Tout*, ed. A.G. Little and F.M. Powicke [Manchester, 1925], pp.301-20).

[29] K.A. Fowler, *The King's Lieutenant: Henry of Grosmont, First Duke of Lancaster 1310-1361* (London, 1969), pp.122-46; the treaty itself is printed in F. Bock, 'Some New Documents illustrating the early years of the Hundred Years War', *Bulletin of the John Rylands Library*, xv (1931), 91-3, while R. Delachenal, 'Premières negociations de Charles le Mauvais avec les Anglais (1354-1355)', *BEC*, lxi (1900), 253-82 and E. Perroy, 'Quatre lettres du Cardinal Guy de Boulogne, 1352-1354', *Revue du Nord*, xxxvi (1954), 159-64 [*Etudes d'histoire médiévale*, pp.336-42] add further valuable documents, of which the dating has been reassessed by Jugié, *BEC*, 145 (1987).

[30] Fowler, *op.cit.*, pp.96ff.

candidate originally supported by the French for the ducal throne of Brittany. He had been captured at the battle of La Roche Derrien in June 1347 and was tiring of his imprisonment in England.[31]

John II was not idle in countering Edward's apparent diplomatic success with these vassals whose opposition or defection he feared. But his task was complicated by serious disagreements amongst his own councillors, fuelled by feuds like that between Charles II of Navarre and Charles de la Cerda, constable of France, murdered in January 1354 at Navarre's instigation.[32] At that moment Charles II was in close contact with Edward with whom he had already agreed a plan for partitioning France. Six weeks later he was reconciled with John II by the treaty of Mantes (22 February 1354), the first of a series of changes of allegiance that punctuated a long career of perfidy persisting to his death in 1387.[33] Now, as later, it was the fate of Navarre's Norman possessions that most concerned the kings of England and France. Both recognized, as a curious correspondence between Henry, duke of Lancaster and Cardinal Guy de Boulogne reveals, the importance of these 'holes' through which the English might slip into France as they had already done through Brittany.[34] By the treaty of Mantes it seemed that John had temporarily plugged them, yet his fears may have continued to make him conciliatory, prompting his offer at Guines.

There is also the question of papal pressure in bringing England and France together. For over a year Guy de Boulogne – a partisan of Navarre – had been working assiduously to this end, though Edward had recently raised the stakes. An envoy had told the pope in 1353 that he now wanted in full sovereignty:

> The restitution of the duchy of Aquitaine as fully as his ancestors had held it, the duchy of Normandy, the county of Ponthieu, all of the lands which he had conquered from his adversary of France, Brittany and elsewhere, and the obedience of Flanders.[35]

In return for all this he was prepared to give up his title to the French throne (and also to Normandy if John could prove his right to it). Hopes for peace after a draft treaty was made at Guines were dashed, however, when the two kings refused to ratify the terms in late 1354. There is no agreement over who is to blame for this failure. There are signs that after

---

[31] Bock, *op.cit.*, pp.84-91.

[32] R. Cazelles, *Société politique, noblesse et couronne sous Jean le Bon et Charles V* (Geneva and Paris, 1982), brilliantly reworks a period which was first magisterially surveyed by R. Delachenal, *Histoire de Charles V*, 5 vols. (Paris, 1909-30).

[33] Delachenal, 'Premières negociations', pp.276-7 for Charles's letter to Lancaster informing him of the treaty.

[34] *Ibid.*, pp.279-80; *Oeuvres de Froissart*, xviii. 360-1; Fowler, *The King's Lieutenant*, pp.127-8.

[35] Fowler, *op.cit.*, p.114 after *Rot. Parl.* ii. 251-2.

initial enthusiasm Edward III became less anxious to settle. Likewise John II had reasons for holding back. By January 1355 all that the clever manoeuvring of Guy de Boulogne had achieved was to bring the English and Navarrese together again.[36]

When the next round of negotiations was held, Edward's bargaining position had been immeasurably strengthened by military success. In Normandy an Anglo-Navarrese party enabled Edward III to set up a provisional government. The garrison at Calais was strengthened. Edward's hold on Brittany tightened. First established in 1342-3 and consolidated by lieutenants like Sir Thomas Dagworth and Sir Walter Bentley, this grasp was reinforced between 1355-8 by one of the king's closest confidants, Henry, duke of Lancaster.[37] In Guyenne the arrival of Edward, prince of Wales, eager to extend his renown as victor of Crécy, led to one of the most successful of all destructive raids or *chevauchées* in the autumn of 1355. Narbonne and the Mediterranean coast were reached as the prince carried the war into a region hitherto untouched except by tax demands. In 1356 an even more ambitious raid was launched into the heart of Valois France. Originally the prince intended to join up with other expeditionary forces led by Lancaster and his father. These never materialized fully and while returning to Bordeaux, laden down with booty, his army was brought to bay by John II. The French king had hurried to meet the prince at the head of superior forces, but suffered an even greater defeat than Crécy near Poitiers on 19 September 1356. The prince's victory was crowned by the capture of the king himself, along with many other notable prisoners. The long list of the dead included many distinguished names. It was a disaster of the first magnitude for the Valois monarchy.[38]

The political and military repercussions of defeat were compounded by internal feuding among the remaining royal councillors, an ominous communal movement in Paris with Etienne Marcel, provost of the merchants, at its head, and rural unrest which culminated in the Jacquerie in the Ile de France and surrounding regions in 1358. Others, like Charles II of Navarre and bands of undisciplined soldiers of uncertain allegiance, also took advantage of royal weakness. Soon the problem of raising enormous ransoms demanded for the king and other numerous prisoners accentuated the desperate financial plight of the kingdom. The currency had already been weakened by frequent devaluation to meet war expenses in the opening decades of the war. The machinery for raising taxation remained rudimentary, especially when compared with that used in England. It is against this background, with England and its allies

---

[36] Fowler, *op.cit.*, p.144; Trautz, *op.cit.*, pp.367ff.

[37] Fowler, *op.cit.*, pp.158-71.

[38] H.J. Hewitt, *The Black Prince's Expedition of 1355-1357* (Manchester, 1958); Delachenal, *Charles V*, i. 123ff; Cazelles, *op.cit.* pp.229ff.

holding the upper hand, that further Anglo-French negotiations were held in the next few years.[39]

In March 1357 an Anglo-French truce was agreed at Bordeaux between the prince of Wales and John II. The prince had been authorized to treat for a 'final peace'. No details of a preliminary agreement that followed are known though some 'secret' instructions from Edward III have survived. In these there is no mention specifically of English claims to the French crown. But there was insistence that whatever lands were conceded should be held in full sovereignty. Subsequently between 1358-60 four more treaties were either projected or arranged: the first and second treaties of London (8 May 1358 and 24 March 1359) and the treaties of Brétigny and Calais (8 May and 24 October 1360). The latter, with one important exception, was simply a ratification of the former. In all of these the principle of territorial concessions in full sovereignty by the French king in return for the renunciation of his claim by Edward III was stated or implied.[40]

The most extensive concessions were those set out in the second treaty of London when, in addition to Guyenne (interpreted in its widest sense), together with other provinces previously listed in the abortive treaty of Guines (Touraine, Anjou, Maine, Ponthieu and Calais), there were also added Boulogne, Guines and Normandy. This would have given Edward III approximately half the kingdom of France, in effect a reconstituted and enlarged Angevin empire. In return Edward was to renounce 'the name, crown and kingdom of France' for himself and his heirs. When this treaty was rejected by the Dauphin Charles and the royal council in Paris as *ni passable ni faisable*, Edward launched his largest force to date on a campaign intended to bring him triumphantly to Reims for his coronation.

Apart from forcing Philip de Rouvres, duke of Burgundy, to make terms at Guillon, where he promised to assist at the consecration of Edward as king of France and to pay 200,000 *moutons* to rid his lands of English forces, the campaign was not a military success.[41] The weather and Fabian tactics prevented Edward from defeating the dauphin in the open field and few towns fell by siege. On both sides the campaign induced a greater sense of realism. Fresh talks were held at Brétigny not far from Chartres. They resulted in an agreement moderating the extreme terms of

[39] John B. Henneman, *Royal Taxation in Fourteenth-Century France*, 2 vols. (Princeton and Philadelphia, 1971-6).

[40] Delachenal, *Charles V*, ii. 402-11 (draft of first treaty of London, cf. Chaplais, *Eng. Med. Dip. Practice, Text*, i. no.201); *Oeuvres de Froissart*, xviii. 413-33 and E. Cosneau, *Les grands traités de la Guerre de Cent Ans* (Paris, 1889), pp.3-32 (second treaty of London); *Foedera*, III, i. 514-18 and Cosneau, pp.33-68 (Calais). The most detailed recent discussion is J. Le Patourel, 'The Treaty of Brétigny, 1360', *TRHS*, 5th ser. 10 (1960), 19-39 [*Feudal Empires*, Chapter XIII].

[41] *Foedera*, III, i. 473-4 (Guillon).

the second treaty of London. John II's ransom was reduced from four to three million *écus* (£500,000). Edward was to hold a sovereign Guyenne, further enlarged by Rouergue, together with Calais, Ponthieu and Guines. But he was to release any title to the other northern parts of the former Angevin empire – Normandy, Anjou, Maine and Touraine – and claims to sovereignty over Brittany and Flanders.[42] Given the skilful policies of Louis de Male, this last was hardly a notable sacrifice. But that of Brittany did represent a genuine loss as Edward had controlled much of the coastline, athwart lines of communication with Guyenne, as well as several inland garrisons. The Breton succession, a cause of dispute for nearly twenty years, was to be settled separately. Balancing Anglo-Flemish and Franco-Scottish alliances were to be abandoned. Castles held by the English in regions remaining French were to be surrendered, whilst Frenchmen deprived of their lands for treason were to be restored. Most significant of all, Edward undertook, as at Guines, to renounce 'the claim to the name and right of the crown and kingdom of France'.[43] There was an urgency about proceedings which augured well for the fulfilment of the treaty, even though terms were still provisional. They were to be ratified after the first instalment of John's ransom had been paid and he had been released. It remained to be seen whether Edward was prepared at last to pay the price to attain one goal, unchallenged sovereignty over Guyenne, by sacrificing another, his claim to the French crown. The events of the next few months suggest that he was not.

When Charles IV died in 1328, prima facie, there was no reason why Edward III's claim to the French crown through his mother should not have been accepted as a valid one. Indeed it apparently was by some of the legal experts then consulted.[44] There were no certain rules governing royal succession in the absence of a direct male heir, simply precedents for the exclusion of female claimants. The question of transmission of claims through the female line was still undecided, but if Isabelle's ability to do so on this occasion was allowed, the prospect that other cadets might present similar ones could not be excluded. It was on these grounds that Charles of Navarre, born in 1332, had a superior claim to both Edward III and Philip VI. What swayed the balance in 1328 in favour of Philip was not the overwhelming legitimacy of his case but his personal qualities. He was the oldest candidate, influential at the French court, and the dying king had nominated him as regent in the event of his wife giving birth to a son.[45] Edward might with a clear conscience feel there were equally compelling

---

[42] Delachenal, *Charles V*, ii. 193ff; Le Patourel, 'Treaty'.

[43] *Ibid.*, p.39.

[44] J. Le Patourel, 'Edward III and the Kingdom of France', *History*, xliii (1958), 175 [*Feudal Empires*, Chapter XII]; R. Cazelles, *La société politique et la crise de la royauté sous Philippe de Valois* (Paris, 1958), p.47.

[45] Cazelles, *Crise*, pp.35ff.

arguments to maintain his claim. The outcome of other contemporary succession disputes reveals how little consistency there was in arriving at decisions and how much political considerations carried the day. Le Patourel's view that 'there was no reason why Edward should not believe in his cause . . . (and) take it up again when circumstances were more favourable' is eminently reasonable. As a Christian ruler there was, indeed, an obligation for him to do so: 'he had no choice, for an inherited right implied a duty'.[46] Since this argument has been considered sympathetically (at least by English historians!) in assessing Henry V's motivation in reopening the war in 1415, it should perhaps be given more of its proper due in 1337.[47]

Then, for what it is worth, the scrappy evidence indicates that it was at the king's personal insistence that the claim was put forward. Whatever meetings preceded the decision, whatever doubts were expressed and whoever influenced the king (and here the contemporary opinion that it was Robert of Artois who persuaded Edward of his rights may need to be taken more seriously than is customary), there can be no escaping the implication of sending Henry Burghersh, bishop of Lincoln, to treat with 'Philip of Valois' in April 1337. This was four months before Edward formally announced the failure of the negotiations and six before he briefly adopted the style 'king of France', only to drop it again when peace talks were resumed.[48] It is this last action that has probably carried most weight in persuading historians that the claim was not sincerely meant. It was correct protocol, however, when there were still those pressing hard for a negotiated settlement, at least on the English side.

Subsequent events were to show that Philip VI was unwilling to yield. In addition to providing protection for his Flemish allies by assuming the title, there were other sound reasons to adopt this course if Edward was to be on equal terms with his adversary.[49] For Le Patourel Edward's letters, proclaiming his decision on 8 February 1340, have the ring of truth; others will continue to detect opportunism in the king's actions. What cannot be denied is that it represented an astute move in the struggle and announced a programme which might rally the discontented in France to Edward's

---

[46] Le Patourel, 'Edward III', pp.175-6.

[47] C.T. Allmand, 'Henry V the soldier and the War in France', *Henry V. The Practice of Kingship*, ed. G.L. Harriss (Oxford, 1985), pp.117-35.

[48] Roy M. Haines, *Archbishop John Stratford* (Toronto, 1986), p.245, citing the *Historia Roffensis*, draws attention to a meeting in the Tower on 23 January 1337 to discuss *de iure quod rex Anglie habet ad coronam Francie* which other sources attribute to the Lenten parliament of 1337. *Foedera*, II, ii. 994 and 1001 (cf. *Oeuvres de Froissart*, xviii. 47-50), commissions issued on 7 October 1337 to the duke of Brabant, marquis of Juliers, count of Hainault and William Bohun, earl of Northampton, used the style *Rex Anglie et Francie* or *Rex Francie et Anglie* but no other letters in this form have been found.

[49] Prestwich, *op.cit.*, pp.169-70 and above p.181.

standard.[50] The chancery clerk who composed the letters knew a great deal about the recent history of France. Le Patourel's cleverly argued case is that by claiming the crown Edward was able to place himself at the head of an alternative government. He discerns a pattern in both diplomacy and military events which, even if it fails to carry complete conviction, has constructively altered perceptions of how the war was fought. In particular, he stressed the importance of Edward's appeal to provincial sentiment when many felt that their private interests or liberties were threatened by the repressive, arbitrary and partial government of the Valois.[51]

Edward's intervention after 1340 in Flanders, Brittany, Normandy, Burgundy and even further afield – in Toulouse, for instance – shows how far he could get by piecemeal subversion rather than by outright conquest. For Le Patourel this was a 'provincial strategy' for gaining the crown. More conventionally it will be seen as depending on such chance factors as a succession dispute in Brittany or the personal grievances of a Godfrey de Harcourt in Normandy. But what is undeniable is its success in attracting those opposed to the Valois. Is it any wonder that Philip VI and John II determined to punish 'treason' severely wherever they found it?[52] In these circumstances Edward could certainly entertain greater hopes than he has sometimes been permitted of obtaining the crown of France. His reluctance finally to renounce that claim, despite several times announcing that he was about to do so, needs to be seen in this context. He had drawn back from ratifying the draft treaty of Guines; he appears to have done so again at Calais.

The circumstances then have been nowhere better explained than by Pierre Chaplais:

> The preliminary treaty of Brétigny provided for the transfer to Edward III of certain lands in full sovereignty and for certain renunciations to be made on both sides at such place and date as should be appointed by common consent at Calais ... when the treaty was ratified ... the twelfth article was deliberately omitted and the word 'sovereignty' dropped throughout the text. These omissions were compensated by the conclusion of a separate agreement known as *clausula Cest assavoir* which postponed the renunciations until specified lands were surrendered by the king of France to Edward III. These lands (in Poitou, Agenais, Quercy, Périgord, Limousin, Gaure) were to be transferred before 1 November 1361 at the latest and formal documents

---

[50] *Foedera*, II, ii. 1108, translated in *English Historical Documents, 1327-1485*, ed. A.R. Myers (London, 1969), p.66.

[51] Le Patourel, 'Edward III'.

[52] C. Johnson, 'An act of Edward III as count of Toulouse', *Essays in History presented to R.L. Poole*, ed. H.W.C. Davis (Oxford, 1927), pp.399-400; Cazelles, *Crise*, pp.133ff; J. Tricard, 'Jean, duc de Normandie et héritier de France, un double échec?', *Annales de Normandie*, xxix (1979), 23-44; S.H. Cuttler, *The Law of Treason and Treason Trials in Later Medieval France* (Cambridge, 1981), pp.142-62.

confirming the renunciations would be issued by 30 November. In the meantime the king of France was to abstain from making use of sovereignty in the lands concerned, and the king of England was to refrain from using the title King of France.[53]

Since Dr. Chaplais's important contribution, the removal of clause twelve and the agreement *Cest assavoir* has appeared more plausibly as evidence of Edward III's fear that John II would not complete his side of the bargain than the French diplomatic victory it was once claimed: 'whoever first thought of modifying the text of the treaty, it is evident . . . that responsibility for the non-execution of the renunciation clauses rests with Edward III'.[54] For Le Patourel this was further evidence of Edward's unwillingness to give up his ambitions and recover what 'he had lost at Brétigny'. To an extent the king was a victim of his own propaganda and success on the battlefield; to contemporaries it did seem that God had blessed his cause. To renounce his rights ran counter to the chivalrous and religious principles by which the king otherwise lived. In any event, both sides had something to gain from the non-implementation of the terms of Brétigny-Calais.[55]

Anglo-French relations from 1360-1415 were dominated by the new treaty in the same way that the treaty of Paris had dominated the years after 1259. A start was made with the cession of territory and sovereign rights. Edward dropped the title of king of France, but neither party acceded formally to the full terms and 'by March 1362 it had certainly been realized in France that Edward aimed at obtaining immediate French renunciations while postponing his own until the king of France had honoured all his obligations'.[56] On 19 July 1362 he invested his son with the principality of Aquitaine. Eventually he established a court of sovereignty to replace the *parlement* of Paris and hear appeals from the prince's judgements.[57] In November 1362 he came to terms with some of the French hostages for Brétigny-Calais, tired of their exile in England, to gain the territories he required.[58] Whilst awaiting ratification of this important subsidiary agreement which pledged additional castellanies in Berry, the princes (Philip of Orléans, Louis of Anjou, John of Berry and Louis of Bourbon) were taken to Calais. When the Estates meeting at Amiens in October 1363 finally rejected the treaty, Louis of Anjou broke

[53] 'Some Documents regarding the Fulfilment and Interpretation of the Treaty of Brétigny (1361-1369)', ed. P. Chaplais, *Camden Miscellany*, xix (1952), 6.

[54] *Ibid.*, p.7.

[55] Le Patourel, 'Edward III', p.179.

[56] 'Some Documents', ed. Chaplais, p.8.

[57] *Foedera*, III, ii. 667; Chaplais, *Essays*, VIII, 89; 'Some Documents', ed. Chaplais, pp.52-4.

[58] *Foedera*, III, ii. 681.

parole. John II, bound by his honour, returned to London and died there on 8 April 1364, his ransom only partially paid and the territorial clauses still far from completion.

Although the next few years saw continuing efforts to implement at least some terms of the 1360 treaty, Anglo-French relations continued to deteriorate. A seemingly satisfactory settlement was reached in Brittany only by arms. Charles V accepted the verdict of the battle of Auray (29 September 1364), which gave victory to the young John de Montfort over Charles de Blois, when he allowed the warring parties to agree the first treaty of Guérande (12 April 1365).[59] Outside France, the struggle in Castile between Pedro II and his illegitimate brother, Enrique da Trastamara, began to draw both sides into conflict once again. Despite victory by Pedro and the Black Prince at Nájera (3 April 1367), Enrique gradually gained the upper hand with French assistance. He sealed a formal alliance with Charles V on 20 November 1368 and within a year had overthrown and murdered his brother. In the 1370s Castilian naval support made a considerable contribution to Valois military success, forcing England to look for similar aid. An alliance was made with Portugal in 1373 and renewed in 1386; it still endures.[60]

The combination of difficulties in implementing the 1360 terms and clashing interests outside France naturally led both sides to prepare for war again. Planning for this appears to have been more thorough at the Valois court than in England. Old alliances were refurbished and new ones struck. Charles II of Navarre continued his habitual intrigues, playing one side off against the other. In 1370 the prince of Wales insisted that his father sever contacts with such an unreliable ally. Rebuffed, Charles accepted the barony of Montpellier as the price of coming to terms with Charles V in the treaty of Vernon (March 1371).[61] In the south-west Charles V worked on the equally fragile loyalties of the lords of Albret and Armagnac, the two most important Gascon lords to be disenchanted by the administration of the prince of Wales in Aquitaine. In November 1368 he accepted their appeals against the prince, fortified in the knowledge that leading lawyers like John of Legnano considered that he was not bound by the 1360 terms.[62] In the county of Flanders the

[59] Michael Jones, *Ducal Brittany, 1364-1399* (Oxford, 1970), pp.1-21.

[60] P.E. Russell, *English Intervention in Spain and Portugal in the time of Edward III and Richard II* (Oxford, 1955) is the best account; see also Goodman above pp.85-8.

[61] Delachenal, *Charles V*, iii-v *passim* and Russell, *op.cit.* for Charles II. *Foedera*, III, ii. 907 = Chaplais, *Eng. Med. Dip. Practice, Text*, i. no.26 for the prince's views.

[62] 'Some Documents', ed. Chaplais, pp.54-5, 70-8; Delachenal, *Charles V*, iv. 60ff; E. Perroy, 'Edouard III et les appels gascons en 1368', *Annales du Midi*, lxi (1948-9), 91-6 [*Etudes d'histoire médiévale*, pp.299-303]. Evidence of the military activities of both sides before the war officially reopened in 1369 is provided in a contemporary newsletter written from Gascony on 19 March 1369: *Anglo-Norman Letters and Petitions from All Souls MS. 182*, ed. M. Dominica Legge (Oxford, 1941), no.138.

struggle which had raged for many years over the hand of Margaret, heiress of Louis de Male, was concluded satisfactorily for France. In 1369 Philip, Charles V's brother, who had already been endowed with most of the former duchy of Burgundy (1363), gained papal approval for marriage to her to the dismay of Edward III.[63] Allied to these diplomatic successes and the rising fortunes of the monarchy abroad, an overhaul of royal finances, coinage, demesne and army, had been undertaken since 1360. Efforts to restore the tarnished image of the monarchy began to bear fruit. The mystique and rituals of kingship were emphasized. Charles V surrounded himself with learned advisers and encouraged the study and translation of works of classical philosophy and political theory to improve government practice and propaganda. Some of the dignity and prestige lost by Philip VI and John II was laboriously regained. The king was even confident enough to plan an ambitious invasion of England, timed for the summer of 1369.[64]

In the conflict which now broke out again and continued, with brief intermissions, until 1389, particular phases may be discerned, but no convincing overall strategy emerges; the war, an ever constant presence, became one of attrition. Between 1369-73 there was an unsuccessful rearguard action by the English to defend the greater Guyenne created at Brétigny. Thereafter, for the rest of the century and beyond, they had to struggle to hold onto its rump, restricted to a narrow band of territory around Bordeaux and Bayonne.[65] From 1372-81 there were also prodigious efforts to prop up or restore the regime of John IV in Brittany. This was more successful even though after 1381 he proved to be at best a lukewarm ally.[66] The idea of a barbican policy attracted some support. This meant the creation from 1378 of a line of important garrisons at Calais, Cherbourg and Brest (these latter fortresses ceded to the English for the duration of the war by Charles II of Navarre and John IV of Brittany respectively). When linked with English Gascony, the intention was to add depth to England's defence by placing the front line south of the Channel. An attempt was later made to extend the system by including Ghent (1385).[67] With garrisons also on the marches with Scotland this proved, however, to be a very costly policy. Even in times of

---

[63] J.J.N. Palmer, 'England, France, the Papacy and the Flemish Succession, 1361-9', *Journal of Medieval History*, 2 (1976), 339-64; Ormrod, *J. Brit. Studies*, 26 (1987), 412-13, 415-17.

[64] Cazelles, *Société politique, noblesse et couronne*, esp. pp.505-16; J.W. Sherborne, 'John of Gaunt, Edward III's Retinue and the French Campaign of 1369', *Kings and Nobles in the Later Middle Ages*, ed. R.A. Griffiths and J.W. Sherborne (Gloucester, 1986), pp.41-61.

[65] M.W. Labarge, *Gascony, England's First Colony 1204-1453* (London, 1980), pp.166-83.

[66] Jones, *Ducal Brittany*, pp.60-142; G.A. Holmes, *The Good Parliament* (Oxford, 1975), pp.21-34.

[67] *Rot. Parl.*, iii. 36; for the war at sea in the 1370s see Russell, *op.cit.*, pp.227-47; Palmer, *England, France and Christendom*, pp.52-62 (Ghent).

relative peace a quarter or more of royal resources were spent on a handful of castles.[68] Not surprisingly this limited what could be spent on more aggressive measures. Sir Thomas Trivet led a small expedition to Navarre in 1378-9 and Edmund, earl of Cambridge left for Portugal in 1381. In 1383 Henry Despenser, bishop of Norwich, led a crusade in the Urbanist cause to Flanders. Yet the impression left by most of this activity is of short-term planning in response to changing circumstances.

Great *chevauchées* were still launched; for private soldiers booty, one of the major incentives for fighting since the war began, could still be won. Often, however, the raids were poorly tied into broader war objectives as evident from the recrimination following the expeditions of Knolles in 1370, Gaunt in 1373-4 and 1378 and Buckingham in 1380-1. Although Edward III intended to venture abroad himself again in 1369 and 1372, on neither occasion did his fleet succeed in getting away. The Black Prince was forced by illness to leave Guyenne in 1371 and, although his influence persisted till his premature death in 1376, he had to leave the fighting to others.[69] There was thus little to show for the enormous outlay on men and munitions during the 1370s. Popular resentment of war taxation and the failure even to protect England's south coast combined in the Peasants Revolt of 1381. Thereafter the scale of military activities slackened and divisions amongst royal councillors began to surface more readily over particular policies in a period of straitened means.

There was controversy over Despenser's expedition in 1383, the military results of which were negligible.[70] French plans to invade England now reached a more advanced stage of preparation than any previous effort. Help was first sent to Scotland in 1384, then again and more substantially in 1385. This called for a response in kind from Richard II.[71] In the same year and the two following the French gathered men and supplies at Sluys. It was only through energetic naval action that their threatened invasion was thwarted. In 1386, after further prolonged debates, John of Gaunt was finally permitted to leave England and make a bid for the crown of Castile. He returned in 1389, enriched by a pension accepted as compensation for releasing his title.[72]

In the interim Richard II had begun to assert himself. As early as 1383 he showed some disinclination for the war with France, signalling a break

[68] J.W. Sherborne, 'The Costs of English Warfare with France in the later Fourteenth Century', *BIHR*, l (1977), 147-9. See also below pp.300-2.

[69] R. Barber, *Edward, Prince of Wales and Aquitaine* (London, 1978).

[70] M. Aston, 'The Impeachment of Bishop Despenser', *BIHR*, xxxviii (1965), 127-48; Perroy, *L'Angleterre*, pp.166-209; J. van Herwaarden, *Froissart: Historian*, ed. Palmer, pp.111ff.

[71] Campbell, 'England, Scotland', pp.207-12; G. Templeman, 'Two French Attempts to invade England during the Hundred Years War', *Studies in French Language, Literature and History presented to R.L. Graeme Ritchie* (Cambridge, 1949), pp.225-38.

[72] Palmer, *England, France and Christendom*, pp.67-104; Russell, *op.cit.*, pp.400-525.

with policies pursued for so long by his father and grandfather. Michael de la Pole, chancellor from 1383-6, has been credited with inaugurating this peace policy, which from the first provoked opposition.[73] In 1387-8 the Appellants, headed by Thomas, duke of Gloucester and Richard, earl of Arundel, two of the most warlike nobles, seized power from the king and his closest confidants and wholeheartedly prosecuted the war at sea. But after the king had lost some of his friends, executed or exiled in the Merciless parliament of 1388, in May 1389 he was able to declare himself of age (he was already 22) and regain control. Once more he quickly showed a conciliatory attitude towards France.[74] Argument has raged over what led the king to make the truces mentioned earlier. As Galbraith once pointed out, 'Richard was not always wedded to a peace policy, nor were all the magnates permanently committed to a policy of war. It was the hard logic of events which made peace first necessary and then obvious'.[75] For Perroy it was 'the pomp of the Valois court and the apparent absolutism of the French monarchy' that 'fascinated this imperious young man' perhaps hoping to gain from Charles VI support for escaping 'the tutelage of his barons'.[76] More recently Dr. Palmer has vigorously argued that both Richard II and Charles VI believed that the conflict could be settled at long last. He has linked their desire for peace in the west with plans for crusade in the east.[77] Others remain unconvinced by a case that has been constructed from very partial evidence and with a wealth of unverifiable hypothesis.

It is difficult, as usual, to extract the motives of participants in the negotiations from the kind of documents surviving, but sufficient evidence does remain to show that once again 'final peace' was under discussion. One of Palmer's arguments is that this was shattered by a Gascon revolt in 1394-5.[78] Dr. Vale has offered a very different interpretation of events which are supposed to have 'wrecked the secret understanding between England and France' that would have resulted in Guyenne being alienated from the crown of England, to be held by Gaunt and his heirs from Charles VI and his.[79] What had prevented the ending of conflict on

[73] Palmer, *England, France and Christendom*, pp.44ff; J.S. Roskell, *The Impeachment of Michael de la Pole, Earl of Suffolk in 1386* (Manchester, 1984), pp.98-109.

[74] Palmer, *op.cit.*, pp.142ff enlarging on 'English Foreign Policy 1388-1399', *The Reign of Richard II*, ed. Du Boulay and Barron, pp.75-107.

[75] Quoted by G.P. Cuttino, *English Medieval Diplomacy* (Bloomington, 1985), p.96.

[76] *Ibid.*, p.97 after Perroy, *The Hundred Years War*, p.197.

[77] *England, France and Christendom*, pp.142ff.

[78] An argument first advanced in 'The Anglo-French Peace Negotiations, 1390-1396', *TRHS*, 5th ser., 16 (1966), 81-94; see also 'Articles for a Final Peace between England and France, 16 June 1393', *BIHR*, xxxix (1966), 180-5. As James Sherborne points out a better description of this document would be 'a working agreement', 'Charles VI and Richard II', *Froissart: Historian*, ed. Palmer, p.62.

[79] Vale, *English Gascony*, pp.27-33 and his penetrating review of *England, France and Christendom* in *EHR*, lxxxviii (1973), 848-53. See also Sherborne's reservations, *loc.cit.*

previous occasions, seems again to have been the most likely cause of failure to achieve peace in the 1390s: the issue of sovereignty and the king's title. Even before the Gascon rebellion, the proposed peace of 1393 had been rejected decisively in parliament where it was said that 'it would be ludicrous for the king of England to do homage and fealty . . . for Aquitaine and other overseas territories and . . . that every single Englishman having the king of England as his lord would pass under the heel of the French king and be kept for the future under the yoke of slavery'.[80]

A war which had been largely feudal and dynastic in origin had become in the course of the fourteenth century one with a national dimension in which royal interests might have to be protected against the king himself. In the interim the best that the peace-makers could do was to patch up a truce. Only after two further generations of almost continual warfare would these national and royal dimensions be brought once again into synchrony for the English.

---

[80] *The Westminster Chronicle 1381-1394*, ed. and trans. L.C. Hector and Barbara F. Harvey (Oxford, 1982), p.519.

Chapter 14

The Letters of the Avignon Popes (1305-1378): a Source for the Study of Anglo-Papal Relations and of English Ecclesiastical History

P.N.R. Zutshi

Papal letters are only one of the many types of sources on which the historian of Anglo-papal relations and of the English church in the period of the popes' residence at Avignon needs to draw. Even if material of English provenance, such as the archives of royal and episcopal government and the chronicles, is not taken into account, it is evident that papal letters only form part of the picture. Various officials in the papal curia issued documents in their own name, notably the cardinal penitentiary[1] and the chamberlain.[2] The documents of the chamberlain and other records of the apostolic chamber, which include accounts of its receipts and payments, provide detailed information on financial questions and the missions of papal *nuntii*.[3] If various kinds of papal records are ignored in the present article, it is not because I wish to imply that the historian can afford to disregard them. In concentrating on papal letters I hope to show that, although their importance has long been recognized, they represent a source which has not yet been adequately explored by English historians.

First, however, it is necessary to indicate how letters of the Avignon popes for English recipients have been transmitted to us. They sometimes survive in the original. About 340 original letters have been traced in English libraries and archives.[4] The majority of these letters are addressed

---

[1] F. Tamburini, 'Note diplomatiche intorno a suppliche e lettere di penitenzieria (sec. XIV-XV)', *Archivum Historiae Pontificiae*, xi (1973), 149-208.

[2] D. Williman, 'Letters of Étienne Cambarou, camerarius apostolicus (1347-1361)', *Archivum Historiae Pontificiae*, xv (1977), 195-215. For letters of an earlier chamberlain, Gasbert de Laval (1319-47), see Vatican Archives, Collectoriae 373, ff.122-45, 156-65^v.

[3] J. de Loye, *Les archives de la chambre apostolique au XIVe siècle* (Paris, 1899); L.E. Boyle, *A Survey of the Vatican Archives and of its Medieval Holdings* (Toronto, 1972), pp.154-72. The accounts are being published by the Görres-Gesellschaft in the series *Vatikanische Quellen zur Geschichte der päpstlichen Hof- und Finanzverwaltung, 1316-1378*. See also *Accounts Rendered by Papal Collectors in England, 1317-1378*, ed. W.E. Lunt (Philadelphia, 1968).

[4] P.N.R. Zutshi, *Original Papal Letters in England, 1305-1415*, to be published by the Vatican Library in the series *Index Actorum Romanorum Pontificum ab Innocentio III ad Martinum V electum*. The introduction contains a detailed discussion of the survival of original papal letters in England, on which the following sentences are based.

to the king of England or members of his family or to royal servants, and are now in the Public Record Office. The number of original papal letters extant outside the public records is rather small. One reason for this is that in England the Reformation led to the systematic destruction of papal letters. The effects of the Reformation, nonetheless, cannot explain why so many more letters from the thirteenth century survive than from the fourteenth: about 1,100 letters of the years 1198-1305 are estimated to be extant.[5] The reason for the imbalance seems to lie in the recipients of the letters. In the thirteenth century, probably most letters were in favour of monasteries and other ecclesiastical institutions. Here the chances of the letters being preserved, at least until the Reformation, were reasonable. In the fourteenth century, on the other hand, letters in favour of individuals – both spiritual concessions and provisions to benefices – began to predominate. After the death of their beneficiaries there would have been little need to preserve such letters. A high proportion of them probably perished through neglect before the Reformation. The loss of so many original letters is regrettable, since the originals provide information which will not be found in copies. An example may be given: common letters (which with certain exceptions were letters issued as a result of petitions) were sometimes endorsed with the signature of the agent, or proctor, who impetrated them in the papal court on behalf of the petitioners. The original letters therefore show which agents Englishmen used to transact their business in the curia.[6]

Many more papal letters survive in England as copies than as originals. One finds them rehearsed in the *acta* of bishops and papal judges delegate. In the fourteenth century, the rise in England of the notary public, who was licensed by papal or imperial authority to transcribe documents, made more widely available a new means of producing authenticated copies of papal letters.[7] Notarial copies of papal letters are not rare. Most cartularies of religious houses include some papal documents and they often have a special section devoted to them.[8] Papal letters were copied by their recipients into registers and letter-books of various types, notably episcopal registers.

We must look at the transmission of papal letters in Vatican sources in

[5] C.R. Cheney, 'Some Features of Surviving Original Papal Letters in England', *Annali della Scuola Speciale per Archivisti e Bibliotecari dell'Università di Roma*, xii (1972), 1-25, at p.2, estimates that there are about 1,600 original letters of the years 1198-1417 in England and Wales. Of these, over 500 are from the years 1305-1417.

[6] P.N.R. Zutshi, 'Proctors Acting for English Petitioners in the Chancery of the Avignon popes', *Journal of Ecclesiastical History*, xxxv (1984), 15-29.

[7] Cf. C.R. Cheney, *Notaries Public in England in the Thirteenth and Fourteenth Centuries* (Oxford, 1972).

[8] C.R. and M.G. Cheney, *The Letters of Pope Innocent III concerning England and Wales* (Oxford, 1967), p.xix; G.R.C. Davis, *Medieval Cartularies of Great Britain* (London, 1958), p.xii.

somewhat greater detail. Vast numbers of letters will be found in the papal registers now in the Vatican Archives.[9] The Avignon Registers contain for the most part common letters. They are written on paper and begin with the pontificate of John XXII (1316-34). Parchment copies of these registers were made, which now form part of the series of Vatican Registers. For John XXII and Benedict XII (1334-42) the copies are more or less complete, but under Clement VI (1342-52) there were omissions in the copying.[10] These omissions increased substantially during the pontificate of Innocent VI (1352-62), while for the last two Avignon popes, Urban V (1362-70) and Gregory XI (1370-78), only a small proportion of the letters registered was copied.[11] The Vatican series contains three other types of registers of papal letters. 1) There are some paper registers which properly belong in the Avignon series.[12] 2) The so-called 'secret' registers are parchment registers containing political correspondence and other curial letters (that is, letters issued not as a result of a petition but on the initiative of the curia). 3) There are also paper registers which contain curial letters, relating to financial matters, the Papal State, papal *nuntii* etc. They are known as chamber registers, but this term is rather confusing since the secret registers are likewise registers of the chamber.

This material – some 200 volumes of Avignon Registers and some 240 volumes of Vatican Registers – has only been published in part. Those interested in letters concerning England will turn first to the *Calendar of Papal Letters*.[13] However, this publication uses only the Vatican Registers, even though from the mid-fourteenth century many of the letters in the original Avignon Registers do not appear in the Vatican Registers. An idea of the extent of the omissions in which the editorial policy of the *Calendar* resulted can be had from the fact that the common letters of the first pontifical year of Gregory XI fill ten volumes of the Avignon Registers but only one volume of the Vatican Registers.[14] This shortcoming in the *Calendar of Papal Letters* is well known[15] but, as we shall

---

[9] For what follows see F. Bock, *Einführung in das Registerwesen des Avignonesischen Papsttums* (*Quellen und Forschungen aus Italienischen Archiven und Bibliotheken*, xxxi (1941), Ergänzungsband).

[10] A detailed concordance is given in *Acta Pataviensia Austriaca*, i: Klemens VI., ed. J. Lenzenweger (Österreichische Akademie der Wissenschaften, 1974), 43-167.

[11] D.E.R. Watt, 'Sources for Scottish History of the Fourteenth Century in the Archives of the Vatican', *Scottish Historical Review*, xxxii (1953), 101-22, at p.112.

[12] Boyle, *Vatican Archives*, p.115 n.29.

[13] *Calendar of Entries in the Papal Registers relating to Great Britain and Ireland: Papal Letters*, ii-iv (H.M.S.O., 1895-1902); henceforth cited as *CPL*.

[14] Reg. Av. 173-82, Reg. Vat. 282. See C. Tihon, *Lettres de Grégoire XI*, iv (Analecta Vaticano-Belgica, xxviii, 1975), iv. 11-18.

[15] E.g., L. Macfarlane, 'The Vatican Archives', *Archives*, iv (1959), 29-44, 84-101, at 37; Boyle, *Vatican Archives*, pp.114-23.

see, its effects have not always been taken into account by historians using information deriving from the *Calendar*. A further problem with the *Calendar* is that some letters in the Vatican Registers which one would expect to be included are omitted.[16] An instance of this is a solemn privilege of Clement VI (a type of document which by this time is extremely rare) in favour of the abbey of Minoresses at Denny.[17] One final defect in the *Calendar of Papal Letters* must be mentioned: the summary of the contents of the letters is sometimes incomplete or inaccurate. To take another example from the registers of Clement VI, a letter of 29 January 1344 reserves a 'dignitatem vel personatum aut officium' in the cathedral of St. Asaph to be conferred on John Trevaur, but in the *Calendar* this becomes a provision 'of a canonry of St. Asaph, with expectation of a prebend or dignity'.[18]

A more ambitious, and in most respects more satisfactory, undertaking is the publication of the registers of the Avignon popes by the École française de Rome. It is intended to cover all the letters registered irrespective of whether they appear in the Vatican or the Avignon Registers. The project is far from complete, and a start has yet to be made on the common letters of Clement VI, Innocent VI and Gregory XI.[19] However, the publication of the common letters of Urban V is well advanced.[20]

Papal letters will be found in the Vatican Archives outside the main series of registers. The *Instrumenta Miscellanea* include original letters and drafts as well as other documents, and there is a calendar of the items relating to the British Isles.[21] A larger collection of original drafts has been bound up to form Reg. Vat. 244 A-N. These are drafts of curial letters from Clement VI to Gregory XI, most of which were registered, but the drafts are of great interest since they sometimes show alterations made in the content of letters before they were issued.

In illustrating what information papal letters can provide about English affairs, I propose to concentrate on three kinds of letters: political

[16] Cf. Macfarlane, 'Vatican Archives', p.34 and n.19.

[17] Reg. Vat. 180, ff.283ᵛ-4, copied from Reg. Av. 97, ff.378ᵛ-9. The date of the privilege is 30 April 1348.

[18] *CPL*, iii. 126. The letter appointing the executors of the provision survives in the original: PRO, Papal Bulls (S.C.7)/13/14 (printed in *Foedera*, III, i. 1-2).

[19] See the list in Boyle, *Vatican Archives*, pp.125-7, which can be supplemented by information in the next footnote.

[20] M. Hayez and others, *Urbain V: lettres communes* (B[ibliothèque des] É[coles] F[rançaises d'] A[thènes et de] R[ome], 1954 ff.). The calendar, in nine volumes, is finished and contains 27,899 entries, but the number of letters is higher than this because an entry often includes more than one letter. The first volume of the index (A-K) appeared in 1985.

[21] C. Burns, 'Sources of British and Irish History in the *Instrumenta Miscellanea* of the Vatican Archives', *Archivum Historiae Pontificiae*, ix (1971), 7-141.

correspondence with the kings of England, letters in favour of ecclesiastical institutions, and provisions to benefices. I am aware that in doing this some areas equally worthy of attention will be ignored. In particular papal letters which reflect the religious life of the period come to mind, including indulgences for visitors to churches and chapels and licences for individual clerics and laymen to choose a confessor, to have a portable altar or to celebrate mass before day-break.

Cooperation is more in evidence than conflict in relations between the kings of England and the Avignon popes.[22] This is most apparent under Clement V (1305-14). Clement honoured the memory of Edward I by having solemn exequies celebrated for him in 1307, the first time, it seems, that a pope did this for a king.[23] Edward I in his lifetime received important financial favours from Clement, as did Edward II.[24] Further evidence of Clement's cordial relations with the English monarchy could easily be adduced. It would be misleading to ignore the cases of friction between Clement and the kings of England: in 1307-9, for instance, Clement complained about Edward II's imprisonment of three bishops and other infringements of ecclesiastical liberty. However, even here, the overriding impression is that the pope felt personally wounded by the business.[25]

The origins of Clement V's favourable disposition towards the kings of England are to be found in his career before he became pope. He had been archbishop of Bordeaux, but his association with the English Crown goes back earlier than this. J.H. Denton has argued that Clement can be identified with the royal clerk, Bertrand de Got, who appears in a petition addressed to Edward I.[26] What Dr. Denton argued from indirect evidence

[22] General surveys of the subject include J. Haller, *Papsttum und Kirchenreform* (Berlin, 1903), i. 375-440, and W.A. Pantin, *The English Church in the Fourteenth Century* (Cambridge, 1955), pp.76-102. There is a wealth of information on the procedure used in Anglo-papal diplomacy in P. Chaplais, *Eng. Med. Dip. Practice*.

[23] W. Ullmann, 'The Curial Exequies for Edward I and Edward III', *Journal of Ecclesiastical History*, vi (1955), 26-36.

[24] W.E. Lunt, *Financial Relations of the Papacy with England to 1327* (Cambridge, Mass., 1939), pp.164-6, 382-418; Y. Renouard, 'Édouard II et Clément V d'après les Rôles Gascons', *Annales du Midi*, lxvii (1955), 119-41.

[25] PRO, S.C.7/11/15 (*Foedera*, II, i. 59): 'quantumcunque personam tuam diligimus ex corde et quantumcunque tuum et regni tui statum prosperum sicut proprium cupiamus, . . . detentionem prelatorum . . . dissimulare salva conscientia non possemus . . .' See also *The Register of John de Halton, Bishop of Carlisle*, ed. W.N. Thompson and T.F. Tout (2 vols., Canterbury and York Society, 1913), i. 309-13; PRO, S.C.7/11/16, S.C.7/12/13 and 16, and BL, Cotton Cleopatra E ii, ff.275-6 (*Foedera*, II, i. 41-2, 60, 97-8).

[26] J.H. Denton, 'Pope Clement V's Early Career as a Royal Clerk', *EHR*, lxxxiii (1968), 303-14; cf. Ch. V. Langlois, 'Documents relatifs à Bertrand de Got', *Revue Historique*, xl (1889), 48-54. For other members of Clement's family in the royal service see J.A. Kicklighter, 'La carrière de Béraud de Got', *Annales du Midi*, lxxxv (1973), 327-34; *idem*, 'An Unknown Brother of Pope Clement V', *Mediaeval Studies*, xxxviii (1976), 492-5.

can be shown directly from Clement's letters to Edward I. In 1306 the pope referred to 'quantis honoribus, favoribus et gratiis ex benigne familiaritatis affectu tua excellentia, temporibus quibus ante suscepte a nobis prelationis officium tuis insistebamus obsequiis, nos iugiter honoravit'.[27] It is clear from this passage that Bertrand's service to the king antedated his appointment as archbishop, and indeed as bishop of Comminges (1295). Also in 1306, Clement referred to himself as being mindful of 'illius . . . domestice familiaritatis qua tibi hactenus minori fungentes officio stringebamur, consiliariorum tuorum utpote ascripti consortio . . .'[28] The allusion to being a counsellor of Edward I is rather vague, although the wording suggests a formal rather than an informal position. It may refer to the Gascon council, of which Bertrand might have been a member as archbishop of Bordeaux,[29] or to the English council, since Bertrand had visited England.[30] On Edward I's death the pope emphasized his gratitude to him in writing to the new king, Edward II: 'dum nos minor status haberet et assisteremus obsequiis dicti regis multis nos graciis et favoribus honoravit, nostrisque consiliis fiducialiter inherebat, ac de vassallis et terris suis utilis traximus nos et nostri.'[31] Finally, in a letter to John de Ferrers, seneschal of Gascony, in 1312 Clement said that before he became pope he promoted the business of Edward I at the court of Philip IV of France ('. . . negotia progenitoris eiusdem in . . . curia . . . regis Francie prosequendo').[32] The association between Edward I and Clement V prior to the latter's election to the papacy is reflected in certain letters from the king to the pope.[33] It forms the background against which Clement's expression to Edward II of his

[27] PRO, S.C.7/11/33 (*Foedera*, I, ii. 1005) and S.C.7/11/34.

[28] PRO, S.C.7/11/12 (*Foedera*, I, ii. 981). J.H. Denton, *Robert Winchelsey and the Crown* (Cambridge, 1980), p.219, draws attention to this passage.

[29] On the Gascon council see J.P. Trabut-Cussac, *L'administration anglaise en Gascogne sous Henry III et Édouard I* (Geneva, 1972), pp.191-4; *The Liber Epistolaris of Richard de Bury*, ed. N. Denholm-Young (Roxburghe Club, 1950), pp.xxviii-xxxi. E.C. Lodge, *Gascony under English Rule* (London, 1926), p.145, states that the archbishop was normally a member of the Gascon council, but there appears to be no evidence for this as early as the reign of Edward I.

[30] Denton, 'Clement V's Early Career', pp.310-11.

[31] *Liber Epistolaris*, ed. Denholm-Young, pp.97-8, no.210.

[32] PRO, S.C.7/12/14 (*Foedera*, II, i. 176-7). This passage is quoted by C. Wenck, *Clemens V. und Heinrich VII.* (Halle, 1882), p.33.

[33] In 1306 Edward mentioned the 'fecunde dilectionis integritas quam ad nos magna experientia vos habere et habuisse probavimus a iam diu' (*Foedera*, I, ii. 997); and in the same year he stated that the pope had been pleased 'de ipso statu [*scil.* nostro] tam pie et tenere cogitare, atque disponere, quod utique ab iuncto sanguine et antiqua gratitudine novimus processisse', W. Prynne, *An Exact Chronological Vindication . . . of our Kings Supream Ecclesiastical Jurisdiction over all Religious Affairs* (3 vols., London, 1665-8), iii. 1147-8. See also *ibid.*, 1069.

affection for the English royal house must be seen: 'non credamus umquam aliquem fuisse summum pontificem temporibus hominum qui tunc vivunt qui tantum dilexerit domum tuam sicut nos diligimus.'[34] It might be thought that statements of this sort simply embody the common form of diplomacy, but this seems to be an unwarranted assumption since Clement did not confine himself to conventional and stereotyped expressions and since his actions were in accord with his words.

It is not possible in this article to examine in detail the relations between the papacy and the kings of England under Clement V's successors; but I shall briefly consider two aspects of these relations which permeate the Avignon period – efforts to secure peace between the kings of England and France, and attempts to launch crusaders. All the Avignon popes took measures to bring about peace between the two kingdoms.[35] Clement V wrote to Edward I in 1306 that one of the reasons why he had not left France for Rome was to establish peace.[36] With the intensification of the conflict from the time of Benedict XII, papal efforts also intensified.[37] In 1376 Gregory XI said that he had postponed his move from Avignon to Rome at the request of the English peace negotiators.[38] The Avignon popes had few conspicuous successes. One problem was that the English doubted their neutrality; hence the frequent claims by Clement VI and his successors that they would consider the case of both sides impartially.[39] Closely connected with the popes' concern for peace between the kings of England and France was their desire to launch a crusade to the Eastern Mediterranean, since peace in the West was seen as

---

[34] PRO, S.C.7/11/16 (*Foedera*, II, i. 41-2).

[35] See P. Chaplais, 'Règlement des conflits internationaux franco-anglais au XIVᵉ siècle', *Le Moyen Âge*, lvii (1951), 169-302 (reprinted in his *Essays*, ch.9); B. Guillemain, 'Les tentatives pontificales de médiation dans le litige franco-anglais de Guyenne au XIVᵉ siècle', *Bulletin philologique et historique du Comité des travaux historiques et scientifiques*, 1957, pp.423-32.

[36] PRO, S.C.7/11/33 (*Foedera*, I, ii. 1005) and S.C.7/11/34. Cf. G. Mollat, *Les papes d'Avignon*, 10th edn. (Paris, 1965), pp.16-17; B. Guillemain, *La cour pontificale d'Avignon* (Paris, 1962), p.75; and the letter cited above n.32.

[37] See E. Déprez, *Les préliminaires de la guerre de Cent Ans* (Paris, 1902); idem, 'La conférence d'Avignon (1344): l'arbitrage pontifical entre la France et l'Angleterre', in *Studies in Medieval History presented to T.F. Tout*, ed. A.G. Little and F.M. Powicke (Manchester, 1925), pp.301-20; G. Mollat, 'Innocent VI et les tentatives de paix entre la France et l'Angleterre', *Revue d'histoire ecclésiastique*, x (1909), 729-43.

[38] PRO, S.C.7/17/4 (*Foedera*, III, ii. 1056). On the negotiations to which the letter refers see É. Perroy, 'The Anglo-French Negotiations at Bruges, 1374-1377', *Camden Miscellany* xix (Camden Third Series, lxxx, 1952).

[39] E.g., Clement VI wrote to Edward III in 1343: 'circa reformationem pacis . . . omni affectione privata et cuiusvis parcialitatis sintilla remotis penitus et exclusis, secundum deum et puram conscientiam nostram intendimus . . . laborare': PRO, S.C.7/13/8 (*Foedera*, I, ii. 981-2, where the letter is assigned to Clement V).

a prerequisite for royal participation in a crusade.[40] Without exception, the Avignon popes showed an interest in the crusade against the Moslems, and there is no reason to doubt the sincerity of that interest. The subject occurs constantly in their letters to the kings of England. However, it does not seem to have had a special priority. The compliant Clement V permitted most of the proceeds of the crusading tenths imposed in 1305 to pass to the English royal family, without Edward I having taken the cross or any stipulations being made about the use of the money.[41] Edward II was able to profit in a similar way from Clement and John XXII.[42] It seems that in 1319-20 John XXII regarded an expedition 'ad prosecutionem negotii Terre Sancte' as a possibility only for the remote future.[43] A letter to Edward III in 1332 indicates that he was still reticent about the idea then.[44] Benedict XII actively discouraged the crusading plans of Philip VI of France.[45] The concept of the crusade could embrace expeditions other than those associated with the Holy Land. Papal enemies in Italy must have often seemed to the popes a more urgent problem than the Moslems in the East, and crusades and other expeditions were launched against these enemies. Innocent VI in 1360-1 requested the assistance of Edward III, as well as of the English church, to resist Bernabo Visconti of Milan.[46]

Papal letters addressed to the kings of England were for the most part curial letters. The character of papal letters in favour of ecclesiastical institutions and individuals was different: they were generally common letters, produced in response to petitions. The pope's role in issuing common letters was not a passive one since he could, and did, modify or reject the petitions presented to him.[47] However, as the initiative in

[40] A letter of 1345 from Clement VI to Edward III reads: 'Rogamus itaque serenitatem regiam et attentius in domino exhortamur quatinus que, quanta et qualia principes catholici ad eiusdem dilationem fidei . . . possent agere hiis temporibus, si guerris et dissensionibus suis cessantibus intendere circa talia procurarent, consideranter attendens, tu . . . ad vias pacificas super guerris tuis animum regium dirigas . . .': PRO, S.C.7/13/17 (*Foedera*, III, i. 28-9). On what follows see K.M. Setton, *The Papacy and the Levant, 1204-1571*, i (Philadelphia, 1976); N. Housley, *The Avignon Papacy and the Crusades* (Oxford, 1986).
[41] See Lunt, *Financial Relations to 1327*, pp.382-95.
[42] *Ibid.*, pp.400-18. Edward II did take the cross: PRO, S.C.7/25/22 (*Foedera*, II, i. 319-20).
[43] A. Coulon and S. Clémencet, *Lettres secrètes et curiales du pape Jean XXII relatives à la France* (BEFAR, 1900 ff.), i, no.1227.
[44] PRO, S.C.7/25/28 (Coulon and Clémencet, *Lettres secrètes et curiales du pape Jean XXII*, no.4835).
[45] Déprez, *Les préliminaires*, especially pp.123, 410-3.
[46] PRO, S.C.7/22/6, S.C.7/35/10 (*Foedera*, III, i. 509, ii. 623-4); W.E. Lunt, *Financial Relations of the Papacy with England, 1327-1534* (Cambridge, Mass., 1962), pp.95 ff.
[47] The registers of petitions, which survive in the Vatican Archives from the pontificate of Clement VI onwards, give the words of the pope's response to those petitions which were granted and show that many requests were modified by him: see *Calendar of Entries in the Papal Registers relating to Great Britain and Ireland: Petitions to the Pope*, i (H.M.S.O., 1896).

issuing common letters did not lie with the pope, great caution is necessary in using them as an index of papal policy. On the other hand, such letters provide valuable evidence about the aspirations of petitioners throughout Latin Christendom and shed light on the countries with which the Avignon papacy was in contact.

Many of the letters in favour of ecclesiastical institutions were letters of justice which, at the request of a party in a dispute, appointed one or more judges *in partibus* to hear the case. The procedure for issuing letters of justice was simpler than for other letters. However, in order to give an opportunity to someone whose position might be harmed by a letter of justice to object to, or 'contradict', it, such letters were publicly read out at the curia (in the *audientia publica*) before their issue.[48] Letters of justice were not registered, and there was little incentive for their beneficiaries to preserve them carefully, since they did not confer any permanent rights but merely instituted a judicial process. Nonetheless, in England occasionally they do appear in cartularies or survive in the original. It must be admitted that letters of justice are problematic as sources. They are often uninformative about the cases to be heard by the judges delegate, and to understand them properly it is necessary to discover from other judicial records to what use they were put. A litigant might impetrate letters in different forms appointing judges.[49] He could then choose which letter to use according to the circumstances of the case. One also finds both parties obtaining papal letters which appointed judges and consequently two rival courts dealing with the same case.[50] However, letters of justice can provide welcome information about obscurer religious houses, hospitals, parish churches and chapels.[51] Some letters of justice tell us something about the cases which the judges delegate had to hear. A letter of Innocent VI, dated 2 December 1358, concerns a dispute between the abbey of Glastonbury and Richard de Tynebury, rector of Pucklechurch, Gloucestershire, over an annual pension and other matters.[52]

---

[48] P. Herde, *Audientia Litterarum Contradictarum* (2 vols., Tübingen, 1970). See also J.E. Sayers, *Papal Judges Delegate in the Province of Canterbury, 1198-1254* (Oxford, 1971).

[49] E.g., two letters of John XXII: Westminster Abbey Muniments, 2763-4 (*Luffield Priory Charters*, ed. G.R. Elvey (2 vols., Buckinghamshire and Northamptonshire Record Societies, 1968-75), i, nos.17-18). Cf. R. Brentano, *York Metropolitan Jurisdiction and Papal Judges Delegate (1279-1296)* (Berkeley, 1959), pp.152-3.

[50] See *ibid.*, especially ch.8.

[51] E.g., a letter of Gregory XI, dated 2 April 1373, orders the prior of Lewes to revoke the illicit alienation of property of the chapel of Maresfield, Sussex: PRO, S.C.7/64/4.

[52] Lambeth Palace Library, Papal Documents 91. The compilation of the 'Great Chartulary' of Glastonbury (ed. A. Watkin, 3 vols., Somerset Record Society, 1947-56) antedates the dispute. For the earlier relationship between the church and the abbey, see *ibid.*, i, pp.xx, 89, 95, 105-6, 108, 156; and see also *Adami de Domerham Historia de Rebus Gestis Glastoniensibus*, ed. T. Hearne (2 vols., Oxford, 1727), ii. 309. I am indebted to Dr. M.J. Franklin for advice on the question.

Much more detailed descriptions of litigation occur in letters which record proceedings in the *audientia sacri palatii*, or Rota. These letters were likewise not registered. A long letter of 27 June 1342 concerns a dispute between the priory of Tutbury and the abbey of St. Pierre-sur-Dives.[53] The letter orders the execution of a judgement supporting the priory's claim to complete independence of the abbey. Although Tutbury was regarded by the king as an alien priory and for this reason in 1343 it was in his hands during the war with France,[54] the monks secured permission from him the following year to publish their letter.[55] However, in the same year (1344) the king revoked his permission and upheld the earl of Lancaster's rights of patronage (which are not mentioned at all in the papal letter) over the priory, enshrined in an agreement made long before between the abbot of St. Pierre-sur-Dives and the then lay patron, the earl of Derby.[56] The king also supported the prior imposed by the abbey, Alexander de Portu,[57] whom the monks of Tutbury regarded as an intruder. The papal judgement in favour of Tutbury is therefore unlikely to have had much effect, although one of the executors of the letter, Thomas Fastolf, threatened the monks sent to the priory by the abbot of St. Pierre-sur-Dives against the wishes of the existing monks with excommunication.[58] Yet by the fifteenth century the priory had been able to establish its independence of the abbey.[59]

In contrast to letters of justice, letters of grace and mandates concerning the implementation of graces were subject to rather elaborate controls in the curia before they were issued. Papal graces for English ecclesiastical institutions survive in such large numbers in the papal registers and elsewhere and are so diverse in purpose that it is not possible to discuss even a representative sample of them. I shall confine myself to considering some letters in favour of colleges in the universities of Oxford and Cambridge. The fourteenth century saw a series of collegiate foundations here and they often occasioned requests for papal support.

[53] PRO, S.C.7/64/13. It was not used by D.J.A. Matthew, *Norman Monasteries and their English Possessions* (London, 1962); nor is there any reference to the dispute in *The Cartulary of Tutbury Priory*, ed. A. Saltman (Historical Manuscripts Commission, 1962). A royal letter connected with the dispute is printed in William Dugdale, *Monasticon Anglicanum* (6 vols., London, 1817-30), iii. 395-6, but ascribed to Edward II instead of to Edward III (cf. *CPR, 1343-1345*, 334). Oswald Mosley's *History of the Castle, Priory, and Town of Tutbury* (London, 1832), pp.264-9, prints a translation of the letter, but at some points it is very garbled.

[54] *CPR, 1343-1345*, 34, 39.

[55] *Ibid.*, 215.

[56] For the agreement see Dugdale, *Monasticon*, iii. 389.

[57] *CPR, 1343-1345*, 329.

[58] *List of Diplomatic Documents, Scottish Documents and Papal Bulls in the Public Record Office* (Lists and Indexes, xlix, reprinted 1963), 295 (for S.C.7/64/76).

[59] Matthew, *Norman Monasteries*, p.136. See also Mosley, *History*, p.273.

The colleges' endowments generally included the advowsons of parish churches. In 1331 John XXII permitted the appropriation to Oriel College, Oxford, of the churches of Aberford, Coleby and St. Mary, Oxford.[60] Clement VI in 1349 empowered the bishop of London to appropriate two, three or four parish churches up to the value of £100 to Pembroke College, Cambridge,[61] and four letters issued by Clement's successors confirmed or amplified his concession.[62] Sometimes the pope did not have sufficient information to act and he commissioned ecclesiastics in England to investigate a request on his behalf. In 1360, ten years after the foundation of Trinity Hall at Cambridge, Simon de Sudbury, as executor of the will of William Bateman, bishop of Norwich and founder of Trinity Hall, petitioned Innocent VI to confirm a document concerning the foundation, statutes and endowment of the college. Since the document could not be sent to the curia without risk because of the wars then raging, the pope ordered the bishops of Winchester and Rochester and the abbot of Westminster to examine it and send him a transcript of it.[63] Similarly, when William of Wykeham in 1371 requested permission to acquire certain ecclesiastical property for the endowment of what was to become New College, Oxford, Gregory XI ordered the bishops of Worcester and Exeter and the prior of Lewes to inquire into the matter and report to him what they found. The letter states that Wykeham's intention was to increase the number of *scolares* at the university of Oxford from sixty to a hundred.[64]

In the Avignon period for the first time common letters in favour of individuals predominate over those in favour of institutions. Among letters in favour of individuals, provisions to benefices have received the

---

[60] G. Mollat, *Jean XXII: lettres communes* (16 vols., BEFAR, 1904-33), x, nos.54082, 54086-7; *Oriel College Records*, ed. C.L. Shadwell and H.E. Salter (Oxford Historical Society, 1926), pp.444, 485, 489; Oriel College Archives, Coleby 21.

[61] *CPL*, iii. 306.

[62] Pembroke College Archives, Waresley A 15 (Urban V), Tylney C 2, Waresley B 1-2 (Gregory XI). These letters were not used by Hilary Jenkinson in 'Mary de Sancto Paulo, Foundress of Pembroke College, Cambridge', *Archaeologia*, lxvi (1914-15), 401-46, or by other historians of the college.

[63] Reg. Av. 144, ff.270v-1, cap. 119. I am very grateful to Dr. Sandra Raban for supplying me with a photocopy of this entry. The letter is rehearsed in a document issued by its addressees which is briefly mentioned in *Warren's Book*, ed. A.W.W. Dale (Cambridge, 1911), p.225.

[64] New College Archives, 9837: 'cupiens . . . numerum scolarium universitatis predicte, qui de sexaginta scolaribus esse dinoscitur, usque ad numerum centum pauperum scolarium indigentium, aliunde vite necessaria non habentium, ac proficere cupientium in artibus supradictis [*scil.* omnibus liberalibus artibus], in dicta universitate de suis propriis sustantiis . . . statuere et fundare . . .' Cf. R.L. Storey, in *New College Oxford, 1379-1979* ed. J. Buxton and P. Williams (Oxford, 1979), p.39 n.11, where it is shown that Wykeham was supporting forty to sixty scholars in 1376-7.

greatest attention from historians.[65] As far as England is concerned, the fourteenth century represents the high-point of papal influence on appointments in the church. This was when the popes established a virtual monopoly of appointments to bishoprics and when many more provisions to minor benefices were made than before or afterwards. Modern writers about papal provisions have examined a number of wide-ranging themes; for instance, papal reservations of benefices and other aspects of papal policy, the procedure followed in the curia in bestowing benefices, and opposition to provisors and the extent to which they were successful in obtaining their benefices. I shall consider a narrower subject which has received relatively little attention: the text and phraseology of the letters of provision themselves. Does the study of these yield any insights of value to the historian of the English church?

Papal letters concerning the appointment of bishops, abbots and priors (*litterae de provisionibus praelatorum*) give an account of the circumstances of the appointment, including a statement of the legal basis of the pope's action. In the case of direct provisions (as opposed to confirmations of elections), this was most often a general or special reservation. Sometimes the letter mentions that the provision followed a disputed or undisputed election which the pope had quashed,[66] but on other occasions when there had been an election it is ignored.[67] The most informative letters are those in which the pope confirmed an election, since an account of it may be given. John XXII's confirmation of the election of Simon de Meopham as archbishop of Canterbury in 1328 records that the monks of Christ Church proceeded *per viam compromissi*. Three monks were chosen and they in turn chose seven other monks as *compromissarii* who elected Meopham. These ten monks are all named.[68] Papal letters confirming elections also

---

[65] See G. Mollat, *La collation des bénéfices ecclésiastiques à l'époque des papes d'Avignon* (BEFAR, 1921), which is the introduction to his calendar of the common letters of John XXII; B. Guillemain, *La politique bénéficiale du pape Benoît XII* (Paris, 1952); L. Caillet, *La papauté d'Avignon et l'église de France: la politique bénéficiale du pape Jean XXII en France* (Paris, 1975). On the application of papal provisions in England see Pantin, *English Church in the Fourteenth Century*, pp.47-75; J.R. Wright, *The Church and the English Crown, 1305-1334* (Toronto, 1980), pt.I. On the earlier period see H. Baier, *Päpstliche Provisionen für niedere Pfründen bis zum Jahre 1304* (Münster im W., 1911); K. Ganzer, *Papsttum und Bistumsbesetzung in der Zeit von Gregor IX. bis Bonifaz VIII.* (Cologne, 1968). G. Barraclough's excellent study *Papal Provisions* (Oxford, 1935) covers both the thirteenth and the fourteenth centuries.

[66] E.g., in 1361 Innocent VI quashed the elections of Lewis de Charlton and John Barnet to the see of Hereford as contrary to his reservation of the see: BL, Cotton Cleopatra E ii, ff.100-1. This letter, and the letters concerning episcopal appointments in the PRO cited in the following notes, are recommendations of the new bishop to the king of England. Such letters closely follow the wording of the main letter addressed to the bishop himself.

[67] E.g., Innocent VI's letter of 1353 in favour of Gilbert de Welton, bishop-elect of Carlisle, does not mention that initially John de Horncastle had been elected: PRO, S.C.7/54/1.

[68] PRO, S.C.7/56/19.

refer to the *processus informativus*, the investigation by three cardinals into the conduct of the election and the character of the elect.[69] Whether provided by the pope or elected, the candidate for episcopal office was expected to be of a high standard of morality and learning.[70] It is not clear what means were used in the Avignon period to examine the qualities of men whom the pope provided to bishoprics,[71] although the letters of provision commonly allude to the provisors, 'litterarum scientia' and 'morum et vite honestas', about which the pope is said to have learnt by reliable testimony. What is clear is that these and other laudatory expressions about the appointee cannot be regarded as expressing the pope's personal view of him.[72] However, letters of provision provide some information about new bishops. With a graduate, the degree that he held is mentioned; and when someone was below the canonical age for promotion to the episcopate his approximate age is given.[73]

While provisions to major benefices resulted from decisions taken by the pope in consistory, provisions to lesser benefices were made in response to petitions submitted to the pope or the vicechancellor. The most elusive provisions are expectatives *in forma pauperum*. These were provisions in favour of poor clerks, that is clerks who did not already hold a benefice.[74] In the fourteenth century such provisions were not registered unless they were in favour of graduates. Few expectatives for non-graduates have been traced compared to the large numbers which must have been issued.[75]

Other provisions will be found in their thousands in the papal registers. They add to our knowledge of the careers and status of their beneficiaries,

[69] Cf. J.B. Sägmüller, *Die Thätigkeit und Stellung der Cardinäle bis Bonifaz VIII.* (Freiburg im Br., 1896), pp.68-9.

[70] Cf. X 1. 6. 6 (*Corpus Juris Canonici*, ed. E. Friedberg (2 vols., Leipzig, 1879-82), ii. 53): 'nullus in episcopum eligatur, nisi qui . . . vita et scientia commendabilis demonstretur'.

[71] The references for the early history of the *processus informativus* given by H. Fokciński, 'Conferimento dei benefici ecclesiastici maggiori nella Curia Romana', *Rivista di Storia della Chiesa in Italia*, xxxv (1981), 334-54, at 335 n.3, all concern papal confirmations of elections or postulations.

[72] N.M. Fryde's comments on John XXII's provision of John Stratford to the see of Winchester ('John Stratford, Bishop of Winchester, and the Crown, 1323-30', *BIHR*, xliv (1971), 153-61, at 154) need to be amended accordingly. See also R.M. Haines, *Archbishop John Stratford* (Toronto, 1986), p.138 n.96. In the case of a bishop translated from one see to another, the general description of his merits was replaced by a reference to his having governed his earlier see well.

[73] Henry de Burghersh, provided to the see of Lincoln in 1320 by John XXII, is described as 29 years old or thereabouts: PRO, S.C.7/56/11 (*Foedera*, II, i. 425).

[74] See C. Tihon, 'Les expectatives *in forma pauperum* particulièrement au XIVe siècle', *Bulletin de l'Institut historique belge de Rome*, v (1925), 51-118.

[75] An example, dated 12 January 1306, is PRO, S.C.7/44/19 (printed from a notarial transcript of this original in Prynne, *An Exact Chronological Vindication*, iii. 1078-9). See also G.P. Cuttino, *English Diplomatic Administration, 1259-1339* (2nd edn., Oxford, 1971), p.38 n.3. The provision is in favour of Elias Joneston.

particularly because any benefices which a provisor already held are listed in one of the *non obstantibus* clauses.[76] The wording of the *arengae* used in letters of provision deserves attention. Johannes Haller pointed this out some ninety years ago, in publishing the *Modus expediendi litteras apostolicas* of 1525 by Jacobus Dittens, but subsequent historians seem to have ignored the implications of this treatise.[77] The *Modus* notes that, if the petitioner was absent from the curia, a single letter of provision with the incipit 'Dignum arbitramur et rationi congruum' was issued, addressed to a prelate or a cathedral canon as executor of the provision. If the petitioner was present in the curia, two letters were issued and three executors appointed, of whom one was resident in the curia. In the case of a graduate the incipit of the letters was 'Litterarum scientia, vite ac morum honestas', otherwise it was 'Vite ac morum honestas'.[78] The comments of the *Modus* can be applied to fourteenth-century letters. A letter of 29 July 1374 with the incipit 'Dignum arbitramur et congruum' orders a bishop to confer a benefice on a cleric, having first examined him to see if he was suitable to hold the benefice.[79] The reference to the examination suggests that the cleric was not present in the curia and so could not be examined there. Conversely two letters with the incipit 'Vite ac morum honestas' were issued in 1346 to provide Richard de Aston to a canonry with expectation of a prebend, one addressed to Aston and the other addressed to three executors.[80] The executors were not specifically charged with examining Aston; no doubt he was present in the curia and examined there. A similar provision for John de Clifford in 1371 has the incipit 'Litterarum scientia, vite ac morum honestas', because he was said to be 'licentiatus in legibus'.[81] Other *arengae* were, it seems, also used in letters for provisors who were present in the curia.[82]

---

[76] This also applies to dispensations which permitted a cleric to hold two or more incompatible benefices: we thus have an impressive list of the benefices which the young Thomas Arundel had accumulated in a letter of 17 March 1372 which formerly served as a wrapper for Cambridge University Library, Ely Dean and Chapter Muniments, 1/A/3. See also M. Aston, *Thomas Arundel* (Oxford, 1967), pp.7-8.

[77] J. Haller, 'Die Ausfertigung der Provisionen', *Quellen und Forschungen aus Italienischen Archiven und Bibliotheken*, ii (1899), 1-40. Cf. K.A. Fink, 'Arengen spätmittelalterlicher Papsturkunden', in *Mélanges E. Tisserant*, iv (Vatican City, 1964), 205-27. The *arengae* are referred to below by their incipits, which are of course also the incipits of the texts of the letters.

[78] Haller, 'Ausfertigung der Provisionen', pp.22-3.

[79] Lewes, East Sussex Record Office, Ashburnham Archives, 2962, concerning a benefice in Italy.

[80] *CPL*, iii. 220. The letter to the executors survives in the original: PRO, S.C.7/13/19 (*Foedera*, III, i. 82-3).

[81] The letter serves as a wrapper for York Minster Library, Dean and Chapter Muniments, M2(3)a.

[82] E.g., 'Sedis apostolice circumspecta', 'Dum ad personam', 'Meritis tue probitatis', 'Probitatis et virtutum'.

The existence of a letter of provision does not necessarily mean that the provision took effect.[83] It was left to the executors, whose powers were considerable, to implement it,[84] and the provisor might face competition or opposition. Nevertheless, letters of provision are a fundamental source for anyone wishing to form a general picture of the English clergy in the fourteenth century. Unfortunately, from the pontificate of Innocent VI until the end of the Avignon period, a substantial proportion of provisions to English benefices is unpublished. The main reason for this has already been mentioned: the reliance of the *Calendar of Papal Letters* on the increasingly selective Vatican Registers. It may be worth considering the implications of this situation in an area which is now receiving much attention, the careers of university clerks. A number of recent writers have adopted a quantitative approach to the subject on the basis of the computerization of information in A.B. Emden's *Biographical Registers* of the universities of Oxford and Cambridge.[85] These admirable volumes do not in general draw on the provisions and other papal letters concerning the careers of university clerks in the unpublished Avignon Registers. It is therefore possible that a statistical analysis deriving from the *Biographical Registers* may present a distorted picture. Mr. Aston and his collaborators noted that the second quarter of the fourteenth century saw a large increase in the proportion of university men who obtained preferment, while the second half of the century saw a fall back to a lower proportion.[86] Is it a coincidence that from the middle of the century large numbers of letters of provision are omitted from the Vatican Registers and hence from the *Calendar of Papal Letters* and publications which depend on it? One must not exaggerate the effect of these omissions on the statistics: some of

---

[83] See F. Baix, 'De la valeur historique des actes pontificaux de collation des bénéfices', in *Hommage à Dom Ursmer Berlière* (Brussels, 1931), 57-66; Barraclough, *Papal Provisions*, ch.3.

[84] G. Barraclough, 'The Executors of Papal Provisions in the Canonical Theory of the Thirteenth and the Fourteenth Centuries', in *Acta Congressus Iuridici Internationalis Romae 12-17 Novembris 1934*, iii (Rome, 1936), 109-53. See also *idem*, *Public Notaries and the Papal Curia* (London, 1934).

[85] A.B. Emden, *A Biographical Register of the University of Oxford to A.D. 1500*, 3 vols. (Oxford, 1957-9), and *A Biographical Register of the University of Cambridge to 1500* (Cambridge, 1963). See T.H. Aston, 'Oxford's Medieval Alumni', *Past and Present*, no.74 (1977), 3-40; T.H. Aston, G.D. Duncan and T.A.R. Evans, 'The Medieval Alumni of the University of Cambridge', *ibid.*, no.86 (1980), 9-86; J.A. Brundage, 'English-Trained Canonists in the Middle Ages', in *Law-Making and Law-Makers in British History*, ed. A. Harding (London, 1980), pp.64-78; A.B. Cobban, 'The Medieval Cambridge Colleges: a Quantitative Study of Higher Degrees', *History of Education*, ix (1980), 1-12. G.F. Lytle, 'Patronage Patterns and Oxford Colleges, c.1300-c.1530', in *The University in Society*, ed. L. Stone (2 vols., Princeton, 1975), i. 111-49, was written without use of the computerization of Emden. See also R.N. Swanson, 'Universities, Graduates and Benefices in Later Medieval England', *Past and Present*, no.106 (1985), 28-61.

[86] Aston, Duncan and Evans, 'Alumni of Cambridge', pp.83-4.

the information about provisions is likely to be available from sources other than the papal registers, notably episcopal registers; and the figures concern all types of preferment, not just preferment to ecclesiastical benefices. On the other hand, it should be remembered that the system of papal provisions tended to favour graduates. Some kinds of graduates could receive a provision without undergoing the usual examination *in litteratura*.[87] Half of the known provisions of Benedict XII to benefices in England were in favour of graduates.[88] It is not surprising that the universities complained vigorously when papal provisions were curtailed from the reign of Richard II.[89] One can indeed expect the omission of the material in the Avignon Registers to have had some influence on the statistics. It can be said with greater confidence that for the same reasons Guy Fitch Lytle's conclusion that there was a sharp decline in papal patronage of Oxford graduates after 1350 is in need of revision.[90] When the publication by the École française de Rome of the indexes to the registers of common letters of Urban V is complete, it will be possible to assess the contribution to be made by the Avignon Registers for one pontificate.[91]

C.R. Cheney in his remarkable essay, 'The letters of Pope Innocent III', noted that his analysis tended to reduce the historical value of the letters.[92] Some considerations regarding Innocent III's letters also apply to those of the Avignon popes. Historians must beware of being over-impressed by the rhetoric, often skilfully deployed, of papal letters. A more serious problem is that it was difficult for the popes to gain accurate information about events far from the curia. The pope's ignorance is reflected in those letters where, using a phrase like 'de premissis certam notitiam non habemus', he ordered an ecclesiastic *in partibus* to investigate the subject of a petition on his behalf.[93] Caution may be necessary as regards the narratives in all types of papal letters from Avignon. Thinking that the see of Down was vacant, Innocent VI provided Gregory O Mochain to it and had him consecrated bishop at the curia. It was then found that the see was not vacant, and O Mochain therefore had the distinction for a short time of being an 'episcopus nullius ecclesie'.[94] Letters of justice, delegating a judge or judges to hear a case *in partibus*,

---

[87] Mollat, *La collation des bénéfices ecclésiastiques*, pp.44-5.

[88] Guillemain, *La politique bénéficiale du pape Benoît XII*, p.82.

[89] See, e.g., E.F. Jacob, *Essays in the Conciliar Epoch*, 3rd edn. (Manchester, 1963), pp.219-20, 239.

[90] Lytle, 'Patronage Patterns', p.128; apparently accepted by Swanson, 'Universities, Graduates and Benefices', p.43.

[91] See above n.20.

[92] C.R. Cheney, *Medieval Texts and Studies* (Oxford, 1973), pp.16-38.

[93] See above p.269.

[94] See his subsequent provision to the see of Elphin: *Vetera Monumenta Hibernorum et Scotorum Historiam illustrantia*, ed. A. Theiner (Rome, 1864), no.628; PRO, S.C.7/54/3.

present the greatest problems. They were issued at the request of one party in a dispute and no doubt his statement of the case tended to be partisan. The opposing party had the opportunity to 'contradict' the letter in the *audientia publica*, but this depended on his having a proctor there. Yet to suggest that papal letters in the Avignon period are over-rated as a source would be unwarranted. For certain pontificates the proportion of papal letters which have been adequately published is small, and relatively few English historians have made use of the unpublished material. Even when letters have been published, a close examination of their contents may be rewarding. The letters of Clement V used earlier to throw new light on his relations with the kings of England have all been published. Finally, papal letters in the fourteenth century were the products of a rather complex administrative machine. A knowledge of the papal administration, and particularly of the process in the chancery and other departments of the curia by which the letters were issued, will assist the historian to avoid misunderstandings about the letters and to maximize the information that can be extracted from them.

Chapter 15

The Effects of War on the Church:
The Case of the Alien Priories in the Fourteenth Century[1]

Alison McHardy

At the parliament held in the early summer of 1379 a committee of prelates and lords was set up, at the commons' request, 'to examine the estate of the king'. Its brief was, 'First to examine the revenues arising from the subsidies on wools', during the financial year beginning Michaelmas 1378, and, 'also, to supervise all the revenues of the realm received during the said time, as well as the revenues of alien priories, and of the ancient maltolt of wools, of the voidance of bishoprics, abbacies and all other profits whatsoever'.[2] It was rare for alien priories to achieve such prominence in national politics. True, alien monks, like other foreigners, attracted unfavourable notice in wartime from patriotic M.P.s.[3] But the political public seldom showed itself aware of the importance of the property and patronage owned by foreign ecclesiastics, an importance which was, however, well recognized by the English crown and its servants from the reign of Edward I. Alien priories are a particularly suitable subject for inclusion in a volume devoted to England and her neighbours from 1066 to 1453; they were the product of the Norman Conquest, and their history from 1295 was shaped, very largely, by the Anglo-French wars. This history may, therefore, be read as a commentary upon the relations between England and France, and also as a contribution to discussion of non-combatants' fortunes in wartime. Two distinguished monographs have not exhausted the rich sources for study of the subject,[4] and the present essay seeks to illustrate some of the

[1] Much of the research on which this paper is based was made possible by a generous grant from the Wolfson Foundation. I wish also to record my thanks to Mrs. Dalton, archivist of New College, for her help and interest in my work on the records of Takeley priory. Thanks are due to the Warden and Scholars of New College, Oxford for permission to print the documents in the appendix, and to Professor J.C. Laidlaw and Dr. G. Hesketh for advice on Anglo-Norman language.

[2] *Rot. Parl.*, iii. 55. The parliament met from 24 April to 27 May, *Handbook of British Chronology*, ed. E.G. Fryde, D.E. Greenway, S. Porter & I. Roy, 3rd ed. (London, 1986), p.564.

[3] For example, in 1346, 1377, 1380, *Rot. Parl.*, ii. 191, iii. 22, 96.

[4] Marjorie Morgan, *The England Lands of the Abbey of Bec* (Oxford, 1946); Donald Matthew, *Norman Monasteries and their English Possessions* (Oxford, 1962).

rewards which these may yet yield.

The piety and generosity of the Norman Conquest's beneficiaries resulted in the creation of religious houses which were dependent on northern French, especially Norman, abbeys, wherever the settlers penetrated. Most of course were in England and along the Welsh Marches,[5] but examples could be found in Ireland,[6] and in Scotland too.[7] Another wave of colonisation, that of southern Scotland by the Anglo-Normans, produced a similar crop of foundations dependent on foreign abbeys; Scotland's equivalent of 'alien priories' were daughter houses of Durham, Reading and Rievaulx.[8] Coinciding with this 'international' generosity, movements of monastic reform, many emanating from France, resulted in greater centralisation among the newer orders. Not all the donations to far-off recipients were of resources sufficient in size to found priories, or even cells; manors, or much smaller pieces of land, rents, advowsons, tithes, town houses, any of these could be, and were, given. And although most grantees were abbeys, other religious corporations, such as hospitals and cathedral chapters, also benefited.[9] Some of these gifts cannot ever have been greatly profitable to their owners, for it needed neither intervening ocean nor problems caused by war to make possession of distant properties a doubtful asset.[10] In some cases administration used up all the revenues arising from income.[11]

These problems became much worse as a result of political intervention by the English crown during the later middle ages. The practice of seizing lands and rights on a large scale began with John's confiscation of all church property following Innocent III's imposition of the Interdict in 1208.[12] Devised by John in a fit of temper, the policy was enthusiastically embraced by governments ever after under a variety of ideological, theological or political slogans. In the later middle ages the cause was 'patriotism', and it was on this pretext that in 1295 Edward I seized all English property held by foreign ecclesiastics.[13] It was Edward I's

[5] And in the Channel Islands.

[6] A. Gwynn and R.N. Hadcock, *Medieval Religious Houses: Ireland* (London, 1970), p.104.

[7] Cambuskenneth, Stirlings., dependent on Arrouaise, D.E. Easson, *Medieval Religious Houses: Scotland* (London, 1957), p.74.

[8] *Ibid.*, pp.49, 53, 55, 64, 65.

[9] E.g., the chapters of Rouen and Coutances.

[10] See the problems posed to Dryburgh Abbey by its property in Northants. in the thirteenth century, Keith Stringer, 'The Early Lords of Lauderdale, Dryburgh Abbey and St. Andrew's Priory at Northampton', in *Essays on the Nobility of Medieval Scotland*, ed. K.J. Stringer (Edinburgh, 1985), pp.44-71.

[11] A.J. Taylor, 'The Alien Priory of Minster Lovell', *Oxoniensia*, ii (1937), 103-17 details one such example.

[12] C.R. Cheney, 'King John's Reaction to the Interdict on England', *TRHS*, fourth series, xxxi (1949), 129-50.

[13] Marjorie Morgan, 'The Suppression of the Alien Priories', *History*, 26 (1941), 205.

government which formulated the excuses under colour of which the seizures were made; coined the term 'alien priories' to describe these properties; and devised the system by which they were exploited to the crown's profit with a minimum of effort by its own servants. The political slogans and administrative procedures of this first period (1295-1303) proved so serviceable that they were employed on those subsequent occasions on which alien priories were taken into the crown's control (1324-7, 1337-60, 1369 onwards). Edward III and his successors during the Hundred Years War were not, therefore, originators of the policy towards alien priories but they developed it considerably.

The excuses for seizure of alien priories during time of war with France were these: that foreign monks were enemy spies and that they exported money from the realm with the result that the English war effort was weakened whilst the enemy profited. The cry of 'spy' accords ill with a succession of examples of alien priors acting as servants of the English crown, as messengers and diplomats,[14] providers of hospitality,[15] collectors of clerical taxes,[16] and, ironically, as commissioners of array 'in view of French imminent invasion'.[17] There was also the episode of the heroic defence of the town of Lewes in 1377 by the French-born prior of Lewes' alien priory.[18] The charge of exporting money cannot be denied since not all priories and properties were insignificant, and it was to support their mother houses that the gifts had originally been made. We may doubt, though, whether their English revenues would greatly have enhanced the French war effort. In any case, during the peace following the treaty of Brétigny the main concern of at least one of the French mother abbeys, Fécamp, was not with bullion but with the import of food.[19]

The real motive for the seizures was greed, and in their dealings with the alien priories the goverments both of Edward III and Richard II showed themselves harsh, muddled, inconsistent and inefficient. The muddle began with the description 'alien priory' – not an ecclesiastical

[14] A.K. McHardy, 'The Alien Priories and the Expulsion of Aliens from England in 1378', *Studies in Church History*, 12 (1975), 134.

[15] The prior of Tickford (Bucks.) lodged Richard II on his way to Scotland in 1385, *CPR, 1385-89*, 201.

[16] But the prior of Albury and his colleague, a local rector, commissioned by the bishop of Hereford to collect the clerical tenth granted in 9 Richard II were in disgrace because they 'do not trouble to account for the said tenth', 12 December 1390, *Calendar of Fine Rolls, 1383-91*, 340.

[17] The prior of Prittlewell was commissioned in the hundred of Rochford, Essex, 26 April 1385, *CPR, 1381-85*, 590.

[18] *Historia Vitae et Regni Ricardi Secundi*, ed. G.B. Stow (Pennsylvania, 1977), p. 48.

[19] Licences for the shipment of 60 gammons of bacon and six dozen cheeses (5 May 1365) and 200 quarters of wheat and 12 dozen cheeses (18 June 1365) in order to sustain the abbot and monks of Fécamp, *CPR, 1364-67*, 106, 128.

term but a political label which was attached to any property in the ownership of foreign ecclesiastics. The seizure of property in 1337 took in 'priories, houses, benefices, lands, places, goods and chattels of religious and other aliens',[20] that is, anything which could be exploited for the crown's gain. Given the complexity of the properties, chattels and rights involved it is scarcely surprising that the royal administration was soon floundering in a morass of manors, jurisdictions, monastic rules, pensions, bailiwicks, advowsons and tithes, and was hitting out with terminological inexactitude in a way which disconcerted contemporaries and confuses posterity. Thus Hornchurch (Essex) was in 1389 described as a 'church or house', and a month later as 'the church, monastery or house'. This confusion created difficulties for the bishop of Aire who had been granted custody 'but which he cannot obtain because he holds the custody and farm under the description of "the church and rectory of Hornchurch with all its possessions in Essex and Kent" . . . and not under the description "the priory of Hornchirche" . . .'[21] References to 'priories or manors' became more frequent in the later fourteenth century as political and, more especially financial, pressures reduced, or even extinguished, monastic life in small houses.[22] Not all confusion began at home; since 'alien' was synonymous with 'enemy' some foreign houses with interests in England found themselves treated as supporters of the French cause when, they claimed, this was not the case. So in 1358 St. Mary's Abbey, Langonnet, Brittany, successfully petitioned for the restitution of a £10 rent seized on account of the war, 'because the king is sufficiently informed the abbot and convent are of his fealty and obedience'. Soon after, the Norman house of St. Fromond recovered a Lincolnshire rectory which had been seized and farmed out to king's clerks, because Edward III's 'kinsman Philip de Navarre has certified by letter that the prior and monks have now come into the king's obedience, and are adherents of his party'.[23] In view of this imprecise terminology and muddled thinking it is perhaps not surprising that the crown's treatment of 'alien religious and others' was inconsistent. There were differing policies towards different orders: Cistercians escaped seizure but Cluniacs did not; houses which paid substantial pensions to French abbeys could go unmolested,[24] while insignificant cells which can rarely have shown a profit were taken into

[20] *CFR, 1337-47*, 36-7.

[21] 5 November, 18 December, 1389, 4 July 1390, *CPR, 1388-92*, 207, 262, 277.

[22] E.g., Cammeringham 'manor otherwise called the priory', 1395, *CPR, 1391-96*, 579; 'the manors called priories of Frampton . . . Paunfeld . . . with the manor called the priory or house of Welle . . .', 17 April and 21 May 1399, *CPR, 1396-99*, 559, 579; Swavesey and Dry Drayton 'which manors under the name of "the alien priory of Swavesey" . . .' *ibid*, 579.

[23] 10 and 30 March 1358, *CPR, 1358-61*, 23, 33.

[24] Spalding (Lincs.) owed £40 *p.a.* to St. Nicholas, Angers, and Thornton (Lincs.) owed £20 *p.a.* to Aumale, *CCR, 1369-74*, 43, 44.

custody; hospitals dependent on a mother house in nearby Boulogne escaped unscathed while those with more distant connections, in Savoy, for example, found themselves in the king's hand during the French war.[25]

Although the crown's hold on alien church endowments was not all-embracing it was, nevertheless, both very widespread and very profitable. The benefits it derived were of two kinds; one was ecclesiastical patronage, the other was money. Ecclesiastical patronage was retained by the crown when it granted away custody of the priories and other properties. This was a universal rule; only a single exception (to be discussed below) has been found. The result was that the crown greatly increased the amount of patronage at its disposal; the Patent Rolls record thousands of presentations made by the crown to benefices temporarily in its hands during the war. Systematic study of these presentations is yet to be made, but it may well reveal that king's clerks were the main beneficiaries.

The other advantage the crown looked for was financial. Having seized the priories and other lands, it granted them to keepers who were to pay an annual farm at the exchequer. It is doubtful, though, if the exchequer actually received much cash, for the crown used the farms to make grants to those whom the king wished, or felt he ought, to favour. The farmers were instructed to hand the money to the grantees, to obtain acquittances and to return these to the exchequer in full or part payment of the farm.[26] The beneficiaries of such grants would repay careful study; although not, of course, the only source of largesse at the crown's disposal, the revenue expected from alien priories offered a welcome, and flexible, extension to its ability to show generosity, yet with no diminution of its own resources. Grants from the farms of alien priories are a good indication of the fortunes of individuals (William Latimer and Simon Burley are good examples) and, it may be suggested, they offer a useful test of the political character of, and changes at, court. A few examples of such royal favour must suffice. In March 1338 the French emigré, Robert of Artois, was granted 800 marks a year, during pleasure, and was to take this sum from ten alien priories, plus Bec's bailiwick of Ogbourne.[27] Early in 1360 John Beauchamp of Warwick, younger brother of Earl Thomas, and one of the original Garter Knights, was granted £300 a year, of which half was to

---

[25] Farley (Beds.) and Ludgershall (Bucks.) dependent on Saintingfeld, David Knowles and R.N. Hadcock, *Medieval Religious Houses: England and Wales*, 2nd ed. (London 1971) pp.320, 326. Seized and farmed was Hornchurch, dependent on St. Bernard, Montjoux, *ibid.*, p.323.

[26] Mandates to pay part of the farm directly to Juliana, countess of Huntingdon, New College, Oxford, Takeley Charters, T.C. 167, 249; and to Thomas of Woodstock, T.C. 253, 279. See Appendix below pp.289-95.

[27] 26 March; the amount payable by each farmer is specified, *CPR, 1338-40*, 32.

come from the farms of alien properties.[28] Richard Pembridge 'who stays continually by the king's side' (he was a chamber knight) was granted £40 a year from the farm of Ware priory 'for good service in the wars as well as elsewhere'.[29] Despite a scandalous past, the king's life retainer John Dalton received £40 a year from the Suffolk house of Stoke by Clare,[30] while John Ipre, steward of the household, was granted 200 marks a year from Ware in 1376.[31]

Beneficiaries might also act as keepers of priories and properties themselves, with the concession that they could keep some, or all, of the proceeds of the farm. Between 1337 and 1382, when priories were in the hand of the English crown, the normal procedure was for the prior, or the proctor of the foreign house, to act as custodian; and there is no evidence that the crown bore ill-will to priors as a group.[32] Indeed commissions to others sometimes explained why the prior had been passed over for the post of keeper: the prior could not cope;[33] the prior had gone to France and stayed there;[34] or the prior's leprosy prevented him from ruling the house.[35] From the beginning of the war, however, there were exceptions to the rule of appointing the prior as keeper; St. Michael's Mount, perhaps for military reasons, was always farmed to laymen,[36] while two royal Isabels, Edward III's mother and daughter, were committed as farmers, the former of Deerhurst, the latter of Minster Lovell.[38] As we would expect, royal servants were chosen as keepers when the office was committed to outsiders. Thus a king's clerk who had suffered losses in the crown's service overseas was given custody of no less than seven west-country houses in a commission of 3 March 1340.[39] John Darcy, formerly

---

[28] 1 March, *CPR, 1358-61*, 328; *Complete Peerage*, ed. V. Gibbs *et al.* (London, 1910-59), ii. 50.

[29] A duplicate letter patent was issued on 7 February 1361 because he had lost the first one, *CPR, 1358-61*, 539; Chris Given-Wilson, *The Royal Household and the King's Affinity* (Yale, 1986), pp.160-1, 170, 173, 208.

[30] He had already surrendered this grant by 2 May 1363, *CPR, 1361-64*, 344. For Dalton's past, see T.F. Tout, *Chapters in the Administrative History of Medieval England* (Manchester, 1928), iv. 130 n.7.

[31] 8 January, *CPR, 1374-77*, 399.

[32] McHardy, 'Alien Priories', 136-8.

[33] Commitment of Swavesey to John Grey of Ruthin because the prior 'has surrendered the keeping into the king's hand, asserting that he cannot answer for the farm and support other charges and praying the king to commit the same to another', 10 April 1348, *CFR, 1347-56*, 77.

[34] Brother William Naget, prior of Panfield and Wells, had gone to France without permission and had left no deputy, but another French monk, Brother William Pougier, was appointed as keeper in his place, 6 August 1351, *ibid.*, 303.

[35] Folkestone, 22 July 1386, *CFR, 1383-91*, 147.

[36] Matthew, *Norman Monasteries*, p.109.

[37] Commission, 20 April 1345, *CFR, 1337-47*, 419.

[38] Dimission of office, 22 October 1366, *CPR, 1358-61*, 474.

[39] Thomas Crosse. His farms varied between 10 marks and £100, *CFR, 1337-47*, 165.

steward of the household, had been granted £40 a year from the farm of Minster Lovell; unable to extract the cash from its prior, he was given the custody himself in 1353.[40] Simon Burley's rise to fortune is symbolized by his acquisition of farms of properties belonging to Fécamp abbey: the Gloucestershire manors of Cheltenham in 1374 and Slaughter in 1378, and an inn in London's Thames Street a year later.[41] The implication must be that, even when paying the full farm, the keeper still expected to realise a profit.

The expectations of outsiders who were granted annuities or keeperships may not, though, have been entirely fulfilled. For in their anxiety to make profits out of the priories, both the crown and the outsiders imposed as keepers inflicted severe economic damage upon them, and it was this, above all, which was responsible for severing the links with mother houses on the continent. From 1342, when efforts were made to raise the farms in force since the beginning of the war,[42] to 1387, when proclamation was ordered in five midland counties soliciting higher tenders for priory farms,[43] the crown sought to maximize income from this source. Laymen responded to this call more readily than did priors,[44] and changes in custody were surely often the result of bargains struck between financial speculators and the exchequer. Outside keepers undertook to provide for the monks they found *in situ*[45] and as the numbers of these were reduced by death and deportation the priories should, in theory, have been capable of supporting modest rises in farms; the interest of parliament in 1379 was probably caused by the expulsion of over 100 French monks in the previous year.[46] Perhaps M.P.s thought that an overall rise in the farms was now possible.

If so, they were very much mistaken. For the evidence is overwhelming that the priories had been farmed at too high a rate since the beginning of the war.[47] Faced with the exchequer's demands, the keepers had two options: to sell off assets and neglect repairs in order to meet current needs, or to allow their farms to pile up arrears of debt to the crown. There is considerable evidence that outside keepers tended to take the former course while priors preferred the latter. Thus in 1340 Tutbury was

[40] There were three John Darcys, Tout, *Chapters*, vi. 220; 18 June, *CFR, 1347-56*, 564.

[41] 12 July 1374, *CPR, 1370-74*, 461; 18 May 1378, 5 July 1379, *CPR, 1377-81*, 223, 371.

[42] There is evidence that at least eleven priories had their farms raised this year; that of Ware increased from £230 to £245 *p.a.*, *CFR, 1337-47*, 259, 266, 267.

[43] Lincs., Leics., Notts., Derbys., Rutland, 5 February 1387, *CPR, 1385-89*, 317.

[44] E.g. *CFR, 1347-56*, 427-8; *CPR, 1381-85*, 396-7.

[45] The rate at Stevington in 1357 was 2s. a week for the prior, and 18d. a week for his fellow-monk; 5s. *p.a.* each for clothing; the keeper to provide fuel, *CFR, 1347-56*, 51.

[46] Matthew, *Norman Monasteries*, pp.153-6.

[47] See Rose Graham's calculations concerning the effect of the farm on Wenlock, quoted by Morgan, *History*, 26 (1941), p.205; and the conclusion reached that for the Bec dependencies 'the farms . . . were unreasonably high', Morgan, *Lands of Bec*, p.121.

returned to the custody of its prior because 'many destructions and damage have been committed by the king's ministers and others'; two years later Wenlock was also restored to its prior for the same reason.[48] In 1355 Brother Michael de Ganiaco, monk of Lyre abbey and its proctor in England, appeared before the council to explain that, 'the manors, woods and other things pertaining thereto, are greatly deteriorated and almost destroyed by reason of the said farm and on account of their occupation by laymen'. The councillors conceded his case and custody was returned to him.[49] From 1375 to the end of the century a stream of commissions was issued to investigate complaints of damage and waste; in many cases names were named, and the apparently-guilty individuals identified as former keepers.[50] The priors preferred the way of indebtedness. This apparent inefficiency was not their fault; not only were the farms demanded unrealistically high, the priors were themselves creditors who had difficulty securing payment of loans and gathering rent.[51] And they did not always receive the support from the crown which their situation merited.[52] Faced by widespread shortfalls in hoped-for revenue, and bombarded by petitions for clemency, the crown worked out compromises with each priory individually. Stratfield Saye had its farm remitted altogether; contrariwise, the proctor of Fécamp abbey was given licence to fell oaks and other trees to the value of £40 to enable him to repay arrears of his farm and to repair his properties.[53] Arrears might be written off,[54] or rescheduled,[55] and farms reduced,[56] if only until the old debts were paid off.[57]

In the light of this unsatisfactory financial situation it is interesting to consider one particular grant of moneys to be drawn from the farms, the £1,000 a year given to Thomas of Woodstock. Edward III's youngest son was created earl of Buckingham at the start of Richard II's reign, on 16

---

[48]　13 April 1340, 5 February 1342, *CFR, 1337-47,* 175, 258.

[49]　*CFR, 1347-56,* 427-8.

[50]　E.g., commission to examine the case against John Bromwych lately farmer of properties of the abbess of Caen in five counties; and pardon to Bromwych's widow and executors of his waste and trespasses while keeper; 29 May and 17 August 1389,*CPR, 1388-92,* 61, 100. For similar examples, see *CPR, 1396-9,* 53, 506.

[51]　The prior of Takeley was given assistance in gathering overdue rents, 10 February 1343, *CPR, 1343-45,* 11.

[52]　Pardons were granted to two debtors of Ware, in June and December, 1384, *CPR, 1381-85,* 394, 479.

[53]　1 July 1359, 12 November 1358, *CPR, 1358-61,* 246, 118-9.

[54]　£168 13s.4d. arrears of Takeley's farm were pardoned, 26 May 1351, *CPR, 1350-54,* 98; Creeting was excused its debt of £22 13s.4d. on 1 May 1360, *CPR, 1358-61,* 356.

[55]　Modbury successfully negotiated such a scheme on 8 December 1356, *CFR, 1356-68,* 24.

[56]　Takeley's increment of £14 *p.a.* was cancelled, 20 September 1343, *CPR, 1343-45,* 117.

[57]　Arrangements of this nature were negotiated by Farley and Wenlock, *CPR, 1358-61,* 82, 230.

July 1377, and on the same day was granted £1,000 a year from the exchequer to support his new status.[58] It has been pointed out that Thomas of Woodstock depended throughout his life upon exchequer grants, never receiving the landed endowment proper to a king's son,[59] but not until we examine this cash grant do we see how ungenerous it was. The money was payable during pleasure, and it was to be derived from the farms of alien priories and other properties of French houses. Woodstock is often perceived as a warmonger, but this grant surely gave him a substantial vested interest in the war's continuance . The £1,000 was to come from eight farms. The lands of the abbess of Caen were to provide £266 13s.4d., and another large sum was to come from Fécamp abbey's English properties (£200). The priories concerned were Ware (£206 13s.4d.), Takeley (£133 6s.8d.), West Mersea and Stoke by Clare (£60 each), Panfield (£40), and Swavesey (£33 6s.8d.).[60] At the time of the grant a number of these houses had already been in serious difficulties. The farm of Fécamp was in debt in 1358.[61] Panfield had run up debts before 1360, and was still paying them off in 1362; the grant to a royal serjeant-at-arms of £20 a year from the arrears suggests that repayment was expected to take some time.[62] The condition of Takeley was probably very serious. Attempts to increase its farm from £126 to £140 in 1342 were abandoned the following year.[63] At the same time the prior had difficulty gathering his rents and was probably leasing property to raise ready money.[64] It had private creditors by the end of 1348,[65] and in 1351, after yet more trouble with tenants, it was pardoned a substantial amount of farm.[66] In 1354 the prior farmed his Middlesex church of Hampton for ten years,[67] and there are references to his debts to the crown, and others, in 1357 and 1358, while in 1359 he was granted a three-year respite from paying the farm.[68] The prior then leased some London properties in an effort to clear his debts to the crown, but was apparently still paying them off in 1363[69] and an amount yet remained in 1384.[70] Thus Woodstock's

---

[58] *CPR, 1377-81*, 60.

[59] Anthony Goodman, *The Loyal Conspiracy* (London, 1971), p.90.

[60] 5 July 1377, *CPR, 1377-81*, 372.

[61] *CPR, 1358-61*, 118-9.

[62] 1 May 1362, *CPR, 1361-64*, 192.

[63] *CFR, 1337-47*, 267; *CPR, 1343-45*, 117.

[64] *Ibid.*, 11; *CFR, 1337-47*, 268.

[65] *CPR, 1348-50*, 216.

[66] Rent arrears, *ibid.*, 525; pardon of £168 13s.4d. 26 May 1351, *CPR, 1350-54*, 98.

[67] New College, Oxford, Takeley Charter no.63.

[68] 24 November 1357, *CFR, 1356-68*, 52; *CCR, 1346-49*, 627.

[69] Houses in Mogwel and Silver Streets, *CPR, 1370-74*, 265; the agreement was made on 1 May 1360; grant to Juliana, widow of the earl of Huntingdon, of 20 marks *p.a.* from the arrears of Takeley's farm, 12 June 1363, *CPR, 1361-64*, 352.

[70] Commission as farmers to the priors of Takeley and of the London Charterhouse, 24 February 1384, 'provided that they pay nothing in respect of arrears before 16 February 1361', *CFR 1383-91*, 39.

grant was not without problems, and despite the assurance that it would be exchanged for a grant of land, this did not speedily happen. The grant was renewed on 24 October 1386,[71] and it was not until 16 November 1390 that £600 of it was exchanged for the manor of Burstwick; in April 1397 Woodstock was still receiving money from Panfield and from Ware.[72] Thus for much of his nephew's reign Thomas had an interest in this group of priories. So it is likely that a commission to five men, headed by Simon Burley as warden of the Cinque Ports, to fell trees on Fécamp property in order to fortify Rye, would scarcely have earned his approval.[73] The Caen properties meanwhile seemed to have suffered a succession of rapacious farmers;[74] it was probably Woodstock's own commission as keeper which brought to light the malpractices of his predecessor, John Bromwych.[75] On the evidence of this royal grant, Thomas of Woodstock, who is often considered something of a political bully, appears as a man with a legitimate grievance against the governments of both the minority and of the majority of Richard II.

The plight of the religious houses which we have been discussing demonstrates how bleak was the outlook for those who had powerful enemies but no firm friends at a time when jingoism was rampant in the political community. What alien priories lacked, almost without exception, was a powerful lay lord close at hand who would protect their interests. The only possible exception was Pontefract, for here the prior and convent were able to retain the advowson of the vicarage of All Saints, Pontefract, the only instance of an alien house retaining any ecclesiastical patronage, and it did so because Henry, duke of Lancaster, petitioned on the prior's behalf.[76] John of Gaunt also took an interest in Pontefract, securing its denization for 100 marks in 1393 – a bargain compared with Lenton's payment of 500 marks in the same cause during the previous year.[77] The only hope of more lenient treatment lay in addressing petitions to the king and to other members of the royal family, the exchequer and the council. From the many references to such requests, it is clear that the documents printed in the appendix are of a type which was once common.

They are petitions, apparently drafts, for they lack dates or any evidence that they were ever sealed; they are stitched together down the left-hand side. Each of the eleven documents is in a different hand, though

---

[71] *CPR, 1385-89*, 233.

[72] *CPR, 1391-96*, 575, 111.

[73] 6 February 1385, *CPR, 1381-85*, 532.

[74] *CPR, 1374-77*, 160; *CPR, 1396-99*, 506.

[75] Commission as keeper to Woodstock 20 September 1388, *CFR, 1383-91*, 278; Bromwych's activities are noted in *CPR, 1388-92*, 61, 100.

[76] Grant, 28 September 1359, *CPR, 1358-61*, 271.

[77] 4 February 1393, 7 October 1392, *CPR, 1391-96*, 215, 196.

several of the headings are in one hand. The writing suggests strongly that these drafts were prepared by king's clerks. This group of documents presents several problems; there seem to be no final versions surviving among the public records; discrepancies between sums of money mentioned in the petitions and in the chancery rolls make it difficult to know if these requests were successful, or indeed, presented; they cannot be dated with precision. They may be discussed in three groups. The first comprises numbers 1, 2 and 6, which are petitions for removal of Lord Latimer from the keepership of the priory, so they can be dated between 3 June 1373 when he was appointed, and 19 July 1376 when the prior succeeded him.[78] The earl of Arundel, to whom no.2 is addressed, was Latimer's father-in-law. Latimer seems to have been an unpopular farmer elsewhere; there was a complaint about his management of Ecclesfield in 1376.[79] The second group, nos.3, 8 and 10, concerns Takeley's interest in Isleworth, part of a substantial holding of Middlesex property. John de Ipre is referred to as farmer of the manor in 13 January 1378 and again in June 1385, though the commission to him to act was dated 19 October 1383.[80] However, a commission to investigate an allegation by the royal steward in Isleworth that the prior of Takeley had withdrawn alms for the king's soul there, was dated back in October 1365.[81] The remaining petitions all concern the farm. They allege that the prior paid £189 at the start of the war – which seems to be true – in order that the priory should not be farmed, and that this agreement was contained in a letter patent in 1340. No such compact exists on the patent roll for that year, though this does not mean that it never existed.[82] It is, however, an unlikely story, for reasons discussed in this essay. Both the references to pestilence in the petitions, and the grants of remission recorded in the patent roll suggest that these date from the decade 1350-60.[83]

The only conclusions to be drawn from the story of the alien priories in the Hundred Years War is that there were no chronological landmarks – neither the 'expulsion' of 1378 nor the 'dissolution' of 1414 were decisive[84] – and that there was no single solution to the problems which the priors, proctors and mother houses faced. The transfer of property took place over more than a century, and was effected with widely varying degrees of eagerness on both sides of the Channel. The story of these houses is thus more varied than has often been allowed, and, it is contended, is of

---

[78] *CFR, 1369-77*, 214, 358.

[79] Matthew, *Norman Monasteries*, p.109 n.1.

[80] *CPR, 1377-81*, 100; *CCR, 1385-89*, 80; *CFR, 1383-91*, 10.

[81] *CPR, 1367-70*, 62.

[82] See *CPR, 1385-89*, 55 for references to two letters patent, concerning Stoke by Clare, which were not enrolled.

[83] And discussed above p.281.

[84] McHardy, 'Alien Priories'; Morgan, *History*, 26 (1941).

considerable interest. If, in pressing this claim, the priory of Takeley has figured most prominently among the examples, that is no more than just. For Takeley was dependent upon the abbey of St. Valéry, in Picardy, where the saint's shrine was housed; and it was, of course, the intervention of St. Valéry in 1066 which caused that favourable wind to blow which carried Duke William's fleet to England.[85]

[85] The story, told by William of Poitiers, may be conveniently consulted in *English Historical Documents*, ii, ed. D.C. Douglas and G.W. Greenaway, 2nd ed. (London 1981), pp.234-5.

Appendix

New College, Oxford, Takeley Charters

In the following documents punctuation has been modernized but spellings have not been standardised. The conventional abbreviation for 'qu' has been extended.

1

1373 × 1376. Petition for the removal of Lord Latimer as keeper,
and restitution of the priory to the custody of the prior.

N.C. 13, 108 (new reference); T.C. 256 (old reference).
No date or any trace of a seal. 29cm wide: 7cm high. Parchment.

La bille de ferme de cent marcz et de stallement de xx marcz par an.[1]

A nostre tresredoute seignour le Roi et a son tresnoble conseil, supplie humblement vostre povre chapeleyn le Priour de Tackele que come graunte fust par vous au comencement de ceste guerre que touz Priours en Engleterre aliens dussent tenir lours benefices de vous pour certeynes fermes. Et puis par voz lettres patentes grauntastes au dit suppliant la dite Priorie de Tackele, rendant a vous par an, durant la guerre, cent marcz et annuelment xx marcz par estallement pour les arrerages de la ferme du guerre passe. Et tresredoute seigneur le dit suppliant ad entendu que vous avetz graunte ore de novell' al Sire de Latymer la dite Priorie a ferme, Pleise a vostre tresgraciouse seigneurie en oevre de charite graunt' a vostre dit Chapeleyn quil puisse pesiblement tenir sa dite ferme selonc la tenure et graunt a lui par vous tresredoute seigneur faitz;[2] eiant regard que sa mere maison est distrute par les guerres.

  [1] This first sentence is underlined and written as a heading above the text on the right-hand side of the parchment.
  [2] The remaining words are written in a different ink.

2

Date and description as above. T.C. 257.
No date or any trace of seal. 29cm wide: 7cm high. Parchment.

A tresnoble et tresgracious seignour, monseignour le Counte Darundel supplie humblement vostre povre Chapeleyn le Priour de Tackele; que come nostre seignour le Roi ad graunte a monsire de Latymer la dite Priorie ove les appurtenauntz duraunt la guerre pour une certeyne ferme par an, Plese a vostre tresgraciouse seigneurie parler a monseignour de Latimer que lui plese graunter au dit Priour sa dite Priorie ove les appurtenauntz duraunt la guerre; Rendaunt au Roi sa ferme et au dit seigneur de Latymer outre la dite ferme xl livres par an, autrement que lui plese graunter au dit Priour iiij manoirs en Essex ove touz les appurtenantz, cestassavoir le manoir de Tackele, Lyndesele, Bryshangers et Bradewelle pour xx livres annuels a lui ordinez pour sa sustinaunce et pour xx livres de ferme apaier au dit seigneur annuelement duraunt la guerre.

3

c.1367 × 1378. Petition for the cessation of proceedings in, and for remission of the fine imposed by, the court of the manor of Isleworth.

T.C. 258. 26.5cm wide: 10cm high. Parchment.

La bille fesant mencioun de almoigne.[1]

A soun treshonoure seignour monsire Johan de Ipre, monstre le povre Priour de Tackelee du countee de Midd' alien, que come altrefoith' en baunk le Roi presentee fut par .xii. que le Priour de Seint Walry dount la dite mesoun de Tackelee est celle, avoit sustret certeinz almoignes quex il fut tenuz de faire come par la dite presentement fut sourmys, Sour quoi le dit priour, alleggea et monstra diverses chartres et confermementz des Rois faitz as predecessours le dit Priour, a tenir en fraunk almoigne, quites de toutes manere charges. Par force des queles chartres, il fut adonques de les dites almoignes deschargee et seit departi quites par iugement en la dite court come en le proces sour ceo ewe pleinement est contenuz, Et nientmoinz, le Priour qorest par malice dascunz est amercie et grevee en la court de Istelworth' dount mon dit seignour est fermour pour meisme la cause que les amercementz a diverses foith' amountent a la summe le ix livres y ceste a an darrein a graunt arrerissement de soun estat et retardacion du paiement de sa ferme due au Roi de sa dite Priorie dount il prie remedie et grace pour dieux.

[1] The heading is underlined and is in the same hand as the heading of nos.256, 259, 262, 263.

4

c.1351 × 1362. Request for the lowering of the rate of the farm.

T.C. 259. 30cm wide: 10cm high. Parchment.

Soit ceste bille bien veuez.[1]

A honourables et graciouses seignours Tresorer et Barounz de Lescheqer nostre seignour le Roi, monstre vostre povre chapelayn si vous plest, le Priour de Takkelee, Come son predecessour apresta a nostre dit[2] seignour le Roi en lan de

[1] Underlined. For a note on the handwriting see no.258 note 1.
[2] 'dit' interlined with caret mark.

son regne quatorszime, une graunde somme dargent en aide de sa gwerre come il apiert par sa patente, pour avoir sa priorie saunz rienz paier la gwerre durant, et neint meyns lan ensuiant la dite Priorie feust seisi es maynz nostre dit seignour le Roi et mys a auxi haute ferme come[3] il feust devant, saunz avoir regard que le dit priour vendist tout son estor et engagea sez manoirs as diverses gentz a terme de lour vies pour chevysance de la dite somme. Et oultre ceo, lez tenantz le dit Prior sount mortz par lez pestilences et lez mesons le dit Priour abatuz par le graunt vent[4] et a ceo le mier ad noee, et degaste une des places le dit Priour a graunt defesance et empoverissment du dit Priour et tout le Covent pour touz iours. Supplie humblement le dit Priour a voz puissantz et graciouses seignouries que vous plese pour dieux et en oevre de charite avoir regard a sez meschiefs avantditz, et lui graunter sa dite priorie pour si resonable et esi ferme paier,[5] si quil puisse honestement vivre et amender sez mesons et tenir hospitalite et faire almoignes et les[6] charges qapartiegnent a sa dite priorie.

[3] 'come' written twice; the first time crossed through.
[4] Possibly a reference to the great gale of 15 January 1361 (C.E. Britton, *A Meteorological Chronology to A.D. 1450*, London, 1937).
[5] Caret mark: C mars.
[6] 'les' interlined with caret mark.

5

c.*1351* × *1359. Petition for the total remission of the annual farm.*

T.C. 260. 29cm wide: 7cm high. Parchment.

A treshonoure seignour Prince de Gales, monstre son povre chapeleyn le Priour de Tackele alien que come lan xiiij[e] du regne nostre seignour le Roi bailla a nostre dit seignour le Roi .c. et iiij[xx] et ix livres [£189] al expedicion de sa guerre tut a une foith' et a lui fust sa Priorie rendu par patente pour lavantdit aprest saunz rendre ascune ferme la guerre durant, et lan apres ensuant fust reseisie et mys a ferme a vj[xx] et vj livres [£126] rendaunt par an saunz avoir regard ne pite du graunt damage que le Priour eust pour avoir les deniers susditz qar il vendi touz ses estores et engagea touz ses manoirs pour avoir avant la mayn les deniers susditz et est tut destrut et ses maisons totes debrisez et nad de quei vivre. Supplie le dit Priour quil pleise a son dit treshonoure seignour qil lui pleise pour dieu et en ovre de charite parler a nostre dit seignour le Roi et a son conseil que sa Priorie lui soit rendue ensicome nostre dit seignour le Roi lui rendi par sa patente ensealle

[Two or three illegible letters at the foot.]

6

c.1373 × 1376. See above, nos.1 and 2.

T.C. 261. 32cm wide: 6.5cm high. Parchment.

A nostre seignour le Roi et a son conseil.[1]

Supplie son povre chaplein frere Gerard de Oissencourt Priour de Takkele le quel
Priore le seignour de Latymer tient a present come ia piece apres laprise des terres
et tenementz des aliens en vostre main pour cause de ceste guerre fust ordine par
vous et par vostre noble conseil que les priours et autres governours des dites
terres duissent pour loneur de dieu et la conservacioun des choses de seinte esglise
avoir la garde de lour terres et tenementz devant touz autres pour paier la ferme
ordine. Et ore ledit Suppliant ad este en ceste terre trois quartiers del an
poursuant ladite priorie et ne poet estre receu ne avoir ascun vivre de quey il poet
estre sustenu, si teinent qil soit povre mendiant si remedie nest mise par vous et il
est prest de bailler plegges suffisantz de paier ladite ferme, cestasavoir vi^{xx} [120]
marcs par an la guerre durante atant come fesoit son predecessour devant que
ledite Priore lui fust oste que plese a vostre treshaute seignourie de lui graunter la
garde des ditz terres et[2] tenementz iuxte vostre susdite seinte et iuste ordinance, et
ceo lui voillez graunter en oevre de charite, afin quil poet vivre et servir dieux et
prier pour vous

[1] In the same hand as the rest of this document; a different hand from the headings to
nos.256, 258, 259 etc.
[2] 'et tenementz' interlined with caret mark.

7

c.1351 × 1359 (?). Petition for respite from payment of arrears of the farm.

T.C. 262. 25.5cm wide: 11.5cm high. Parchment.

Soit ceste bille veuez par bon conseil.[1]

A nostre seignour le Roi et son conseil, supplie son povre chapeleyn le Prior de
Tackele alien que come il eit eu sa dite Priorie a ferme de nostre dit seignour le Roi
la guerre duraunte pour cent vint et sys livres rendaunt par an, les qeux deniers
unques ne poait il paier tant fust le secle si bon, ne lever sa dite ferme de revenues
de sa dite priorite, quil ne covenist chescun an vendre devant la mayn graunt
partie de sa dite priorite, et sovent de temps est alee vivre a sa miere eglise purceo
qeu ceo pays navoit dount prendre sa sustinaunce et estre ceo que en lan nostre
seignour le Roi quatorzisme le dit prior fust requis par le conseil de eyder et bailler
sa ferme de trois termes avant la mayn a nostre dit seignour le Roi al esploit de sa[2]

[1] The same hand as the heading to nos.258, 259, 263.
[2] 'sa' interlined with caret mark.

guerre, et que sa dite Priorite lui seroit peisiblement renduz saunz nulle ferme paier a nostre seignour le Roi la guerre durante, et pour acomplier la volunte nostre dit seignour le Roi nientcontre esteantz les meschiefs ou il estoit, sil se mist aplus graunt meschief, et engagea ses manoirs a sept anns devant la mayn pur cent quatrevintz et neif livres [£189] pur les trois terms avantditz de amacer la dite summe et paier a nostre dit seignour le Roi pur quele paiement restitucion de sa dite Priorite lui estoit graunte et faite par patente, la quele il ad devers lui et sudeynement en lan ensuaunt, saunz avoir regard, compacion, et pite as greves meschiefs susditz estoit sa dite priorite reseisie, sauns cause en la mayn nostre seignour le Roi, et estre ceo si est le secle par mortalite qad estee taunt destrute que ses fermers ount lessez ses manoirs dount ses terres gisent friches et tot degastez, et ne trove homme que les voille prendre pur nul denier a ferme et pur quels destresses des viscountes et autres minstres nostre dit seignour le Roi pur les arrerages susditz qils fount sur le dit Prior nad dount vivre et est a derere de sa ferme de cent et douze livres sauns le terme de Pasche avenir quest sessaunt et trois livres et ensi est sa dite Priorite destrute as touz iours si dieu et nostre seignour le Roi par son bon conseil neyent pite et merci de y mettre hastive amendement

8

c.1367. Complaint of unjust prosecution concerning works of charity in the church of Isleworth.

T.C. 263. 27cm wide: 11cm high. Parchment.

Soit ceste bille veu pour lalmoigne demande de Istelworth'[1]

A chaunceller nostre seignour le Roi supplie vostre povre chapelayn le Priour de Tackelee comoigne Labbe de Saint Valleri et datif que come ils et lour predecessours ount tenutz leglise de Istelworthe et pluseours autres tenementz en la countee de Midd' par les chartres des progenitours nostre seignour le Roi et quites santz nulle charge faire par quelles chartres il ad este descharge des pluseours presentementz sur luy et ses predecessours faites de subtractioun des certeines almoignes dont il fust accuse devant les Justices par diverses enquestes en baunk nostre dit seignour le Roi et ore les ministres le Roi a Istelworth[2] luy destreignent illoeques de iour en autre et lui ount amercie a chescun court par long temps tancques a la somme de noef livres pour diverses almoignes queles ils diont qil deust paier, encountre la tenour des dites chartres et encountre la prohibicion nostre seignour le Roi sur la dite chartre exemplie faite, et a eux livere; plese a vostre treshonoure seignourie de les faire venir devant vous doier

---

[1] The same hand as the headings of nos.256, 258, 259, 262.
[2] At this point there is a largely illegible amendment interlined in a different ink. [. . .] de les[tenauntes[. . .].

lours resons de lour destresses et de luy faire droit selonc la chartre avandite pour[3] lamour dieu et en eovere de charite quil[4] ne soit destruyt par tielles destresses qar autrement il ne pura paier sa ferme a nostre seignour le Roi pour la Priori[e] avantdite.

[3] 'pur lamour . . . de charite' interlined, in the same ink as is used for the illegible interlineation above.

[4] From 'quil' until the end, the words are crossed through in the same ink as is used for the two interlineations.

9

c.1357. Petition for respite from payment of all arrears of the farm.

T.C. 264. 26.5cm wide: 8cm high. Parchment.

A nostre seignour le Roi et a son bon conseil, monstre son povre chapelleyn le Priour de Tackele alien que come lan de son regne quatorzisme le predecessour le dit priour apresta a nostre dit seignour le Roi c iiij[xx] et ix livres [£189] al expedicion de sa guerre tut a une foiz et a lui fust sa Priorie rendue par patente saunz rien rendre la guerre durant pour quele aprest issint avoir devaunt la meyn son dit predecessour lessa a ferme touz ses manoirs et ses possessions et[1] vendy touz ses estors, et lan apres mesme la Priorie fust reseisie et mys a ferme a cxxvi livres [£126] saunz avoir regard ne pite a nulles des meschiefs avauntditz et saunz avoir regarde que puis la Pestilence ils vaillont le meyns et ses mesons sont touz eschevys et ruynouses et le dit Priour nest pas de power de les reparailler, rendaunt la ferme avauntdit. Par quei supplie le dit Priour pour dieu et en eovre de seynte charite quil plese a vostre tresgraciouse seignourie avoir regard et compassioun as meschefs susditz et respiter les arrerages la guerre duraunt, et lui mettre a tiel ferme quil poet vivere du remenaunt et partie des autres damages et meschiefs avauntditz amender et outre faire le service divin[2] come atient a un religious

[1] 'et . . . estors' interlined with caret mark.

[2] Probable reading; the ms. is a minim short.

10

c.1367. See above, no.8.

T.C. 265. This document is in the same hand as the emendations to no.263. Irregular shape: 30.5cm wide: 13cm high. Paper: written with a very blotchy pen.

A chanceler nostre segnour le Roi supplie vostre povre chaplein le Prior de Tackele comoigne Labbe de Seint Walleri et datif, qe come ils et lours predecessours ount tenutz leglise de Istelworth et plusours autres tenementz en la countee de Middelsex' par les chartres des progenitiours nostre seignour le Roi, quites saunts nulle charge faire, par[1] queles chartres il ad este descharge de plusours presentements sur lui et[2] ses predecessours faites de subtraccion de certeins almoigne dount il fust encuse devaunt les justices[3] par diverses enquestes en bank nostre dit[1] segnour le Roi, et ore les ministres le Roi a Istelworth lui destregnent illesques de jour en autre et lui ount[1] amercie a chescun court par long' [sic] tanqe a la summe de neof liveres pour diverses almoignes quels ils dieunt quil dut paier encountre la tenour de dite chartre et encountre la prohibicion nostre seignour le Roi sur la dite charte exemplie faite et a eux livere. Plese a vostre treshonoure, de les faire venir devaunt vous doner lours resouns de lour destresses et de lui faire droit selonc la charte avantdit, qil ne soit destruit par tiels destresse qil[4] ne poura[5] paier sa ferme a nostre segnour le Roi pour la Priorie avantdite

Dorse, in another hand: Copie supplicacionum.

[1] Interlined with caret mark.
[2] 'et ses precesessours' interlined with caret mark.
[3] 'les justices' interlined with caret mark followed by 'eaux' crossed out.
[4] Followed by 'quil ne priour de' crossed through.
[5] 'il ne poura' interlined with caret mark.

11

c.1351 × 1362. Request for the farm of the priory to be reduced to 100 marks.

T.C. 266. 27cm wide: 9.5cm high. Parchment.

A honourables et graciouses seignours Tresorer et Barounz de lescheqer nostre seignour le Roi, monstre vostre povre chapelayn, si vous pleist, le priour de Takkelee, come soun predecessour apresta a nostre dit seignour le Roi, en lan de son regne quatorszime, une grande somme dargent en aide de sa gwerre, come il apiert par sa patente, pour avoir sa priorie saunz rien paier la gwerre durant, et nient meyns lan ensuant, la dite Priorie feust seisi es maynz nostre dit seignour le Roi et mys a auxi haute ferme come il feust devant, saunz avoir regard que le dit Priour vendist tout son estor et engagea sez manoirs as diverses gentz a terme de lour vies pour chevysance de la dite somme. Et oultre ceo les tenantz le dit Priour sount mortz par les pestilences et lez mesons le dit Priour abatuz par le graunt vent et a ceo le mier ad noee, et degaste une des places le dit Priour,[1] a graunt defesance et empoverissement du dit Priour et tout le covent pour touz iours. Supplie humblement le dit Priour a voz poissantz et graciouses seignours que vous[2] pleise pour dieu et en oevre de charite avoir regard a cez meschiefs avantditz et lui graunter sa dite Priorie, pour cent marcz, si que puisse honestement vivre et amender sez mesons et tenir hospitalite et faire almoignes et les charges qapartiegnent a sa dite Priorie.

[1] Almost certainly this refers to East Hall, a manor on the Essex coast which was liable to flooding. During the period of ownership of Tackley by New College there were constant disagreements between the Warden and Fellows and the tenants of East Hall about the maintenance of the sea wall, and this manor was one of the first places to be sold by the college following the passing of the act of 1858 which enabled endowments to be disposed of. I am grateful to Mrs. Dalton for this information.
[2] 'vous' interlined with caret mark.

Chapter 16

The End of the Hundred Years War:
Lancastrian France and Lancastrian England*

Maurice Keen

'Today it is told Cherbourg is gone, and we have now not a foot of land left in Normandy': so James Gresham wrote to John Paston on 19 August 1450.[1] It was then just twelve months since Charles VII of France, at Roches Tranchelion on 31 July 1449, had declared himself no longer bound by the truce with the English, on the ground of their armed escalade of the town of Fougères in Brittany, and their refusal to make reparation for this breach of the truce or to disavow the capture.[2] In the intervening year all that was left of the wide lands that Henry V had won with the 'blood and treasure' of England was overrun by the French, in a militarily decisive campaign.

James Gresham's use in his letter to Paston of the 'royal we' – *we* have not a foot of land left – shows nicely how Englishmen had come to identify their king's claims in France not just with his private dynastic rights but with the crown in its collective sense, embodying the community and its interest, whereby 'the leste lyge man, with body and rent, He is a parcel of the crowne'.[3] It is not surprising, therefore, that the ignominious collapse of English Normandy sent powerful shock waves through the country. Well before the surrender of Cherbourg the duke of Suffolk, Henry VI's chief minister whose incompetent diplomacy had culminated in the sack of Fougères and so offered the French their *casus belli*, had been toppled, and subsequently murdered. In the anger of the moment, incredible rumours of his treachery circulated, that he had plotted with Dunois, Guillaume Cousinot and others to depose King Henry, that he had 'steered' the duke of Orléans to excite the French to attack Normandy; rumours which were solemnly brought forward as formal charges when he was impeached in the spring parliament of 1450.[4] Somerset, the lieutenant

---

*I must acknowledge a deep debt of gratitude to Dr. C.T. Allmand for his invaluable counsels and criticisms of a draft of this paper.

[1] *Paston Letters*, ed. J. Gairdner (London, 1872), i, no.103.

[2] On the taking of Fougères see A. Bossuat, *Perrinet Gressart et François de Surienne, agents d'Angleterre* (Paris, 1936), pp.301-35; M. Keen and M. Daniel, 'English Diplomacy and the Sack of Fougères in 1449', *History*, lix (1974), 375-91.

[3] *Political and Other Poems*, ed. J. Kail (EETS, London, 1904), p.51.

[4] *Rot. Parl.*, v.177-8.

and commander in Normandy whose loss of nerve at Rouen (and subsequently) had ensured that the French won back the duchy with a minimum of fighting, was never formally impeached; but there was a widespread demand that he be brought to account, and charges were prepared against him.[5] Already at the moment when he was treating for the evacuation and surrender of Caen, Cade's rebels in July 1450 were demanding punishment of the traitors by whose means Normandy, Anjou and Maine had been 'delivered' and 'our true lords, knights and esquiers, and many a good yeoman lost and solde ere they went'.[6] The anger against Somerset did not go away: in his Shrewsbury manifesto of 1452 York called on all men to consider 'first the worship, honour and manhood asserted of all nations to the people of England, whilst the kingdom's sovereign lord stood possessed of his lordship in France', and then to compare with this the 'derogation, lesion of honour and villainy reported generally unto the English nation for the loss of the same, namely unto the duke of Somerset, when he had commandance and charge thereof'.[7] Mowbray of Norfolk returned to the same charge in 1453, reminding the council of the 'overgreat dishonour and losses that be come to this full noble realm of England' as a result of Somerset's misconduct, and that the traditional punishment for those who showed cowardice in the face of the enemy was death.[8]

So the blame for the disaster in France was laid squarely at the doors of Suffolk and Somerset. But was it justly so laid? No one would wish very vigorously to defend either the diplomatic mismanagement of the one (Suffolk's domestic abuse of his influence being in this context irrelevant), or the military loss of nerve of the other, yet a puzzle remains. Both Suffolk and Somerset clearly appreciated the vulnerability of Normandy, and what needed to be done there. Back at the beginning of 1445, Suffolk had urged on York, Somerset's predecessor as lieutenant in Normandy, the need to use the respite from hostilities afforded by the truce of Tours to put the defence of the duchy into good order.[9] Somerset received similar, and emphatic advice on his going into Normandy:

> that it be purveied fore here in England of ordinaunce for the felde al maner thing that longithe to the werre, as speres, bowes, arowes, axes, malles, ribawdkyns and alle other stuffe necessairie . . . and that alle youre principalle places be stuffed of alle manner of artillerie, furnysshid withe vitaile for alle manere of doubtes, [and] that soche places as bene frontures upon the

[5] *Letters and Papers illustrative of the Wars of the English in France*, ed. J. Stevenson (RS, 1861-64), ii, pt. II, (718-22) (questions to be put to Somerset); *Paston Letters*, i, pp.lxxvii-lxxx (detailed charges prepared by York, which he hoped in 1452 to have prosecuted).

[6] J. Stow, *Annales* (London, 1631), p.390.

[7] *Paston Letters*, i, p.lxxxiii.

[8] *Ibid.*, i. no.191.

[9] *Rot. Parl.*, v.74.

marches, as Pounthorson, Averaunshes and other places . . . be fortiffied and repaired sufficeauntlie that thei may be stronge and habille to resiste the Kingis ennemies.[10]

Somerset was an experienced commander and the advice was not lost on him: in the spring of 1449 we find him desperately appealing to England for aid, complaining that 'ther is no place in the King's obeissaunce purveied, nother in reparations, ordenaunce ne eny maner artillerie', and reminding all and sundry of the effort that England had put into the conquest of 'that land . . . whereof the shamefulle losse . . . shuld not oonly be to the irreparable hurt of the commyn profite but also an everlastying spite and perpetuell denigration of the fame and renoune of this noble Reme'.[11] Yet there was no response, even at this late date. It was not until July, when open war was clearly imminent, that the parliament of 1449 increased its grant of a half subsidy to a whole one, abated by 6,000 marks.[12] It was not until early in 1450 that any force could be despatched to reinforce Somerset, and then it was a mere 3,000 men that went with Sir Thomas Kyriell, to be cut to pieces by the French before they could join the lieutenant, at Formigny. The real fault, it begins to appear, lay not with Suffolk and Somerset, rather with their countrymen whose response to the needs that these two both well understood was too slow and too slight, but who were to be so ready to blame them.

There is thus a kind of partial defence, at least, for these two much denigrated men. They may have mismanaged things, but that was not the real reason for the swiftness and the totality of the collapse, which was what raised popular anger to such a pitch of fury. The reason why things were not 'seen to' in 'this time of abstinence' (i.e. the truce of Tours), as Suffolk advised, was at root not lack of leadership but a lack of will and concern in that sector of the community that formed the political nation of fifteenth-century England, the gentry whose representatives sat in the Commons and held the purse strings that allowed government to do things that needed to be done. And that will, it would seem, was already lacking when the 'abstinence' was agreed. My object, in the rest of this essay, will be to try and trace its failure back to its origins. Lack of will and concern is, I am aware, by no means a novel explanation of the final ignominious defeat of the English in the Hundred Years War, in the wake of which first Suffolk and then Somerset were dragged down. All I wish to do is to follow up some of the leads offered by recent research, notably that of Christopher Allmand, Michael Powicke and Robert Massey, which seem to me both to have underlined the significance of this factor and to

---

[10] *Letters and Papers*, ii, pt.II, (592-3).
[11] *Rot. Parl.*, v.147-8.
[12] *Ibid.*, 143-4.

have made it easier to understand.[13]

Gerald Harriss has lately and with admirable clarity explained why it was, in cash terms, that nothing could be done about repairing the defence of Normandy after Suffolk came away from Tours with a truce in 1444.[14] The expenses of Henry VI's marriage, the king's own over-lavish patronage and his spending on his colleges, combined with an unscheduled fall in the revenue from the customs, meant that the truce did not relieve the pressure on crown finances in the way that it must have been hoped it would. Indeed the new treasurer appointed on 18 December 1446, Marmaduke Lumley, bishop of Carlisle, was soon having to take drastic steps in order to prevent the position from deteriorating further and disastrously. But the problem of lack of will and concern does not go away in the light of this exposé, nor does Harriss suggest that it should. As has been said, the indications are that it was not a new problem in 1445. It is one that needs to be seen in a wider chronological context, and that belongs to a broader canvas than that of financial history only, and one on which the brush stokes have, necessarily, to be more impressionistic.

Perhaps as good a way as any of introducing the nature of the problem will be via a comparison between the English reactions to adverse fortunes in the war in the fourteenth and fifteenth centuries respectively. The two great peace treaties of the Hundred Years War, of Brétigny and of Troyes, were both followed in England by periods of financial insouciance (with rather more justification in the former case, since the years 1360-9 were a good deal more like a peace, from an English point of view, than the years 1420-9). Then, after the re-opening of the war in 1369, as after the English reverse before Orléans in 1429, the tide of military success turned against the English, and their conquests, in the south west of France in the one case and north of Loire in the other, came under pressure. There, however, the similarity ends abruptly, for the reaction to ill-success in the two instances was entirely different.

Faced with the shock of unexpected reverses, the English in the 1370s,

---

[13] C.T. Allmand, *Lancastrian Normandy, 1415-50* (Oxford, 1983); 'The Collection of Dom Lenoir and the English Occupation of Normandy', *Archives*, vi (1964), 202-10; 'The Lancastrian Land Settlement in Normandy', *Economic History Review*, 2nd ser., xxi (1968), 461-79; 'La Normandie devant l'opinion anglaise à la fin de la guerre de Cent Ans', *BEC*, cxxviii (1970), 345-68; M.R. Powicke, 'Lancastrian Captains', *Essays in Medieval History presented to Bertie Wilkinson*, ed. T.A. Sandquist and M.R. Powicke (Toronto, 1969), pp.371-82; R. Massey, 'The Land Settlement in Lancastrian Normandy', *Property and Politics: Essays in Later Medieval English History*, ed. A.J. Pollard (Gloucester, 1984), pp.76-96. Massey explores the subject in much greater detail in his thesis which I had the privilege of examining: 'The Lancastrian Land-Settlement in Normandy and Northern France, 1417-50' (Liverpool Ph.D. thesis, 1984).

[14] G.L. Harriss, 'Marmaduke Lumley and the Exchequer Crisis of 1446-9', *Aspects of Late Medieval Government and Society*, ed. J.G. Rowe (Toronto, 1986), pp.143-78.

largely through parliamentary grants, literally poured money into their war effort. Continuing lack of success did not deter them. After the disaster that overtook Pembroke's expedition in 1372, after the fiasco of Gaunt's march across France from Calais to Bordeaux in 1373, after the aborting of the Breton expedition of 1375, and even after the exorbitant Poll Tax of 1380-81 had triggered off the Peasants' Revolt, they remained ready to pay for more. The indignation of chroniclers like Walsingham and of the Commons in Parliament against those upon whose unpatriotic and self-interested conduct they blamed reverses – Latimer and his lieutenants at St. Sauveur and Bécherel, or alleged traitors like John Menstreworth and Thomas Catrington, or Despenser and the captains of his disastrous 1383 expedition to Flanders[15] – testify to a widespread sense of involvement and commitment, as do the independent efforts of, for example, the London merchant Philipot to equip ships to clear the seas of Scots and Spanish raiders.[16] So, in a different and perhaps more telling way, do the arguments advanced in the 1371 Parliament and subsequently, in which Wyclif took such an interest, that in the Kingdom's necessity it might be legitimate to force a contribution from the endowments of the possessionate clergy.[17] Altogether the 1370s were a period of unusually sustained and intensive assented taxation for war purposes, perhaps only comparable with the middle years of Henry V's reign, when he was victoriously laying the foundations of the Lancastrian conquest in France. The mood of commitment outlasted them: it was not until the late 1380s that the popular appeal of sabre rattling began to dwindle. If willingness to pay is an acceptable index of involvement throughout the period there seems to have been no lack of will or concern on the part of Englishmen to maintain their footholds on the soil of France.

The reaction of England and of Englishmen to military set-backs in the fifteenth century, in the decade and a half following the relief of Orléans, contrasts sharply with that of their forebears. In 1380 the Commons, faced with a request for £160,000 (principally for Buckingham's expedition to Brittany) agonised and haggled, but ultimately came up with a poll tax of 'groats' through which they expected to raise £100,000;[18] in 1434, when Gloucester offered to take charge of affairs in France and right the situation if £48,000 could be raised for his expenses, he was told by the

---

[15] *Chronicon Angliae*, ed. E. Maunde Thompson (RS, 1874), pp.77 (Latimer), 135-6 (Menstreworth), 261-4 (Catrington); *Rot. Parl.*, ii. 324-6 (Latimer); iii. 324-6 (Despenser and his captains).

[16] *Chronicon Angliae*, p.199.

[17] John Wyclif, *De Civili Dominio*, ed. J. Loserth (Wyclif Soc., London, 1900), ii. 7; V.H. Galbraith, 'Articles laid before the Parliament of 1371', *EHR*, xxxiv (1919), 579-82; A. Gwynn, *The English Austin Friars in the Time of Wyclif* (Oxford, 1940), pp.210-24.

[18] *Rot. Parl.*, iii. 88-90.

treasurer that it would not be possible to raise half the sum.[19] It is true that when, in the aftermath of Orléans, Henry VI was about to cross to France for his coronation there, and again in 1436 in the indignant aftermath of the breakdown of the Burgundian alliance at Arras, the Commons were relatively generous, granting a double subsidy in the first instance and a subsidy combined with a graduated income tax in the second;[20] but the general pattern of taxation in the period 1429-44 was of grants at a reduced rate and with collection spread over an extended period. As Steel has shown, the picture is if anything even more dispiriting if one looks at it in terms of the readiness of local gentry and borough communities to lend to the crown.[21] The observations of Hue de Lannoy in 1436 bear this out; he told the duke of Burgundy that in his opinion 'all the commons of their realm are tired and wearied out with the war'.[22] By the time of the Calais peace conferences of 1439 it was clear that, in the interest of obtaining relief from the pressures of war, the English were prepared to consider very substantial concessions, including the renunciation, in return for an adequate settlement, of the title to the crown of France which they had so aggressively reasserted scarcely eight years earlier by crowning Henry VI in Paris. Alternatively (and rather preferably) they were prepared to consider suspension of the use of the title for the duration of a long truce.[23] There was still a good deal of rhetoric at those conferences about the title itself, about St. Bridget's prophecy of an English succession in France and about the judgements of God given in England's favour on the field of battle.[24] But this was mere rhetoric, as the ambassadors' readiness to look at suggestions like those mentioned above attests. They knew that England was no longer in this matter ready to put her money where her mouth was, in the way she had been in the fourteenth century.

The contrast I have been drawing, between the fourteenth and the fifteenth centuries, must not be pressed too far. In terms of customs revenues, of the comparative burden of bad debt, perhaps most of all in terms of what we would now call 'economic confidence', the 1370s were clearly a much more propitious period in 'public finance' than the 1430s and 40s, and that must go some way at least to explaining why parliament was so much more generous. Even so reasons can be put forward that would support an a priori expectation that the English reaction to reverses

[19] *Proceedings and Ordinances of the Privy Council*, ed. N.H. Nicolas (6 vols. London, 1834-7), iv. 214.

[20] *Rot. Parl.*, iv. 336-7, 486-7.

[21] A. Steel, *The Receipt of the Exchequer, 1377-1485* (Cambridge, 1954), Chapter vi esp. pp.259-65.

[22] Quoted by Allmand, *BEC* (1970), 363.

[23] Cf. C.T. Allmand, 'The Anglo-French Negotiations, 1439', *BIHR*, xl (1967), 1-33; and *idem*, 'Documents relating to the Anglo-French Negotiations of 1439', *Camden Miscellany*, xxiv (1972), 79-149.

[24] *Ibid.*, 115-7.

should have been sharper in the 1430s than in the 1370s, not less so. The treaty of Troyes and the coronation of Henry VI in Paris clearly committed English honour even more seriously than Edward III's royal claim and his assumption of the arms of France had done. Henry V's conquest of Normandy had brought benefits that were more tangible to Englishmen than had been the extension, by the treaty of Brétigny, of the frontiers of the duchy of Aquitaine: as Colin Richmond has written 'it gave the coastal shires of England about thirty years of security . . . It was a wise strategy that kept the war as deep into France as possible.[25] The commercial advantages that control of both shores of the channel afforded were widely appreciated: it dispelled the fears that had disturbed Chaucer's merchant so much, about the keeping of the seas 'betwix Middleburgh and Orwell'.[26] In addition, in consequence of Henry V's conquest, a substantial number of Englishmen had acquired titles, lands and house property in France, and in Normandy in particular; and for these the French advances put not just national reputation but personal wealth and livelihood at risk.

This Lancastrian land settlement relates with another matter that is nowadays regularly brought into the picture when English interests in the maintenance of the war in this period are under discussion, that is the lure of gains of war. As McFarlane long ago pointed out (using Fastolf's career as a prime example) it was possible, at any rate for individuals, to make very considerable profits out of war even in periods when the war generally was going badly for the English, as it was in both the 1370s and the 1430s.[27] This matter of gains of war is worth some consideration, I believe. For if I am right, there is here again a contrast between the fourteenth and the fifteenth centuries, but one whose implications run in the opposite direction to what I have suggested above, and will so help to explain why the reaction to adversity in the later period was less sharp and concerned than in the earlier one, not more so.

Gains of war, like other property, may be divided into two broad categories, moveable and immoveable. The distinction between the two was understood very clearly in the period of the English wars in France, and different rules applied to them;[28] they are not always so clearly distinguished in modern historical writing (largely because it has been so much conerned with gains as an inducement to war service, where the distinction is at its least important). Into the moveable category fall booty,

[25] C.F. Richmond, 'The Keeping of the Seas during the Hundred Years War, 1422-40', *History*, xlix (1964), 284.

[26] Geoffrey Chaucer, *The Canterbury Tales*, General Prologue, lines 276-7.

[27] K.B. McFarlane, *The Nobility of Later Medieval England* (Oxford), 1973), pp.31 ff.; 'The Investment of Sir John Fastolf's profits of War', *TRHS*, 5th ser., 7 (1957), 91-116.

[28] M. Keen, *The Laws of War in the Later Middle Ages* (London, 1965), p.139.

prisoners and their ransoms, and such profits of war as *appatis* (tribute levied by garrisons on a locality): into the other category lands and lordships, titles and tenements. In the fourteenth century, a very high proportion of what was won in France in the moveable form was brought back to England. Writing of the years after Edward III had returned from his expedition of 1346-47, Walsingham described how in England 'there were few women who did not possess something from Caen, Calais, or other overseas towns, such as clothes, furs or cushions. Table cloths and linen were seen in everyone's houses. Married women were decked in the trimmings of French matrons, and if the latter sorrowed over their loss, the former rejoiced in their gain'.[29] Knighton tells us that Henry of Lancaster built the great palace of the Savoy out of his French winnings;[30] William Berkeley told Leland that his house at Beverstone was built out of the ransoms of the prisoners that his great grandfather had won at Poitiers.[31] These examples are taken from the great years before 1360, it must be admitted. But in the 1370s the flow had not dried up entirely; memories of the dramatic windfalls of the recent past were still green, and the evidence of them was visible in high profile.

Though quantitative comparison is not possible, it seems apparent that in the fifteenth century the proportion of the moveable profits of war that found their way back to England was much smaller. This was because the nature of the fighting, on the English side, had changed, from the time of the treaty of Troyes onwards. The age of the *chevauchées*, of the expeditionary host raised in England and which returned home when the campaign was over, laden (hopefully) with prisoners and booty, was now past: the Agincourt expedition was the last of them. The great English captains of the fifteenth century, Talbot and Scales, John Fastolf, William Oldhall, Matthew Gough and their ilk spent years on end, sometimes nearer decades, in service in France, and so did a high proportion of the archers and men at arms who served under them.[32] These captains, and a good many of their subordinates too, acquired offices, estates and houses in France, possessions which were often more extensive than what they held in England (many of the lesser men held nothing there). What they won in France was, in consequence, for the most part spent there likewise: it did not come back to England. There were of course those who, like that famous pair John Winter and Nicholas Molyneux, did make careful plans to send their winnings home, to be invested in the 'purchase of manors',

[29] Quoted by H.J. Hewitt, *The Organisation of War under Edward III* (Manchester, 1966), p.110.

[30] *Chronicon H. Knighton*, ed. J.R. Lumby (RS, 1895), ii. 118.

[31] J. Leland, *Itinerary*, ed. L. Toulmin Smith (London, 1909), iv. 133.

[32] A.J. Pollard, *John Talbot and the War in France* (London, 1983), Chapter 5.

but they were the exceptions rather than the rule.[33] French outgoings often ate too deeply into profit for there to be much left over to send back, even in the case of men of standing. Indeed even Talbot, with his captaincies, his offices and his right in all the prizes he and his men took did not, by Dr. Pollard's calculation, do much better than break even after he had met the expenses of his household in France, of estate and garrison administration, and carried his arrears of pay.[34]

The very incomplete and unsatisfactory evidence with regard to the extent of the sums accruing to Englishmen from moveable gains of war renders any sort of overall quantitative analysis of their importance quite impossible. It has been questioned, probably rightly, whether they were ever of such an extent as to have any impact of significance on the English economy.[35] If there ever was such a time, one would expect it to have been in those years in the fourteenth century when instalments on the huge ransoms of the kings of France and Scotland were still coming in, certainly not in the fifteenth century. But for individuals gains of war could be spectacularly important financially: and they also had a powerful psychological impact. Even in their least durable form, as of those table cloths and trimmings that Walsingham remarked on, they caught the eye. In the fifteenth century this impact was inevitably blunter in England than it had been in the past, because there was less to be seen there.

What was true of gains of war in moveable form was even truer of gains in the immoveable category, and not only in the visual sense. These were, of course, much more important in the fifteenth century than they had been in the fourteenth, on account of the deliberate policy of Henry V and Bedford of settling Englishmen in the areas conquered from the French.[36] Their liberal grants of lands, lordships and houses not only to peers and captains but also to many relatively humble Englishmen were not and could not be sources of clear profit in the sense that, say, the ransom of a valuable prisoner could be.[37] Major grants, like Salisbury's county of Perche or the three *vicomtés* of Aubec, Orge and Pontaudemer that Thomas, duke of Clarence obtained from his brother, or the county of Maine that later came the way of Edmund Beaufort, might constitute a

---

[33] K.B. McFarlane, 'A Business Partnership in War and Administration, 1421-45', *EHR*, lxxviii (1963), 290-310. The compact between Molyneux and Winter stipulated that clear profit gained in France was to be repatriated 'pour acheter des heritaiges au royaume Dangleterre' (p.309).

[34] Pollard, *Talbot*, ch.6, esp. p.120: 'he was perhaps able to make a slight profit out of the war . . . he was certainly not a major profiteer . . . in the end something more akin to a survivor'.

[35] M.M. Postan, 'The Costs of the Hundred Years War', *Past & Present*, 27 (1964), 34-52, esp. 43-50.

[36] Massey, *Property and Politics*, ed. Pollard, pp.77-81; Allmand, *Lancastrian Normandy*, ch.3.

[37] *Ibid.*, pp.61-2.

real accretion to disposable seigneurial income, though at the same time, naturally, they often generated new calls on it. Smaller grants, like the numerous enfeoffments recorded on the Norman Rolls after the fall of Rouen or those that were distributed as rewards to soldiers who had been at the field of Verneuil, were expected to generate an income on which, after outgoings had been set against it, a serving man of arms might hope to maintain himself and his family, but not to generate a clear profit over and above that (that sort of profit, it was originally intended, should go to the crown, but the lands were often wasted and there seldom was much).[38] There were of course men who, like Fastolf, saw the way the wind was blowing in the 1430s and succeeded in realising substantial sums by the sale of their French properties, which they reinvested in England, but again they were the exceptions. The ordinances that Henry V and Bedford made, inhibiting the sale of properties held by Englishmen to others than their co-nationals, helped to ensure that they should be.[39] The consequence was straightforward, that preservation of the Lancastrian conquest in France came to be of very great, indeed vital, importance to those Englishmen who spent most of their time there; and, conversely, to be of relatively little importance, except perhaps psychologically, to those Englishmen who spent most of their time in England. These latter came, in consequence, to be progressively less and less eager to make substantial contributions towards the maintenance of the conquest, from which no profit came their way.

This seems to me to be among the most important points that recent research into the Lancastrian land settlement in France (especially that of Christopher Allmand and Robert Massey) has clarified. As Massey explains, the settlement policy was a French, not just a Norman one;[40] indeed it had to be, since part of the object was to involve English captains and soldiers in the preservation of the conquests that had been won by their arms, wherever these might be (no one else was likely to commit themselves with much enthusiasm to their defence). Hence it was extended beyond Normandy into the Paris region as Henry V advanced and after Verneuil into Maine. What the grantees became thus involved in, however, was the maintenance of the Lancastrian interest in France, not in England, and the deeper the conquest drove into Normandy and beyond, the sharper the separation of those two interests became. Allmand has suggested that the policy of settlement may have been

---

[38] Grants were usually not made outright but up to a given value, e.g. 800 *livres tournois*. The idea was that if the declared income from the lands granted exceeded the figure named, then the sum in excess would be due to the crown. But I know of no instance where this occurred; receipts were usually well below the grant valuation.

[39] L. Puiseux, *L'émigration normande et la colonisation anglaise en Normandie au XVe siècle* (Paris, 1886), p.75.

[40] Massey, *Property and Politics*, ed. Pollard, pp.81-2.

influenced, in part, by English experience in Ireland, and this seems quite plausible.[41] Certainly – unless Henry V or his successor should succeed, and rapidly, in gaining general recognition as king of France – it was calculated to have the same effect that English policy (or lack of policy) had with regard to settlement in Ireland: that is, of creating a 'middle nation',[42] resented by the natives as alien intruders and by their English cousins as having insufficient kinship with them, certainly too little to justify levying major fiscal contributions in England in order to enable them to preserve their 'foreign' possessions. The growing anxiety of the Anglo-Irish settlers' appeals for assistance from England,[43] and the increasing deafness of the English ears on which they fell, is a recurrent theme of late medieval Irish history: it is not a happy analogy for Lancastrian France and its prospects.

The English of Normandy, at the end of the Hundred Years War, were by no means as yet as foreign to England as the contemporary 'English' of Ireland, though if Allmand is right in his delineation of the feelings of a good many of the lesser among them, things were beginning to go that way: 'the duchy was their homeland, the source of their livelihood . . . they had the sense of belonging in the country'.[44] In another and more important sense the difference in their positions was absolute. In Ireland the 'English', facing the aggressiveness of Gaelic princes whose ambitions were local and who were incapable of concerting with one another for long, could be left largely to fend for themselves. The English in Normandy, faced in Charles VII with a truly formidable enemy and a more and more united country behind him, could not. That was the root of the problem facing Henry VI's councillors. Desperate appeals from the Anglo-Irish of the Pale they could afford to ignore, and did: simply to desert to their fate the English of Normandy and France, while the glory of Henry V's victories was so fresh in memory, was not thinkable. No government would be likely to survive the psychological shock, domestically, of such an abandonment, as 1450 showed. On the other hand, they knew that the funds that would be necessary for such a massive military task as the long term defence of the conquest looked to be would not be forthcoming from England. They were caught on the sharp horns of dilemma. Either they must face realities, abandon territory and honour, and risk reaping the whirlwind of popular rage; or seek to maintain honour in spite of interest being lacking, a course which, however

[41] Allmand, *BEC* (1970), 355.

[42] The phrase 'middle nation' first occurs in O'Neill's Remonstrance to Pope John XXII, 1317; see E. Curtis, *A History of Medieval Ireland*, revised edn. (London, 1938), p.192.

[43] E.g. the appeal of 1435 discussed by A.J. Otway-Ruthven, *A History of Medieval Ireland* (London, 1968), p.369.

[44] Allmand, *BEC* (1970), 348.

laudable it may be in the case of individuals, tends to be politically disastrous.

Traditionally, the reaction of the English government in this situation has been described in terms of tensions beween a 'war party' and a 'peace party'. These terms need to be handled with care, especially in the context of the findings of Allmand and Massey. The phrase 'peace party' in particular is potentially misleading. The experience of the two men who are usually credited with the leadership of such a party, Cardinal Beaufort and after him Suffolk, was not such as to incline them at all toward a policy of mere capitulation, of getting out as best they could. Suffolk had had a long and distinguished military career, had been granted substantial lands across the Channel, and had lost a brother and a father in the war:[45] while Beaufort had contributed more funds, from his private resources, towards the making and maintaining of the conquests of his nephew Henry V than had any other single individual.[46] But they both were realists and saw, as Lannoy had put it, that the 'affairs of France cannot long continue in the state they are'.[47] At Calais in 1439 Beaufort seems to have been prepared to toy – though he toyed only – with the possibility of recognizing that Normandy and Gascony were held of the French crown, which would mean the restitution of the Frenchmen put out of their lands by the English conquest, but only if the French would contribute a major part of the sum that would have to be paid in compensation to the English settlers.[48] When it became clear that they would not do so, the next best thing seemed to be to try to distract Charles VII by efforts to rekindle troubles beween the French king and his princes and among the princes themselves: this was almost certainly a major (if tacit) reason for the release of the duke of Orléans from his long captivity in 1440. By the time that it became clear that the duke's liberty would not have any such effect, and nor would the feelers put out towards the count of Armagnac, the need for a truce had become imperative. It is probable that Suffolk, in order to get it, was ready, informally, to agree that Maine should be ceded,[49] calculating perhaps that he could just about get away with that,

---

[45] See Suffolk's own defence in Parliament in 1450, *Rot. Parl.*, v. 176; his grants in France included Hambye and Briquebec (sold in 1430, Allmand, *Lancastrian Normandy*, p.67), the county of Dreux, and Chanteloup and Créances in the Cotentin, *Complete Peerage*, xii, part i. 444.

[46] G.L. Harriss, 'Cardinal Beaufort: Patriot or Usurer?', *TRHS*, 5th ser., 20 (1970), 129-48.

[47] *Letters and Papers*, ii, pt.I, 239.

[48] Allmand, *Camden Miscellany*, xxiv. 145-6.

[49] See T. B. Pugh, 'Richard Plantagenet (1411-60), Duke of York, as the King's Lieutenant in France and Ireland', *Aspects of late Medieval Government*, ed. Rowe, p.122. I am informed by Dr. M.K. Jones that there is an earlier reference to the possibility of the cession of Maine in Edmund Beaufort's commission to be lieutenant and governor (Bibliothèque Nationale, MS. Nouv. acq. fr. 3642 n.800 A, 19 July 1442).

and that anyway it would establish, together with the marriage of Margaret, a new English link with another French princely house, that of Anjou. It seems likely that misplaced hopes of creating tensions in French aristocratic circles are once again the best explanation of his disastrous attempt later, in 1449, at intervention in Breton politics.[50] This is hardly a 'peace' policy: rather it seems to be a record of a quest, fruitless in the end, for a means of preserving most, at least, of what was left of the English conquest, without charging England more than she was prepared to pay.

In England there was one man who was consistently critical of the concessions that Beaufort and Suffolk, in their difficult conduct of diplomacy, were prepared to consider: Humphrey, duke of Gloucester, Henry V's last surviving brother. He can hardly be called the leader of a 'war party' however. Once he had been a great power in the land, but by the 1440s he had become something of a one-man band. Those who have sometimes been associated with him, as York and John Holland, duke of Exeter, do not seem during his lifetime (or in York's case perhaps before the end of 1446) to have been estranged from the court, as he was; and their view of things was probably closer to that of Suffolk than to his posture of belligerence. Holland was ageing, had come home from Gascony before the completion of his term as lieutenant, and was much involved with his own financial and family arrangements; he had never shown strong political partialities.[51] His promotion in 1443 to the rank of duke, and his tenure of the offices of Constable of the Tower and Lord High Admiral suggest that he remained persona grata with the court.[52] York, when he came back to England in 1445, did not come, as he would in 1450, as a critic of the courtiers, and had every reason to believe that he had the king's and their goodwill; his two eldest sons had just been created earls of March and Rutland respectively, and he was clearly hoping that he would be favoured with the renewal of his Norman lieutenancy. At the same time he was involved in negotiations for the marriage of his heir to a French princess, hardly a warmonger's overture.[53] There was of course a real war party in Normandy, under the influential leadership of captains who had made their fortunes in the war and who had substantial properties in the duchy, and who were close to the council in Rouen – but not very close to the court or council of Westminster (or to Gloucester, for that matter). There may have been one or two of the higher English aristocracy who saw eye to eye with them, almost certainly Talbot, who had spent so much of his career in service in France, perhaps also Somerset, who had likewise a long service record and whose landed

[50] Keen and Daniel, *History*, lix (1973), 387-90.
[51] Holland's position is carefully analysed in M. Stansfield, 'The Holland Family: Earls of Kent and Huntingdon, and Dukes of Exeter' (Oxford D.Phil. thesis, 1987).
[52] Pugh, *Aspects of late Medieval Government*, ed. Rowe, esp. pp.122-5, 127.
[53] *Letters and Papers*, i.79-86.

wealth was more amply secured in France than in England.[54] Neither of these was close to Gloucester, and when he died Talbot was in Normandy and Somerset about to set out thither. Gloucester apart, the history of the 'war party' in the later 1430s and 1440s, such as it is, belongs to the story of Lancastrian France rather than of Lancastrian England, and those are, as I have been trying to suggest, distinct and separate stories.

That separation has been my theme and I must conclude on it. The suddenness of the final collapse of Lancastrian France, which so shocked and enraged contemporaries, was deceptive. The seeds of the dissolution of Henry V's conquest had been planted at its inception, because of the plans for a measure of English settlement that were an integral part of his policy of conquest. Such settlement created an English interest in that conquest that was important to some Englishmen (those enfeoffed in France) but was quite separate from that of the community of the English homeland. The lands that they held were French lands, held mediately or immediately of the French crown, and there was no significant advantage to England in their holding them. Yet in the long term there was no way of maintaining their possession, except with English arms (and money), because their possession brought no advantage at all to France or to Frenchmen. The tensions inherent in this situation did not become really apparent, in England and to English councillors, until the 1430s, though the petition of the commons, in 1421, that the crowns of England and France should in perpetuity remain separate and independent of one another, was a warning shot across the bows.[55] The fact that, at the early stage, so many prominent Englishmen found themselves, in consequence of Henry's victories, in possession of considerable estates on both sides of the channel helped temporarily to obscure the underlying but real division of interest. Their trans-Channel possessions were however only a flimsy coupling between the two worlds of Lancastrian France and Lancastrian England, because for all men, perhaps above all for the prominent, there came a time when they had to choose between priorities. Some men naturally did their best to keep a solid footing in both worlds, as for a long time did Fastolf, whose splendidly recorded acquisitiveness, in combination with his irresistible instinct to proffer unsolicited advice, have perhaps allowed him to colour too much our vision of his age. But he was rather exceptional, and finally even he had to make his choice (though he grumbled bitterly to the end about his French losses).

As Michael Powicke has trenchantly pointed out, a substantial proportion of the greater captains of the Agincourt expedition (as of the

---

[54] Somerset's extensive French interests are examined in M.K. Jones, 'The Beaufort Family and the War in France, 1421-50' (Bristol Ph.D. thesis, 1982).

[55] *Rot. Parl.*, iv. 127.

subordinate leaders of most of the major fourteenth-century hosts) were the kind of men who formed local opinion and swayed local politics in England, whose careers combined with occasional military service membership of parliament, the tenure of shrieval office, and sitting as J.P.s on the commissions of the peace in their counties.[56] But from 1417 onward men of this sort become rarer and rarer among the leaders of the soldiery in France. Men like Matthew Gough, Fulk Eyton and Osborne Mundford were too busy in France to have a chance of being able to discharge these sorts of offices in England. They were men of the same stamp and background as others who stayed at home and dominated their county communities, but their paths had led them in a different way and their situation shaped for them different priorities. It is in this light, I believe, that one must read that often quoted passage of William of Worcester:

> But now of late daies, the grettir pite is, many one that ben descendid of noble bloode and borne to armes, as Knightis sonnes, esquiers, and of othir gentille bloode, set hem silfe to singuler practik . . . as to lerne the practique of law or custom of lande, or of civil matier, and so wastyn gretlie theire tyme in suche nedelese besinesse, as to occupie courtis halding, to kepe and bere out a proude countenaunce at sessions and shiris halding . . . And who can be a reuler and put hym forthe in suche matieris, he is, as the worlde goithe now, among all astatis more set of than he that hath despendid xxx or xl yeris of his daies in gret jubardies in youre antecessourys conquestis and werris.[57]

Worcester is not here telling us, as he seems to be, about a sea change that has come over English upper class society; only about how, as a result of Henry V's conquests, the preoccupation of English gentlemen who chose to take their part in their counties drew them apart from those other gentlemen who chose to take their chance in the king's wars overseas. He is also, as he intended though perhaps not in the way he intended, telling us something very important about why Lancastrian France collapsed as it did, like a pack of cards, in 1449-50. Englishmen who bore out a proud countenance at sessions and shire holdings were quite capable of bearing arms too, as they showed at Wakefield and Towton and Tewkesbury; they let Lancastrian France go to its fate not because they had turned soft, but because they had too little to lose there.

---

[56] Powicke, 'Lancastrian Captains', *Essays presented to Bertie Wilkinson*, ed. Sandquist, pp.371-82.

[57] *The Boke of Noblesse*, ed. J.G. Nichols (Roxburghe Club, London, 1860), pp.77-8.

Index